The BiblioLife Network

This project was made possible in part by the BiblioLife Network (BLN), a project aimed at addressing some of the huge challenges facing book preservationists around the world. The BLN includes libraries, library networks, archives, subject matter experts, online communities and library service providers. We believe every book ever published should be available as a high-quality print reproduction; printed on- demand anywhere in the world. This insures the ongoing accessibility of the content and helps generate sustainable revenue for the libraries and organizations that work to preserve these important materials.

The following book is in the "public domain" and represents an authentic reproduction of the text as printed by the original publisher. While we have attempted to accurately maintain the integrity of the original work, there are sometimes problems with the original book or micro-film from which the books were digitized. This can result in minor errors in reproduction. Possible imperfections include missing and blurred pages, poor pictures, markings and other reproduction issues beyond our control. Because this work is culturally important, we have made it available as part of our commitment to protecting, preserving, and promoting the world's literature.

GUIDE TO FOLD-OUTS, MAPS and OVERSIZED IMAGES

In an online database, page images do not need to conform to the size restrictions found in a printed book. When converting these images back into a printed bound book, the page sizes are standardized in ways that maintain the detail of the original. For large images, such as fold-out maps, the original page image is split into two or more pages.

Guidelines used to determine the split of oversize pages:

• Some images are split vertically; large images require vertical and horizontal splits.
• For horizontal splits, the content is split left to right.
• For vertical splits, the content is split from top to bottom.
• For both vertical and horizontal splits, the image is processed from top left to bottom right.

Items should be returned on or before the date shown below. Items
not already requested by other borrowers may be renewed in person,
in writing or by telephone. To renew, please quote the number on the
barcode label. To renew online a PIN is required. This can be requested
at your local library.
Renew online @ **www.dublincitypubliclibraries.ie**
Fines charged for overdue items will include postage incurred in recovery.
Damage to or loss of items will be charged to the borrower.

Leabharlanna Poiblí Chathair Bhaile Átha Cliath
Dublin City Public Libraries

Comhairle Cathrach
Bhaile Átha Cliath
Dublin City Council

Tl   te

Due Date	Due Date	Due Date

The Alps in 1864. A private journal. [With maps.]
Moore, Adolphus Warburton
British Library, Historical Print Editions
British Library
1867
vi. 360 p. ; 8°.
10059.d.34.

Rre

Rev: A.J. xxi h.139

THE ALPS IN 1864.

A PRIVATE JOURNAL

BY

A. W. MOORE.

1867.

PREFACE.

THIS Journal of my Alpine wanderings in 1864 is not intended for general circulation, but I cannot submit it to even friendly critics without a few words of apology for its manifold defects.

My object in originally writing it was to compile a narrative, the subsequent perusal of which might recall to my own recollection the various details of my mountaineering campaign of that year. With this view I recorded at full length all the trivial incidents which form the staple of such a tour, and constitute its charm. But these details, though full of interest to myself, will be very dull reading to other people, and had I at the time had any idea that the narrative would ever emerge from the obscurity of manuscript, I should have omitted most of them. Want of time has prevented me re-writing the book on an entirely different principle, and it is, therefore, printed almost word for word as it originally stood. I can only trust that the intrinsic interest of most of the expeditions described will induce my friends to wade through the attendant mass of comparatively unimportant matter. For the numerous faults of composition which will, I fear, be found in the volume, I can only plead in excuse that I have throughout sacrificed elegance, and sometimes, perhaps, correctness of expression, in order to obtain minuteness of topographical detail. I have only further to add with reference to my speculations as to the accessibility of various mountains, most of which have been falsified by subsequent events, that I have allowed them to remain as written, in order to show how worthless is the opinion on such points of even a fairly-experienced observer. In all such cases, an explanatory note is appended.

CONTENTS.

MAPS.

THE ALPS IN 1864.

Saturday, *18th June*.—I left Brighton at 5. p.m., reached Redhill Junction at 5.45, remained there till 7.6, when the Dover train came up and deposited me at the latter place at 9.20, I went forthwith on board the boat, and managed to get into a sleepy state before it sailed, at 10.35.

Sunday, *19th June*.—The fates were propitious, the sea was calm, and the boat reached Calais at 0.35 a.m. without my having been compelled to pay the usual tribute to Neptune. On arriving at Paris at 7.20 I went to the Hotel de France et d'Angleterre, in the Rue des Filles St. Thomas, where I found the Walkers and Morshead, with whom was a young fellow of the name of Gaskell, who had been intrusted to Morshead for introduction to the High Alps. The day passed as pleasantly as a day in Paris always does. We astonished "Mossoo" by appearing in all our Alpine glory in the Bois de Boulogne, and, at intervals, prepared ourselves for hardships to come by the consumption of large quantities of strawberries and cream ice. William Mathews and his party were at Meurice's, en route to the Pyrenees, so that, altogether, the Alpine Club was well represented. After dinner Morshead started for Basle, having arranged to meet me at Evolena on or about the 9th July; and at 8.40 the rest of the party left for

B

Chambery and St. Michel. We had hoped to keep the carriage to ourselves, but, just as the train was on the point of starting, we were joined by a most remarkable-looking female, English, tolerably young, tolerably good-looking, arrayed, as to her head, in a pork-pie hat with a huge red feather, solitary, and encumbered with multitudinous packages. I believe that each member of our party passed a large portion of the night in speculating about this mysterious stranger. We compared notes in the morning, but utterly failed in arriving at a satisfactory conclusion, so finally christened her the "Enigma," by which name she goes unto this day. The weather all day had been threatening, but, as the night advanced, the clouds disappeared until the full moon was left shining in a perfectly clear sky.

Monday 20th June.—No one of us did much in the way of sleep, and the usual scalding coffee at Macon roused us thoroughly. Culoz was reached at 8.48; and there, standing ready to meet us, were Whymper and our old friends Christian Almer and Melchior Anderegg,—Melchior attached to Mr. and Miss Walker, and Almer to Horace Walker and myself. Leaving Culoz at 9.12, we reached Chambery at 10.0, where Mr. and Miss Walker, with Melchior, left us en route for the Grande Chartreuse. At Chamousset we picked up Whymper's guide, Michel Croz of Chamouni, a large, pleasant-looking man, whom we forthwith introduced to Almer; but, as each was ignorant of a single word of the other's language, their mutual communications were somewhat limited. The country through which the line passes is picturesque, but the heat and dust made the journey tedious; and in spite of some entertaining conversation and behaviour on the part of the "Enigma," who was bound for Turin, we were all glad to reach St. Michel, the present terminus of the line, at 12.10 p.m. Here there was much to be done; baggage had to be arranged, provision laid in, and the last tolerable dinner we had to expect for some time consumed. This latter operation was performed satisfactorily at the excellent, but expensive, restaurant attached to the station. And finally, at 2.40 p.m., the greater portion of our baggage being left to await our return, which might be expected in about ten days, we turned our backs upon civilization, and plunged into the wilds. An ice-axe is a rare spectacle on the Cenis road, and many curious glances were cast at our party as we passed along the straggling main street of St. Michel. We had no very precise notion where we should pass the night, our intention being to ascend the Combe de Valloire as long as daylight lasted, and trust to find an opportune chålet at nightfall. This Combe de Valloire opens out on the left bank of the Arc, just opposite to St. Michel, but terminates in a mere gorge through which there is no path. To get at all into the inhabited part of the valley it is necessary to climb to a great height over the intervening hill-side, an arrangement which appears common to many of the lateral valleys of this district, and cannot be too strongly condemned. Having crossed the Arc, here a considerable stream by a substantial stone bridge, we at once commenced the ascent. The path, after passing some scattered houses, mounted rapidly through meadows and luxuriant woods, which, however, afforded but scanty protection from the sun, whose scorching beams were pouring down upon us from an almost cloudless sky. We were all more or less heavily laden, and to luckless individuals fresh from a sedentary life in England, the walk was as trying a one for a first essay as could well have been selected. Nevertheless, with occasional short halts, and a draught from a tolerable spring in a shady nook, we managed to toil upwards, and were soon astonished to see at how great a depth below the valley lay. The scenery throughout was charming, and the path, though steep, good, and apparently much frequented, as we passed several parties of natives on their way down. In due course the woods were left behind, and a stiff pull over the open ground above them brought us at 4.45 to the crest of the ridge, marked by a small chapel and three very tall crosses. The ascent from St. Michel, itself 2533 feet above the sea, cannot be less than 3000 feet.

B 2

The view from this point, which may conveniently be called Col de Valloire, was unexpectedly fine. Looking back, at our feet lay St. Michel, plainly visible, backed by the extensive and not very interesting-looking valley lead-ing up to the Col des Encombres, to the left of which was a rocky peak, with curiously-contorted strata. But the prospect in the opposite direction absorbed the larger share of our regards. Looking straight up the long valley of Valloire, and over the ridge of the Col du Galibier at its head, our attention was drawn to a solitary summit, towering upwards into the sky. Croz instantly recognised it as the Monarch of the Dauphiné Alps, the Pic des Ecrins, 13,462 feet in height, whose conquest we hoped to effect. The face of the mountain above the Glacier Blanc, which the explorations of Messrs. Bonney, Mathews, and Tuckett had determined to be the only one offering any chance of a successful attack, was turned towards us, and though the distance was much too great to allow us to form any reliable opinion of our chances of victory, yet the little we could make out with the aid of my glass was the reverse of encouraging. The final peak appeared to be protected by a huge bergschrund, running completely across the slope below it, and above this obstacle was a wall of ice and rock, arranged to a certain extent on the couloir pattern, and evidently very steep. We were unable to trace a single couloir right up to the arête; everyone stopped short, leaving an interval of rock, slightly sprinkled with snow, the ascent of which might or might not be practicable. The arêtes right and left of the summit appeared to be fearfully thin and serrated; in fact as unpromising as possible. One thing only was clear, that the mountain would prove no easy conquest. And having arrived at this conclusion, we turned to another part of the view in which we were almost as much interested. Some distance up the valley was the village of Valloire, built at the base of a curious sort of hillock. To the right of, and far behind, the village, towered a singular group of peaks which could be nothing but the Aiguilles d'Arve, a nearer acquaintance with which we hoped to make on the morrow. The most conspicuous point visible was one of the most remarkable peaks I have ever seen—a vast dome of rock, sliced off on one side as though the operation had been performed with a knife, with an enormous excrescence on the top of the dome, strongly resembling the top of a pepper-box. To the left of this "lusus naturæ," and rather in advance of it, was a snow-peak, which I imagined to be the highest summit of the group. Whymper, however, disagreed with me, and (rightly, as afterwards appeared) assigned the supremacy to a second dome of rock, which was rather imperfectly seen between this snow-peak and the pepper-box above mentioned, to which latter, so far as apparent difficulty of access went, it bore a striking resemblance. From this group three lateral valleys radiated, and all finally opened out into the main valley of Valloire. After some discussion, we determined that the base of the Aiguilles might be most advantageously approached by the most southerly of these three valleys, which bears on the Sardinian map the appropriate name of Vallon des Aiguilles d'Arve. Its entrance appeared to be some distance above Valloire, but we resolved to use every exertion to get at least so far before nightfall.

To accomplish this there was no time to lose, so at 5.5 we picked up our traps and commenced the descent, the path being better and decidedly less steep than on the side of St. Michel. The views of the valley in descending were charming, and the curious ravine in which it terminates was well seen. After passing two considerable villages, we reached Valloire, in the bottom of the valley, at 5.45, and went to a rough little inn on the "place," where we hoped to lay in provisions. The resources of the establishment proved to be an unlimited supply of good bread, cheese, and red wine, eggs but no meat. In addition to satisfying the present pangs of hunger we had to superintend the preparation of the stores to be taken with us, as Almer, owing to his ignorance of the language, was helpless, and Croz was rather apathetic. The people of the inn were excessively civil and anxious to supply our wants, but scarcely seemed to appreciate the value of time to us. The egg-boiling was a very long process, so, while it was going on, we went out into the "place," where the curé and some members of the local aristocracy were playing at bowls under difficulties on a piece of ground tilted up at a considerable angle, and of the roughest and most uneven character. All the preparations being at length completed, we left Valloire at 6.50. The path now crossed to the left bank of the stream, and wound through a picturesque gorge between the curious hillock before mentioned, at the base of which the village is built, and the side of the valley. On the top of this hillock, in a very striking position, is a large chapel, the ascent to which must rather take it out of those natives whose piety may induce them to visit it. The evening was fine, and the walk on very pleasant. At 7.40 we came to a small village, and obtained from one of the inhabitants, the colour of whose nose bore witness that its owner had certainly not taken the pledge, the information that there were occupied châlets at the entrance of the Vallon des Aiguilles d'Arve, and also directions how to reach them. In accordance with these instructions we shortly left the main track, and commenced a rapid ascent over the shoulder of the hill that intervened between us and the Vallon. The track was both rough and steep, and the distance greater than we had anticipated. Corner after corner was turned, but there was no sign of the wished-for huts. Darkness, too, was coming on apace, and it was, therefore, with no small satisfaction that we at length saw a group of buildings looming through the gloom, and at 8.25 reached our destination. The châlets were situated at the entrance of, but fairly within, the Vallon, which opens out into the main Valley of Valloire opposite to, but at a higher level than, the hamlet of Bonnenuit. The woman in charge received us civilly, and showed us a large barn, furnished with a fair quantity of hay, where we could pass the night. She only insisted on one condition, that we should not

introduce any light into the place for fear of setting fire
to the loose hay. Her anxiety on this score was remarkable,
and we had to promise emphatically over and over again,
both to go to bed and get up in the dark, before she was
satisfied. That point settled, she took us to another châlet,
and warmed a quantity of milk, with which and our own
stores we made a very satisfactory supper. Hunger
appeased, there was no temptation to remain up, so we
soon retired to our dormitory, and took up our positions
side by side on the hay, through which the hard boards
made themselves painfully perceptible. Of ventilation also
there was more than enough, and we were not at all too
warm. Possibly owing to these two circumstances it was
long before I fell asleep, notwithstanding that I had passed
the two previous nights in travelling. But I at last dropped
off, and doubtless soon commenced to swell the nasal uproar
which had been for some time proceeding from my
companions.

Tuesday, 21st June.—However uncomfortable a bed or
its substitute may be, there is one moment when it appears
luxurious, and that is, when, at an unearthly hour of the
morning, one is called upon to leave it. So it came to
pass, that, after a restless and uncomfortable night, when,
at about 3.0 a.m. the voice of Almer proclaimed the break
of day, and the consequent necessity of rising, I was very
loth to obey his summons, which was not more welcome
to the other members of the party. However we all turned
up, and performed our toilette, an operation neither long
nor extensive, consisting merely of a vigorous shake in
order to get rid of the loose particles of hay that were
making themselves felt on various parts of our persons.
Having breakfasted on bread and butter and cold milk, we
paid our hostess a very moderate sum, bade her farewell,
and at 3.55 started on our way, accompanied (not as guide)
by an ill-favoured native whose business called him some
distance up the Vallon. It was a lovely morning, the sky
cloudless, and the air so deliciously fresh that it did more
in a few moments to restore our energies than had been

accomplished by our night's rest. The valley for some
distance in front was perfectly level, and the walking over
luxuriant pastures was very pleasant. On our right was a
ridge, separating us from a similar valley; in fact the
central of the three glens which radiate from the Aiguilles
d'Arve. The most conspicuous point in this ridge was
the snow-peak which I had yesterday from the Col de
Valloire supposed to be the highest of the Aiguilles, most
erroneously however, for it now showed itself in its true
character as comparatively insignificant, and merely an
outlier of the main group. The ridge on our left, separating
us, I imagine, from the valley leading to La Grave by the Col
de Golèon, was far more lofty, especially at its further end,
where it circled round to the head of our valley. From its
general level three points rose conspicuous, close to each
other, which are called on the French map " Les trois
Pointes d'Aiguilles." The Aiguilles d'Arve themselves
were invisible, hidden by a turn in the valley. At 4.30 we
left the pastures behind us, and commenced a steady
ascent over a singular expanse of stone-covered ground,
which was scored in a remarkable way by deep channels,
undoubtedly cut by torrents descending from " Les trois
Pointes." These channels ran transverse to our line of
march, and as it was necessary to descend into and cross
each one in succession, the walking was very laborious.
This lasted an hour, and brought us at 5.30 to the last
bit of level very near the head of the valley, where it
became necessary to make up our minds as to the exact
course we would follow. We, therefore, halted for the
double purpose of looking about us and giving Whymper,
who was not well, an opportunity of recovering himself.

Our immediate object was to make the ascent of the
highest of the three Aiguilles d'Arve, and descend either
towards St. Jean d'Arve, or better still, if possible, direct
to La Grave, on the high road of the Lautaret. The three
peaks are close together, springing from an elevated ridge,
the general direction of which is, speaking roughly, north
and south. The southern peak is the highest, attaining

11,529 feet, but it only very slightly exceeds the central summit, which, by the same authority, is 11,513 feet. Neither on the French nor Sardinian maps is there any sign of the third or northern peak, although its height can be little inferior to that of its brethren, while from most points of view it is equally conspicuous.

On the Sardinian map, indeed, only one summit is depicted, just north of the watershed between the Maurienne and Dauphiné, not far out of its true position. We knew nothing about the Aiguilles from personal knowledge, and had chosen our line of attack in consequence of having read in Joanne's "Itinéraire de Dauphiné" a somewhat vague account of an ascent of what, from the height given, appeared to be the central peak from the side of St. Jean d'Arve, which wound up with the statement that it was possible to get down to Valloire. We, therefore, concluded that, in the event of the highest point proving inaccessible, we should be able to climb the second, and certainly descend on the other side by a route, which Joanne stated to be "relativement facile." The idea that the account in Joanne might be mythical and both peaks inaccessible had never entered our heads, and we were, therefore, somewhat taken aback at the scene displayed to our admiring eyes from our halting-place at the head of the Vallon des Aiguilles d'Arve. As we sat, looking about due north, on our left towered the two highest of the Aiguilles, apparently so equal in height that, but for the map, we should have been at a loss to determine their relative claims to supremacy. I never saw more remarkable peaks than those two perfectly symmetrical piles of rock, which were so like each other that they might have been cast in the same mould. They rise abruptly from a ridge which circles round from "Les trois Pointes;" over this ridge the ill-favoured native, who had left us some time before, had declared that there was an easy pass direct to La Grave. It may be *possible* to get over, but there is not a single well-marked depression in the ridge, the general level of which cannot be much

under 10,000 feet, while the rocks which fall from its
summit to the valley below are so precipitous and smooth,
that we all, Almer and Michel included, doubted the
practicability of ascending them at any point. Of one thing
we were certain, that the native had, after the manner of
the country, lied, and that whether or not it might be
possible to force a passage, no one had ever crossed that
way to or from La Grave. Between the Aiguilles, peaks
1 and 2, was a most fascinating gap of no very great
width from which fell towards the valley a small but
beautiful glacier.   It was a perfect reproduction in
miniature of its larger brethren in other parts of the Alps.
Below the gap was a formidably steep ice-wall, cut off by
the orthodox bergschrund from the névé. This latter in
due course ended in an ice-fall, very steep and shattered,
which terminated on low cliffs, succeeded by the usual
slopes of rock, stones, and grass, on which at this early
period of the season there was a good deal of snow. To
the north of peak No. 2 a ridge circled round towards the
snow-peak before mentioned, which was now almost in
front of us, but a ridge much more practicable than the
one above described.   Slopes of considerable steepness led
up to a series of extensive snow-fields, which it appeared
easy to follow up to their origin at any point. It will be
understood from the above description that the ridge at the
head of the valley sweeps round in an almost perfect semi-
circle, the Aiguilles d'Arve being in the centre of the arc,
while one of "Les trois Pointes" and the snow-peak face
each other at either extremity of the chord.

A very few moments convinced us that, as regarded the
Aiguilles, the southern arête and the eastern face of peak
No. 1 were equally inaccessible, while the northern arête
that fell to the gap above the glacier was a simple
precipice.   The gap itself we thought accessible with
difficulty, as the glacier and ice-wall leading up to it
promised a tough piece of work, while, when it should be
attained, the southern arête of peak No. 2 appeared no
less unpromising than the northern arête of peak No. 1.

The eastern face, too, of the latter offered as little prospect
of success as that of its companion; and, but for one
circumstance, we should at once have given up all hope of
reaching its summit. This was, that from our point of
view we could not see the true northern arête, which falls
to the ridge connecting the central peak with the northern
or lowest of the Aiguilles No. 3; the arête, ridge, and
peak were all invisible, masked by the most advanced
portion of the snow-fields before mentioned. Now, it was
by this northern arête that I gathered from Joanne the
ascent had been made, although the vagueness of the
description, combined with the total absence of any reliable
map, rendered it impossible to be certain. However, we
were all willing to be persuaded that such was really the
case, and as the Aiguilles were evidently inaccessible on
all other visible sides, we determined to make for the gap
between Peaks 2 and 3, which, although invisible, we knew
must exist, and try our luck from there, never doubting
that in any event we should be able to get down on the side
of St. Jean d'Arve. Accordingly, at 6.10 we resumed our
march, steering considerably to the right towards my deceptive snow-peak, under which it seemed possible to get on
to the snow with less difficulty than more to the left under
Aiguille No. 2, where the supporting cliffs appeared more
precipitous. Steep slopes of scanty grass were succeeded
by still steeper ones of stones, covered here and there with
patches of the winter's snow. Occasionally some very faint
traces of a track, probably made by sheep or goats, were
visible, but never for long, and we had to select for ourselves
the most eligible way. After keeping to the right for some
time and mounting to a considerable height, we began working round to the left, and finally at 6.50 reached the snow,
on which the sun was playing with full force, warning us of
the necessity for spectacles and gaiters. During a halt of
ten minutes these were put on, and thus, fully equipped for
work, we bent our knees to tackle the apparently endless
slopes in front of us, making for a point immediately to the
right of Aiguille No. 2. The slopes were steep, the rays of

the sun hot, and we heavily laden, so that, although there
were no difficulties to be overcome, the work was severe,
and whoever of the two men happened to be pounding the
steps turned round frequently to rest a moment and survey
the view which was rapidly opening out behind us. At
length, after passing over a patch of shattered rocks, the
last upward step was taken, and at 8.45 we stood in a gap
some fifty yards wide between Aiguilles Nos. 2 and 3.

Our first glance was down on the other side, and our first
impression was that we were regularly "sold," and that we
should have to return the way we came. From our feet the
rocks fell in an absolute precipice, apparently cutting us off
completely from the smiling valley, or rather combination of
valleys, that lay between us and the fine group of the Grandes Rousses, the highest of which Croz greeted as an old
friend. A careful inspection, however, showed us two very
steep snow couloirs, by either of which we thought it might
be practicable to effect the descent; so, dismissing that question for the present, we turned our attention to Aiguille
No. 2. The nature of the descent towards the valley of St.
Jean d'Arve had convinced us at once that the ascent
referred to by Joanne could not have been made from our
present position, as he speaks of gentle pastures being
followed to the very foot of the peak, whereas the nearest
pastures were some two thousand feet below at the foot of
a precipice. We were, therefore, not particularly astonished
on looking up at the Aiguille which rose immediately above
us to find that its northern face offered scarcely more prospect of success than its southern, eastern, and western sides.
We estimated the gap in which we were sitting to be about
10,200 feet in height, so that the summit of No. 2 was still
1300 feet above us. It might have been possible to scramble
up for some distance, but not to attain a height sufficiently
great to repay us for the attendant risk, which would have
been considerable, the narrow ledges along and up which we
must have gone being covered with a thin layer of snow.
Almer and Michel were strongly opposed to such a proceeding; so, having determined at a glance that the lowest

of the Aiguilles, No. 3, was from this side as inaccessible
as his brethren, we bestowed a malediction on Joanne, and
settled ourselves on some loose rocks to admire the gorgeous view that lay extended before us.　Looking east, the
centre of the picture was occupied by Monte Viso, at a
great distance, towering over numberless intervening ridges
from which numerous other fine peaks rose, which, however, shrank into comparative insignificance in the presence
of their chief.　To the left of the Viso was the great
mass of the Tarantaise Alps, a " terra incognita " to all of
us except Croz.　Of all the crowd of peaks the only one we
identified to our satisfaction was the Dent Parassée, on the
other side of the valley of the Arc, with a great field of
glacier at its base, no doubt the Glacier de la Vanoise.　To
the right of the Viso, but very much nearer to our position,
our delighted eyes were regaled with a cloudless view
of a considerable portion of the great Dauphiné group of
Alps.　First in importance and in interest towered the
Monarch of the group, the Pic des Ecrins, looking as impracticable as from the more distant Col de Valloire.　Long and
carefully we examined the monster, and when the glass was
finally laid down, our hopes of ever being able to attain its
summit were rather faint.　Behind the Ecrins was the
double-headed Pelvoux, presenting to us the magnificent
precipice of black rock, only streaked here and there with
snow, which falls from the very top of the mountain to the
Glacier Noir.　Even more imposing and striking in form
was the peak to its immediate right, which has been likened
by some to a gothic cathedral, the highest point of the so-
called Crête du Pelvoux, 12,845 feet in height.　An attempt
to reach its summit would give some very pretty practice
in rock-work and the enterprising climber a remarkably
good chance of breaking his neck.　The last peak visible in
this direction was the Meije, in height only inferior to the
Ecrins, just seen over the shoulder of Aiguille No. 2, which
shut out from us the Brêche, Rateau, and Grand Glacier du
Lans.　Looking west, the view was less remarkable, the
only object of interest being the long range of the Grandes

Rousses, containing two summits of apparently equal height, and sending down considerable glaciers towards the valley of St. Jean d'Arve which lay extended in all its beauty below us.

The weather was lovely, and the temperature agreeably warm; there was no object in a very early arrival in the valley below, so that we lay basking in the sun in a state of bliss and enjoying the view until 11.30, when we turned to descend, having first christened the col, Col des Aiguilles d'Arve. The two couloirs from which we had to select a way were both equally unpromising in appearance, very steep, and with ugly patches of rock cropping here and there out of the snow, suggesting a rough reception in case of a slip. After some discussion we selected the one nearest to Aiguille No. 3, and having put on the rope, started, Croz leading, while Almer brought up the rear. Near the top the snow was perilously thin over the rocks, causing the steps to be very insecure, and suggesting the idea that later in the season, when there would probably be no snow at all, the ascent or descent might be quite impracticable, while the rocks right and left offered no alternative route.* Lower down, however, the snow was deeper, and soft enough to give good footing, so that in spite of its great steepness, which in places must have been at least 55°, we made good progress. About two-thirds of the way down the couloir suddenly narrowed to a width of certainly not more than two feet, and at the same time took a sharp twist in a remarkable manner to the right, where we had to pass with more than ordinary caution. But once through this curious hole matters mended, and the couloir gradually widened out into an ordinary steep slope of snow. On getting clear of the rocks we opened out to the right, one of the most superb views of the chain of Mont Blanc I ever saw. From the

---

* Later in the same year Mr. C. Oakley made an unsuccessful attempt to ascend the central peak of the Aguilles d'Arve from this col. At that time the descent on the side of St. Jean d'Arve did not appear practicable, the couloir by which we descended being then bare of snow.

Col du Bonhomme to the Col Ferrex every part of the range was clear, while Mont Blanc himself soared in the centre above all his satellites, an object of surpassing magnificence. This glorious scene was a complete surprise, and lent an unexpected interest to this side of the pass. The sight of the long slope of snow below us, of course, suggested the question of a glissade, but neither of the guides quite approved the notion, considering the slope too steep. However, after some discussion, Walker, whose ability at a glissade is extraordinary, started off alone, standing, and soon reached the bottom safely. Almer, Whymper, and myself followed, ignominiously sitting down, while Croz declined both ways, objecting to our mode because it would wet his trousers. We then, at 12.30, got off the snow, the descent from the col having occupied exactly an hour, and halted for twenty minutes on a level plain covered with some huge rocks, and watered by the streams caused by the fast-melting snow. Looking up from here the couloir by which we had descended appeared so precipitous that no one would have supposed it possible to traverse it, while the three Aiguilles displayed themselves in all their glory. Resuming our way, we passed along the top of a very curious grass-grown ridge, suspiciously like an old moraine, and, then, bearing well to the left, pushed rapidly on over steep stone-covered slopes, succeeded by thin grass, until at 1.25 p.m. we came to a group of inhabited châlets situated at a considerable height above the Combe de la Sausse which forms the head of one of the many tributary glens that unite to form the main valley of St. Jean d'Arve. Three women appeared to be the only inhabitants of the place; they were sitting outside one of the châlets busily engaged with some needle-work, and beyond staring in astonishment at our appearance, took not the slightest notice of us, not uttering a syllable. Our request for milk was at first received with solemn silence, as if they did not understand what we wanted; but after some time an idea of what we meant appeared to dawn upon them, and copious supplies were brought, and quickly consumed. On making enquiries about night-quarters, we with some difficulty elicited that there were some châlets down in the Combe de la Sausse, where we could probably sleep ; so, as they would be more convenient for the morrow's journey, and there was little temptation to prefer those of our informants, who on their part seemed decidedly anxious to get rid of us, we determined to descend to them. Whymper, however, was anxious to make a sketch of Aiguilles and Col, so, leaving the guides at the châlets, we three mounted a certain distance up a grassy hill behind until a favourable spot was found, where Whymper set to work, Walker and I going a few yards higher up. It would have been difficult to find a more eligible position from which to contemplate the Aiguilles, and the range running from them round the head of the Combe de la Sausse, and I spent some time in a careful examination of the group, which for its height is certainly one of the most remarkable and picturesque in the Alps. On the French map the word " signal " is placed against Peak No. 2, but neither from our present position, nor the col, nor the valley on the other side, could any of us detect anything on the summit at all resembling the work of human hands. Here for the first time I got a good view of Aiguille No. 3, which is double-headed, and as precipitous as the other two, but more massive and less graceful in form. I puzzled myself in vain to trace out any practicable line of ascent up either of the Aiguilles, but the north side of No. 3 was invisible ; and I finally came to the conclusion that if the account in Joanne is not (as I can scarcely believe it is) entirely mythical, it refers to Peak No. 3, to which the height of No. 2 has been erroneously given. But that this is, as he says, " relativement facile" I much doubt. The heat was scorching, and Walker's replies to my observations degenerated from sentences into monosyllables, and from monosyllables into snores. Evil example is contagious ; and, so soon as I had satisfied myself about the Aiguilles, I stretched myself on the grass, with a handkerchief over my face, and fell asleep, until in due course

the slumbers of both of us were broken by the voice of
Whymper, proclaiming that he had finished his sketch, and
was ready to go down. It was 4.0 p.m., so, running down
to the châlets, we stirred up the guides, and, after another
draught of milk, resumed our journey at 4.25. A steep
path led down towards the Combe de la Sausse, and then,
keeping to the right, brought us, at 4.50, to a second group
of châlets, situated on a grassy knoll at a considerable
height above the gorge through which the torrent flows
before joining the main stream, which comes down from
the Col des Infernets. The approach was unpromising
through a sea of filth, but never were first appearances
more deceptive; for, once past this unpleasant moat, we were
received with the utmost cordiality by the two honest-
looking women in charge, and were shown for night-
quarters a large clean barn, with an abundance of soft hay.
Having deposited our traps, we went into the châlet, a
model of cleanliness, to superintend the making of tea, and
during the operation endeavoured to get some information
about the country from our excellent hostesses; but, with
every desire on their part to communicate all they
knew, we could not learn much, except that the châlets
were the Châlets de la Sausse, and those higher up the
Châlets de Rieublanc, and also that there was such a pass
to La Grave as the Col de Martignare, which was passable
for mules, and, therefore, presumably easy. We fared
sumptuously on tea and quantities of milk, hot and cold,
helped down by bread and butter from our own stores, and
nothing could have surpassed the civility with which we
were attended to. Tea over, I went to the edge of the
grassy knoll, overhanging the gorge, the black shaly cliffs
on the other side of which were remarkable, and sat there
for some time, returning to witness a most gorgeous
sunset, and one of the finest bits of colour on the Aiguilles
d'Avre I ever saw. The air soon became chilly, so we
retired to our barn, and, burrowing in the soft hay, were,
with the addition of our plaids, shortly warm enough, and
soon slept the sleep of the just.

c

Wednesday, 22nd June.—Our couches were luxurious, and even our guides experienced an unusual reluctance to get up, and in consequence did not call us till 3.0 a.m., by which time we had hoped to start. However, I cannot honestly say that the additional hour's rest was at all unwelcome. After a copious supply of hot milk for breakfast, we had a most desperate struggle with our hostesses to persuade them to accept some remuneration for the good fare and accommodation we had had. For some time they obstinately refused to take anything, but we at length succeeded in forcing upon them the merest trifle; and, finally, at 4.15 took our departure under a shower of good wishes, and with many injunctions to come again if we were ever in the neighbourhood.

Our object now was to cross to La Grave on the high road of the Lautaret, from Grenoble to Briançon, and, en route, ascend some point sufficiently high to give us a good view of the Dauphiné Alps in general, and the grand chain of the Meije in particular. Before leaving England, a careful preliminary study of "Joanne" had elicited the fact that the shortest route from La Sausse to La Grave was by the Col de Martignare, which crosses the chain to the east of the better known Col des Infernets; also, that from the aforesaid Col it was possible with very little difficulty to ascend a lofty summit, called the Bec du Grenier, *or* Aiguille du Goléon. On referring, however, to the Sardinian survey, I found there, depicted to the east of the Col de Martignare, not *one* peak bearing the above two names, but *two* distinct summits; one just above the Col, the Bec du Grenier, the height of which is not stated, the other still further to the east, and somewhat to the south of the watershed between the Maurienne and Dauphiné, the Aiguille du Goléon, 3429 mètres, or 11,251 English feet in height, with a very considerable glacier—the Glacier Lombard—between the two. On the French map, on the other hand, neither of the above names is to be found, but a peak called Aiguille de la Sausse, 3321 mètres, or 10,897 feet in height, is placed in the position assigned to the Bec du Grenier in the Sardinian map, while, further to the east, is a second and lower nameless peak, 3304 mètres, or 10,841 feet, not at all in the position given to the Aiguille du Goléon, of which and the glacier Lombard there is not a sign. All this was very puzzling and unsatisfactory, but, as we had no doubt of being able to climb some point to the east of the Col de Martignare, we determined to make that Col the basis of our operations.

Leaving the châlets, we followed a faint track towards the head of the Combe de la Sausse, and soon opened out as savage a scene as can well be conceived. From the southern Aiguille d'Arve a great wall of shaly precipices ran, speaking roughly, in a south-westerly direction, for a considerable distance. From this wall, two peaks, built on much the same pattern as the Aiguilles, rose pre-eminent. Suddenly the ridge, abandoning its previous direction, turned due west, forming the watershed between the Maurienne and Dauphiné, and falling in a series of precipitous slopes to the valley below. On this portion of the ridge two rocky peaks were also conspicuous, and at the summit of one of them we hoped eventually to arrive. Standing at the entrance of the Combe de la Sausse, and looking south, the first section of the ridge above described was on our left,—straight in front of us was the second section,—while on our right was an immense buttress, projecting from the latter, crowned with pastures, which appeared completely cut off in the most extraordinary manner from the main valley in which we were.

The Combe de la Sausse was thus shut in by three walls of cliff, on none of which was there a sign of vegetation. On all sides the eye was met by exceedingly steep slopes of hard black shale, or rather grit, split up into numerous ravines, and seamed with immensely long snow couloirs. We saw from here that the descent on this side from the gap, between peaks Nos. 1 and 2 of the Aiguilles d'Arve would have been long, difficult, and laborious, lying for a long distance over slopes of the above nature, steep throughout, and, low down, almost perpendicular. After traversing a dreary expanse of stones, we got on to the most enormous bed of avalanche snow I ever saw. It stretched away an a great hummocky mass to an immense distance, and, I should think, can never be entirely melted, even late in the summer, as in such a profound gorge the sun can play on it for only a very brief period every day. After advancing over this for some time, we held a consultation as to the best course to pursue, in order to get on to the main ridge in front of us. Whymper suggested pushing straight forwards and climbing up the steep rocks and snow couloirs so as to hit the ridge very high up, as near as possible to the most easterly of the two peaks we hoped to climb. The appearance of the place was very uninviting, suggesting a long-continued grind of a most excruciating character, and the possibility of finding the snow in the couloirs either too thin over the rocks, or else soft and avalanchy. Neither Walker nor myself, therefore, was at all sorry to find that Almer and Croz objected to such a course, and preferred climbing the buttress on our right, and following it or its continuations to the main ridge, against which it finally abutted. Steering, accordingly, to the right, we got off the snow, and commenced climbing diagonally along the side of this buttress. I have rarely done a more laborious, not to say difficult, piece of walking. The soil was hard black grit, very steeply inclined, and without the faintest vestige of path. The footing was, consequently, so bad that it was no very easy matter to get on at all without slipping into the ravine below. The only way was to make a series of rushes, not stopping to pause before each footstep; and as, in addition to the lateral inclination being great, we mounted tolerably straight up, the constant series of efforts became most fatiguing, and finally landed me on the better ground above, more winded than I have often been. However, what we had undergone clearly showed how we should have been victimised had we adopted the course first proposed; so, duly congratulating ourselves on our superior wisdom, we went on our way rejoicing.

We were now above the cliffs which I had looked at last night from the grassy knoll near the châlets, of which from our present position we had a good view. It was a

considerable relief to find ourselves again on grass, poor
though it was, and a still greater one to discover a faint
track, which led us over comparatively level ground to the
crest of the buttress, from which we looked down into a
long valley, with a ridge at its head, over which lay the
Col de Martignare. The track led down into this valley,
and we followed it for some way, but, as we did so, the
idea of making so considerable a descent in order to
traverse a long dreary valley, and finally mount again to
the Col, became more and more distasteful to us, and at
length we determined to climb again to the top of the
buttress, and follow it as long as possible towards the main
ridge. We came to this decision against the opinion of
the guides, who, preferring present ease, wished to descend
and make for the Col. The event, however, proved that
we were undoubtedly right, and later on our friends can-
didly admitted it. A steep and toilsome scramble brought
us at 5.50 once more on to our buttress, here narrowed to
an arête, overlooking on the right the valley we had left
behind, and on our left the Combe de la Sausse, while in
front it stretched away towards a rocky point on the main
ridge, which we should have to get over or circumvent in
order to reach our wished-for summit. This arête is very
well marked on the Sardinian map, where it bears the
singular name of the "Arête Letolé" (sic). It is not the
least narrow, that is to say, there is ample room for one
person to pass along at a time in comfort, nor is it for
the most part at all steep, and is composed of fine shale,
along which the walking is most agreeable. Altogether I
never traversed a more pleasant pathway, and as we looked
down into the valley on our right and the ravine on our
left, we felt that on each occasion when we had had to choose
a way we had chosen well. As we advanced, the view in
front, of course, remained unchanged, but behind we
gradually opened out that superb view of the chain of
Mont Blanc which we had yesterday enjoyed, and which
is one of the greatest attractions of all the expeditions in
this part of the Alps. From no other direction does Mont

Blanc show to such advantage, or display so fully his supremacy over all the other neighbouring peaks. But this was not all, for in advance of Mont Blanc was the extensive group of the Graians, presenting a crowd of fine summits, to us unknown, with the exception of the Paradis, which was unmistakeable. After three quarters of an hour of the most luxurious walking, with only an occasional bit of stiff ascent, our way became less easy, the slope increased formidably in steepness, the shale gave place again to hard grit, and, to make matters worse, water trickling over this from the snow higher up had frozen, forming in many places a thin coating of ice, where great care was necessary in passing. We were now approaching the rocky point on the main ridge against which the arête finally abuts, and began to doubt the propriety of pushing straight up to it, as it appeared uncertain whether we should be able to work round either side of it, and so get on to the ridge. After some discussion, we abandoned the arête at 6.50, and commenced crossing the side of the buttress diagonally towards a point on what appeared to be the main ridge, rather to the right of the rocky point. The piece of work that ensued was far from easy, for the slope of the ground was so steep, and there was so much ice, that we found it difficult to keep our footing, and avoid an ugly slip. Walker and Croz followed a slightly different route to that pursued by Whymper, myself, and Almer, whose axe was brought vigorously into play. There was not much to choose between them in point of difficulty, but ours had the trifling advantage that it brought us to one spot, where the snow trickled over the rocks in sufficient quantity to enable us to get a good draught and refresh ourselves a little. At length, after considerable trouble, we got on to the ridge at 7.20, and found that it was only a shoulder of the peak above, and that the main ridge was a little further on, but accessible with ease over steep slopes of snow, filling the angle between the two. As, however, it was not certain that, even when on the ridge, we should be able to get along it, the guides went on to reconnoitre, while we sat contem-

plating the great glacier of Mont du Lans, of which we now
for the first time got a view. It is certainly a fine object, a
vast billowy field of névé, occupying the summit of a great
rocky plateau, and pouring down steep and narrow glaciers
through the numerous gorges which run down towards the
Combe de Malaval, and the road of the Lautaret; but on the
whole we were disappointed, I scarcely know why, but
there was a something wanting to produce an entirely
satisfactory effect. The men soon returned, reporting that
in front all was well, so at 7.35 we resumed our way, carefully traversed the slope of steep snow, and were very
shortly on the main ridge, where we were at once met by
the anxiously looked-for chain of the Meije; but, as the
same was seen to much greater perfection higher up, I will
reserve description. Turning to the left, we now passed
under the southern face of the point we had been so long
approaching from the opposite side, and in due course found
ourselves standing at the edge of a series of long snow slopes,
stretching up to the base of a fine rock-peak, for which we
determined to make, concluding it to be one of those which
we had inspected from the Combe de la Sausse. The
slopes were very steep, and the snow in the worst possible
condition, hard on the surface, but soft and powdery below,
so that the footing gave at every step, and the work was
very fatiguing. Nevertheless, with occasional short halts
to take breath, we mounted until we reached the rocks
forming the final peak. Skirting the snow at the base of
these, we at last took to them, and commenced climbing
straight up towards the summit. The rocks were steep,
but much shattered, presenting no difficulty, and merely
calling for the exercise of ordinary care; nor were they
particularly long, and, after a pleasant scramble, the last
one was surmounted, and a few steps of very gentle ascent
over snow brought us, at 9.15, to the summit of our peak, a
sharp snow-point, cut away in formidable precipices on the
side of La Sausse.

As we had expected, we were not on the highest point in
the neighbourhood, but exactly where we were it was im-

possible from the map to make out, as the lay of the land by
no means corresponded with the features laid down by
either the French or Italian authorities. In a south-
easterly direction from us, and separated by a considerable
glacier, which also clothed it to the very summit, was a
fine conical snow-peak, apparently about 200 feet higher
than our position, *certainly* on the watershed, but otherwise
corresponding tolerably to the position assigned on the
Sardinian map to the Aiguille du Goléon. On the summit
there appeared to be a "signal," and I have very little
doubt that it really is the Aiguille du Goléon, 11,251 feet
in height, and that we were on the Bec du Grenier, the
height of which, by comparison with the neighbouring peaks
and ridges, we estimated at about 11,000 feet. We might
have reached the higher point without any difficulty in,
I suppose, about two hours, but we already commanded
so admirable a view that we did not consider that the extra
height to be gained would repay us for the labour to be undergone. The view was one of the most gorgeous I ever
saw, and we could not possibly have had more favourable
weather for enjoying it, the sky being absolutely cloudless,
and the temperature agreeably warm. It was most extensive towards the north, where Mont Blanc towered above all
his rivals in unparalleled magnificence, with, in front, the
countless peaks of the Graian and Tarantaise Alps, amongst
which latter Croz now picked out his old conquest, the
Mont Pourri, while, in close proximity to us, the rival and
parallel groups of the Grandes Rousses and Aiguilles
d'Arve formed a foreground of no ordinary interest. The
latter especially are extraordinary objects; in fact, small
Matterhorns, quite as steep and rugged, and more symmetrical than the genuine Matterhorn, while they, the
two highest peaks at least, are quite as inaccessible.* But,
however attractive this portion of the panorama, it could
not long detain us from the prospect south, where the whole
chain of the Meije, seen from a height and distance sufficiently great to allow us to form some idea of its real eleva-

---

* This observation is, of course, no longer applicable.

tion, lay extended in perfect beauty before us. Having established ourselves on the highest rocks in comfortable attitudes, my glass was got out, and we prepared for a thorough study of the range. Straight in front of us was the great mass of the Meije itself, the second mountain in Dauphiné, rising to a height of 13,081 feet, or only 201 feet lower than Les Ecrins, one of the finest walls of mingled crag and glacier in the Alps. There is no one distinct summit, but many pinnacles crown the ridge, three of which appeared to be so equal in height, that without the map we should probably have been unable to decide upon their relative claims to supremacy. There, however, the palm is given to the western peak—we thought on the whole correctly—though whether it exceeds the eastern point by so much as 249 feet, as stated, may be doubted. Between the eastern and western peaks, which are of bare rock, rises the third summit, on which is much more snow. It appeared to us little, if at all, lower than either of its neighbours, and might, *perhaps*, be scaled from La Grave with great difficulty. From the very top of the western peak, the ridge falls in a tremendous precipice to a remarkable narrow gap, beyond which it rises less steeply to the long-shattered crest of the Rateau. To this gap the name of Brêche de la Meije, and the height of 11,054 feet are given on the French map, and through it we hoped to make a direct pass from La Grave to La Berarde, descending on the other side by the Glacier des Etançons. Photographs, and the description of travellers who had preceded us, had led us to expect considerable difficulties in the undertaking, but I think that none of us were quite prepared for a place so utterly impracticable-looking as that we now saw. From the Brêche, a steep ice-wall, with a large bergschund at its base, fell to the glacier below. The upper slopes of this were gentle, but did not long remain so, for they gradually merged into an ice-fall of the steepest and most shattered character, which continued without the slightest intermission to the foot of the glacier. To gain the Brêche by ascending straight up this was obviously impossible, but at first sight there appeared to be no alternative route. The great field of ice, enclosed between the Meije, the Rateau, and the spur from the latter supporting the Glacier du Mont du Lans, is divided into three distinct branches by an enormous bi-forked buttress running up into it from the direction of La Grave. The western prong stretches in the direction of the Rateau, and the eastern one towards the Brèche, while in the actual fork hangs the central and least extensive branch of the glacier, steeper but less crevassed than the branch falling from the Brèche itself, with which it is connected by slopes of névé. The result of our examination was that, first by the rocks between these two branches, and then by the central branch, our goal must be reached, if at all. The rocks, it is true, looked bad, and were reported by previous travellers to be "moutonnés," but there did not appear to be any other route offering the slightest chance of success. To the west of the Rateau was the Col de la Lauze, or de La Selle, leading to St. Christophe, over the extremity of the Glacier du Mont du Lans, which stretched away from it to the right for miles, a vast level field of névé. At the far end of this glacier, but some distance beyond it, a crowd of fine peaks were seen, of whose names even we were ignorant, but we supposed them to be somewhere near the head of the Combe des Arias, on the other side of the valley of the Venéon. Curiously enough I have no note on the subject of either the Ecrins or any peak of the Pelvoux group, which must, however, have been visible; but the precipices which hem in the short but very broad Glacier d'Arsines, over some point on which goes the difficult Col du Glacier Blanc to Val Louise, were very striking. I am sorry to say that a careful comparison of the scene before us with the French map very much shook our confidence in the accuracy of the latter, so far as the chain of the Meije is concerned. The eastern end of the Glacier du Mont du Lans appeared to be laid down very inexactly, while the glacier that falls direct from the Brèche de la Meije is terribly cramped, especially in its lower portion. But far more serious errors have been made about the mass of the

THE RANGE OF THE MEIJE AND ECRINS.

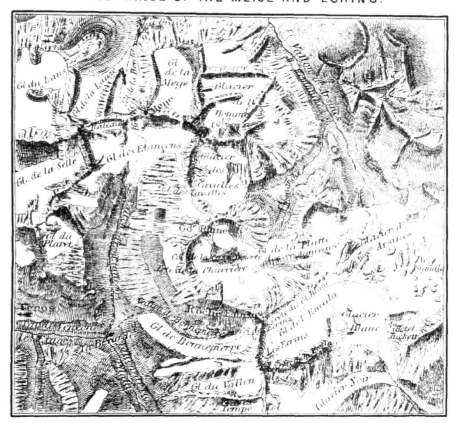

Meije itself, where the Glacier de la Meije, which hangs
from the northern face of the mountain, is depicted as about
twice its true size, and as running at its south-eastern angle
into a gap behind the second or eastern peak, communicating
with the Glacier des Etançons on the south side. Now, in
point of fact, on the north side there is absolutely no such
recess as that depicted on the map, but the space devoted to it
is really occupied by a confused mass of precipitous pinnacles,
couloirs, and hanging glaciers, which completely cut off the
Glacier de la Meije from the Glacier des Etançons. We
had thought of making a return pass from La Berarde to
La Grave by these two glaciers, but the idea was, of course,
very summarily knocked on the head. On the accompanying
map I have corrected to the best of my ability the most
glaring errors on the French map, but have no confidence
that my map represents the real state of things, which can
only be made out with proper instruments.

After an hour and three quarters spent in most perfect
enjoyment, we turned to descend at 11.5 a.m., but, wishing
to avoid the rocks by which we had mounted, bore to the
left, and got down to the glacier-clad ridge connecting our
peak with the supposed Aiguille du Goléon. From this
a formidably steep slope of snow fell towards the valley, and
in its upper part required the greatest care in traversing,
in order to avoid causing an avalanche, the sun having
acted upon the snow with such effect, that at every step
we went in up to our waists. However, the steepest part
was soon over, and we were at length able to indulge in a
long glissade, which carried us rapidly down to the level
snow-plain below, where at 11.35 we halted, taking up our
position on some loose masses of rock lying about. During
a quarter of an hour's halt, Walker and I amused ourselves
by shying stones at a large stone set up a certain distance
off as a mark, but I am bound, as an impartial historian,
to confess that, as in glissading, so in stone-throwing, his
skill was far greater than mine. At 11.50 we were again
on the move, and, always bearing to the left, descended
rapidly, until after another glissade, and traversing a most

unpleasant tract of mingled stones and snow, we finally quitted the snow and took off our gaiters. We were now at the head of a long straight lateral valley, which opens out into the valley of the Romanche, rather below La Grave. Tracks were visible on both sides of the torrent, but we selected that on the left bank, intending eventually to pass through one of several gaps in the ridge, which we supposed would bring us straight down upon La Grave. The valley was intersected by numerous small ravines, which were troublesome, as the path, not a very good one, had to dip into every one of them, adding materially to the labour. The distance, too, was great, and the view of the Meije in front scarcely redeemed the walk from dulness. At any rate no one was sorry when, at 1.25, the gap in the ridge was reached, and we found ourselves looking down upon the Lautaret road, and in a position almost more favourable for surveying the Brêche than higher up. We had another good look at it, and were confirmed in our opinion that the rocks, bad as they appeared to be, offered the only chance of success. A very long steep slope of avalanche snow on the right bank of the glacier under the Meije attracted our attention, but a glance at the enormous mass of débris at its base and the séracs above showed that it was too dangerous to be seriously thought of as a road. Notwithstanding the apparent difficulties, Almer appeared tolerably sanguine that we should find some sort of way over, and we were willing enough to be persuaded of the correctness of his opinion, so, at 1.50, went on our way. The faintly-marked track led over rough and barren ground, keeping to the right until the foot of the descent was nearly reached, when we had to make a long zig-zag to the left, which finally brought us into the track from the Col du Goléon (?), close to a considerable village which we had supposed to be La Grave. That place, however, was some way further down, and we had a hot, tiresome, stony, and very steep descent, before we at last dropped into the Lautaret road, close to the village, and walked into the little inn "chez Juge" at 2.40 p.m.

We were agreeably surprised at the appearance of the inn, which we had been prepared to find so poor that we had intended passing the night at some châlets on the other side of the Romanche, where we should be nearer our morning's work. We were shown into a very tidy "salon" beyond the common room, and three clean-looking bedrooms, the sight of which quite determined us to remain where we were, especially as going on to the châlets, which were not yet inhabited, would not shorten the next day's journey materially. Accordingly dinner was ordered, and during its preparation we killed the time in consuming lemonade largely, admiring the grand view of the Meije and its glaciers, which is to be had from the very door of the inn, and lastly in discoursing with the natives. We informed them of our designs upon the Brêche, but found an apathy on the subject which astonished us amongst a population numbering in its ranks several of (in their own opinion) "les plus grands chasseurs du monde." One and all united in declaring the project utterly impracticable. Some chaffed us mildly as amiable lunatics, while the officials of the "Gendarmerie Impériale" condescended to be particularly jocose on the subject. While sitting in the common "salle," Walker and I were accosted by a stout, not to say podgy, individual, who, in ignorance of our names, informed us that he and others had been invited by a Monsieur Renaud of La Bessée, to meet Messrs. Walker, Whymper, and Moore at Ville Val Louise on the 26th June, for the purpose of ascending the Pic des Ecrins, and that he was now on his way there, adding that he was an experienced mountaineer, having ascended the Rigi, and walked a good deal in the country about Zurich! Our alarm at this piece of news was considerable, nor was it diminished on our friend further observing that Monsieur Renaud had engaged *four-and-twenty of the most renowned* guides of the country to accompany us. We were at a loss to understand how anything could have transpired regarding our movements, until Whymper explained that before leaving England he had written to Monsieur Renaud, inviting *him* to join us on a *pass* we proposed to make from Val Louise to La Berarde, and casually mentioning that we also intended to have a look at the Ecrins; but, of course, he never meant M. Renaud to extend the invitation to strangers. However, we managed to shake off our stout friend, and carefully abstained from revealing ourselves, or mentioning that we hoped, all going well, to have the top of the Ecrins in our pockets by the evening of Saturday the 25th, so that he, Renaud, and the four-and-twenty renowned guides would find themselves left "out in the cold." After dinner, which was very fair indeed, we had an interview with "the most unblushing liar in Dauphiné," Alexandre Pic by name, a sturdy, good-looking fellow, who immediately began giving us specimens of his peculiar qualifications by stating various topographical facts in connection with the neighbouring glaciers, five out of six of which, we, of our own knowledge, knew to be grossly incorrect. Notwithstanding his want of veracity, he appeared a good stout walker, so we engaged him to carry all our traps round to Rodier's house at La Berarde, where he undertook to deposit them by an early hour the next afternoon. All other arrangements having been made, we went to bed, not altogether happy about the weather, which looked unsettled, but general opinion was in favour of a fine day for the morrow, so I got between the sheets for the first time since the previous Friday night, hoping for the best.

Thursday, 23rd June.—I had apparently only just closed my eyes, when I opened them again, and sounding my watch, found that it was 1.0 a.m., and that, consequently, our short night had already come to an end. It was an unpleasant fact, and, as I sat up in my bed, hugging my knees, a hard inward struggle went on before I could resolve not to lie down for another half-hour. However, virtue triumphed, and I crawled out of bed and went to the window, when a state of things not very satisfactory was disclosed. Rain was not falling, but the sky was obscured with heavy clouds, while those objectionable little white mists, which are so ominous to mountaineers, were creeping slowly down the valley along the flanks of the mountains. Whymper had particularly requested that, in the event of its being uncertain whether or not we should start, he might not be disturbed, so I went into Walker's room, woke him up, and putting our heads together out of window, we meditated on what it was best to do. We should have found some difficulty in making up our minds, but, while anxiously scanning the heavens, there was a sudden break in the clouds, which revealed the moon shining up above in a clear sky, and summarily settled the question. Whymper was roused, and, as there was no sign of movement in the house, I took a candle and went off to perform a similar pleasant operation on the guides. I made my way into the kitchen, where a fire was still smouldering, and was saluted by the combined buzzing of some thousands of blue-bottle flies, whom my light had roused from their slumbers on the white-washed walls. These vermin, I at first thought, were the sole occupants of the apartment; but as my eyes by degrees penetrated the gloom, they rested upon an old woman sitting in a chair, who, with mouth wide open, and eyes almost projecting from their sockets, was fixedly staring at me, with terror depicted on her venerable visage. What she took me for, unless a midnight murderer, I cannot tell, for she appeared unable to speak. However, the sound of my mellifluous voice broke the spell, and I at last succeeded in making her comprehend that she was to wake up Almer and Croz, and prepare breakfast while we were dressing. I am afraid that poor Whymper's breakfast must have been considerably spoiled by the behaviour of his boots, which obstinately declined to allow his feet to get into them. The more he worked and pulled, the more they would *not* go on, until we at last were becoming seriously alarmed lest he might have to attack the Brèche with one boot half on and the other in an even less advanced position. However, perseverance and unparliamentary language finally prevailed, the obnoxious articles were in their proper places, breakfast was finished, the provisions were packed and arranged, and at 2.40 a.m. we left La Grave in high spirits, the weather having almost entirely cleared.

A slight descent brought us down to the Romanche, which was crossed by a wooden bridge, and a good path led rapidly up the steep grass slopes on the opposite side, bearing rather to the right towards the entrance of the gorge, through which the drainage from the glaciers of the Brêche and Rateau flows to join the main stream. Before reaching the châlets at which we had intended to sleep, we struck down to the bank of the torrent, and, crossing to the left side of the gorge, followed a rough track over stones and through scattered pinewoods, towards the great glaciers in front. We were surprised to see how very much further back these lay than we had supposed when looking up from La Grave, and also at how great an elevation the ice terminated. Whilst steadily advancing we had an exceedingly fine view on the other side of the gorge of the Glacier de la Meije, and of the side of the Meije itself. The glacier, though extensive, is quite one of the secondary order, and ends at a far higher level than that which comes down from the Brêche. It is a continuous ice-fall from top to bottom, but its ascent would be quite practicable, and by it we thought that it might be possible to get very high up, if not to the summit of the central peak of the Meije. On to the highest point of that superb mountain-mass there did not appear to us any possibility of arriving from this side. In fact, I have rarely seen such hopelessly impracticable precipices. Leaving the route to the Col de la Lauze on our right, and passing the foot of the Glacier de la Brêche, which was so covered with moraine and débris that it was difficult to say where terra firma ended and the glacier began, our path became more and more vague, difficult, and laborious, until, after picking our way through and over a wilderness of stones, we got fairly on to the moraine of the glacier at 4.0 a.m., stumbled along it for ten minutes, and then stopped to

look about us. I have rarely seen a more glorious spectacle
than that presented by the great ice-fall of the eastern arm
of the Glacier de la Brêche, at the foot of which we were now
standing. Of less breadth than the celebrated ice-fall of
the Col du Géant, it is far steeper and longer, and, hard as
it may be to believe, infinitely more shattered. It receives
at about half its height a considerable tributary from
the side of the Meije, quite as dislocated, and even
steeper, so that huge towers and pinnacles of ice are perpetually pushed over and dashed down to the lower level.
The result is, that in one place a very long steep slope of
avalanche débris has been formed, stretching far up into
the confused sea of séracs; and we had at one time thought
that this might offer a practicable route to the upper and
comparatively level plateau above the ice-fall. The sight
of the huge cliffs of ice that impended over this slope, ready
to rake it at any moment, now finally put an end to any
such idea, especially as we for the first time realised the
length and steepness of this apparent high road, which
would have required many hours of step-cutting to surmount, and, after all, would not have brought us to the
very top of the fall. A near view, therefore, only confirmed
us in the opinion we had formed yesterday on the Bec du
Grenier that the ascent must be made by the western arm
of the glacier, which is enclosed in the fork of the buttress
before mentioned. This arm of the glacier, originating
under the eastern end of the long crest of the Rateau,
communicates in its upper portion with the Glacier de la
Brêche on the east, but on the west is cut off by a spur of
the Rateau from the third great arm of glacier, which for
present purposes I shall call Glacier de la Lauze. From
its source it falls very steeply in somewhat crevassed
slopes of névé and ice, until it ends abruptly in a precipitous and very narrow tongue of ice. Over the rocky wall
supporting this curious finale huge blocks of ice are hurled
periodically, and the result here also is a long steep slope
of débris, stretching far over the level tract below. It was
clearly impossible to approach this glacier at its very end,

D

much less get on to it, nor had it been possible, would there
have been any advantage in doing so, for the ice immediately above was so steep and broken that no passage up it
could have been forced. But above a certain height the
glacier, though steep, was evidently practicable, and we
saw to our no small satisfaction that, if we could only
manage to get on to the ice above that point, there would
be no further serious difficulty to encounter, until we
reached the ice-wall leading to the Col. But how to get
on to it ? There in truth was the rub ! The rocks looked
more and more detestable as we came near them, yet up
those on the right bank of the glacier, that is to say, up
the most eastern of the two spurs, must we find a way, if
the goal was ever to be attained.

It did not take long to realise all this, and at 4.20 we
resumed our way over the moraine, which, for moraine,
was by no means bad. Nevertheless, at 4.40 we quitted
it without regret, and commenced a series of short zig-zags
up a slope of avalanche-snow which stretched up to the
very edge of the rocks on which our fate was to be decided.
The slope was steep and the snow hard, but a kick from
Croz, who was leading, was sufficient to give good footing,
and we mounted rapidly, so that, when at 4.55 we stood
at the edge of the rocks, I was quite surprised to see how
much we had risen above the glacier in the last quarter of
an hour. The first few steps, after quitting the snow, required care, but, after scrambling up for five minutes, we
once more halted in an eligible position to take breath, and
prepare for the tug of war. Our spirits, like our bodies,
had risen considerably, for we had already discovered
that these dreaded rocks, which were supposed to be
"moutonnés," and ground quite smooth in consequence
of having once been covered by the now shrunken glaciers,
were composed of rough granite, which, though steep, gave
particularly good foothold. At 5.10 we were ready for the
fray, and started off to try conclusions with our enemy.
We were soon busily engaged in a most agreeable climb,
winding about wherever the passage seemed easiest; en-

countering no serious difficulty, but at the same time keeping hands as well as feet hard at work, we steadily advanced. Some places from below had seemed almost impassable, and had troubled severely the minds of both Almer and Croz, but now, when it came to the point, some of these ugly bits were altogether avoided, while others were circumvented by help of opportune gullies and patches of snow, which from the lower level had been invisible. It was really quite a pleasure to scale such delightful rocks; the stone held the boot so well that, even in the steepest places, I, who am by no means a first-rate performer, felt that, without making a positive effort to do so, it would be almost impossible to slip. So things went on flourishingly until 6.5, when we found ourselves at the foot of a slope of hard snow, covering the rocks, which would evidently lead us right on to the glacier, at the very point we had below settled to be the most eligible. Before attacking this, it was thought prudent to put on the rope, and, although the precaution was not strictly necessary, it was undoubtedly wise, as the slope was very steep, and the consequences of a bad slip to an untied individual would have been unpleasant. Cutting diagonally up and across the slope, we passed under a great overhanging pinnacle of ice, and at 6.20 stepped on to the glacier, which from La Grave had looked so hopelessly inaccessible, without having encountered any serious difficulty at all. There was some talk about breakfasting here, but, at the urgent request of the guides, we determined to postpone that tempting operation as long as possible, as they were anxious to get on to the upper plateau of the glacier before the sun should have softened the snow. We were all in high spirits at the unlooked-for facility with which our present position had been attained, and Whymper, who, in a desponding moment at La Grave, had bet Walker and myself each two francs that the time occupied in reaching the Col would be nearer thirteen hours than eight hours, was anxious to know for how much, down on the nail, we would let him off, but we held him to his bargain, and chuckled. The slopes, which now stretched upwards in front of us, were steep, but the snow was in admirable order, and we went straight up without zig-zags in a more direct line than I ever remember to have followed on any former occasion. A few crevasses had to be crossed or circumvented; but, although later in the season the state of things might be vastly different, there was no difficulty worth mentioning, and the labour inevitably attending the ascent of so steep a slope was the sole obstacle to still more rapid progress. The guides took it in turn to lead, and by 7.15 had brought us to a point where they at last allowed us to stop for breakfast; not a bit too soon, as the interiors of all were beginning to wax rebellious, so much so, that Walker, probably from having waited too long, so soon as he *had* eaten something, was violently sick, to our no small alarm. He, however, very soon revived, and felt all the better for the operation.

It was a glorious morning, and Mont Blanc in the distance looked more superb than ever, while the three peaks of Les Aiguilles d'Arve appeared as inaccessible as from most other points of view. At 7.45 we resumed our march, and now, for the first time, struck off to the left, in order to get on to the head of the eastern arm of the Glacier de la Brêche, which was connected with our arm by steep slopes of névé, intersected by some very considerable crevasses. Our route led just above one of these chasms, a monster, with gaping jaws fringed with icicles, quite ready to receive the whole party, in the event of any one slipping from the insecure and slippery staircase that was cut along and above the upper edge. On rounding the last of these slopes, we obtained, for the first time since getting on to the rocks, a view of the Col, which was now not far above us, but separated by a considerable expanse of almost level snow-fields, extending to the foot of the final wall. We took our turn at guessing the amount of time likely to be expended in gaining the ridge. Walker estimated one hour and a half, while I, resolving not to be under the mark, allowed three hours. For a considerable time we had been exposed to the full power of a rather scorching sun, but, traversing the snow-fields towards the Col, we soon fell under the shadow cast by the great wall of the Meije, so took the opportunity to halt for a few seconds, while the guides hastily made up their minds as to the exact point at which it would be best to attack the bergschrund, which, as usual, ran like a moat along the base of the ice-wall. The ground steepened as we advanced, and a few large crevasses had to be avoided, but at 8.30 the lower edge of the bergschrund was reached, and we stood at the base of the last obstacle between us and the wished-for goal, a wall of ice, covered with snow, rising to a height of, perhaps, 150 feet above the glacier. Our course had been well chosen, as we hit the chasm at a point where it was almost choked with snow, so that there was no actual difficulty in crossing; but right and left the gulf yawned with open mouth, and rather later on in the season would be a most formidable, if not impassable, obstacle. As it was, we found far less difficulty in getting over than in hanging on when the other side was reached. I have not often been on a slope of snow steeper than this was immediately above the bergschrund. The angle there must have been at least 55°, and higher up, where the inclination was not so great, I tried it with my clinometer and found 48°, steeper than any part of the celebrated wall of the Strahleck. Fortunately the snow was in excellent condition, and exercising every caution, we worked gradually straight up, and, at 8.50 a.m., stepped with a yell of triumph into the narrow gap not many yards wide. The Brêche de la Meije was won.

We had been only six hours and a quarter from La Grave, including halts amounting in the whole to about one hour, so that Whymper had to shell out his money to Walker and myself; but I doubt whether he ever paid anything in his life with such satisfaction and good will. The height of the pass, according to the French map, is 3,369 mètres, or 11,054 English feet, probably not far from the truth; and, assuming it to be so, we were able to

fix the height of the Bec du Grenier with tolerable accuracy
at 11,000 feet. Yesterday, looking across *from* it to the
Brêche, we had been unable to determine which was the
higher point of the two, and now, looking *at it* from the
Brêche, we were in an equal state of uncertainty, a tolerable
proof that there is not very much difference between the
two. The Col is, or rather was at this time, a very narrow
snow-ridge, with a few patches of rock cropping out, and
on one of these we took up our position, so soon as we had
relieved our excited feelings by yelling till we were almost
black in the face. The view, looking north, was pretty
much what we had seen coming up, and was slightly obscured by clouds, the Grandes Rousses alone being quite
clear; but to the south it was far more interesting. The
Glacier des Etançons fell away from our feet, and a very
cursory inspection showed that no very great difficulty
would be encountered in descending by it to the Vallon
des Etançons and La Berarde. Two spurs, running down
from the Rateau and Meije respectively, divide the upper
portion of the glacier into three bays, of which the eastern
one is much the most extensive. The Col is at the head of
the central one. The Pic des Ecrins was very well seen,
towering over the ridge to the north of what we supposed
to be the Grande Ruine, one of several wonderful pinnacles
of rock which rise out of the lofty ridge on the left side of
the Vallon des Etançons. The Pelvoux was quite invisible, but to the right of the Ecrins was the huge mass
of the Ailefroide, certainly the finest feature of the view.
This glorious mountain bears a strong resemblance to the
Meije, inasmuch as, like its loftier neighbour, it is a con-
glomeration of peaks, so nearly equal in height that it is
hard to say which is the true summit, and is, moreover,
equally precipitous and inaccessible in appearance. To
the right of the Ailefroide, the great Glacier de la Pilatte lay
extended in all its length and breadth, closed at its head
by a lofty ice-covered ridge, considerably higher than that
on which we were sitting, and crowned by several fine
peaks. The ridge bears on the French map the singular

title of "Crête des Bœufs Rouges," and over some portion of it we hoped to make a new pass from Ville Val Louise to La Berarde. There were several well-marked gaps in the ridge, but none very promising in appearance, so far as regarded the descent on to the Glacier de la Pilatte. To the right of that glacier was a very fine group of peaks, standing at the head of the Glaciers du Chardon and du Vallon, over each of which it seemed that passes might be made to the Val Godemar with no very great difficulty. In our immediate vicinity the most striking object was the long ridge which runs up from the Col to one of the lower peaks of the Rateau. I have never seen so shattered and serrated a ridge; in places it was a mere knife-edge of rock, and all along so rotten that it seemed as if a puff of wind or a clap of thunder must dash the whole fabric to pieces. The pinnacle, too, to which it led, was worthy of it, a marvellously-sharp spike of rock, on which a man might comfortably impale himself. The corresponding ridge from the Meije on the east side of the Col was far more solid, and at the same time much more precipitous, falling abruptly from the western peak of the mountain, whose height from a point so immediately below we were of course unable fairly to realise.

A cool breeze was blowing over the Col, and, although our position was tolerably sheltered, we found ourselves getting chilly, so, at 9.50 a.m., took a final look at La Grave, and commenced the descent towards La Berarde. A short but steep snow-slope * fell from our feet to the Glacier des Etançons below, and we commenced the descent close under the rocks of the Rateau; in fact, when about half-way down, we took to the rocks for a few steps. The snow was very soft, but there was no other difficulty, and we soon found ourselves safe over the small bergschrund that intervened between us and the comparatively-level fields of névé. We now struck straight across the glacier

---

* Later in the year this would probably be found a wall of bare rock, and its descent might be troublesome.

towards the long southern spur of the Meije, but to reach it had almost to wade through the soft snow, which was considerably crevassed. Once under the rocks we descended rapidly, pursued by a shower of stones from the Meije, which had to be dodged, and made us by no means sorry when the long spur was turned, and we were fairly on the eastern arm of the glacier, out of harm's way. The great southern face of the Meije, overhanging this arm of the glacier, is a wonderful object; a long line of cliff, totally unlike anything I have seen in any other part of the Alps. The range of crags, forming the left bank of the glacier, is seamed by several snow couloirs, leading up to gaps in the ridge. The most northerly of these was especially tempting, and, according to the map, ought to have communicated with the Glacier de la Meije at its south-eastern angle. This, however, we had seen from the Bec du Grenier, could not possibly be the case, and we were quite unable to guess where any one, reaching the gap from the south, would really find himself in relation to the glaciers on the north side of the chain. The range on the right bank of the glacier is as lofty and even more precipitous than the other. It is a long spur, running south from the Rateau, and completely cuts off the Glacier de la Selle, which drains towards St. Christophe, from the Glacier des Etançons. This ridge is not laid down on the French map, where its place is assigned to a glacier, bearing the curious name of "Glacier du Col," which, in reality, does not exist. It is very doubtful whether any passage can be forced in this direction from the Vallon des Etançons to the Vallon de la Selle, as the intervening barrier is of a most impracticable character, with short and steep hanging glaciers clinging to the cliffs. Nothing could well be easier than the central portion of the Glacier des Etançons, down which we went at a great pace, avoiding without difficulty the few crevasses that were not entirely snowed over, until, steering towards the right bank, we got clear of the snow-covered ice at 10.55, and, as nothing but open and easy glacier lay before us, halted for ten minutes to take off the rope, invariably a welcome operation. The glacier was in a horribly wet condition, and at every step we went above our ankles into slush, which was equally trying to our tempers and our boots. Towards the end crevasses became more numerous, and we at last took to the central moraine, the walking along which was simply loathsome. The moraine gradually spread over the whole end of the glacier, and then both moraine and glacier gradually came to an end, or rather died out on a level stone-covered plain. We had landed on the left bank of the torrent or torrents, which were of no great breadth, and selected the first eligible spot for getting across to the right bank. This accomplished, we soon had the felicity of crossing back again, and then pushed steadily down the valley, till we reached, at 11.40, a perfect oasis in the desert, a small plot of scanty grass with loose rocks lying about, just at the foot of the steep descent from the Col des Cavalles. On seeing this haven of rest, the traps were instantaneously thrown down, and we determined to make a long halt, as there was no object in a very early arrival at La Berarde, which was now within easy reach.

We certainly acted up to our determination, for we never budged till 3.10 p.m., and I don't think I ever spent three hours and a half more enjoyably. The view, looking up the valley, of the Glacier des Etançons, the Brêche, and the Meije, was of the most superb character, and I am happy to say that Whymper utilised the time, which Walker passed in sleeping, and I meditating, in the laudable occupation of sketching the scene, the fame of which, in any tolerably frequented part of the Alps, would draw crowds. The Meije on this side is even steeper than on the north, and falls sheer from summit to base in a long line of black precipices, on which there is scarcely a single patch of snow. The range forming the left side of the valley is scarcely less remarkable, and the huge splintered pinnacles of the Grande Ruine, Tête de la Charrière, and other less important summits, tower into the air defiantly. We were in a very good position for examining the descent from the

Col des Cavalles, and agreed unanimously that, of all dreary and detestable passes, it must be the dreariest and most detestable. The rocks and stone slopes must, whether in the ascent or descent, be most wearisome. Croz pointed out the point between the Tête de la Charrière and Grande Ruine which Mathews and Bonney reached last year from the other side and christened the Col de la Casse Deserte. They did not like to descend, but I must say that, seen from below, the descent seemed far preferable to that from the Col des Cavalles. The valley was apparently closed at its lower end by a remarkably fine group of mountains between the Glaciers du Chardon and du Vallon, the highest peak of which is called on the map Montagne du Clochatel, and is assigned a height of 11,729 feet. At 3.10, overcoming our laziness, we started off, and crossed for the last time to the right bank of the stream, expecting an easy and agreeable walk thenceforward to La Berarde. Never were we more out of our reckoning; the whole bed of the valley is covered with stones of all sizes, from that of a cricket-ball upwards, without the faintest sign of a path. It was impossible to take our eyes off our feet, and if an unlucky individual so much as blew his nose without standing still to perform the operation, the result was either an instantaneous tumble, or a barked shin, or a half-twisted ankle. There was no end to it, and we became more savage at every step, unanimously agreeing that no power on earth would ever induce us to walk up or down this particular valley again. The scenery, nevertheless, is throughout of the highest order of rugged grandeur, and, were a tolerable path only made, as might easily be done, the tourists who, after toiling up the somewhat monotonous valley of the Venéon, arrest their steps at La Berarde, whence there is literally nothing to be seen, would not fail to continue their route, at least as far as the little patch of grass where we halted so long. There are some very fine waterfalls from the cliffs on the right side of the valley, one like the old Cascade des Pelerins at Chamouni, the falling water making a similar rebound; but even these picturesque objects were sources of annoyance, as they formed considerable streams, which run down to join the main torrent, and each one in succession had to be crossed as best it might. Passing the entrance of the Vallon de Bonnepierre, we got a good view of the glacier of the same name, and also of the Ecrins. Very shortly afterwards we really fell into what might by courtesy be called a path, which led us by a very steep and rugged descent over the shoulder of the intervening hill down to the little hamlet of La Berarde, situated just at the point where the Vallon de la Pilatte and the Vallon des Etançons unite to form the main valley of the Venéon. It was just 4.55 p.m. when we entered the house of young Rodier, who always receives the casual visitors to this out of the way spot.

We were cordially received by him and his wife, and *affectionately* by his mother, an ancient hag in her dotage, who lavished her endearments on the party in general and poor Walker in particular rather more freely than was agreeable. Rodier, who seemed in bad health, manifested some slight interest on hearing of the route by which we had passed from La Grave, and made no difficulty in communicating all he knew about the neighbouring glaciers, which was not much. Our programme for the next day was, to cross the Col de la Tempe between the Ecrins and Aile-froide, and reach Tuckett's gîte on the left bank of the Glacier Blanc, with a view of attacking the Ecrins from there. Whymper, however, wished to try and make a pass nearer the Ecrins, mounting by the Glacier du Vallon, and descending on to the northern branch of the Glacier Noir. No one knew anything about the practicability of either side of the proposed pass, but it was well known that a descent on to the Glacier Noir was not practicable from all points of the long ridge which separates it from the Vallon de la Pilatte. Under these circumstances, and considering that a failure would entail the loss of three entire days, the following day being Saturday, and we not wishing to attack the Ecrins on Sunday, the voice of the majority decided against the Col du Vallon. Croz then suggested that we should bivouac on the top of the Col des Ecrins to-morrow night instead of at Tuckett's gîte, and be so much nearer the peak. This would entail the abandonment of the Col de la Tempe, which Walker and I were both anxious to pass in order to see the northern face of the Pelvoux, but, on the other hand, it would allow us to get one full night's rest at La Berarde, and would be undeniably a far better starting point for the peak. An additional reason for agreeing to Croz's proposition was, that Pic had not arrived with our traps, without some of which we could not possibly .start; so things were finally settled as he proposed. Our day's walk had by no means impaired our appetites, and shortly after our arrival we made Madame Rodier prepare us a large omelette; but we found that even this, with copious draughts of milk, was not sufficient to appease our hunger, so, having routed up a large ham, Walker and I proceeded to cook a dish of ham and eggs, which, in spite of our deficient culinary knowledge, turned out most excellent. Thanks to these various occupations, we found the time, till it was the hour for retiring, hang by no means heavily on our hands. We stopped up as long as possible waiting for Pic, who came not; so, invoking a blessing on the head of that mendacious one, at 9.15 we requested Rodier to show us our sleeping quarters. He led us to a capacious barn close by, where there was an abundance of clean straw, held a candle while we arranged ourselves for the night, not a very long operation, and then took his departure.

Friday, 24th June.—Having gone to sleep in the blissful consciousness that there was not to be an early start in the morning, I never opened my eyes till 8.0 a.m., and immediately closed them again till 9.0, when I shook off dull sloth, and emerged into the open air. On entering Rodier's house, we found that our friend, " the unblushing one," had arrived at 5.0 a.m., having passed the night at St. Christophe. On enquiring why he had not appeared last night, as agreed, he assumed a bilious and generally dilapidated air, and stated that he had been taken so ill on the road that he had actually fainted, and remained for some time insensible, so that he found it quite impossible to get beyond St. Christophe. We were, I regret to say, uncharitable enough not to believe a word of this, and imputed his non-appearance to the fact that he, in common with the other natives of La Grave, had been so firmly convinced that we should be unable to get over the Brèche, and must return, that he had probably not started till we were seen on the top, and of course had not had time to accomplish the distance, which is very considerable. On opening the knapsacks, it was found that out of a large number of cigars which Walker and Whymper had sent round, at least two-thirds had been purloined en route. This was too bad, so Walker said casually to Pic, "Monsieur Pic, je pense que vous avez fumé beaucoup hier," to which the fellow replied with an air of surprise and total innocence quite delightful, "Moi! je ne fume jamais, jamais!" Of course, after that nothing more could be said, but we mentally resolved that if he did not smoke, he chewed, and that pretty vigorously. He certainly acted up to the character he had assumed of a man indisposed, and on that account declined serving as our porter to the top of the Col des Ecrins, saying that otherwise he should have been most happy to accompany us, but that, as it was, he should only be in our way. For once we believed him. We paid him fifteen francs, the sum agreed upon, and let him depart in peace, which he did the same afternoon. It was absolutely necessary to find a porter, so we entered into negociations with Rodier. He, however, said that his health was so bad that he should be afraid to pass a night in a position so exposed as the top of the Col des Ecrins, and, moreover, advised *us* not to do it either, observing, with perfect truth, that at this early period of the season we should probably find the rocks, which Croz had seen when he crossed with Tuckett, entirely covered with snow. He strongly recommended us to change our plans so far as to sleep at the foot of the steep couloir leading to the Col, instead of at the top of it, assuring us that on the upper plateau of the

Glacier de Bonnepierre we should find some admirable sites for a bivouac, and offering to come with us so far with coverings, &c., for fifteen francs. It must be confessed that the idea of a night on the snow with scanty coverings, at an elevation of more than 11,000 feet, preparatory to what would probably be a very hard day's work, was the reverse of inviting, and Rodier's counsel so commended itself to our common sense, that, with the full concurrence of Croz and Almer, we agreed to his proposition, and ordered him to prepare all the coverings, and boil all the eggs, that could be collected in La Berarde.

The situation of La Berarde itself is most uninteresting, as, although standing in a little plain at the junction of three valleys, there is neither a single glacier nor any peak of importance visible from it. The tourists who occasionally come up from Bourg d'Oysans, and look upon it as the end of the world, must be most grievously disappointed. It stands very high, 5702 feet according to the French map, so that vegetation is stunted and scanty, while the pine forests, which in the Swiss Alps give such a charm to the lower slopes of the mountains, are here entirely wanting, their place being supplied by long dreary slopes of stones and débris, as displeasing to the eye as they are ruinous to the feet and boots.

The morning was passed in superintending the preparations of the commissariat, the staple of which was eggs, and in discussing the weather, which, though still very fine, showed signs of changing, a large mass of cloud at the bottom of the valley, towards St. Christophe, making strenuous, but fortunately so far ineffectual, efforts, to force its way up to our more elevated regions. Rodier managed to collect sundry most suspicious-looking coverings, and at last all was declared ready; so, after another meal of hot milk, we started at 1.20 p.m., the larger portion of our personal effects being left in charge of Madame Rodier to await our return, which we hoped would take place on the following Monday. La Berarde is in the angle formed by the junction of the torrents from the

Vallon des Etançons and the Vallon de la Pilatte, and our route lay up the left bank of the stream from the first-named valley. For some distance there was a fair though rough and stony path, which mounted rapidly towards the entrance of the short Vallon de Bonnepierre over steep slopes of wretched grass and stones; but, as we climbed the track gradually vanished, leaving us to choose the line of march which pleased us best. At this time of the day the grind was severe, and no one seemed at all inclined to force the pace or to object to a short halt when the first, and, as usual, steepest part of the ascent was accomplished. In front of us the fine Glacier de Bonnepierre showed its extreme end, covered from bank to bank with moraine, while below it dreary slopes of stones stretched downwards in the usual fan-shape towards the main valley. Amongst this mass of débris the torrent from the glacier forced its way, not in one grand stream, but in several considerable ones, and as we had to get over somehow to the opposite or right side of the Vallon, we looked anxiously out for a favourable spot to effect the passage. When Tuckett first crossed the Col des Ecrins *from* Val Louise, he encountered considerable difficulty here, and got thoroughly soaked, a catastrophe which it was most important for us to avoid, as the consequences of a bivouac at a great elevation in wet garments might be serious, putting aside the discomfort of such a state of things. We saw no point that pleased us for some time, but at last, when not far from the foot of the glacier, we struck down to the bank of the first torrent, and commenced the passage. There were four distinct streams, separated by high moraine-shaped mounds of stones, and we contrived to pass them all in succession with less difficulty than we had expected, and without a serious wetting. Tuckett crossed a good deal lower down, after the streams had coalesced, but I should think that our route would always be found preferable. The torrents passed, we took at once to the enormous moraine of the Glacier de Bonnepierre, one of the most extensive I ever saw, and quite as unpleasant to traverse as most of its

kindred. We thought it well, however, to reconcile ourselves to the inevitable, as Rodier informed us that we
should have very little relief from it, until we reached our
proposed night-quarters. We shortly diverged for a time
on to the slopes of the valley on our left, and worked along
them, collecting, as we went, quantities of dry juniper
branches, wherewith to make a fire up above. Croz and
Almer loaded themselves with such a mass of these, that,
as they walked side-by-side, they looked just like a peram-
bulating shrubbery, presenting an appearance that would
have been very alarming to a person of Macbethian turn
of mind. Having secured wood enough to keep up a
roaring fire all night long for a week if necessary, we
returned to the moraine, which now rose very steeply in
front. We toiled up it, expecting momentarily to find a
level spot again where we could rest, but the further we
mounted the more distant did the summit-level appear,
until, at 3.25, we halted in despair. Unfortunately, while
we had been mounting, the clouds had not been idle. The
high peaks in front were all enveloped, while behind us the
great mass, which had been struggling all day to force a
passage up the valley, appeared at last to have succeeded;
La Berarde was already obscured, and the enemy was
slowly but surely creeping up to us. This untoward state
of affairs compelled us to shorten our halt, and at 3.35 we
resumed our march along the moraine, which soon became
more level, and had alongside of it a companion like unto
itself. We were getting along pretty rapidly, when down, or
up, came the mist, and enveloped us instantaneously in its
clammy folds. This at first did not check our pace, but
Croz and Rodier soon showed by their manner that they
were uncertain of their ground, and, finally, at 4.5, Croz
honestly admitted that he was uncertain whether we ought
to go to the right or to the left, or straight forwards, and
that we had better wait a little in hopes of a clearance, or
at least a temporary lift. So down we sat, not feeling
particularly happy in our minds, yet trying to persuade
ourselves that the mist was merely local, and that we

should soon get rid of it. Croz, meanwhile, was evidently thinking hard, and endeavouring to recall his recollection of the ground, and at last, at 4.25, came to the conclusion that we could not go very far wrong by keeping straight forwards along the moraine as far as possible ; so, off we went again in the direction indicated. The moraine had hitherto been pretty much like other moraines, neither more nor less objectionable, but it now assumed a specially detestable character, narrowing to a mere knife-edge of hard grit, along the top of which we must perforce go, as the slope on either side was too steep to give footing without the use of the axe. A painful series of Blondin-like manœuvres had to be gone through in order to pass along this objectionable arrangement, but all my care could not prevent me from coming down several times in a straddling position on the narrow edge, an attitude certainly unpleasant, but agreeable compared with the consequences of adopting the only alternative, viz., rolling on either side down to the crevassed glacier at an unpleasant depth below. I, for one, was not sorry when the moraine expanded into a level space, covered with loose masses of rock, some of enormous size, and piled one upon another, in a manner that suggested any number of charming sites for a bivouac. The mist remained as thick as ever, but we could not be very far from the head of the glacier, and we might not find so eligible a spot further on, so it was resolved to pitch our tent amongst these hospitable stones, and at 5.0 p.m. the traps were deposited, and every man started off to find a hole big enough to hold the whole party, or, failing that, a burrow for himself.

Walker and I went off together, and although unable to find a " Grand Hotel," discovered a small " Auberge," containing just sufficient accommodation for two, which we at once resolved to appropriate to ourselves. Several rocks had fallen together, forming a perfect hole, with a not too wide entrance, and the floor sunk considerably below the general level, so that we had to get down into it, and, once in, were completely sheltered from any wind that

E

could blow. The floor, indeed, had been left in a horribly unfinished state, but, by getting rid of some of the sharp-pointed stones, and replacing them by flat ones, we hoped to improve matters so as to make it tolerably comfortable. We were working away, and the place was beginning to assume quite a palatial aspect, when the mist suddenly lifted a little, and disclosed a somewhat similar patch of rocks a considerable distance further on. The guides at once determined to go on there, so all our labour was thrown away, and at 5.25 we somewhat sulkily turned our backs on our "Auberge," picked up our respective loads, and went on our way. After all, it was scarcely worth while moving, as in ten minutes, at 5.35, our goal was reached, and we halted for good under a huge mass of rock, inclined at a slight angle with the ground, which was at once selected as head-quarters. By comparison, however, with our abandoned "gîte," the place was wretched, so Walker and I went prowling about to see if we could not find something better. Our search was long fruitless, and we had a highly exhilarating scramble over the neighbouring rocks before we found what we liked in the shape of a hole, similar to our former one, but less extensive, requiring much more arrangement, and altogether less satisfactory. Still nothing better was forthcoming, so we set to work arranging the floor. The shape of the hole was such that we should be obliged to lie with our heads towards the entrance, and, therefore, not so much sheltered as we could have wished, but still fairly protected against everything but heavy rain, which was scarcely to be expected. The levelling of the floor was a rather difficult operation, and the result after all was only negatively good. By placing ourselves as we intended to lie at night, we found out what was wanted, and managed—not to make a smooth couch, that was impossible—but to arrange the stones so that they fitted pretty well into the crevices and sinuosities of our respective carcases.

While engaged in our building operations, the mist that enveloped the glacier and surrounding peaks was becoming thinner; little bits of blue sky appeared here and there, until suddenly, when we were standing before our front entrance, and looking towards the head of the glacier, far far above us, at an almost inconceivable height, in a tiny patch of blue, appeared a wonderful rocky pinnacle, bathed in the beams of the fast-sinking sun. We were so electrified by the glory of the sight that it was some seconds before we realised what we saw, and understood that that astounding point, apparently miles removed from earth, was one of the highest summits of Les Ecrins, and that we hoped, before another sun should set, to have stood upon an even loftier pinnacle.* As the mist gradually cleared away, and disclosed the spotless fields of névé, forming the upper plateau of the Glacier de Bonnepierre, and the wall of cliff rising from it, crowned by a ridge, broken into the most fantastic forms and peaks, I thought I had never gazed upon so sublime a scene; and writing now in cool blood, and after witnessing other glorious spectacles, I am not disposed to change my opinion. The mists rose and fell, presenting us with a series of dissolving views of ravishing grandeur, and finally died away, leaving the glacier and its mighty bounding precipices under an exquisitely pale blue sky, free from a single speck.

We saw, to our no small satisfaction, that Croz had steered discreetly, and that the steep couloir leading to

---

* I do not think the position of the Ecrins, with reference to the surrounding glaciers, has ever been quite exactly described. The mountain has three summits, whose respective heights are 13,462, 13,396, and 13,058 feet, but the second is very insignificant, and scarcely worthy of distinct recognition. The highest summit does *not* look down upon the Bonnepierre Glacier, and is not, I believe, visible from it. The noble pinnacle of rock, which is so imposing from that glacier, is the third summit, which, on the side of the Glacier de l'Encula, shows as a dome of snow. A rugged ridge stretches in a westerly direction from this peak, and separates the Glacier de Bonnepierre from the parallel Glacier du Vallon. The highest summit does not lie on the watershed at all, but in the ridge thrown out from it to the eastward between the Glacier de l'Encula and the Glacier Noir. To the west of the highest point is the so-called second summit, which is a mere projection from the ridge. This *is* on the watershed, and overhangs the Glacier du Vallon. A glance at the map will make these details clear.

the Col des Ecrins was very slightly to our left, only separated from us by a perfectly level field of névé. On going
up to head-quarters, we found that Whymper had constructed a charming "gite" for himself close at hand, and
that the men, having built a low wall of stones round their
position, had lit a fire, and were now busy making preparations for supper. Not far off we found a tolerably
copious stream of water, so, proceeded to boil up a lump
of portable soup we had brought from England, together
with half a cake of "Chollet's" compressed vegetables.
From preliminary trial in London, we had discovered that,
at the best, this concoction only produced a scalding liquid,
with a very strong taste of nothing in particular, and a
very slight one of meat and vegetables, and that to obtain
even this result large quantities of salt must be thrown
into the mixture. We were, therefore, disgusted, though
scarcely surprised, to find that not a grain of that article
had been brought with us, and that our "potage" must go
without seasoning. The labour of boiling it was considerable, as the fire manifested at first a strong desire to go
out altogether, and then persisted in burning most fiercely
just at the point where the pot was not, a difficulty which
was got over by two of the party on opposite sides keeping
up a vigorous blowing with their hats, so as to drive the
flame into the middle, and the smoke into each other's eyes.
At last the soup boiled, and though the most partial cook
could not call it nice, it was at least warm and comforting.*
From our position there was a delicious echo from the
cliffs of the Ecrins. The answer came, not immediately
after the call, but after the lapse of a considerable interval,
when no reply was expected, and in a note wonderfully
clear and musical. It was dark before our supper was at

---

* In the way of portable soup I have never come across anything equal
to the "soup tablets," sold by McCall and Son, of Houndsditch. They are
very portable; and each tablet, when boiled up with the proper proportion of
Chollet's vegetables, makes a quart of excellent soup. Mr. H. Walker and
I took out a large quantity in 1865, and the more we used it, the more were
we impressed with its merits.

an end, and, in spite of the fire, we soon found ourselves getting chilly, a fact not to be wondered at, seeing that our quarters could not be much lower than 9500 feet. I accordingly took off my boots, put on a pair of warm sleeping socks and a pair of slippers, buttoned up my coat, tied my hat down over my ears with a handkerchief, and then, with Walker, went down to our hole, accompanied by Almer bearing two blankets, which, in spite of our remonstrances, he and Croz insisted that we should have. One blanket was placed over the stones, on the top of which we wrapped, in our plaids, took up our position, the other blanket and my mackintosh sheet were then thrown over all, Almer wished us good night, and we were left to our meditations. I cannot honestly say that our couch was comfortable, as, notwithstnding all our exertions, one or two impracticable stones had been left, which touched us up most unmercifully between the ribs. Moreover, without disarranging all the coverings, it was almost impossible to vary the position we had first taken up, and a cautious wriggle was the only movement either of us could venture to indulge in. Much sleep was, therefore, not to be thought of, and for a very long time we both lay silent, but very wide awake, meditating upon what the morrow was likely to bring forth. At last, however, Walker's heavy breathing announced that he had dropped off, and shortly afterwards I myself lapsed into a happy state of oblivion.

Saturday, 25th June.—Shortly after midnight I woke, and moving my head, could see the vast cliffs of the Ecrins, bathed in the light of the moon, which was fast approaching the last quarter. The effect was wonderful, and was enhanced by the solemn, and almost oppressive silence that reigned around us. There was not a sound, and we might have been miles away from any other human being but ourselves. Suddenly, and without any sort of warning, the silence was broken by the thunder of what must have been a gigantic avalanche falling from the other side of the Ecrins. The reverberation had scarcely died away, when—crash! the echoes were again aroused by a still more tremendous fall, the sound from which rose and fell for many minutes before absolute silence again prevailed. We waited anxiously, hoping for yet another fall, but we hoped in vain, and nothing more occurred to disturb the tranquillity around. I don't think that either of us got much more sleep after this, but we lay, getting momentarily colder and more uncomfortable, until 3 a.m., when the voice of Almer, up above, was wafted down to us in a very good imitation of the early village cock. We were nothing loth to move, so, throwing off the coverings, we emerged from our den into the open air, and made our way up, over some patches of snow which had frozen hard in the night, and required some art to cross in slippers, to head-quarters, where we found a blazing fire, with some wine warming over it, and round it the rest of the party looking particularly cold and sleepy. Whymper had passed the night pretty much as we had, but I fancy that the men had not had much sleep, and had found it sufficiently cold. One of the greatest objections to a bivouac is, that it is impossible to persuade the guides to make anything like an impartial distribution of such coverings as there may be. They invariably leave themselves with almost nothing, in their anxiety for the comfort of their employers. I have never, however, heard a good guide utter a syllable on the subject of his nocturnal discomforts, and Almer and Croz, and even Rodier, were no exceptions to the rule; on the contrary, they were certainly the most cheerful members of the party. The hot wine put life into us all, and, after forcing some bread and butter down our throats, we made preparations for a start. Everything not likely to be required was left for Rodier to take down to La Berarde, amongst other things my mackintosh sheet. I had intended to get rid of my plaid also, but, on second thoughts, determined to be prudent, and retain it, especially as, carried on my back like a knapsack, in a very convenient arrangement of straps I had had made in England purposely, it would cause me very slight inconvenience. At last all was ready. The superfluous wood was laid in a heap for the benefit of future comers, if there should ever be any; we paid Rodier, who gave us an emphatic, but quite unnecessary, caution to be careful; and at 3.55 a.m. left our refuge, all roped carefully together, Croz leading.

It was a glorious morning, the sky cloudless, and the atmosphere perfectly still, so that as regarded weather our prospects could not have been more favourable. Personally I felt anything but fresh and up to work, as usual, after a night on hard stones, from which, even under the most propitious circumstances, very little real rest can be derived. The exposure is a trifle, but the cruel hardness of the couch tells severely. Picking our way over a wilderness of stones, we were soon on the glacier, which was very slightly inclined, and completely covered with snow. Not a crevasse was visible, and we had no difficulty in pushing on at a good pace towards the foot of the couloir up which lies the only means of egress from the glacier. Though not so mysterious and imposing under the matter-of-fact morning light as they had appeared last night when partially veiled by mists, the long line of cliffs which hem in the head of the Bonnepierre Glacier is singularly grand. From the Roche Faurio to and beyond Les Ecrins, the mighty wall is seamed with numerous snow couloirs, of varying breadth and steepness, of which all, save the one which, by a merciful dispensation of providence, leads up to the very lowest point in the ridge, are probably impracticable. Not that the appearance of even this is by any means fascinating. On the contrary, as we approached it, it assumed an aspect more and more repulsive, and appeared both steeper and loftier than we had supposed from a distance. In less than an hour of easy walking we were close to the foot of the wall. We were now obliged to make frequent short halts to take breath, the slope being scarcely steep enough to render step-cutting absolutely necessary, yet too steep for us to progress, except most laboriously, without it. At length, after rounding a patch of rocks, we were fairly committed to the couloir, which was of the usual funnel shape, tolerably broad at the bottom but gradually narrowing,

until at the top it became a mere cleft. Once in this
limited channel, *our* work became easy and pleasant enough,
as we had simply to put our feet in the steps which Croz
and Almer cut, but the two latter, doubtless, looked at the
matter from rather a different point of view. The couloir
was fortunately not filled with ice, or we should have taken
hours to scale it, but with very hard snow, in which steps
had to be cut, but with a far less expenditure of labour
than would have been required by ice. Nevertheless it
was a long and toilsome piece of business, and, looking
down, it seemed a very long time before we had made any
perceptible way. The greatest care had to be exercised,
and the steps cut large and deep, as the slope was formidably steep, and a slip on to those nasty jagged rocks
which we had passed below would have made a summary
end of our expeditions. I tried the angle with my clinometer in two separate places, and found it to be 52°
and 54°. I don't think it ever varied much, so that, even
had the footing not been so precarious, the mere labour
of lifting oneself from step to step on such a slope would
have been considerable. All this time we were completely
in the shade, and found the temperature uncomfortably
cold, especially for our hands and feet, which were also
brought into contact with the ice of the couloir. But our
men worked admirably, one hewing out the rough step
first, the other improving and polishing it up for us; so that,
except by gross carelessness, we could not well slip. The
narrow gap, which from below had seemed so high above
us, sensibly diminished its distance, the channel in which we
were became more and more confined, near the top a little
soft snow helped us on, and at 5.55 a.m., just two hours
from our " gite," the final step was cut, and we stood on the
Col des Ecrins, a mere cleft in the ridge between the Roche
Faurio to the north, and the Ecrins to the south.

In spite of the great elevation of this point (11,206 feet,
according to Tuckett's observations), the distant view on
either side is very inconsiderable; the real attraction is the
extraordinary difference in the character of the ground on

the east and west sides. On the west we had just mounted
by a very precipitous couloir, certainly not less than 1200
feet in height, while on the east a gentle slope fell away
very gradually to an exquisitely pure field of névé, extending almost on a level for a great distance in front. This is
called on the French map Glacier de l'Encula, but is
really nothing more than the upper plateau of the Glacier
Blanc. The ridges that bound it right and left are very
striking, the Crête de l'Encula, running out from the Ecrins,
and the Crête du Glacier Blanc, from the Roche Faurio;
the former especially is a wonderful mass of crag and
broken glacier. Straight in front, beyond the Glacier
Blanc, the most prominent object was a remarkably fine
mountain, with a rocky summit, which had also attracted
our attention from the Col des Aiguilles d'Arve and the
Bec du Grenier. This appeared to agree in position with
a peak considerably to the east of the Col du Glacier Blanc,
called on the French map Pic Signalé, which is equivalent
to no name at all, as the unimaginative engineers have
applied the same title to some dozen peaks in the Dauphiné
Alps. It attains a height of 12,008 feet, and is well worthy
the attention of mountaineers. Overhanging Monetier,
between Briançon and the Hospice du Lautaret, it might,
perhaps, be most advantageously attacked by the Glacier
du Casset. Immediately to the north of the Col rose the
Roche Faurio, 12,192 feet in height, which, if accessible,
must command a most interesting view, as it stands in the
angle between three very extensive glaciers, de la Bonnepierre, de la Platte des Agneaux, and de l'Encula. But to
the south of the Col was the object on which our thoughts
were intent. There rose the monarch of the Dauphiné Alps,
the highest summit in France proper—the Pic des Ecrins,
soaring to a height of 13,462 feet, or 2256 feet above our
position. A greater contrast than that presented by
this mountain, as seen from the side of La Berarde,
and as seen from the Glacier de l'Encula, can scarcely be
imagined. The western face of the peak that falls to the
Glaciers de Bonnepierre and du Vallon is one of the

sheerest precipices in the Alps; neither glacier nor snow
can find a resting-place on it, while the eastern face on
which we were now looking, is entirely covered with snow
and glacier, steep certainly, but not excessively so.   The
final peak seemed to be defended by an ugly bergschrund,
above which rose, what appeared from below to be a by no
means lofty nor steeply-inclined wall of snow or ice,
seamed here and there with ribs of rock protruding very
slightly from the surface of the snow.   In fact, the mountain on the eastern side seemed as easy of access, as from
the west it had appeared impracticable, and, had we not
been warned by the misfortunes of our predecessors, we
should have certainly looked upon the work before us with
contempt.   As it was we estimated that, under the most
unfavourable circumstances, four hours would see us on
the top, and two hours and a half more back again at
the Col.

The exciting ascent of the couloir had freshened us up
wonderfully, and although, under ordinary circumstances,
it would scarcely have been eating time, we felt the effects
of our scanty meal at starting, and now, while studying
the view, were quite ready for the contents of the provision-
bag.   At 6.25 we turned up in the direction of the peak,
but in a few minutes again halted to deposit the "impedimenta," in the shape of knapsacks, plaids, &c., to await
our return.   Almer filled with snow a metal vessel we had,
and set it up, in hopes that the sun, which was already
powerful, would have melted it by the time we descended.
Then we fairly bent our minds and legs to the work before
us, and, Croz leading, started up the steep slopes of névé,
bearing rather to the left.   The object of this course was to
avoid some enormous ice-cliffs which towered in the most
threatening manner high up on the right, and which gave
us palpable evidence of their capability for mischief in the
shape of a vast tract of recent débris, across which we had
to flounder.   This was very likely the result of the two
falls, the noise of which had so startlingly broken upon
our repose.   Although the slope up which we were mount-

ing presented not the slightest difficulty in itself, it was
sufficiently steep to make the ascent laborious, and we
found it necessary to make frequent short halts for breath.
The snow was in first-rate order; indeed, we should have
been better pleased had it been not quite so good, as a
more moderate pace must have been kept. We were
obliged to cut round the edge of an occasional crevasse,
but, on the whole, this part of the mountain was very
much less broken up, and altogether easier than, from the
accounts of our predecessors, we had expected to find the
case. This was very likely owing to the almost unprecedentedly large quantity of snow which there appeared to
be this year in the high Alps. It stood us in good stead on
the Brêche de la Meije, and now, again, undoubtedly gave us
no small assistance. The result was, that we mounted
rapidly. Already the lofty ridges which enclose the Glacier
de l'Encula had sunk beneath us, and over the northern of
these ridges the three Aiguilles d'Arve, the great mass of
the Graians, and, above all, the towering form of Mont
Blanc, once again greeted us. It must be confessed that
the higher we climbed, the greater became our contempt
for our peak. It certainly seemed that, once over the bergschrund, we ought very soon to be on the top, and so
persuaded was I of this, that I hazarded the opinion that
by 9.30 we should be seated on the highest point. Whymper
alone was less sanguine; and, probably encouraged by the
result of his former bet, on hearing my opinion, offered to
bet Walker and myself two francs that we should not get
up at all, an offer which we promptly accepted. We were
now sufficiently near to the bergschrund to be able to form
some idea of its nature and difficulty. It certainly was a
formidable-looking obstacle, running completely along the
base of the final peak, or rather ridge from which the peak
itself rose. For a long distance the chasm was of great
width, and, with its upper edge rising in a wall of ice,
fringed with icicles, to a height of, perhaps, thirty-feet above
the lower edge, was obviously quite impassable. But, on the
extreme right (looking up), the two lips so nearly met that

we thought we might be able to get over, and, on the extreme
left, it seemed possible, by a considerable detour, to circumvent the enemy, and get round his flank. We finally determined on the latter course, as, to the right, the slope
above the chasm seemed to be steeper than at any other
point. After the first start, we had been steering tolerably
straight forwards up the centre of the glacier, and were
now approaching the bergschrund, just under the highest
peak of the mountain, at about its most impracticable
point. The more direct course would have been to attack
it on the right, but, for the reason above stated, we chose
the opposite end, so had to strike well away to the left
diagonally up the slope. We here first began to suspect
that our progress would not be quite so easy and rapid as
we had hoped, as the snow became less abundant, and the
use of the axe necessary. Still we worked away steadily,
until, at 8.10 a.m., in one hour and forty minutes from the
Col, we turned the bergschrund, and were fairly on its
upper edge, clinging to an ice-step which promised to be
only the first of an unpleasantly long series.

Above us the slope stretched up to some rocks, which
continued without interruption to the main ridge, a prominent point on which was just over our heads. The rocks
looked quite easy, and it seemed that, by making for them
just under the small peak, we should be able to work round
the latter, and get on to the main ridge to the right of it
without serious difficulty. Almer led, and wielded his axe
with his usual vigour, but the ice was fearfully hard, and
he found the work very severe, as the steps had to be cut
sufficiently large and good to serve for our retreat, if need
be. After each blow, he showered down storms of fragments,
which came upon the hands and legs of his followers with
a violence that rendered their position the reverse of
pleasant. Still the rocks kept their distance, and it was a
long time before we scrambled on to the lowest of them,
only to find that, although from below they had appeared
quite easy, they were in reality very steep, and so smooth
that it was scarcely possible to get along them at all, the

hold for hands and feet being almost "nil." The rocky peak, too, above us turned out to be much farther off than we had supposed, and, to reach the point on the main ridge to the right of it, we had before us a long and difficult climb up and along the face of the rocks. The prospect was not pleasant, but we scrambled along the lower part of the rocks for a short time, and then Almer started off alone to reconnoitre, leaving us rather disconsolate, and Walker and myself beginning to think that there was a considerable probability of our francs, after all, finding their way into Whymper's pocket. Croz did not approve of the rocks at all, and strongly urged the propriety of getting down on to the ice-slope again, and cutting along it above the berg-schrund until we should be immediately under the peak, and then strike straight up towards it. He, accordingly, cast loose the rope, and, crawling cautiously down, began cutting. I am not very nervous, but, as I saw him creeping alone over the ice-covered rocks, I felt an unpleasant qualm, which I was doomed to experience several times before the end of the day. Just as Croz had begun to work Almer returned, and reported that things ahead were decidedly bad, but that he thought we could get on to the arête by keeping up the rocks. We passed his opinion down to Croz, and, while he was digesting it, we communicated to Almer what Croz had been saying to us. Now, up to the present time no two men could have got on better, nor more thoroughly agreed with each other than Croz and Almer. We had been slightly afraid that the natural anti-pathy between an Oberlander and a Chamouniard would break out upon every occasion, and that a constant series of squabbles would be our daily entertainment. We were, however, agreeably disappointed, as Almer displayed such an utter abnegation of self, and such deference to Croz's opinion, that had the latter been the worst-tempered fellow in the world, instead of the really good fellow that he was, he could not have found a cause of quarrel. Upon this occasion, although Almer adhered to his own opinion that it would be better to keep to the rocks, he begged us to follow the advice of Croz, who was equally strong in favour of the ice, should he, on further consideration, prefer that course. Croz protested emphatically against the rocks, but left it to us to decide, but in such a manner that it was plain that a decision adverse to his wishes would produce a rumpus. The position was an awkward one. The idea of cutting along a formidably-steep slope of hard ice immediately above a prodigious bergschrund was most revolting to us, not only on account of the inevitable danger of the proceeding, but also because of the frightful labour which such a course must entail on the two men. On the other hand, a serious difference with Croz would probably destroy all chance of success in our attempt. So convinced, however, were we that the rocks offered the most advisable route that we determined to try the experiment on Croz's temper, and announced our decision accordingly. The effect was electric; Croz came back again in the steps which he had cut, anger depicted on his countenance, giving free vent to the ejaculations of his native land, and requesting us to understand that, as we had so chosen, we might do the work ourselves, that he would do no more. Affairs were evidently serious, so each of us cried "peccavi," and to calm his irritation, agreed, it must be confessed against our better judgment, to adopt his route. Almer was more amused than annoyed, and concurred without a word, so the storm blew over; the sky was again clear, and we resumed our labours, which, during the discussion, had been suspended for a few minutes.

The half dozen steps that led us on to the ice were about the most unpleasant I ever took. The rocks were glazed with ice; there was nothing in particular to hold on by, and without the trusty rope I should have looked a long time before trusting myself to move. As it was, I was very considerably relieved when we were all standing in the steps, and Croz, again roped on to us, began, at 9.35, to cut in front. I must do him the justice to say that, so soon as we were committed to his line of march, he worked splendidly, bringing the whole force of his arm to bear in

the blows with which he hewed the steps. Never halting
for a moment nor hesitating, he hacked away, occasionally
taking a glance behind to see that all was right. We could
not but admire the determination with which he laboured,
but the exertion was fearful, and we became momentarily
more of opinion that our original decision was the wisest.
The slope, on which we were, was inclined at an angle of
50°, never less, sometimes more, for the most part of
hard blue ice, bare of snow. This was bad enough; but
far worse were places which we occasionally came to, where
there was a layer of soft, dry, powdery snow without cohesion, so that it gave no footing, and steps had to be cut
through it into the ice below—steps which were filled up
almost as soon as cut, and which each man had to clear
out with his hands before trusting his feet in them. All
the time the great bergschrund yawned about a hundred
feet below us, and the knowledge of this fact kept us well
on the alert, although, from the steepness of the slope
below, the chasm itself was not visible. One hears people
talk occasionally of places where the rope should not be
used, because one person slipping might entail the loss of
the whole party ; but I never heard a guide give vent to
any such idea, and certain I am that had any one of us
now proposed to take off the rope and go alone on that
account, Almer and Croz would never have allowed it, and,
indeed, would not have advanced another step. It must be
admitted, however, that, all along this slope, had one of
us unfortunately slipped, the chance of the others being
able to hold him up would have been very small, and the
probability of the party in their fall being shot over instead
of into the bergschrund still smaller. But, in my opinion,
the use of the rope on such places gives so much more
confidence, if it is no real protection, that the chances of
a slip are much diminished, and certainly a party can progress more rapidly. For an hour Croz kept on his way
unwearied, cutting the steps for the most part beautifully,
but occasionally giving us rather a long stride, where every
one held on like grim death, while each man in succession

passed. But, at last, even his powerful frame required rest; so Almer relieved him, and went to the front. All this time we had risen but little, but we were now very nearly under the highest peak, and it was necessary to think of getting on to the ridge; so we at last fairly turned our faces to the slope, and began cutting straight up what appeared to be a great central couloir. Unlike most couloirs, this one did not run without interruption to the ridge above, but came to an abrupt termination at a considerable distance below it, leaving an intervening space of rock which promised some trouble. But we were yet far from the lowest point of these rocks, and every step towards them cost no small amount of time and labour. I have rarely been on harder ice, and, as blow after blow fell with so little apparent result in raising us towards our goal, an inexpressible weariness of spirit and a feeling of despair took possession of me. Nevertheless, we *did* mount, and, at 11.30, after two hours of terribly hard work (for the guides), we grasped with our hands the lowest of the crags. To get on them, however, was no easy task, as they were exceedingly smooth, and coated with ice. Almer scrambled up, how I know not, and, taking as much rope as possible, crawled on until he was "fest," when, by a combined operation of pulling from above and pushing from below, each of us, in turn, was raised a few steps. We hoped that this might be an exceptional bit, and that higher up matters would improve. But it was a vain hope; the first few steps were but a foretaste of what was to follow, and every foot of height was gained with the greatest difficulty and exertion. As we climbed, with the tips of our fingers in some small crevice, and the tips of our toes just resting on some painfully-minute ledge, probably covered with ice or snow, one question gradually forced itself upon us, almost to the exclusion of the previously absorbing one, whether we should get to the top of the mountain, and this was, how on earth we should ever get down again—get down, that is to say, in any other state than that of débris. The idea that it would be possible to descend these rocks again, except with a rush in the shape of an avalanche, seemed rather absurd; and at last, some one propounded the question to Almer and Croz, but those worthies shirked the answer, and gave us one of those oracular replies which a good guide always has at the tip of his tongue when he is asked a question to which he does not wish to give a straightforward response, to the effect that we should probably get down somehow. They were, perhaps, of opinion that one thing at a time was sufficient, and that they had work enough to settle the question of how we were to get up. Our progress was unavoidably slow, and the positions in which one was detained, while the man in front was going the full length of his tether, were far from agreeable; while hanging on by my eyelids, the view, seen between my legs, of the smooth wall of rock and ice on which we had been so long engaged, struck me as being singularly impressive, and gave me some occupation in discussing mentally where I should stop, if in an oblivious moment I chanced to let go. But to all things must come an end, and, at 12.30 p.m., with a great sigh of relief, we lifted ourselves by a final effort on to the main ridge, which had so long mocked at our efforts to reach it, and, to our huge delight, saw the summit of the mountain on our right, led up to by a very steep arête of rocks, but evidently within our reach.

The work of the last four hours and a half had been so exciting that we had forgotten to eat, and, indeed, had not felt the want of food; but now the voice of nature made itself heard, and we disposed ourselves in various positions on the ridge, which in many places we might have straddled, and turned our attention to the provisions. As we sat facing the final peak of the Ecrins, we had on our left the precipice which falls to the head of the Glacier Noir. Without any exaggeration, I never saw so sheer a wall; it was so smooth and regular that it might have been cut with a knife, as a cheese is cut in two. Looking over, we saw at once that, as we had thought probable, had we been able to get from La Berarde on to the ridge at the head of the

F

Glacier du Vallon, it would have been impossible to get down on to the Glacier Noir, as the cliffs are almost as precipitous as those down which we were looking. On the right bank of the Glacier Noir towered the dark crags of the Pelvoux, Crête du Pelvoux, and Ailefroide, a most glorious sight, presenting a combination of, perhaps, the finest rock-forms in the Alps; I certainly never saw so long and steep a line of cliffs, rising so abruptly from a glacier.

At 12.50 we started again, Almer leading. We had first to cross a very short but very narrow neck of snow, and Almer had scarcely set foot on this, when a great mass of snow, which had appeared quite firm and part of the ridge, suddenly gave way, and fell with a roar to the Glacier Noir below. Almer's left foot was actually on this snow when it gave way. He staggered, and we all thought he was over, but he recovered himself, and managed to keep steady on the firm ridge. It is true he was roped; but the idea of a man being dropped with a sudden jerk, and then allowed to hang suspended, over that fearful abyss, was almost too much for my equanimity, and for the second time a shudder ran through my veins. This little isthmus crossed, we tackled the rocks which rose very steeply above our heads, and climbed steadily up along the arête, generally rather below the edge, on the side of the Glacier de l'Encula. The work was hard enough, but easier than what we had gone through below, as the rocks were free from ice, and the hold for hands and feet was much better, so that there was no fear of slipping. I don't think a word was said from the time we quitted our halting-place until we were close to the top, when the guides tried to persuade us to go in front, so as to be the first to set foot on the summit. But this we declined; they had done the work, let them be the first to reap the reward. It was finally settled that we should all go on together as much as possible, as neither party would give way in this amicable contest. A sharp scramble in breathless excitement ensued, until, at 1.25 p.m., the last step was taken, and we stood on the top of the Ecrins, the worthy monarch of the Dauphiné Alps.

In that supreme moment all our toils and dangers were forgotten in the blissful consciousness of success, and the thrill of exultation that ran through me, as I stood, in my turn, on the very highest point of the highest pinnacle— a little peak of rock with a cap of snow—was cheaply purchased by what we had gone through. Close to us was a precisely similar point, of much the same height, which scarcely came up to the rank of a second summit. It could have been reached in a few seconds from our position, but, as our point was actually the highest of the two, and was also more convenient for sitting down, we remained where we were. I must confess to a total inability to describe the wonderful panorama that lay extended before us. I am not one of those happily con- stituted individuals who, after many hours of excitement, can calmly sit on the apex of a mountain, and discuss simultaneously cold chicken and points of topography. I am not ashamed to confess that I was far too excited to study, as I ought to have done, the details of a view, which, for extent and variety, is altogether without a parallel in my Alpine experience. Suffice it to say that over the whole sky there was not one single cloud, and that we were sitting on the most elevated summit south of Mont Blanc, and it may fairly be left to the imagination to conceive what we saw, as, at an elevation of 13,462 feet, we basked in the sun without the cold wind usually attendant at these heights. There was not a breath of air, and the flame of a candle would have burnt steadily without a flicker. In our immediate neighbourhood, after the range of the Pelvoux, before described, the most striking object was the great wall of the Meije, the western summit of which from here came out distinctly the highest. The Aiguilles d'Arve stood out exceedingly well, and, although 2000 feet lower than our position, looked amazingly high. Almost the only trace of civilization we could distinctly make out was the Lautaret road, a portion of which, pro-

bably near the entrance of the valley leading to the Glacier
d'Arsines, was plainly visible. On the side of the mountain towards La Berarde, what principally struck us was
a very great and extensive glacier, apparently not marked
on the map, which appeared to be an arm of the Glacier
du Vallon, but far more considerable itself than the whole
glacier is depicted on the French map. Of the extent of
the view, and the wonderfully favourable condition of the
atmosphere, a fair idea may be gained from the fact that
we clearly identified the forms and ridges of the Matterhorn
and Weisshorn, the latter at a distance of 120 miles, as the
crow flies, and that those were by no means the most distant objects visible.

So soon as the first excitement consequent on success
had subsided, we began seriously to meditate upon what
during the ascent had frequently troubled us, viz., the
descent. With one consent we agreed that unless no other
route could be found, it would be most unadvisable to attempt to go down the way we had mounted. The idea of
the rocks, to be followed by the ice-slope below, in a doubly-
dangerous state after being exposed all day to the scorching sun, was not to be entertained without a shudder.
The only alternative route lay along the opposite arête to
that which had led us to the top, and, although we could
not see far in this direction, we determined, after very
little discussion, to try it. Accordingly, after twenty
minutes' halt, we each pocketed a small fragment of the
stone that was lying on the snow, and, regretting that we
had no bottle to leave, and no materials with which to construct a cairn, took our departure at 1.45 from the lofty
perch which, I fancy, is not likely to receive many subsequent visitors. Passing immediately below the second
point before mentioned, so that our hands almost rested
on it, and also several similar pinnacles, our work commenced. I never, before or since, was on so narrow an
arête of rock, and really from step to step I was at a loss
to imagine how we were to get on any further. We kept,
as a rule, just below the edge, as before, on the side of the

Glacier de l'Encula, along a series of ledges of the narrowest and most insecure character; but we were always sufficiently near the top to be able to look over the ridge, down the appalling precipices which overhang, first the Glacier Noir, and later, the Glacier du Vallon. Of course, every single step had to be taken with the greatest care, only one person moving in turn, and the rest holding on for dear life, Croz coming last to hold all up. In spite of the great difficulty of the route, the obstacles were only such as required more or less time to surmount, and although the slightest nervousness on the part of any one of us would have endangered the whole party and delayed us indefinitely, in the absence of that drawback we got on pretty well. We were beginning to hope that the worst was over, when Almer suddenly stopped short, and looked about him uneasily. On our asking him what was the matter, he answered vaguely that things ahead looked bad, and that he was not sure that we could pass. Croz accordingly undid the rope, as also did Almer, and the two went forward a little, telling us to remain where we were. We could *not* see what was the nature of the difficulty, but we *could* see the countenances of the men, which sufficiently showed us that the hitch was serious. Under any other circumstances we should have been amused at Almer's endeavours to communicate his views to Croz in an amazing mixture of pantomime, bad German, and worse French. He evidently was trying to persuade Croz of something, which Croz was not inclined to agree to, and we soon made out that the point at issue was, whether we could get over this particular place, or whether we must return to the summit, and go down the way we had come. Croz was of the latter opinion, while Almer obstinately maintained that, bad as the place was, we *could* get over it, and proceeded to perform some manœuvres, which we could not clearly see, by way of showing the correctness of his opinion. Croz, however, was unconvinced, and came back to us, declaring plainly that we should have to return. We shouted to Almer who was still below, but he evidently had not the slightest intention of returning, and in a few moments called upon us to come on, an injunction which we cheerfully obeyed, as, in our opinion, anything would be preferable to a retreat, and Croz, perforce, followed. A very few steps showed us the nature of the difficulty. The arête suddenly narrowed to a mere knife-edge of *rock*, while on one side a smooth wall, some 4000 feet in height, fell sheer towards the Glacier du Vallon, and on the other side, above the Glacier de l'Encula, the slope was not much less steep, and equally smooth. To pass below the ridge on either side was obviously quite impossible; to walk along the ridge, which was by no means level, was equally so, and the only way of getting over the difficulty, therefore, was to straddle it, an operation which the sharpness of the ridge, putting aside all other considerations, would render the reverse of agreeable. However, there, perched in the middle of this fiendish place, sat Almer, with one leg over the Glacier du Vallon and the other over the Glacier de l'Encula, calm and unmoved, as if the position was quite an everyday one. He had not got the rope on, and as he began moving along the ridge, we shrieked at him to take care, to which he responded with a "ja, gewiss!" and a chuckle of satisfaction. We threw him the end of the rope, and then cautiously moved, one at a time, towards him. I must confess that when I found myself actually astride on this dizzy height I felt more inclined to remain there for ever, contemplating the Glacier du Vallon, on to which I might have dropped a stone, than to make my way along it. The encouraging voice of Almer, however, urged me on, and I gradually worked myself along with my hands, until I was close up to him and Walker, with no damage save to the seat of my trousers. Whymper and Croz followed. From this point forwards we had for half-an-hour, without exception, the most perilous climbing I ever did. We crept along the cliffs, sometimes on one side of the ridge, sometimes on the other, frequently passing our arms over the summit, with our feet resting on rather less than nothing. Almer led with wonderful skill and courage, and gradually brought us over the worst portion of the arête, below which the climbing was bad enough, but not quite such nervous work as before, and we were able to get along rather quicker. At length, at 3.45, in two hours from the top, we were not far above the well-marked gap in the ridge, between the highest peak and the one marked on the French map 3980 mètres, or 13,058 feet. There we thankfully left the arête, and, turning to the right, struck straight down the ice-slope towards the bergschrund. Almost every step had to be cut, but, in spite of all he had done, Almer's vigour seemed unimpaired, and resolutely declining Croz's offers to come to the front, he hacked away, so that we descended steadily, if slowly. We could not see the bergschrund, and were, therefore, uncertain for what exact point to steer, for we knew that at only one place would it be possible to get over at all, where from below we had seen that the two edges nearly met—at all others the breadth and height would be far too great for a jump. For some distance we kept straight down, but after a time bore rather to the left, cutting diagonally along the slope, which was inclined at an angle of 52°, and, below us, curled over so rapidly that we *could* see the glacier on to which we wished to descend, but *could not* see what lay between us and it. Passing over a patch of ice-covered rocks which projected very slightly from the general level of the slope, we were certain that we could not be far above the schrund, but did not quite see how we were to get down any further without knowing whether we *were* above a practicable point or not. It was suggested that one of the party should be let down with the rope, but, while we were discussing who should be the one, Almer cut a few steps more, and then, stooping down and craning over, gave a yell of exultation, and exclaimed that it was all right, and that we might jump over. By a marvellous bit of intuition, or good luck, he had led us to the only point where the two edges of the chasm so nearly met that we could get across. He cut down as low as possible, and then, from the last step, each man, in turn,

sprang without difficulty on to the lower edge of the
crevasse, and at 4.45 the problem of getting off the mountain was solved.

When Messrs. Mathews and Bonney made an attempt
on the Ecrins in 1862, they determined the bergschrund to
be 525 feet below the summit. We all thought this below
the mark, and that the distance was nearer 700 feet. But,
however this may be, nothing can give a clearer idea of
the magnitude of the difficulties we had overcome than
the fact that we had taken no less than eight hours and a
half, including halts to the amount of less than one hour,
to get up and down this comparatively trifling distance.
We all felt vastly relieved to find ourselves over our last
serious difficulty, and the guides fully shared our satisfaction. Indeed, Croz now, for the first time, admitted that
the Ecrins was really defunct. The Col des Ecrins was
our next point, and towards this we hurried as fast as possible; but the snow was in a very different condition from
what we had found in the morning, being very soft, so that
we plunged in deep at every step; nevertheless, we jumped,
trotted, and walked at such a pace, that at 5.25 we reached
the point just above the Col, where eleven hours before
we had deposited our baggage. Our thoughts had been
for some time intent on the vessel full of snow which had
been left to melt, and our disgust may be imagined, when
we found the vessel upset, and void alike of snow or water,
so that our parched palates would have to wait for some
time longer for the much-needed moistening. We now
had to descend by the Glacier de l'Encula and Glacier
Blanc to the Val Louise, and hoped to reach Ville Val
Louise, the " chef lieu" of the valley, about midnight,
but our ability to accomplish this depended largely upon
whether we could get well clear of the glaciers before dark.
We knew that we should have hard work to do this; so,
after only ten minutes' halt, we reluctantly shouldered our
respective loads, and at 5.35 resumed our way over the level
snow-fields of the Glacier de l'Encula. This is one of the
most extensive glacier plateaux in the Alps, and the ridges

of the Crête de l'Encula and Crête du Glacier Blanc, which surround it, are very fine. It is almost free from crevasses, but is very long; and, although the snow was in far better order than we had expected, it was 6.55 before we reached the point where the glacier abandons its easterly direction, and takes an extraordinary turn due south, at right angles to its former course, round the corner of the Crête de l'Encula, assuming at the same time the name of Glacier Blanc. From here the Ecrins stood up very well, and, turning round, we took what was destined to be our last near view of our vanquished foe. But I regret to say that, at the moment, our attention was more than equally divided between the mountain and the sound of falling water, which was audible close by. We made for a small patch of rocks that cropped out of the ice, and, to our infinite delight, found a tolerably clear stream running over them, with which we did our best to quench our thirst, and took the opportunity of washing down a mouthful of food. At 7.10 we were off again, and, picking our way through the crevasses, which were becoming numerous, were soon compelled to get off the glacier on its left bank, in order to avoid the seracs of the upper ice-fall, the natural result of the extraordinary turn which the glacier is obliged to make in order to reach the Val Louise. Moraine, avalanche snow, and débris offered us an easy line of descent, which we followed at a great pace, I coming occasional croppers in my haste, until, at 7.30, we emerged on to the little open plain on which is situated the Hotel Tuckett, a very tolerable hole, where we had originally intended to pass the night before attacking the Ecrins. Fortunate was it, however, that we had varied our plans, for we found that the stream, which was considered one of the great advantages of the spot, had, in an erratic moment, taken a turn into the hole, filling it with water, and, of course, rendering it altogether uninhabitable.

From here, the natural course would still be to follow the left bank of the glacier, but no way has yet been found along the rocks on that side of the ice-fall, and it is necessary to cross to the right bank, and descend by the lower slopes of the Crête de l'Encula to the moraine of the Glacier Noir, which almost meets the lower end of the Glacier Blanc. The passage of the glacier is an easy operation, as, most opportunely, just at this point there is a level and quite uncrevassed plateau between the upper and lower ice-falls. Accordingly, at 7.45 we found ourselves on the opposite side, having enjoyed during the passage a perfect view of the superb upper ice-fall. A few minutes brought us, just as it was getting dusk, to the brow of the steep descent leading down to the level of the Glacier Noir. This, always trouble- some and never particularly easy, in the rapidly-increasing darkness was simply detestable, especially to a person so shortsighted as myself. To this day I cannot understand how I got down the steep slopes of débris and stones, over- grown here and there with juniper, and varied by smooth faces of rock, without a serious fall. In the worst places Almer guided my feet into the proper steps, which I was quite unable to see myself, and Walker, like a trump, stuck to me, in spite of all my entreaties to him to go ahead. The sagacity with which Croz hit off the exact line of descent was marvellous, and, without his local knowledge, I don't think we could have got down till daylight. From a point about half-way down we got a gorgeous view up the Glacier Noir of the Pelvoux range, the Ailefroide, and Crête de la Berarde, their summits tinged by the last rays of the sun, while the glacier and valleys below were already enveloped in darkness. At 8.45 we landed on the moraine of the Glacier Noir, but it was by this time quite dark, and there was no chance of a moon to help us out, while we had no lantern nor light of any description; in fact, we were just half-an-hour too late.

Our proper course would now have been to keep along the side of the moraine to its end, then cross the torrent from the Glacier Blanc, and descend the valley along the left side of the main stream, where we knew we should find a constantly-improving track which would lead us in due course to Ailefroide and Ville Val Louise. But, for some reason,

Croz objected to pass the torrent, and determined instead to cross the whole width of the moraine of the Glacier Noir, and descend by the right side of the valley where there is no path at all. The idea of traversing one of the most rugged and extensive moraines in the Alps in pitchy darkness in order to descend the pathless side of a savage and rarely-visited valley, struck me as simply monstrous, and, if we wished to reach Ville, perfectly suicidal. Croz, however, insisted that there was no other way, so we commenced our task by ascending the very lofty and steep side of the moraine, hoping for the best. The whole lower end of the Glacier Noir is covered with moraine from one side to the other, exactly like the Zmutt, Zinal, and other similarly offensive glaciers in the Swiss Alps, and from this circumstance it derives its name. Even by daylight the passage would be no easy task; what it was by night can be imagined. Ridge after ridge was passed, until Walker, myself, and Almer reached the top of the last one, and had only to descend along its side to *terra firma*. Whymper and Croz were already down, and we followed. The height was probably fifty or sixty feet, and the footing was horribly bad, while immense blocks of stone were lying on the slope in a most uncertain state of equilibrium. Almer and I were about half-way down, doing all in our power to avoid dislodging the stones, when, suddenly, the whole side of the moraine came down with a run, right upon us. I do not hesitate to say, that I never in my life was in such peril. The smaller stones swept along with such violence that they took me clean off my legs, just as a torrent might have done, and carried me down, *nolens volens*, along with Almer, who was as powerless as myself. All we could do was to keep fast hold of each other, and avoid being thrown down. On all sides of us the huge blocks came down helter-skelter, dashing against each other, and creating a fiendish din, which added to the terrors of the moment. Every instant I expected to be knocked over and disabled, if not killed outright, and I have never been able to understand how we escaped. But, providentially, the missiles,

Ville Val Louise, but determined to cross the torrents at once, and so get on to the proper side of the valley. There were several streams, but we contrived to get dry-footed over all of them but the last, which was wide and rapid. But over we must go; so, turning up our trousers, we went in and waded across. The water was cold, and the current rapid, but the stream came very little above our knees, and we were soon safely landed on the left bank, where our eyes were instantly greeted by the welcome path. Our boots were, of course, full of water, but we did not stop to empty them, as we should walk them dry before arriving at Ville. As we looked at the opposite bank of the torrent which we had just left, we congratulated ourselves on our superior wisdom in having stopped for the night where we did; but our congratulations were mingled with some anxiety about Whymper and Croz, as we could scarcely believe that they had been able to find a way in the dark over the waste of ruin that encumbered that side of the valley. Rocks upon rocks were piled together in the wildest confusion, completely blocking up the narrow tract of very steep ground that sloped down from the side of the mountains towards the torrent, which rushed furiously along over its uneven bed. I should be sorry to have to find a way along this savage ravine by daylight, much more in the dark, so that we were not surprised, after we had gone a short distance, to hear a voice hailing us, and on looking across saw our friends under a large stone, where they had evidently passed the night. They were just preparing to start, but could not possibly cross over to us, as the torrent had become so deep and rapid as to be quite unfordable, so we were obliged to keep apart for the present. The scenery of the Vallon d'Ailefroide, as this arm of the Val Louise is called, is exceedingly fine, the tremendous cliffs of the Pelvoux on the right side being objects of extraordinary grandeur. The valley, although savage and barren, is far more agreeable to traverse than the generality of the Dauphiné valleys, as it is not only not steep, but the track is a very tolerable one, and by no means particularly stony. We took it very easy, and enjoyed the walk much, until we at last reached a little open plain, at the point where the Vallons de Sapenière and Ailefroide unite to form the Val Louise proper, crossed to the right bank of the torrent, and at 5.15 reached the filthy châlets of Ailefroide, where Whymper had arrived a few minutes earlier, after a very fast walk of the most rugged and painful character. He and Croz were naturally hungry, and not caring for milk, which was all the châlets could supply, very wisely started off for Ville, in order to have breakfast ready as soon as possible, leaving us to follow at our ease. An old fellow of the name of Sémiond appeared to be the dignitary of the place, and through him we got some tolerable milk. We informed him of our yesterday's exploit, which did not appear to interest him much, but he was profoundly sceptical as to the Ecrins being higher than the Pelvoux. He had lived all his life under the shadow of the latter mountain, in the firm conviction that it was the highest of the Dauphiné Alps, and now, in his old age, did not care to have his belief shaken, and a new, and to him unknown, peak raised to the supremacy. At 5.25 we left the châlets, having seen enough to convince us that, under almost any circumstances, our " gite " would be far preferable to the foul accommodation afforded by them. Below Ailefroide is a good mule-path, which, however, we contrived to get out of once or twice with no worse result than being obliged on one occasion to cross a furious torrent by a single pine tree, thrown over at a considerable height above the stream, an operation which I preferred to perform straddling, and found almost as detrimental to my trousers as the arête yesterday. Throughout the scenery is charming, and the vegetation improves rapidly until we at last found ourselves walking through groves of walnut and cherry trees, the fruit on the latter not yet ripe. Just above Claux, where the valley leading by the low Col de l'Echauda to Monetier falls in, we crossed again to the left bank of the stream, and, passing through the village, made tender enquiries for cherries, but were informed that there were not yet any, but that we should find them lower down. The view, looking up from about here, is very picturesque, the superb mass of the Pelvoux standing up well behind the foreground of luxuriant vegetation, itself a sufficiently rare spectacle in Dauphiné. In spite of the early hour of the morning, and of our being still in the shade, the walk onward was hot and dusty. We met numerous natives, most of whom, especially the females, were extremely garrulous. One toothless old hag, in particular, impressed upon us, in an almost unintelligible patois, the necessity of going to an inn at Ville, kept by a friend of hers. We were not sorry when we crossed for the last time to the right bank of the stream by a good bridge, leading into Ville Val Louise, and, turning down the bank for a few yards, walked into the little inn " chez Giraud " at 7.0 a.m., just three hours from our " gîte."

In the not very inviting salle-à-manger we found Whymper and Croz, who, having ordered breakfast for the party, had been indulging in a preliminary and much-needed repast on their own account. There was some delay before our breakfast arrived, and when it did begin to make its appearance, a huge soup-tureen of boiled milk was for a long time all we had to feast upon; but, at last, divers sorts of strange and unknown meats were brought in, on which we in vain endeavoured to make a good meal, as the only recognisable animal, a chicken, was utterly spoiled by having been cooked in garlic. However, what we could not eat ourselves we transferred to the guides, who made short work of everything. While break-fasting, the room gradually filled with natives, who took little notice of us, but got into conversation with Croz, who, from having been here before, was not quite a stranger. Our mountaineering gear was a great mystery to them, and Croz chaffed them unmercifully on the subject, assuring them, in answer to enquiries, that we carried the rope in order to harness the chamois after we had caught them, a fact which was considered remarkable, but was believed implicitly. When the room was nearly full, an old fellow, bearing the stamp of frequent potations on his countenance, joined the company. He was already half-seas over, and a very little more finished him, when he began singing a song, of which the burden was, the triumphs over the English of the great Napoleon, under the title of the "Petit Caporal." It was evidently intended for our edification, as the performer every now and then stopped short, and, turning to us, said, with an air of mock politeness, irresistibly ludicrous—"Il ne faut pas vous facher, Messieurs." Numerous letters had to be written, and afterwards Walker and I sallied out into the "Place," opposite the church, where we found a congregation of the inhabitants, but not engaged in religious duties. A regular fair was going on, the principal articles on sale being nails and cherries. We invested largely in both of these, the former for our boots, the latter for our interiors, took a look at the church, the exterior of which is *adorned* with some horrible daubs, and were then glad to beat a retreat out of the scorching sun, and at the same time avoid the admiring populace, who, as we moved about, formed a circle round us. I scarcely know how we passed the morning, but it was dreary work. To remain in the Salle was impossible, as the row that was going on was perfectly maddening, so we took up our position on a log of wood outside under the shade of the house, and congratulated ourselves that our stay in this horrible hole was to be so short.

Our object now was to ascend the Val d'Entraigues, which joins the Val Louise at Ville, and from its head to make a new pass to La Berarde, over the long ridge of the Crête des Bœufs Rouges, which forms the southern boundary of the great Glacier de la Pilatte. Although up this valley there is a tolerably well-known pass to the Val Godemar by the Col du Célar, we could not get the slightest information out of the natives. They could not even tell us how far up were the highest châlets of Entraigues; some said two, some three, and some five hours. This uncertainty was an excuse for an early start, so we ordered dinner to be ready at 1.0, intending to be off at 3.0 p.m. The dinner bore a strong resemblance to the breakfast; but had it been a sumptuous banquet we could not have done justice to it in the midst of such an uproar as was going on around us. The room was crammed to suffocation with people more than half drunk, and the scene of riot and confusion was something indescribable. It made us quite ill, and so soon as we had wound up with some of the excellent liqueurs, which are the best things the house affords, we fled once more to the open air, and waited patiently till the guides were ready. There was some trouble in collecting the provisions, but at last everything was packed, and having, in consideration of the great heat, engaged the landlord's brother to take the things on his mule as far as the châlets, we called for the bill. When this was brought, we found ourselves called upon to pay about double as much as we should have been charged at Zermatt; so we cut it down one-third, and after a long argument with the land-lord forced him to admit that he was well paid. He requested the pleasure of taking a farewell glass of "Chartreuse" with us, and we parted excellent friends. But all this had taken up time, and it was 3.30 p.m. when we joyfully quitted Ville Val Louise after what will always live in my recollection as the most miserable Sunday morn-ing I ever passed.

The path wound gradually round to the right into the Val d'Entraigues, and in a few minutes we were fairly out of the Val Louise. The former is considerably narrower and wilder than the Val Louise, but is none the less attractive on that account. On the contrary, we were charmed with the scenery, and found the walk most enjoyable after the weary hours of idleness we had been condemned to pass. The rocks on either side of the valley are very fine, and, for a wonder, their lower slopes are clothed with luxuriant pine-woods, and other trees. The torrent, of great size, rushes along at a tremendous pace, but is rarely visible, as its bed consists for the most part of a series of profound gorges, one of which, some way up the valley, presented a scene of savage grandeur, such as I have rarely seen surpassed. Altogether we were delighted, but, perhaps, in our joy at getting away from Ville, estimated the scenery at a higher rate than we should have at another time. We three pushed on at our own pace, leaving the guides and mule to follow at their's, but, during a halt we made to get some milk, they passed a-head of us. The old woman at these châlets was an extraordinary character; almost toothless, she chattered away, notwithstanding, with a volubility that was quite alarming, especially as her remarks were totally unintelligible. Our demand for milk was answered by a flow of verbiage, which we endeavoured to stop by paying beforehand the supposed value of the milk, but the sight of the money only made her worse, and she talked, grimaced, and gesticulated until we were almost in despair. The milk, rather sour, was, however, at last brought, and, having drunk it, we retired, pursued by the old woman's tongue, in happy ignorance of what she had been so earnestly endeavouring to impress upon us. Thenceforward we took it rather easily, as Walker was not very well, the milk having disagreed with him, but, in spite of all delays, we reached the châlets of Entraigues at 5.55 p.m., in less than two hours actual walking from Ville Val Louise. The châlets are pleasantly situated on a slight eminence in the centre of a little plain, just where the valley forks. The southern branch, called the Combe de la Selle, opens out from a mere cleft in the side of the main valley, which no one would imagine could lead anywhere, but I believe there is a pass in this direction to Champoléon. The northern branch is much more considerable, and is closed at its head by steep cliffs and two extensive glaciers. The glaciers are separated by a long spur, running down from the fine Pic des Opillons. To the south of this summit lies the direct route to the Val Godemar by the Col du Célar, a pass exceeding 10,000 feet in height; and to the north of it a still higher pass might undoubtedly be made into the same valley, but it would be a rather more circuitous route, as the descent would be into the lateral valley, through which lies the way from La Berarde by the

Col du Says. The ridge, forming the left side of the Val d'Entraigues over which we hoped to pass, looked extremely unpromising, being very lofty and precipitous, but we could form no conclusion as to our prospects of success, as it sends down numerous long spurs, forming a series of ravines, and we could not see what lay between them, whether glaciers, or couloirs, or impracticable rocks. We knew that we must cross as far west as possible, as the Crête des Bœufs Rouges forms the boundary not only of the Glacier de la Pilatte but also of the Glacier du Sélè, and, by reaching a point on the ridge too far east, we should find ourselves above the latter glacier, just where we did not wish to be. Before determining our exact line of march, it would, therefore, be necessary in the morning to ascend the valley nearly as far as the foot of the Col du Célar, and we trusted that from there we should discover some means of access to the ridge.

Nothing could have exceeded the hospitality with which we were received at the châlets, which were models of cleanliness, and the two women in charge seemed as if they could not do enough to make us comfortable and anticipate our wishes. They were both middle-aged, and bore the marks of toil on their faces, but I have rarely seen more prepossessing countenances; honesty and good-temper were stamped on them. All sorts of châlet luxuries were set before us—milk, cream, séracs, curds and whey, and most excellent cheese. While we were discussing these, they cooked us a huge omelette, and then lent us every facility for brewing some tea. At about 8.15 p.m., we retired to a large clean barn close by, where they had arranged an immense quantity of perfectly new straw for our couches. Nothing could have been more luxurious, and, with our plaids, we were soon packed side-by-side, like birds in a nest. The guides were equally comfortable, and the united party were very soon asleep.

Monday, 27th June.—I never passed a more comfortable night, and felt anything but amiably disposed towards the intruders, when, at 2.15 a.m., there was an irruption

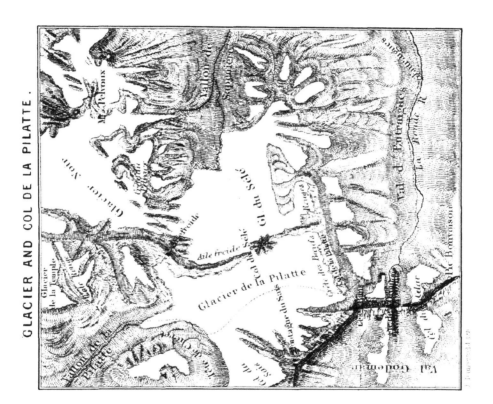

GLACIER AND COL DE LA PILATTE.

of people into our barn, who summarily put an end
to our repose. Through the gloom I made out that one
of the objectionable individuals was a man, who shortly
resolved himself into Monsieur Jean Reynaud of La
Bessé, a friend of Whymper, whose reported engagement
of "four-and-twenty of the most celebrated guides of the
country" had so alarmed us at La Grave. He had come
up yesterday afternoon to Ville Val Louise to meet us
in accordance with Whymper's invitation, and, finding
that we had already started, pursued us, arriving at
Entraigues very late at night. He had heard at Ville
of our ascent of the Ecrins, and congratulated us on the
same, saying nothing to lead us to suppose that he had
ever intended to accompany us; so we said nothing about
our conversation with the "podgy man" at La Grave, and
that mystery accordingly remains unsolved. Our indefatigable hostesses had prepared us some excellent coffee
for breakfast; having done justice to which, we bade them
farewell, after having with the greatest possible difficulty
forced them to accept the smallest trifle, and at 3.35 a.m.
started on our way.

The morning, though fair, was by no means perfect;
there were a few clouds in the sky, the general appearance of which presaged a change, and there was a rainy
feeling in the wind, which made us glad to reflect that this
would be the last occasion for several days on which we
should be absolutely dependent on fine weather. We were
accompanied for a short distance by a man who had come
up from Ville with M. Renaud, and whom he utilised as a
beast of burden so long as his way lay with ours.
Entraigues is situated in the centre of a small plain, just
below the junction of the Combe de la Selle with the main
valley, which latter above the junction contracts to a mere
gorge. The torrent has brought down vast quantities of
stones and débris, which lie scattered over the plain; and
over this rough ground we had first to pick our way,
following a very faint track along the left bank of the
stream. At the mouth of the gorge the ascent became

steep, but, so soon as we were fairly within it, the track kept for a long time almost on a level. The châlets of Entraigues are themselves high, and above them the vegetation is very scanty, the valley, which is nothing more than a glen, presenting a scene of the dreariest and most unattractive character, so that we had no temptation to waste time on the road, and, pushing rapidly on, were soon engaged in a toilsome and disagreeable scramble along the rough and stony slopes on the left side of the valley. The track had by this time died away, but our route was obvious. Near its head the valley takes an abrupt turn from west to north-west, and we had to get round the shoulder of the hill in the angle, beyond which we hoped to be able to form some idea of the practicability of our proposed pass. Having traversed the steep side of the hill, we found ourselves looking into the last bit of level ground at the head of the valley, and, as we expected, in full view of the surrounding peaks and glaciers. In the middle of a dreary flat, through which shallow streams meandered promiscuously, was an enormous old moraine, evidently a relic of the good old days before the glaciers had shrunk to their present comparatively attenuated proportions; and on the top of this, at 4.55, we took up our position, turning our faces almost due north.

Westward towered the exceedingly lofty and rugged ridge, which, running from the Pic de Bonvoisin on the south to Les Bans on the north through the Pic des Opillons, forms the barrier between the Val d'Entraigues and the Val Godemar. From between the Pic de Bonvoisin and the Pic des Opillons a very steep and shattered glacier falls towards the valley, but does not reach it, as it terminates above steep cliffs, succeeded by long slopes of débris. Over the head of this glacier lies the Col du Célar, which the good people at Entraigues informed us was passable for sheep and goats. Looking at the place, we certainly found it hard to believe this, as the glacier itself would be difficult enough for even men to pass, and the rocks right and left, by which, I believe, the ascent is made, looked scarcely more promising.

The ridge between the Pic des Opillons and Les Bans is loftier but certainly not more inaccessible than that of the Col du Célar. From it a steep snow-slope falls to a glacier of a similar character to its neighbour, terminating in precisely the same manner. The Pic de Bonvoisin and the Pic des Opillons appear to be of the same elevation, 11,503 feet, but Les Bans is a far more considerable summit, rising to the height of 11,979 feet, and presents a very imposing appearance on this side, where it shows as a long rugged crest, almost free from snow. From this, the long range of the Crête des Bœufs Rouges runs east, and forms the southern boundary of the Glaciers de la Pilatte and du Sélè and the north side of the Val d'Entraigues. Along the Crête rise several considerable peaks, of which the western, a very striking, sharp-pointed summit, is the highest, and seemed little, if at all, inferior to Les Bans, to which it is contiguous. This cannot possibly be the summit to which on the French map the height of only 11,332 feet is given, as so material a difference between it and Les Bans would have certainly been perceptible from our position, from which both were almost exactly equidistant. With regard to the possibility of passing over the Crête, we could make out less than we had hoped, partly in consequence of an envious mist having perched itself just in this direction, and still more owing to the character of the ground. On the map a very short but broad strip of glacier is represented as lying along the face of the ridge; but this has no foundation in fact. The real state of the case is, that there are a number of steep secondary glaciers, commencing some distance below the top of the ridge, separated from each other by long spurs of rock, and terminating at a considerable height above the valley, in very narrow and precipitous ravines. Along the whole length of the ridge we could not make out one single point which *looked* at all like a pass, but, after much discussion, discovered two gaps, by one of which we agreed the attempt must be made, if at all. The first of these lay between Les Bans and the highest point of the Crête,

and, we imagined, must be the top of a couloir, rising out
of the head of a glacier, whose tail was just visible, projecting over the rocks; but we could not be certain, as the
wall at the head of the glacier was masked by a rocky
spur coming down in front of it. The second gap was
further east, on the other side of the highest point of the
Crête, and this also we could not clearly see how to
approach, no glacier being visible above the lower wall of
rocks, which must evidently be the first step in the ascent.
We fancied the first gap, but, as it was not desirable to
make a mistake, Almer started off to the other side of the
valley, towards the foot of the Col du Célar, to try and
get a view up the ravine, glacier, and couloir, which led up
to it. We saw him making his way along the steep slopes
of débris below the two glaciers (which might conveniently
be called Glacier du Célar and Glacier des Opillons), but
finally lost sight of him. Some time passed, and he did not
re-appear, so we concluded that all was right, and, at 5.30,
followed in the same direction, but kept to our own side of
the valley.

Passing along the grass-grown top of the moraine, we
shortly reached the foot of a long slope of snow, the remains of the winter avalanches, lying along the base of the
rocks in which we wished to find an accessible point.
This slope offered a most convenient mode of approach, so
we turned straight up it, keeping always near the foot of
the rocks, over which a series of fine cascades fell, caused
by the melting snows of the glacier above. We now caught
sight of Almer again, at a great height above us, crossing
the upper part of this slope, towards a recess in the rocks
on our right, where we accordingly guessed he had found
an assailable point. The snow was very hard, and the
inclination considerable, so that, mounting without steps
being cut, our progress was toilsome and slow. Croz and
myself were in front, and, talking as we went on various
topics, never for an instant supposed but that the other
three were at our heels, until, chancing to look round to
see how high we had risen, to our surprise we found that

for some reason they had dropped behind, and were only
at the foot of the slope, which we were half way up. There
was evidently nothing the matter, as they were coming up
steadily in our steps, so we did not think it necessary to
stop, and went on our way towards where Almer was waiting for us. When we were two-thirds of the way up, we
passed underneath the projecting snout of a glacier which
terminated abruptly in ice-cliffs, just above our heads, and
I should think must occasionally send a few blocks over
down on to our slope, which in that case would be rather
warm quarters. As it was, an occasional stone came
whizzing past, of whose approach we were always warned
by a shriek from Almer, which we in our turn passed to
our friends below. As we neared Almer's position, the
slope became steeper and harder, so that it was impossible
to advance without using the axe, seeing which he began
cutting steps down to meet us, while Croz cut up, until we
finally joined him, when we bore to the right, and, at 6.50,
got on to the rocks, where we waited for the others, who
were still a long way below. Almer reported that from
below he had been able to get a view of the glacier above,
and also of a couloir rising from its head, which he thought
we should be able to ascend. He had not, however, seen
quite to the top, and was rather apprehensive that there
we might find the snow so thin over the rocks that they
might not be passable, so warned us not to be too sanguine.
I was not much afraid of a failure from this cause, but
was seriously uneasy at the appearance of the weather;
clouds were gradually obscuring the sky, and thick mists
were creeping up the valley at our feet, and were making
strenuous efforts to reach our position. The only point in
our favour was, that a strong north wind was blowing in
the upper regions, and struggling for the mastery with the
objectionable " Vent du Sud," and we trusted that the
contest, if it was not at once decided in favour of the
north, might be prolonged sufficiently to allow us to find
our way down on to the Glacier de la Pilatte. At 7.15 the
rest of the party arrived, and we immediately turned our

attention to the provisions, which I had most meritoriously refrained from attacking, notwithstanding the pangs of hunger which had for some time been tormenting me. Walker and I varied the entertainment by our usual pastime of stone-throwing, and, for the first and only time while we were together, I succeeded in decisively beating him; a victory, however, which must be ascribed, not to my superior skill, but to the fact that he was very much out of sorts from the bad living in which we had been indulging.

At 7.50 we were off again, and commenced climbing the rocks above us, which, though steep, gave good hold for hands and feet, and could not consequently be considered difficult. As we climbed, we found considerable patches of snow, one of which we at last selected as the most convenient line of ascent, and, pounding laboriously up it, gradually emerged from the ravine, and found ourselves at 8.25 on a slope of snow, stretching down to the right side of the glacier, beneath whose foot we had passed. The glacier was very small, exceedingly steep, and much broken up, enclosed on three sides by the superb naked cliffs of Les Bans and the Bœufs Rouges, which rose from it in a tremendous wall, along which we could see no gap nor accessible point. We began to fear that Almer had made a mistake in the direction of his couloir, but he was quite confident, and assured us that it was hidden round a corner, and that so soon as we were in the centre of the glacier we should get a view of it. The rope was accordingly put on, we carefully descended the slope, dropped over a small bergschrund, and, under Croz's guidance, committed ourselves to the ice. Making for the middle of the glacier, we at last unmasked on the extreme left, at its north-western angle, close under the peak of Les Bans, an exceedingly lofty, steep, and narrow couloir, stretching up to the ridge, and defended at its base by a formidable bergschrund, running completely from one side to the other. A more unprepossessing place I never set eyes on, and we all agreed that the work before us was likely to prove rather exciting, possibly more so than would be quite agreeable. But, before getting near the foot of the couloir, we had something to do in threading a way up and through the huge chasms into which the glacier was broken. Croz was here thoroughly in his element, and led the way with great skill and determination, passing one obstacle after another, and bearing gradually to the left towards the enemy. At every step we took, it became more apparent that nature had never intended any one to pass this way, and had accordingly taken more than usual pains to render the approach to the couloir difficult and dangerous. Below the highest bergschrund were a series of smaller ones, arranged systematically one above the other, stretching completely across a very steep slope, so that they could not be turned, but must each in succession be attacked "en face." Fortunately, at this early period of the season, and with so much snow, the difficulty was less considerable than it would have been under other circumstances, and, exercising every precaution, we finally passed the last of the outer lines of defence, and had nothing but a short steep slope between us and the final "schrund," above which the couloir rose more unfriendly than ever, as we approached it nearer. I had been sorely puzzled in my mind how we were going to get across this chasm, as from below it appeared to have a uniform width of about ten feet, the upper edge, as usual, much higher than the lower, and no visible bridge at any point. On getting up to it, however, we found that on the extreme right it had been choked by a considerable mass of snow, the small remains of which, at one point, formed a narrow, rotten, and most insecure bridge, over which Croz cautiously passed, and made himself firm in the soft snow above. Walker, Whymper, Mons. Renaud, myself, and Almer, then followed, as if we were treading on eggs, and all got safely over, much to our relief, as there really appeared no small chance of the bridge going to grief before we were all across, which would have been awkward for those on the wrong side.

It was just 9.30 when we fairly took to this extraordinary gully, which, above the bergschrund, was certainly not more than twelve feet wide, and gradually narrowed in its upward course. For the first few steps we trod in a sufficiency of soft snow in good condition, but, to our dismay, this soon sensibly diminished both in quantity and quality, until at last there was nothing but the old, disgusting, powdery snow resting on hard ice. The axe accordingly came into play; but, if steps were cut of the ordinary size, we should never get to the top till night, so Croz just hacked out sufficient space for the feet to cling to, and worked away as fast as possible, cautioning us emphatically to look out, and to hold on well with our axes while each step was being cut. Another argument in favour of rapid progress arose from the palpable danger in which we were. The centre of the couloir was occupied by a deeply-scored trough, evidently a channel for stones and avalanches, while the space on either side was so narrow that in case of a large fall we could scarcely expect to escape unharmed. Looking up to see what was likely to come down, we discovered at the very head of the couloir a perpendicular or slightly overhanging wall of névé, some thirty feet in height, and, lower down, projecting over the rocks on our left, an enormous mass of icicles, on which the sun was playing, and, of course, momentarily loosening their tenure to the rocks. At the moment we were exactly in the line which they must follow, if they fell, as they evidently would before long, so we lost no time in crossing the stone channel to the other side, where the great mass was scarcely likely to come, and we might probably ward off any stray fragments. I received a lively hint as to the effect of a *large* mass of ice coming suddenly down on one's head, by the effect of a blow from a comparatively small piece, which Croz hewed out from one of the steps. Being so far down in the line, it had time to gain momentum before it struck me, which it did on the head with such violence that for a few moments I felt quite sick and stupid. The incident will give a very good idea of the steepness of the slope on

which we were. I had too much to think of to measure it
with a clinometer, but it was certainly steeper than any
part of the couloir leading to the Col des Ecrins, the
greatest inclination of which was 54°. At one point a
little water trickled over the rocks, which the two front
men managed to get a suck at, but those behind were out
of reach, and the footing was too precarious for more than
a minute's halt, not to mention occasional vollies of small
stones which shot by us, and might be the precursors of
large ones. I don't think that I ever experienced a greater
feeling of insecurity than during the whole of this ascent,
which was unavoidably long. What with the extreme steepness of the slope, and the necessary vagueness of the steps,
which were made additionally unsafe by the powdery snow
which filled them up as soon as they were cut, I felt that a
slip was a by no means unlikely contingency, and was glad
enough upon occasions to find Almer's hand behind, giving
me a friendly push whenever a particularly long stride had
to be made. When we were nearing the top, our attention
was attracted by a tremendous uproar behind us, and,
looking round, we were just in time to see a prodigious
avalanche falling over the cliffs of the Pic de Bonvoisin, on
the other side of the valley. It was at least a quarter of a
mile in length, and many minutes elapsed before the last
echoes of its fall died away. We were now so near the
great snow-wall that it was time to begin to circumvent it ;
so, crossing the couloir again, we clambered up the rocks
on that side in order to get out of it, hoping to be able
from them to get on to the main ridge to the left of the
wall, which itself was quite impassable. As Almer had
expected, the snow was here very thin over the rocks, and
what little there was, was converted into ice, so that the
climbing was most difficult and perilous, and we had no
small trouble to get on at all. However, we managed to
scramble up, and found ourselves overlooking a gully
running parallel, and of a similar character, to the one we
had been ascending, but free from snow and ice, and much
more precipitous. On our side it was quite impossible to

get on to the main ridge, as an impracticable rock rose above our heads, and it was, therefore, necessary to step across this second couloir. I never made a nastier step; the stride was exceedingly long, there was nothing in particular to stand on, and nothing at all but a smooth face of rock to hold on by, so that we had literally to trust to the natural adhesiveness of our hands. Fortunately there was sufficient rope to allow the man in front to cross and get on to the main ridge, and make himself fast before his successor followed, so we attacked the difficulty in turn. I got over somehow, but did not like it at all; lifted myself on to the ridge, Almer followed, and at 10.45 a.m. the Col was gained.

During our ascent of the couloir, the weather, though doubtful, had not been unfavourable, but, just as we got on to the ridge, a cloud swooped down, and enveloped us in its dense folds, and at the same moment it began to snow violently. Luckily Croz, who was first on the top, had been able to satisfy himself that we *were* above the Glacier de la Pilatte, and got a glimpse of what lay between us and it; but the state of the atmosphere was nevertheless sufficiently disappointing, as we were unable to fix with accuracy the exact position of our gap with reference to the peak of Les Bans, and the highest point of the Bœufs Rouges, or to determine its height. From the Brêche de la Meije, we had seen clearly that we were then considerably lower than any point on the ridge south of the Glacier de la Pilatte, and, taking this into consideration, together with the apparent height of our gap, seen from the valley below, we estimated the height of the Col, which we proposed to call Col de la Pilatte, at about 11,500 feet. It is certainly not much below this, and is, therefore, probably the highest pass yet effected in the Dauphiné Alps.

It was no less provoking to have missed the view of the Ecrins and Ailefroide, which we had expected to be particularly fine. But there was no help for it, and no prospect of immediate improvement; so, without halting for a minute, we commenced the descent in the same order as before. All we could see was a steep ice-wall, stretching downwards from our feet, the actual ridge not being more than a couple of feet wide. What was the length of the wall, or what lay below it, we could not discover, but had a shrewd suspicion that we should anyhow find a considerable bergschrund. Croz steered to the left, and began cutting steps diagonally downwards. The snow was in a much worse condition than it had been in the couloir; there was more of it, but it was so exceedingly soft, that our feet pressed through it to the hard ice, as though it had been water, and we were very rarely able to trust to it without cutting a step. We should have been better pleased had there been no snow at all, as the whole slope, the angle of which was about 50°, was in just the proper condition for an avalanche. I never saw Almer so nervous, and with reason; for, as he himself said, while he implored us not to move from one step into another, before we felt that one foot at least was secure, this was just one of those places where no amount of skill on the part of Croz or himself could entirely prevent the chance of a serious accident. It was a wonder how we did manage to stick to some of the steps, the objectionable character of which was increased from their being cut along the side of the slope, a position in which it is always more difficult to get from one to the other than when they are cut straight up or down. As we got lower down there was more snow, which, though softer than éver, was so steep that we could tread tolerably secure steps in it, by help of which we worked down, until we found ourselves brought up short on the upper edge of the expected bergschrund. Croz had hoped to hit this at a point where it was partially choked, but he was disappointed, as the chasm yawned below us, entirely unbridged. A glance right and left showed that there was no more assailable point within reach, so Croz gave out the unwelcome intelligence that if we wished to get over we must jump and take our chance. The obstacle appeared to be about ten feet wide, of uncomfortable depth, and the drop from the upper to the lower edge about fifteen feet. From the lower edge the glacier sloped away, only less steep than the wall on which we were, of which it was a continuation, but cut off by this sudden break. There was, however, so much soft snow that we should fall easy, and the only difficulty, therefore, was, to take a sufficiently fair spring to clear the chasm; for good as I believed my rope to be, I should have been sorry to see any one suspended by it, with a sudden jerk, over such a gulf as that we had beneath us. Walker was untied, so as to give rope enough to Croz, who, then, boldly sprung over, and landed heavily on the lower edge in the snow, where he stood to receive the rest of the party. Walker followed, and then Whymper, leaving Mons. Renaud, myself, and Almer above. Mons. Renaud advanced to the edge, looked, hesitated, drew back, and finally declared that he could not jump it; he felt perfectly convinced that he should be unable to clear the distance, and should jump in instead of over. We encouraged him, but without effect, and at last proposed to lower him down, when the others would hook hold of his legs somehow and pull him across. Almer and I, therefore, made our footing as secure as possible, anchored ourselves with our axes, and made all ready to lower our friend, but his courage failed him at the last moment, and he refused to go. We were now obliged to use stronger arguments, as it was snowing fast, and time was passing, so we pointed out that, if we wished to return ever so much we could not get the others back across the "schrund," and that, in point of fact, there was no chance,—over he *must* go. Again did he advance to the edge, again drew back, but finally, with a despairing groan, leaped, and just landed clear of the chasm, but, instead of letting his rope hang loose, he held it in one hand, and thereby nearly pulled me over, head foremost. Then came my turn, and I must confess that, when I stood in the last step from which I had to spring, I did not like the look of the place at all, and, in fact, felt undeniably nervous. But I had not been one of the least backward in objurgating Mons. Renaud, so felt

constrained to manifest no hesitation myself, whatever
might be my private feelings.   I, therefore, threw over my
axe and spectacles, gathered myself up, and took the leap.
The sensation was most peculiar.   I had not the faintest
idea whether I should or should not clear the chasm, but
the doubt was soon solved by my landing heavily on the
further side, rather to the right of the rest of the party.
The heavy load on my back sent me forwards on my face,
and I shot down the slope with tremendous velocity, head
foremost, until I was suddenly stopped by the tightening
round my waist of the rope, the other end of which was
held by Almer above.   My first impression was, that half
my ribs were crushed in ; as it was, my wind was so completely bagged by the severity of the jerk that I could not
speak, but laughed hysterically, until nature's bellows had
replenished my unlucky carcase.   The incident was so far
satisfactory that it showed the enormous strength of the
rope, and also how severe a shock, a man, like Almer,
standing in a most insecure position, can bear unmoved,
when he is prepared for it.   My weight, unloaded, is ten
and a half stone, and the strain on the rope was certainly
nearly as great as though I *had* jumped into the crevasse.
Almer now followed us over, and at 11.35 we were all together without accident below the " schrund," which, with
the wall above it, was as ugly-looking a place as I would
wish to see.

We now floundered down the slope of soft snow, without
taking much care, as we imagined that henceforward it was
all plain sailing, but were abruptly checked in our pace by
coming upon a huge crevasse, of great length and breadth,
but covered over in places.   Several attempts were made
to cross at one of these points, but without success, as the
breadth was too great, and the snow unsubstantial in the
extreme, and a long detour was necessary before we were
able to get over near its eastern extremity.   This proved
to be the beginning of a new series of troubles, as the
chasms became more and more numerous and complicated,
until the slope which we had imagined would be so easy,

H

resolved itself into a wall of gigantic sèracs, the passage of which tasked our energies to the utmost. The difficulty of the position was increased by our still being enveloped in a mist so thick that we could not see a distance of twenty feet below us, and were in a happy state of ignorance as to whether we were steering properly, or were only plunging deeper into the mire. Nothing, however, could exceed the energy and skill with which Croz threaded his way through the labyrinth which surrounded us. He never once had to retrace his steps, but, cutting along the sides of some crevasses and underneath others, he steadily gained ground. In spite of the generally deep snow, a good deal of step-cutting was necessary here and there, and we had nearly an hour of most exciting work before the inclination of the glacier diminished, and at 12.30 p.m., for the first time since leaving the Col, we stood at ease upon a flat plain of snow. But how long would it last? A fog on an unknown glacier always suggests to my desponding mind the probability of marching round and round in a circle, and finally having to pass the night in a crevasse, so that I, personally, was particularly relieved when, just as we emerged from the sèracs, the mist suddenly lifted sufficiently to let us see a long way over the glacier in front, which displayed itself to our admiring eyes perfectly level and uncrevassed.

The Glacier de la Pilatte is divided at its head into three great bays; one, between the Tête de Cheret and the Montagne du Says, over which goes the Col du Says; the second between the Montagne du Says and Les Bans; and the third, which we had just descended, east of Les Bans. The ridge, forming the right bank of this latter, runs north from the Crête des Bœufs Rouges, towards the Ailefroide, and over its lowest point goes the Col du Sélè to Ville Val Louise. In spite of the improvement in the weather, the Ailefroide and other high peaks remained invisible; so, having no temptation to lose time, we pushed on rapidly over the level snow-fields, gradually making for the left bank of the glacier. The snow was at first both deep and soft, and we all sunk in a good deal, especially poor Mons. Renaud, who had several times almost to be dug out. He was exceedingly tired, and no wonder, as he was utterly out of condition, and had not had much sleep before starting; nevertheless, his cheerfulness and good temper had never varied, and, except above the bergschrund, he had throughout been a most agreeable companion. Fortunately the snow improved as we went on, and we made such good progress that at 1.0 p.m. we got on to a large patch of rocks on the left bank of the glacier, and, with one consent, called a halt. Mons. Renaud enquired whether we were going to light a fire, though where he thought the material was to come from I don't know, and, finding that we were not, he announced his intention of going on to La Berarde so as to change his clothes; so Croz, having given him minute instructions as to the route, and particularly told him that he must get off the glacier on the *right* bank, he started off, while we turned our attention to feeding. There was a cold wind, which swept over our halting-place, so, having satisfied the pangs of hunger, we were glad to move on, and at 1.30 started off again. Just at this point there was a considerable fall in the glacier, which was consequently too much crevassed to be traversed with comfort, so we kept to the left bank, descending rapidly over moraine and steep slopes of débris, varied by long patches of snow, on which we got an occasional glissade, which was most generally brought to an end by our suddenly plunging up to our middles between two rocks, whose warmth had weakened the snow above. At the earliest opportunity we took to the glacier again, lower down, where it was perfectly smooth and level, the ice not even presenting the hummocky appearance usual in such positions, so that nothing could exceed the ease with which we got along. We traversed it to its extreme end, where it curled over in a steepish bank of ice, down which we cut a way, and at 2.10 got off the last glacier we were to tread in Dauphiné on to the "gazon," on the right bank of the torrent.

The "gazon" was, as usual, represented by a perfect

waste of stones of all shapes and sizes, which appeared to extend an unpleasantly-long distance in front, so we prepared ourselves for another feet-punishing and temper-trying walk. As we were stumbling along, we were astonished to see Mons. Renaud on the opposite bank of the torrent, he having, after all, quitted the glacier on the wrong side. This was awkward, not only on account of the roughness of the ground, but also because there was no bridge across till some way below La Berarde, the only facility for crossing above that place being the remains of an avalanche, which Rodier had told us was still firm enough to traverse, but which Mons. Renaud, not being aware of, might very easily miss. However, when we came to it, some way lower down, Whymper remained behind to direct his friend's attention to it. Nothing occurred to disturb the monotony of our walk except the successive passages of the lateral torrents from the Glaciers de la Côte Rouge, de la Tempe, and du Vallon, beneath which our route lay, which were accomplished without much trouble. The Vallon de la Pilatte is scenically far less interesting than the opposite Vallon des Etançons, but, by way of compensation, is also a degree less unpleasant to traverse—the stones, though bad enough, not being quite so rough. But we had, nevertheless, had quite enough of it by the time La Berarde appeared in sight, and were delighted when at 3.55 p.m. we once more found ourselves at Rodier's door.

Our object was, therefore, accomplished, but I don't think the Col de la Pilatte is likely to supersede the Col du Sélè as a direct route between La Berarde and Ville Val Louise. It is considerably longer in point of time, and far more difficult, but is certainly more exciting, and is therefore, perhaps, more interesting. It should not be attempted late in the season, as with little or no snow the Couloir on one side and the ice-wall on the other would be very troublesome, while the bergschrunds on both might be found insuperable obstacles. The pass would, I think, be found more difficult taken from La Berarde, and the way down by no means easily discovered. Personally, I should be very sorry, indeed, to have to descend the upper part of the couloir by which we mounted.

We had all along intended, should time permit, to push on at once to Venos, below St. Christophe, where we understood that there was a tolerable inn; so, having drunk some milk, and collected all our belongings, we bade farewell to the Rodiers, and at 4.40 Walker and I started, Whymper, Mons. Renaud, and the guides following shortly. The weather looked threatening, and we were apprehensive of a wet walk, but, although there was an occasional slight shower, there was nothing to hurt us, so we were so far fortunate. A tolerable path along the right bank of the stream led down the valley of the Venéon, with which we were rather disappointed, though undoubtedly a fine valley; but it is a mere gorge in the mountains, without any variety of scenery. Its flanks are throughout very lofty and steep, scantily clothed with vegetation, so that after a time the long continuance of desolation becomes monotonous. Passing the wretched and half-ruined hamlet of Les Etages, from which we ought to have got a superb view of the Ecrins, the path descended gently, until we reached the point at the entrance of the Vallon de la Muande, where the main valley takes an abrupt turn from west to northwest. From here the path became much rougher, and, which was more irritating, began a steady ascent, which soon raised us to an enormous height above the stream, and continued without intermission as far as St. Christophe. We got fine glimpses of unknown glaciers and peaks up the Vallon de la Muande and the Combe des Arias, but our powers of enjoying scenery were considerably weakened by a rather violent and very cold wind which blew straight in our faces, so that we could with difficulty keep our eyes open. At 6.55 we reached St. Christophe, the chief place of the valley, where we found Almer and Croz who had passed us some time before. Croz remained to wait for Whymper, while Almer went on with us to secure beds and supper at Venos. Below St.

Christophe we came upon a grand scene, where a bridge is thrown over the torrent as it leaps from the mouth of the Vallon de la Selle. The torrent and bridge are both appropriately called "Torrent and Pont du Diable," as the bridge is thrown over a frightful abyss, and the stream issues from a gorge, a mere fissure in the rocks, nearly as contracted and forbidding as the celebrated one of Pfeffers. We now began to go down in earnest, and a steep but most welcome descent soon brought us to the bed of the valley, on a level with the stream upon which we had been so long looking. The scenery became more and more wild, until we gradually entered a gorge of most savage grandeur. Rocks were piled upon rocks in the wildest confusion, as if a whole mountain had been shattered by some convulsion, while the stream rushed furiously along in the midst of the chaos with a sullen roar, with difficulty overcoming the obstacles in its way. We were in the centre of this wonderful defile, and it was getting dusk, when the path suddenly appeared to come to an abrupt termination, and it was some time before we discovered that it made a sharp turn between two huge rocks, and crossed to the left bank of the stream by a natural bridge, formed by some immense masses of rock which have fallen together across it. Thenceforward the path became rougher than ever, and some care was really necessary in the obscure light to avoid a plunge into the furious stream alongside of us, so that, in spite of the amazing grandeur of the scene, the lights of Venos, glimmering in the distance, were a welcome sight. It was a long time before we seemed to get any nearer to them, and, when we did at last cross the bridge which leads into the village, we found, to our infinite disgust, that the inn "chez Paquet" was at the very top of the hill, on the side of which the place is situated. We had some difficulty in finding it, but at last a friendly woman led us to the door, which we entered at 8.40 p.m., after a walk of four hours from La Berarde.

We were received by Mons. Paquet himself, an old fellow of more than 80 years of age, of whom our first impression was not favourable, as his garrulousness was, to tired travellers, almost insufferable. But he showed us the bed-room accommodation, which consisted of one room with four beds in it, two rooms with a bed a-piece, and two beds in the salon. We ordered supper, and, as Whymper and Croz arrived ten minutes after us, having deposited Mons. Renaud at St. Christophe, it was not long before we were sitting down to a most excellent meal. In spite of the good fare, that supper was a rather dreary one, as we were all half asleep, and no wonder, our day's work having extended over seventeen hours. However, two or three glasses of " Chartreuse" set us up, and we finally retired, feeling by no means over-fatigued. We had not had our clothes off since the previous Wednesday night, so our appreciation of clean beds may be left to the imagination.

Tuesday, 28th June.—I was awoke at 7.0 a.m. by the sun streaming in at the window, so jumped up, pulled Walker out of bed, and went to perform a similar kind operation on Whymper, but, on entering his room, found that he was very unwell, and, at the moment, quite unable to get up. We sent him in some tea and toast, which was all he could take, and sat down ourselves to a capital breakfast, which old Paquet came in and superintended. He appeared in a far more amiable light than last night, and was most anxious for all our wants to be well attended to. He was very curious to know what had made us come to *his* inn; and when we told him that it was recommended in an *English* guide-book, his delight knew no bounds. We took the opportunity of impressing on him that what English travellers looked to most was cleanliness; that the food and beds might be coarse or rough, but that they must be clean. We certainly had no reason to complain on that score, and the charge for all we had had was extra-ordinarily moderate. Our programme for the day was, to walk to Bourg d'Oysans, and take a carriage from there as far as the top of the Col du Lautaret, where we proposed to sleep at the Hospice, preparatory to crossing the Col du Galibier to St. Michel to-morrow. After breakfast we found Whymper better, but still far from well, so it was arranged that we and Almer should go on to Bourg, secure a carriage there, and bring it to the point where the path from Venos falls into the Lautaret road, where he and Croz would be waiting for us. Accordingly, at 9.50 a.m., after an affectionate farewell from Mons. Paquet, for whom we really began to entertain quite a regard, we set off. The path for a considerable distance ran along the right bank of the stream, and, indeed, does so the whole way. But, on arriving at a bridge, we found a notice stuck up that further passage along the right bank was " defendu " because of works in progress, and we, in our innocence imagining that the notice was meant to be attended to, crossed over to the left bank. We had in consequence a rougher, but, I believe, rather shorter, walk, but were told by a native whom we met that we need not have regarded the notice. The scenery was throughout pleasing but in no way remarkable, the track leading through several hamlets buried in trees, the inhabitants of which stared at us as though we had been strange monsters, our axes, I fancy, puzzling them considerably. Near the junction of the Venéon with the Romanche the valley gradually opens out into a flat, sandy plain of considerable extent, which must be a perfect furnace, as it is hemmed in on all sides by a steep wall of cliffs. Just here the path became vague, and finally disappeared, having, doubtless, been washed away by the river, which gave manifest evidence of being occasionally somewhat erratic in its movements. We had in consequence a rough and rather disagreeable scramble along the hill-side, but at last fell into a good but dusty road, which brought us into Bourg d'Oysans and the Hotel de Milan at 12.25 p.m., after a walk of two hours and a half from Venos.

On entering the salle-à-manger we were almost knocked down by the stench of garlic; so, having impressed upon the fat and oleaginous landlord that we had not eaten for a week, and required food, we fled over the way to Mons. Michaud, the chemist and photographer of the place, to see

what we could find interesting in his collection. He was
most civil, and informed us that he was going up to La
Berarde to photograph, under the impression that all the
high peaks and glaciers were within sight of that place.
We disabused him of this notion, and gave him a list of
good points of view, particularly desiring him to visit
the Vallon des Etançons and take a view of that side of
the Meije, which he promised to do, and send us specimens to England. We got very fair photographs of the
Brèche and Bourg, but his collection was most rich in
views of the Grande Chartreuse. By the time we returned
to the hotel, luncheon was ready, and, having done justice
to its merits, we went and stood at the door, waiting for
the arrival of the carriage we had ordered, and here we
had the good fortune to meet in the flesh a celebrated
character of whom we had heard, but whose existence we
had supposed mythical.

At the door was standing a young Frenchman, with
whom we got into conversation, observing that we had just
made the ascent of the highest mountain in the country.
"Oh," replied he, "sans doute le Pic de Belledonne;" a
rather elevated Rigi in the neighbourhood. We informed
him that our conquest was not the Pic de Belledonne, but
the Pic des Ecrins, on hearing which he smiled blandly,
never having heard the name before, and, evidently meditating how he might avoid showing his ignorance, finally
contented himself with a spasmodic "Ah!" After a short
pause, he enquired whether we had been up Mont Blanc,
and, on *my* replying in the negative, went on to say that
HE had, about ten days before. We were astonished, as,
without wishing to reflect on the appearance of the worthy
Gaul, I must say that he did not give us the idea of a
man capable of such a performance. However, we, in our
turn, smiled blandly, and enquired whether, so early in the
season, he had found the ascent difficult, and whether he
had had a good view from the *summit*. "From the
summit!" said he, "I did not go to the summit." We
ventured to enquire how high his wanderings had reached.

" Mon Dieu," replied he, " jusqu'au Montanvert !" Our
politeness was not proof against this, so we broke off the
conversation abruptly, and retired to indulge our merri-
ment unchecked.

There was a long delay before the carriage made its
appearance, and, when it did, we found there was only
room for three, and, as we were five, this was obviously of
no use, so the horses had to be taken out, and a larger
vehicle, with some difficulty, found. This entailed a further
most vexatious delay, and the consequence was, we did not
get away till 2.30 p.m., exactly an hour after the time we
had agreed with Whymper to pick him up. Having crossed
the Romanche, we rattled along over the level and dusty
road as far as the point of junction of the path from
Venos, where we found Whymper and Croz in a rather
disconsolate frame of mind. They had been there nearly
an hour and a half, and, naturally, were inclined to think
we had not been quite so diligent as we might have been,
whereas the detention was on our part quite unavoidable.
From the look of the country a stranger would imagine
that the sources of the Romanche must be looked for up
the valley of the Venéon, which is the natural continuation
of the main valley above Bourg, from which place no other
outlet is at first visible. But the parent stream actually
forces its way through a cleft in the side of the valley,
whose existence would scarcely be suspected. This is the
defile of Les Infernets, forming by far the most picturesque
section of the Lautaret road, which is carried most
skilfully along its precipitous flanks, at a great height
above the bed of the stream. Several villages are perched
in most inaccessible looking positions at various points
along the north side, and serve to give variety to the
scenery. The road is well made and kept, and along this
portion of the route passes several projecting spurs by
means of short galleries pierced through the rock, which
are, however, by no means waterproof. Passing through
the wretched hamlets of Freney and Le Dauphin, where
the squalid appearance of the inns is only equalled by the

pretension of their names, we gradually entered the celebrated Combe de Malval. The great expectations we had formed of this gorge, which has been compared to the Via Mala, were much disappointed. The rocks on either side are neither so steep nor so lofty as we had imagined, while the long-continued scene of desolation becomes monotonous in the extreme. There is not a shrub nor a tree visible, nor is a single habitation passed with the exception of a few wretched miners' huts. The cliffs on the south side support the Grand Glacier du Lans, and the tongues of glacier which, fed by that great reservoir of névé, are forced down through the several gorges and openings in the supporting wall, are the most interesting objects in the scenery. We kept a careful look out for a waterfall, called the " Saut de la Pucelle," but were unable to identify it, as, although we passed several considerable ones, none was so pre-eminent in height and volume of water as to be distinguishable from its fellows, and our driver could not assist us. The road is not at all steep, but, wherever there was the slightest pretence of a rise, our never very rapid pace degenerated into the slowest of walks, so, as there was a cold wind blowing in our faces, Walker and I got down and walked some way through the Combe. The Rateau and Meije, with its glaciers, gradually came in sight, and at 6.35 p.m. we reached La Grave, where we went again to the inn " chez Juge," and, having ordered dinner, hurried to the Post-Office, to see after letters and newspapers.

The worthy postmaster instantly recognised us as the party who had attacked the Brêche, and insisted on our coming into his private room, and talking it over. He informed us that we had been seen climbing the last slope, and on the Col, and that the sight had created the greatest excitement in the village, where a passage in this direction had always been considered impracticable. On at last emerging into the street again, we found that the news of our arrival had spread, and that our exploit had really caused more enthusiasm than we could have supposed to have been possible in so apathetic a population. The amount of hand-shaking we had to go through was almost painful, and, at last, one excited individual seized hold of us, and, having proclaimed himself to be the " plus grand chasseur du monde," insisted upon our coming into his house, where he had something to show us. He at the same time apostrophised us by the most endearing epithet in the native vocabulary, which had so powerful an effect on us that we felt constrained to humour him. What our friend had to exhibit was a telescope affixed to his window, commanding a view of the Brêche, through which we traced the greater portion of our route. He also forced us. to take a glass of Cognac with him, and then let us go ; his swagger and conversation during the interview having been something really too delicious. After a rencontre with our friends of the " Gendarmerie Impèriale," who, again, condescended to be mildly facetious, we went in to our dinner, which was a very tolerable one, and, so soon as that was done, ordered the trap to be made ready.

The driver had an exaggerated idea of the amount of rest the horses required, so took his time about putting them to, and it was 8.30 before we were able to start, when it was of course nearly dark. A short distance on, the road passes through two tunnels, of which the second is of immense length (more than 600 yards), indeed, I believe, far longer than any other in the Alps, and lit by lamps at intervals. I shall not forget that drive in a hurry. The cold was most intense, and Walker and I, who sat in front alongside the driver, were perfectly perished, in spite of the protection of our plaids. He and Whymper had the " pipe of peace" as a consolation, which was denied to me. Croz had never had his pipe out of his mouth since leaving Venos, and was, consequently, now in a state of torpor, while Almer fell asleep with his usual facility. The road mounts steadily the whole way, so that we never got out of a walk; and the night, though clear and cloudless, was very dark, so that we saw nothing—no great loss I imagine. Altogether it was the dreariest thing possible, and the distance, although only ten miles, seemed endless. The driver

walked near his horses' heads the whole way, and, had we
been wise, we should have done the same thing, as it was
freezing hard. As we neared the top of the Col, we got
into a trot, which finally landed us, at 11.0 p.m., at the
Hospice du Lautaret, a large massive stone building, in
which there was not a single light, or any sign of life
visible. On getting down, I could scarcely move from cold
and stiffness, and never in my life was so glad to have
arrived. But it seemed for a long time that, after all, we
should have to pass the night in our trap, as our repeated
knockings met with no response. A big dog outside at
first made hostile demonstrations, but was at last persuaded that our intentions were pacific, and then declined
even to bark, for which we should have been really grateful
to him. Finding that mild measures were of no avail, I
caught hold of the knocker and played "Aunt Sally" on
the door for nearly ten minutes without stopping, using
first one arm, and then the other. The popular melody
was effectual, and the door was at last opened by the man
in charge, who abused us heartily for the noise we had
made, while we returned the compliment for his delay in
opening. Visitors not being expected, we had to wait a
long time while beds were being prepared, so passed the
interval in heating a good supply of wine, which put fresh
life into *our* chilled frames, and good humour into our
landlord, whom we invited to join us in its consumption.
We were in due course shown to rooms, lofty and bare but
clean, and were not long in turning into our beds which
were also clean, though coarse, damp, and icy cold.

Wednesday, 29th June.—Shortly after 7.0 a.m. I tumbled
out of bed, my slumbers having been undisturbed, save by
a deluded cock, who crowed at intervals during the night
in a sepulchral tone, which suggested that he was suffering
from a violent indigestion, and that any one who would
wring his neck would perform an act of kindness. A
glance out of window showed that it had frozen hard in
the night, the ground being covered with hoar-frost, and
also that there was a promise of a day, for our last walk in

Dauphiné, as fine as those with which we had all along been blessed. The view from the Hospice, which is built on the very top of the Col du Lautaret, 6740 feet above the sea, is not very extensive, and interesting only in one direction, viz., towards La Grave, where the north-eastern angle of the Meije is well seen. The eastern face of the mountain was the only one we had not hitherto seen, and the view we now got of it enabled us to clear up a topographical mystery which had puzzled us considerably. It will be remembered that, on the passage of the Brèche de la Meije, our attention had been drawn, while descending the Glacier des Etançons, to several couloirs leading up to gaps in the ridge forming the right bank of that glacier, the most northerly of which looked especially tempting, and ought, according to the French map, to have communicated with the Glacier de la Meije, on the north side of the Meije itself. Our observations, however, from the Bec du Grenier had shown that this could not possibly be the case, and we had ever since speculated as to where any one, attaining the gap in question, would really find himself. Looking now at the eastern face of the Meije, we saw a very extensive glacier, steep and crevassed, divided into two arms by a projecting ridge of rock, which could be nothing but the Glacier de l'Homme of the French map. In the ridge at the head of this were several gaps, of which one, particularly well marked, just to the south of and close under the eastern peak of the mountain, was beyond all doubt our old friend. We all agreed that a pass to La Berarde from the side of the Lautaret road might be made through this gap. The ascent would be difficult, as the glacier is broken up into steep cliffs of névé, and the height is great, but the thing certainly could be done, and, the gap once gained, the descent to the Glacier des Etançons would, probably, not be found very difficult. On the other hand, the pass would certainly be longer than the Brèche de la Meije and also less interesting, but it might be convenient at times, when the Brèche is, as I think it will sometimes be found, impracticable. The people of the Hospice gave us an excellent breakfast, of which a large dish of fried potatoes was the principal feature, and the charge for everything was absurdly moderate, the bill for us three—for breakfast, beds, attendance, and the wine last night—amounting to only thirteen and a half francs. Whymper was better this morning, but preferred following us at a rather later hour; so, as soon as we had finished breakfast, Walker, myself, and Almer, took our departure at 9.20 a.m.

Our route lay for ten minutes down the high road of the Lautaret towards Briançon, but at the end of that time we struck away to the left towards the ridge over which passes the Col du Galibier. There was at first no path, but we soon fell into a faint track, over rich and luxuriant pastures, steering to the left in order to cross a small torrent, between us and a group of châlets, which we had been told at the Hospice we must steer for. A rather long detour was necessary before we could cross the deep gully which the torrent has made through the friable soil, but, once on the other side, we made straight for the châlets, which were squalid and miserable in the extreme. From here it seemed that it would be easy to get on to the ridge anywhere, but a cross, perched on a point of it, well to the left, determined us to select that line of march. Nothing could have been easier or more utterly devoid of incident than our route, and we plodded leisurely on, over rough and rather steep ground, until we reached the foot of the final slope. We might with facility have gone straight up this, but we were heavily laden, and in consequence slightly lazy, so carefully kept to the series of very easy zig-zags which were faintly marked along the side of the shaly slope. These soon came to an end, and brought us, at 11.5, to the Col du Galibier, 9154 feet in height, a broad stony ridge, on which we threw ourselves to admire the beauties of nature.

The view to the north was not remarkable, which rather disappointed us, but clouds had risen in the distance, so, perhaps, we did not see so much as we might have done under more favourable circumstances. To the west was a confused mass of tolerably lofty peaks, rising from a considerable tract of snow, which we imagined to be part of the group of which the Aiguille du Goleon and Bec du Grenier are prominent members, but we could not come to any satisfactory conclusion on the subject, and no map that we had threw any light on it. Any one who does not fancy hard work, but likes mild climbing and gorgeous views, could not do better than explore the long ridge which forms the boundary between the Maurienne and Dauphiné, and determine the true relative positions of the extraordinary complication of peaks, ridges, and valleys that radiate from it towards the Maurienne. Towards the south the view was more interesting, as we looked almost straight up the long valley which runs from near Villard d'Arène to the Glacier d'Arsines, and source of the Romanche. The glacier itself, which is almost as broad as it is long, and, to all appearance, perfectly smooth and level, was also well seen ; and, above the tremendous precipices at its head, which are extremely fine and inaccessible in appearance, towered our vanquished enemy—the Ecrins, which presented to us its face above the Glacier Blanc. No position could have been more favourable for retracing the route we had followed to the summit, as the whole of the mountain above the great bergschrund was seen to perfection at a comparatively small distance. We made out the point where we had turned the bergschrund on the ascent, the rocks we had first touched, the ice-wall up which we had toiled so long, the rocks above them, the gap between the peaks above which we had quitted the arête in descending, the slope down which we had cut our way to the bergschrund, and the exact point at which we had finally leaped over that formidable obstacle. We looked at our conquest with proud satisfaction, which Almer fully shared. He took a last look at the glorious mountain with my glass, and, on laying it down, exclaimed, emphatically, that it was indeed a " Teufel,"—which it certainly was. The Meije also came out well, and the gap at the head of the Glacier de l'Homme looked more than ever like a pass. Almer, indeed, quite ridiculed the idea of any serious difficulty being found in effecting it, but we thought that, in this case, he allowed his sanguine disposition to carry him too far, as it seemed to us that the ascent of the Glacier de l'Homme would require a good deal of diplomacy. We ought to have seen Monte Viso, but some clouds had gathered in that direction also, and we were obliged to imagine it, contenting ourselves with the long zig-zags of the Lautaret road, on its descent towards Monetier. A cold wind was blowing over the Col, so we took in all there was to see as rapidly as possible, and at 11.15 bade farewell to the Alps of Dauphiné, and turned to descend to Valloire and St. Michel.

We had a choice of two glens into which to descend, which appeared to unite lower down. Of these the one to the left is called by Joanne "Combe de la Lauzette," and that to the right, "Combe de Valloire." The descent into both appeared equally practicable, and châlets were visible in the Combe de la Lauzette, but we chose the track to the right, wrongly, as I thought at the time, but rightly as appears from a subsequent study of Joanne, who, on a pass so comparatively frequented, may probably be believed. Passing over steepish banks of shale, on which patches of snow were still lying, we soon landed on pastures where the diversity of paths was puzzling, but seeing some châlets on our right, we allowed our natural desire for milk to influence our choice of a route, and steered for them. They were soon reached, and, after some trouble, their occupants, in the shape of two women and a girl, were discovered, but proved to be the most uncivil specimens of their class we had yet come across. Our request for *cream* was received with jeers and laughter, as though the idea was an exceedingly good joke, and the small quantity of milk that was at last brought us was poor in the extreme, and far from fresh. We were, nevertheless, charged an extortionate price for it, and so evidently looked upon as intruders, that we had no temptation to

I

make a long halt, and in a very few minutes took ourselves off. We were surprised to see a man and woman very busy picking the violets which grew all round in profusion, and still more surprised to hear that they had crossed the Col on purpose, and actually found it pay to take them to Bourg d'Oysans for sale. The descent below the châlets became very rapid, and the path struck well away to the left, along the side of the spur which divides the Combe de Valloire from the Combe de la Lauzette. The former was at our feet, and, as we descended into it, we got a view of the rugged range at its head, over which goes the Col des Rochilles to Briançon. A good deal of snow was visible at the head of the Combe, and the pass must be more laborious, and, I should think, less interesting than the Galibier, which is, however, a rather less direct route to Briançon. The path led us down by steep and rough zig-zags to the level of the stream, to the right bank of which we crossed by the first bridge, and were then fairly in the main valley of Valloire. The track thenceforward fell very gently, and brought us, at 12.45 p.m., to the deserted hamlet of Bonnenuit, the highest in the valley, situated exactly opposite the entrance of the lateral Vallon des Aiguilles d'Arve, on the opposite side of the stream. Looking up this we had an exceedingly fine view of two out of the three Aiguilles, and the small hanging glacier between them. Their boldness of form was as remarkable as from all other points of view, and we left them behind us, feeling tolerably confident that they would remain unscaled for many a long day. At a short distance below Bonnenuit we crossed to the left bank of the stream, and were once more on familiar ground. Our former agreeable impression of the scenery of the valley was confirmed, and we thoroughly enjoyed the walk onwards to the village of Valloire, which we reached at 1.55 p.m., having met, *en route*, our hostess at the châlets in the Vallon des Aiguilles d'Arve, who told us that she ascended and descended regularly every day.

We lunched at the little inn off bread, butter, and a peculiarly excellent cheese, almost like a Stilton, which we made look rather foolish by the time we had done. We

were astonished to meet in this out of the way spot a specimen of the "Commercial Traveller" genus, who was very
busy displaying his samples to the landlord and a gathering of the villagers, and appeared to be receiving liberal
orders. At 2.30 p.m. we took our departure, and leisurely
followed the capital but rather steep path, leading up to
the chapel and lofty crosses which mark the Col de Valloire,
where we arrived at 3.15. We had hoped from here to
get a last view of the Ecrins, but were doomed to disappointment, as heavy clouds covered the sky in that direction. A storm was apparently brewing on the other side
of the Arc, and warned us to hasten our steps if we wished
to reach St. Michel, which was visible far below us, with
dry garments. We accordingly made good use of our legs,
and rattled down the steep and stony track as fast as possible, over the open ground, through pleasant woods, and
past the scattered cottages at the base of the hill, until the
main valley was at last reached. The river was crossed,
and at 4.10 p.m. we walked into St. Michel, which we had
left just nine days before. The passage from the Hospice
had taken just six hours' actual walking, and from Valloire
one hour and forty minutes.

We went to the Hotel du Bon Samaritain, opposite the
station, and having secured bed-rooms, our first business
was to order dinner to be ready at the Buffet, which is kept
by the same proprietors, at 6.0, by which time we concluded
that Whymper and Croz would have arrived. We then
ordered up unlimited water, and indulged in the first wash
we had had for more than a week, and, that not unnecessary operation over, sat ourselves down to write despatches
to friends in England, to report progress so far. Shortly
after 6.0 Whymper and Croz arrived, and we soon sat
down to the first dinner, worthy of the name, we had had
since leaving Paris. There was nothing to mar the pleasure of that dinner. Whymper was much better, and we
had the satisfaction of seeing Almer and Croz sitting
at an adjoining table, also enjoying the fleshpots, and
poking fun at each other. The two men had contracted

a thorough liking for each other, and, although unable to express their ideas in language, contrived, by pantomime and various little devices, to show their mutual regard. Our various victories were, of course, celebrated in bumpers of champagne, and the health of the Ecrins was drunk with especial honour, and, I am sure, with a feeling of the greatest respect on the part of all five of us. After dinner we discussed our future movements. Our programme was, to cross to-morrow the Col des Encombres to Moutiers Tarantaise and Bourg St. Maurice, where Walker was to leave us, to join his father and sister at Aosta. On Friday, Whymper and myself were to go over the Col du Bonhomme to the Pavillon Bellevue, whence we hoped, on Saturday, to make the ascent of Mont Blanc, and descend to Chamouni in the day. To reach Bourg would be a long day's work, and an early start would be necessary, which was fixed, after some discussion, for 3.30 a.m. The champagne had had its effect on Croz, who was in a state of glorious excitement, but became at last so noisy and loquacious that we were relieved when he finally took himself off to his well-earned slumbers. Whymper and myself packed and sent off by train to Geneva and Chamouni all our baggage except our plaids, and, at length, every preparation for the morning's start having been made, we all went to bed. At any time our beds would have been thought comfortable, but, after all our toils, we agreed unanimously that we had never lain on more deliciously-luxurious mattresses.

Thursday, 30th June.—The time to be devoted to our comfortable beds was but too short, and at 2.30 a.m. a loathsome tap at the door warned us that, for us, the night was over. However, painful experience has taught me that reflection only makes the sad necessity of getting up more sad, so without delay I responded to the knock, lit our candles, and commenced the labour of dressing. On going down to breakfast and receiving the bill, we found that our repast of last night was charged for item by item, and the total, consequently, raised to a most extortionate sum, about three times what we should have paid elsewhere for a similar dinner. We protested vigorously against this, but without success, so were obliged to submit in a very bad temper, which was not improved when we found that the guides had been treated in a similar fashion. They were naturally horrified to find that in one night they were each mulcted of more than an ordinary day's pay; but remonstrance was as unavailing on their part as on ours, and they had to pay up. We were unable to get Whymper up, and were, therefore, reluctantly compelled to start without him, as we had a long distance to get over in the day. Accordingly, at 3.55 a.m. we set off with Almer, half an hour later than had been arranged, leaving Croz in a disconsolate frame of mind outside the Buffet. The appearance of the weather was not very promising, but it looked as though it might improve, and, at any rate, we could not well come to any harm, as there was said to be a track right over the Col. Passing up the long main street of St. Michel, we turned up a dirty and narrow lane to the left, which led us through the mean and squalid part of the town to the open country behind, where the number of paths would have been puzzling, had not Almer last night very discreetly gone over the first part of the route with Croz and a native, and obtained directions on the subject. So soon as we were well out of the town, the path continued for a long distance by the side of a small stream, passing through luxuriant woods, and mounting steadily, until we were at a great height above the town, close to a tall, solitary tree, which is very conspicuous from below, and had been pointed out to us as a landmark for which we must make. The view from here of the valley of the Arc at our feet was very pleasing, and made a short halt to take breath after the steep pull up specially agreeable. The entrance to the Valley of Valloire was exactly opposite to us, and we could trace all the windings of the path from the Col, down which we had yesterday hurried.

We now gradually penetrated into an extensive upland valley, shut in on both sides and in front by rocky ridges of considerable height, from which low peaks rose here and there. The Col was visible straight in front, presenting no apparent difficulty, but separated from us by a long tract of desolate country, the passage of which promised to be monotonous and tiresome. Walker was laden with all his baggage, no slight weight, and certainly not to be carried up hill longer than necessary, so at the last village we hired a good-looking youth for a trifling sum to act as a beast of burden as far as the top of the Col. All this time the weather, after a transient improvement, had been getting gradually worse, until at last down came the mist, and blotted out the landscape, such at it was, from our vision. We consoled ourselves with the reflection that our loss was not great, and that, in point of fact, we were lucky not to be favoured with a broiling sun, which would have been far more disagreeable. Nothing could exceed the dreariness of the scenery, when an occasional clearance let us see a little way ahead. Of vegetation there was nothing save the coarse grass slopes up which our route lay, and there was not a single object of interest to relieve the monotony of the way. So we mounted along the rough track, which rose steadily but never steeply, looking forward to the châlets, which we supposed we should come to sooner or later, where we flattered ourselves we would go in heavily for milk. But on mentioning the subject to our native, he summarily dissipated our pleasant dreams, by the information that the cows were ill, and produced either no milk at all, or such as was unwholesome, adding that many persons had already been made ill by incautiously drinking it. We came to the châlets in due course, but there were none of the ordinary signs of Alpine life about them. The cows were invisible, and the occupants stood listless and silent at their doors as we passed. Shortly after, we emerged from the mist, and found ourselves apparently close to the Col, to the left of which was the fine mass of the Rocher des Encombres, with a stone man visible on the top of it. The distance, however, was greater than we had supposed, and our consequent disappointment, of course, magnified it still more. But all things must come to an end, and, following the gentle zig-zags, we reached, at 7.25 a.m., the ridge of the Col des Encombres, in three hours and a half from St. Michel. The height of the pass must be over 8000 feet, but there is not much view in either direction; to the north none at all, and to the south, some snow-covered peaks in the neighbourhood of the Combe de Valloire, which, in the cloudy state of the sky, we could not identify.

At our feet grass slopes stretched away to the head of the long Val des Encombres, into which we should naturally have descended. But we had been told at St. Michel that the better plan was to strike the ridge which forms its right side, and separates it from the parallel Val de Belleville, follow it until we came to a stone man, and then turn down to the village of St. Martin de Belleville in the latter valley. Our native told us the same story. So, having sent him on his way rejoicing, we started off in the direction indicated, having only halted a very few seconds. Skirting the head of the valley, we soon fell into a faint track, which was visible for a long distance in front, always near the crest of the ridge, but on the Encombres side. It led over gently undulating ground, and the walking would have been pleasant, if a fine rain had not come on, followed by a slight fall of snow, which the wind blew into our faces. We looked anxiously out for some signs of the path taking the looked-for turn down into the Val de Belleville, but, although we passed several stone men, the track ignored them all, until at 9.0 we actually did pass through a sort of Col, between two eminences on the ridge, on to the Belleville side, and congratulated ourselves that we were going to descend in earnest, the last hour not having brought us twenty feet lower than the Col. We were, however, disappointed, as we gradually wound round again, until we once more overlooked the Val des Encombres at a great depth below us. It presented a most remarkable appearance, as both its steep flanks were scored by a series of very narrow and deep ravines, the effect of which was very singular. We were beginning to think that we must have missed the way, when we met a party of peasants, who told us that we were all right; and, shortly afterwards, the path took a decisive turn to the right, and led us by a rapid descent to some châlets on the slopes above the Val de Belleville. I put my head into one, with a view to milk, and found its occupants sitting over a fire, doing nothing, but staring so fixedly at the flames that my approach was at first not noticed. There was a general air of misery about the people and place, the cause of which was sufficiently explained by the answer, given in a despairing tone to my request for milk, to the effect that all the cows were and had been for some time ill, and gave no milk at all. In the valley below two villages were visible, one on the right bank of the stream, rather higher up than the other on the left. We were not certain which of these two was St. Martin; so, on our way down, we enquired of a hideous old hag, who was prowling about the hill side, arrayed in a steeple-crowned hat, of the conventional witches' pattern, at least three feet high, and a capacious cloak to match. I have no doubt the old lady's intentions were of the most amiable character, and that the information she communicated was most valuable, but she signally failed to make us understand a word of what she said, which, indeed, seemed to us an amazing flow of gibberish. We went on our way not much wiser than before, but interpreted some of her gesticulations to mean that the higher village *was* St. Martin, and so steered accordingly. Below the châlets the descent was very rapid, over steep grass slopes, by a well-marked track, which, as we approached the brow of the final descent above the stream, suddenly vanished and left us rather puzzled how to proceed. There was nothing for it but to follow our noses and trust to luck, which, for a wonder, did not fail us, as, after floundering through some fields of long grass, we fell into a broad path, which led down to a bridge over the stream, crossing which a sharp ascent brought us up to the village, which turned out, as we had supposed, to be St. Martin de Belleville.

It was just 10.35, and we had eaten nothing since our early breakfast at St. Michel, with the exception of a small piece of bread which Almer chanced to have in his pocket; we therefore looked out anxiously for some sort of an inn, and seeing a bush (the usual sign) suspended over the door of a corner house in the little " place," near the church, went in there. We were received by a gaunt, middle-aged female, who took us into a stuffy inner room, and set before us bread, butter, cheese, and some red wine, while she prepared an omelette. Fortunately we had our own cutlery, or we should have been obliged to eat it with our fingers, as the place only boasted of one rusty old knife, which had only half a handle. However, we were not inclined to be particular, and were thankful to get anything at all to eat, so consumed our omelette, and sat, pitching into the bread and cheese, until we could really eat no more, and, thereupon, at 11.10 went on our way. The path onwards down the Val de Belleville is exceedingly good, almost worthy to be called a Char road, and we trotted along it merrily, the weather having improved, and the scenery, though not remarkable, being pretty. We kept throughout to the right bank of the stream, I believe, correctly, although there was an apparently equally good path on the other side, passing through several rather considerable villages. We occasionally abandoned the main road to try a short cut, but I don't think we ever gained much, and once, certainly, lost by the manœuvre, after which we gave it up, and stuck to the highway. This, for the first hour and three quarters, ran tolerably on a level, only rising and falling according to the necessities of the ground. At the end of that time we began to go down in earnest, and soon developed the unpleasant fact that Walker was seriously lame. Ever since leaving the Col he had been complaining of an uneasy feeling in his knee, and now the steep descent over a stony path jarred him severely at every step. Our progress was unavoidably slow, and it was with great difficulty he got on at all. He most unselfishly pressed me to go on, but, of course, that was not to be thought of, and, indeed, was the less necessary, as, when we were once down on a level with the stream, the pain of walking was not so great, so that we travelled as fast as was needful. The river had carried away the path in places, and men were busy working at it, but we had no difficulty in picking a way amongst the débris as far as the point of junction with the Doron, which flows down from Pralognan and the great glaciers of the Tarantaise. Once over this, a broad plain lay between us and Moutiers, which was soon traversed, we crossed the already broad stream of the Isère, walked through the town, and finally reached the Hotel de la Couronne, on the " Grand Place," at 2.15 p.m., after a walk of ten hours and a quarter from St. Michel.

Having ordered dinner, our first enquiry was about means of conveyance on to Bourg St. Maurice, when we were told that the courier would start at 4.15, and had three seats vacant in his carriage, which we had better secure. We did not do so at once, as we hoped that Whymper might arrive, in which case we should hire a vehicle to ourselves, so we simply gave orders that the seats should not be disposed of without reference to us. They gave us an extensive and most excellent dinner, which we did justice to, completely clearing out each dish in succession, much to the gratification of the waiter, whose civility and attention were beyond all praise. Time passed, and there were no signs of Whymper; so, when the courier came in and said we must make up our minds about the seats as there were applications for them, we had no option but to engage them. Just as we were going to start Whymper and Croz arrived, but it was too late for us to change our minds, so they stopped to dine, and at 4.20 we three started in a clumsy sort of omnibus, holding four inside and one on the box alongside the driver. Upon this occasion the fourth seat was occupied by a loquacious female, who was returning after a long absence to her home at

Tignes, which she described as an earthly paradise, with several first-rate hotels,—an account which by no means coincided with what we had always heard on the subject. The cause of her loquacity was explained by the appearance of a bottle out of a basket which she had with her, at which, spurning the conventionalities which require the use of a cup, she took frequent and hearty pulls, upon the first occasion offering us second suck. These potations had their natural effect, and she soon found our society somewhat slow; so, much to our relief, she effected an exchange of position with the occupant of the fifth seat outside, and, for the rest of the journey, lavished her endearments upon the more appreciative driver. The valley for a considerable distance above Moutiers is very picturesque, densely wooded, and in many places contracted to a mere gorge, at the bottom of which the river roars at a great depth below. But after a time the scenery became dreary and uninteresting, and I went to sleep, notwithstanding the general discomfort of the vehicle, and especially the cramped accommodation for our legs. I awoke to find our conveyance halting for a few moments at a village, name unknown, and the rain falling heavily, which filled me with anxiety for the fate of my proposed attack on Mont Blanc on Saturday. Resuming our route, I again lapsed into a happy state of oblivion, from which I was only aroused by our arrival, at 8.30 p.m., at Bourg St. Maurice, in darkness and pouring rain. We went to the Hotel des Voyageurs, and were shown good bed-rooms, and furnished with a tolerable supper, after which we speedily retired, the day's journey having been a long and fatiguing one, to be followed on the morrow, in my case, by one scarcely less so.

Friday, 1st July.—The rain came down incessantly all night long, and, when we got out of bed, shortly after 4.0 a.m., there appeared no immediate signs of a clearance, but by the time we had dressed things looked a little better, and we ventured to indulge in the hope of a dry, if dull, day. Walker's leg was so painful that he very wisely determined to take a mule over the little St. Bernard to Aosta, whither he was bound, in the hope that a day's rest would remedy the evil. We had a very fair breakfast, and for it and our other accommodation were charged a by no means extortionate sum. I said good-bye to Walker, with the greatest possible regret that our pleasant companionship was for the present over, and at 5.30 a.m. started with Almer for the Col du Bonhomme. Our route lay for a short distance along the road to the little St. Bernard, and in our mutual ignorance we kept along it too far, and had to retrace our steps to the point where the track turns off to the left, and mounts steeply into the narrow glen which leads to Chapieu. This is a mere cleft in the mountains, scantily clothed with pine trees, and has not the slightest pretence to beauty or picturesqueness, but we found the walk singularly pleasant, the path being good, and the air deliciously fresh after the rain.

As we went along, we discussed the probabilities of success on our proposed attempt to effect the ascent of Mont Blanc in a single day from the Pavillon Bellevue, above the Col de Voza, thus avoiding the necessity of passing a night, either at the Grands Mulets, or, worse still, on the Aiguille du Goûté. Although it would undoubtedly be a long and hard day's work, we both agreed that the thing could be done, but I was sorely troubled by the absence of Whymper and Croz, as we might find a difficulty in getting a reliable man to accompany us without going down to Chamouni for one. At last, I said to Almer, "What shall we do if Herr Whymper and Croz do not arrive in time?" "Do!" said he, in reply, "wir mussen es versuchen allein" (we must try it alone). I was perfectly astounded at the idea, which would never have entered my head, especially as Almer had never traversed any part of the Aiguille du Goûté route to the summit, and must confess that, on first hearing it, I doubted the prudence of two individuals alone undertaking such an expedition, but I said nothing, and the matter dropped for the time.

The weather steadily improved until the sky was almost clear, the few clouds visible being fine weather clouds, such as caused us no anxiety. At 8.40 we reached the wretched little hamlet of Chapieu, situated at the junction of the routes from the Col du Bonhomme and the Col de la Seigne, and went into the larger of the two little inns to get some food. The place has a bad reputation, and, according to our experience, deservedly so. I ordered an omelette and a bottle of red wine, and, in lieu of the latter, was furnished with a "chopine" of what was perfect vinegar, of the sourest and most undrinkable character, which not even a copious mixture of water could make palatable, much less wholesome. The charge for the whole was extortionate, and at 9.15 we departed, congratulating ourselves that we were not compelled to make a long halt in such a den of thieves, the situation of which is most dreary and devoid of interest. Our route lay up the western arm of the valley, and immediately began to mount by a rough and steep track over luxuriant pastures on which an immense number of cows were grazing, and which presented a marked contrast to the scene of desolation a little higher up. In front, for a long distance, stretched dreary slopes of barren land and shale, on which large patches of snow were still lying, over which the path meandered in a most promiscuous way, occasionally vanishing altogether. Considering that this is one of the most frequented mule-routes in the Alps, being an unavoidable section of the ordinary "Tour of Mont Blanc," it is astonishing that more trouble has not been used to construct a permanent way. It is true, the direction to be followed is indicated by a series of poles, and a cross on the ridge is conspicuous some way off, so that in clear weather there is no difficulty, but, in a fog or bad weather, any one unacquainted with the ground might very easily go astray, and wander for hours over the monotonous and dreary waste without hitting off the Col. We, however, were fortunate in a fine day, and, following the poles, leaving the route of the Col des Fours to Mottet on our right, reached the Col du Bonhomme, 8195 feet in height, at 10.55 a.m. We had hoped to get from here a good view of the Mont Pourri, which rises behind Bourg St. Maurice, but were disappointed, as in that quarter the clouds still remained heavy.

The natural line of descent from the Col is into the Val de Beaufort, which leads down to Albertville, the opening into the Val Montjoie not being visible, until several ridges have been turned. The descent was at first gradual, over deep snow, but became more rapid after we had left the Col well behind, until we were fairly in the Val Montjoie, when a decent path led us through most dreary scenery, past a huge mound of stones, said to have been raised by successive travellers to mark the spot where, years ago, a party of ladies perished in a snow-storm, whence the spot is called the "Plan des Dames." At 12.10 we came to the first signs of civilization in the shape of the châlets of Montjoie. Here we halted for five minutes to get some "niedl," which was most delicious, but the quantity brought was limited, and the price charged very high, two little facts which showed but too clearly that we were once again on the beaten track of tourists. The view looking down the valley from the châlets is most charming. The valley is carpeted with the greenest and most beautiful turf, worthy, of an English Park, while the lower slopes of the mountains, right and left, are clothed with pine woods, which, perhaps, struck us the more from our having hitherto this year been strangers to anything of the sort. Above the trees, on the right, appeared, resting on precipitous cliffs the extremity of the lower ice-fall of the great Glacier de Trélatête, over which lies a pass to the Col de la Seigne, by which the Col du Bonhomme may be entirely avoided. Below the châlets the pastures were dotted with cows, which were worthy of the scenery amidst which they were placed, as, even for Alpine cows, they were singularly fine and clean looking,—their appearance fully accounting for the superior excellence of the "niedl." The walk onwards

was most enjoyable, and the sensation of once more treading a grassy Alp, after the mean apologies for that article
with which we had lately been obliged to be content, was
most luxurious. Below Nant Bourrant, which we passed
at 12.50, the beauty of the valley culminated, the path
leading through a superb gorge. On our left the woods
were denser and more luxuriant than before, while, in their
midst, the torrent rushed furiously over its uneven bed, at
the bottom of a deep ravine, forming numerous fine falls.
We quite agreed that this portion of the walk amply repaid us for the monotony and dreariness of the earlier
part of the route. On our right we passed the glen,
at the end of which once was the Glacier d'Armencette.
Its place is marked by a vast expanse of moraine and
débris, showing the former greatness of the glacier,
which is now represented by an insignificant patch of
snow. The path throughout is most villainous, but, bad
as it is, must have taken some trouble to make, as it is
for the most part hewed out of the solid rock in a series
of long smooth slabs, which must be rather trying for
mules.

At 1.55 p.m. we reached Contamines, a considerable
village, where we determined to dine; so we went to the
Hotel du Bonhomme, kept by Madame Mollard, the wife
of the well-known Chasseur, whose name figures so often
in the accounts of the early attempts to ascend Mont Blanc
from the side of St. Gervais. Madame Mollard intended
to be very civil, but her manner was peculiar. She walked
about the house like a person having a "silent sorrow,"
which she was doing her best to conceal, but which *would*
occasionally crop up; or, like an unappreciated genius,
struggling under the misconceptions and prejudices of an
unsympathising world. After some time, I was supplied
with a tolerably good dinner, of which she was apparently
cook and servitor. In the middle of it she suddenly inquired of what nation I was, and, on hearing that I was
English, abruptly threw down the dish she was carrying,
seized hold of the visitor's book, and, with an air of

triumph, thrust it down before me, pointing to an entry of the visit of the " eldest son of the Queen of England" under the title of Baron Renfrew.

Dinner over, we set off again at 3.40 down the road leading to Bionnay. Very shortly we met an English gentleman and his daughter, mounted on mules, attended by an exceedingly nice-looking Chamouni guide, who inquired whether I thought the Bonhomme was yet passable for mules, as his travellers proposed crossing. He informed me that there had been no ascents of Mont Blanc this year, but that some of the guides had been up to the Grands Mulets, to look after the hut, a rather disagreeable piece of news, as we had fully calculated on finding a track down from the summit to the Mulets. After passing the stream, which carries down the drainage from the Glacier de Miage, we left the road at 4.20, and struck up to the right through fields, towards the entrance of the valley, which is closed at its head by the Glacier de Bionnassay. The track was steep and shadeless, and the heat of the sun scorching, and, after a hearty dinner, I found the pull up rather punishing, but we gained the valley at last, at a point just opposite the village of Bionnassay. The Aiguille du Goûté was now straight in front of us, and a glance showed that there was an enormous and most unusual amount of snow on it; in fact, it was perfectly white. Almer looked at it, and then merely observed, " Etwas schnee!" (some snow), an oracular remark, to which I made no reply. The truth was, that neither of us liked to communicate to the other the unfavourable impression this state of things made on him, and there was always the chance that on nearer approach things might not turn out so bad as they looked from a distance. We kept on the left side of the valley, along the lower slopes of the ridge separating us from the basin of the Glacier de Miage, and having the Col de Voza and the Pavillon Bellevue clearly in view on the opposite side.

As we went along we had a final discussion about Mont Blanc. Almer was stronger than ever in his desire for us to try the thing alone, and nothing that I said shook his confidence. I pointed out that as regarded the ascent I had no fear, since, once at the base of the Aiguille, we had simply to exercise our climbing powers to reach the summit, but that the descent to Chamouni was a very different affair. On that side there was no actual difficulty, but a great number of concealed crevasses, and, although I was perfectly sure that, in the event of my slipping through into one, he would be able to stand the jerk and pull me out, yet I felt that, with every exertion and care on my part, I could not be confident of my ability to do the same by him should he meet with a similar misfortune, which, as leader, was of course extremely probable. "Oh," said he, "I do not fall very easily into a crevasse;" and wound up with, " es muss gehen!" After which nothing more was said, but it was understood that, weather permitting, we were to do our best.

At 5.35 we crossed to the other side of the valley by a bridge near its head, not far from the moraine-covered end of the Glacier de Bionnassay, and, striking up the steep grass slopes, soon entered the grateful shade of the dense woods which clothe the side of the hill. We took it easily through the wood, as the way was steep and the shade pleasant, but in due course emerged on to the open moor-land above, when a very few minutes brought us to the Pavillon Bellevue at 6.20 p.m., in ten hours and a half actual walking from Bourg St. Maurice.

Almer and I had agreed that in the dark we should be unable to hit off the narrow track along the Mont Lachat, by which alone it is possible to approach the base of the Aiguille, and that for that portion of the route we must hire a native acquainted with its intricacies. We accordingly told the good people of the Pavillon to find us such a man, and their exertions soon produced one François Battendier, who professed unlimited knowledge of the way, and whom we, therefore, engaged to go as far as the Tête Rouge, at the very foot of the Aiguille, beyond which he would probably be more of an encumbrance than an aid to

K

us. Having supped off the eternal omelette, I sat outside watching the sunset, which was tolerably favourable, and gave us cause to hope for a fine day on the morrow. We both agreed that it would not do to be caught in clouds on the summit, as Almer did not profess to be well enough acquainted with the Chamouni side of the mountain to be able to find his way down over those vast snow-fields in any weather. The people of the Pavillon were struck dumb with amazement when they first heard of our project, but entered into it most heartily, and expressed the greatest anxiety for its success, as they foresaw considerable advantage to themselves if others were persuaded thereby to follow our example. I soon found the air uncomfortably chilly, and retired in-doors, where there was nothing to detain me from bed, an early visit to which was the more advisable, as we were to start as soon after 1.0 a.m. as possible. Like the rest of the building, the tiny bed-rooms were models of cleanliness, and the beds, though coarse, were soft and comfortable, and furnished with a sufficiency of coverings, no slight consideration at such an elevation; altogether, I was well satisfied, as warm as a toast, and soon asleep.

Saturday, 2nd July.—At twenty minutes after midnight Almer came into my room, and, in reply to my anxious inquiry about the weather, stated that it was " Nicht ganz gut," being rather cloudy, but asked me to go outside and see what I thought about it myself. I, accordingly, tore myself from my warm bed, and, standing on the little wooden balcony that runs round the Pavillon, long and carefully scanned the heavens. Immediately over our heads the sky was clear and studded with stars, but towards St. Gervais it was overcast with threatening clouds. I did not know what to think. The natives were quite positive that the clouds meant no harm, and we should have a fine day; but, in their case, " the wish was father to the thought;" and Almer, when appealed to for his opinion, took refuge in the oracular—" Man kann nicht bestimmt sagen," " one cannot say for certain." The risk of being

MONT BLANC.

caught in the clouds when up above was not to be run
lightly, so I at last decided that we would at least wait for
half-an-hour, and see how matters looked then. The result
of this arrangement was, that I was able to give myself
another warming in bed. But the respite was not long, as,
at 12.55, Almer again appeared with the joyful news that
the weather was much better, and that we would certainly
start. It was quite true, the clouds were breaking up, and
everything presaged a glorious day. All our preparations
were rapidly made, breakfast consumed, and I wrote a
note to be taken down to the excellent manager of the
"Hotel Royal," along with my plaid and Almer's effects.
Our bill was most moderate, the provisions for the day,
including three bottles of wine, coming to only eight and a
half francs, about one-fourth of what we should have paid
at Chamouni, where the great object is, not to put up what
is strictly necessary, but what will run up a bill.

At length all was ready, and at 2.0 a.m. we started,
Battendier being armed with a lantern, as the night was very
black, and there was no moon. Making our way silently
over the open grass-land that stretches from the Bellevue
towards the Mont Lachat, we reached the point where the
ascent begins to get rapid, just as the first faint signs of
dawn were appearing in the eastern sky. The long valley
of Chamouni lay buried in darkness on our left, but over
the Col de Balme was an exquisite tinge of light which
presaged the coming day. On our right we could just
make out, in the gorge below us, the great moraine-covered
tongue of the Glacier de Bionnassay, whose right bank is
formed by the precipices of the Mont Lachat. The ascent
became very rough, and the track more and more vague,
and finally disappeared altogether, when Battendier's movements, which had been for some time those of a man
uncertain of his ground, became so very erratic that I at
last asked him whether he had not missed the way. Now,
my experience in 1863 had taught me that along the precipitous side of the Mont Lachat there was a path, very
narrow it is true, but well marked, and not difficult to

traverse; but the difficulty was, to hit off the exact point where this path begins, and it was on this account we had hired our native, being conscious of our own inability to find the way in the uncertain light. As it turned out, however, we should have got on better without him, as he was now in a glorious state of doubt as to the locality of the wished-for track. I felt certain that we were much too low down, but our friend thought differently, and led us a nice dance down·the steep and slippery hill-side, until I began to think we were going right down to the Bionnassay Glacier. Of course, no path was found, so up we toiled again, but not sufficiently high, and crept along the side of the hill for a short distance, as best we could. But the walking was too difficult to last; indeed, at every step we were getting more hopelessly involved; so, untaught by the former failure, Battendier again began to lead us down. But by this time my patience was exhausted, and I insisted that he should try a good deal higher up, which he, grumbling, did, with the expected result, as, after a stiff scramble, we found ourselves in the track, having lost nearly half-an-hour of precious time in the search. Once in the path, it is not easy to get out of it, except purposely, and with intent to break one's neck, as it is exceedingly narrow, while on the left the cliff rises in a wall, and on the right falls for a great depth in a similar manner. Of course, care is necessary, but there is not the slightest difficulty, and we made good progress, until by 4.0 we were at the edge of a vast expanse of stone-covered ground, which forms the upper part of the Mont Lachat, having left behind us the principal difficulty to be encountered before reaching the base of the Aiguille.

A few sheep generally pick up a wretched sustenance on this dreary spot, but had not yet been driven up, fortunately for them, as there was a great deal of snow still lying about. The walking here is ordinarily easy and pleasant enough, but we found an unexpected difficulty. In the heat of the day the melting snow around gives rise to numerous shallow streams, running over and amongst the rocks. As evening advances, these diminish in volume, but, of course, leave the rocks on each side damp with water. This had frozen in the night, and the result was a thin, and almost invisible, coating of clear, glassy ice, which rendered the greatest care necessary in placing the foot. My blind eyes did not allow me to see this at first, and, before I was warned, I got one severe fall, just on my hip-bone, of which I felt the effects for some days. All this time the Glacier de Bionnassay was an object of surpassing beauty on our right; its ice-pinnacles sparkling in the sun, and some of the more insecure ones occasionally toppling over with a crash. The lower ice-fall is hopelessly im-practicable, being very shattered and steep, but the central portion of the glacier above is comparatively level, and easily traversed. Our manœuvres had enabled us to cir-cumvent the ice-fall, and, after traversing the waste of stones before mentioned, we got on to the central plateau, just at the angle where it runs up in a sort of bay under the Aiguille du Goûté and the promontory of the Tête Rouge. The main branch of the glacier comes down in a superb cascade of séracs from between the Dôme du Goûté and the Aiguille de Bionnassay, and a highly exciting pass might (or might not) be made over it to the Southern Glacier de Miage, descending by an ice-fall of a similar but even more complicated character. The Dôme du Goûté, not-withstanding its height, is almost masked by the Aiguille in front of it, and a careless observer would suppose that the ridge at the head of the glacier started from the latter peak. The Aiguille de Bionnassay is a most superb but ungraceful object, and is seen to great advantage at the point where the glacier is entered, clothed from summit to base with steep hanging glaciers.* The ice, where we took to it, was completely covered with a spotless layer of snow, concealing every crevasse, (and to our no small satisfaction,

---

* The Aiguille de Bionnassay was ascended in 1865, by Messrs. Buxton, Grove, and Macdonald. They climbed the very steep glacier which covers the face of the mountain to its northern arête, and followed it to the summit, descending towards the Northern Glacier de Miage.

as it boded well for the state of things up above), perfectly hard and firm frozen, not yielding in the least under our feet. In less than a quarter of an hour we again took to the rocks on our left, and commenced a laborious climb up immense shattered masses, with patches of snow between them, where the axe occasionally came into use. The Tête Rouge is a promontory, jutting out from the Aiguille du Goûté, with a steep, rocky pinnacle at its northern extremity, round which we worked for some time, but at last struck straight up it, and, passing nearly over its summit, descended on the other side, and, at 5.45 a.m., were standing on the ridge at the base of the Aiguille, and halted on the spot, where, under ordinary circumstances, the ruined cabin, erected many years ago by Mons. Guichard for painting purposes, affords a rough shelter. I say under ordinary circumstances, for on the present occasion there was not a sign of the building in which last year I had taken refuge for an hour from the furious blast which then raged. In fact, it was completely covered with snow to such a depth that we might have been sitting above its walls for all we knew to the contrary, and, of course, the ridge, which is ordinarily bare of snow, was equally transformed in appearance.

As we sat on the hard snow, munching our bread and butter, we carefully scrutinized the Aiguille, which rose immediately above our heads to a height of about 2000 feet. It was completely covered with snow, so much so, that the long arêtes of rock, forming the divisions between the several couloirs that seam its face, were in many places scarcely distinguishable. Curiously enough, neither Almer nor myself at all realised the effect this state of affairs was likely to have on our rate of progress. Knowing that last year, with heavily laden porters and a large party, we had taken less than two hours and a quarter to reach the summit, I thought myself liberal for now allowing two hours and a half, while Almer exultingly exclaimed, "In two hours we shall be up there." Had we had the slightest idea of what lay before us, our expedition would have ended there and then, so that the ancient proverb about ignorance being bliss received a new illustration. Our native was very anxious to be taken on with us, but, not having acquired a high opinion of his powers, we were deaf to his hints, and, having paid and sent him on his way, carefully roped ourselves together, leaving an interval of about fifteen feet between us, and at 6.15 set off alone; the remainder of the rope (which was 100 feet long) being coiled round me, so as to leave Almer free for work.

A series of short zig-zags up a snow slope brought us to the edge of the great couloir, which runs from the top of the Aiguille to the crevassed Bionnassay glacier at its base. It is necessary to cross to the left side of this, as the rocks on its right side are impracticable, and the passage, under ordinary circumstances, is the only serious difficulty in the ascent of the Aiguille. The difficulty, or rather danger, arises from the fact of the couloir being the channel for falling stones, loosened from the upper part of the Aiguille, which sweep down its frozen surface with great velocity and such force that any one, struck by one of these missiles while crossing, would stand very little chance of escaping serious, if not fatal, injury. Fortunately, however, the width of the couloir is not very great, and, by biding their time, a party can get over, each man in succession, without much risk. Indeed, I believe there is no case on record of any one having been struck. At so early an hour of the morning we had not been apprehensive of danger from this source, but were certainly astonished to see on the hard snow which filled the couloir no signs of any stones having fallen this year at all, the surface of the snow being quite smooth and unfurrowed. We were still more surprised to find, instead of a well-defined channel of moderate width, an exceedingly broad curtain of snow, the rocks on each side, ordinarily bare, being completely covered so that it was hard to say where the couloir proper ended and the bounding rocks began. Almer set to work vigorously, and began cutting a way across, cautioning me to take heed to my steps. The sun had not yet reached this portion of the Aiguille, and the snow was, therefore, still very hard, but one good blow was sufficient to make a fairly secure step, so no time was lost in unnecessary polishing up. After *one hundred* steps had been made, or more than double the number usually necessary, we came to the conclusion that it was time to turn our steps upwards, and managed with some difficulty to obtain a lodgment on a patch of very slippery rocks.

In a very few minutes, we, for the first time, realised the precise nature of the piece of work we were committed to, as a glance upwards showed us the rocks above our heads glistening with ice. Instead of a steep but tolerably easy staircase of broken rock, where it is only necessary to be careful not to knock down the loose stones, which is the ordinary condition of the Aiguille, the whole mountain was so fast bound with snow and ice that, without making strenuous exertions, we could not have loosened a single stone. We could not advance a step without first knocking the ice off the rocks with the axe, so as to make some sort of foothold, and it was scarcely ever possible to find a dry piece of rock on which we could get a secure grip with the hands, and so compensate, to a certain extent, for the insecure position of our feet. The work was extremely hard, but Almer hacked away with unflagging spirit, sparing no pains to make the way as easy for me as possible, and ever on the watch in the worst places to give me either a helping hand or a tug with the rope. We tried to keep straight up the arête, which we had first struck after crossing the great couloir, but found it so bad that Almer at last bore away to the right, and crossed a second but much smaller couloir, in hopes of finding the rocks beyond it easier. There was not, however, much difference, but we kept to them, knowing that all the ridges converge near the top of the Aiguille. We were completely in the shade, and suffered much from the cold; as a violent wind completely swept the face of the Aiguille, and almost froze the blood in our veins. I had only one glove, and as both hands had to be used for clinging on, the unprotected one became so numbed, that

I was seriously afraid of its being frost bitten. As if to mock us, we could see the sun playing brilliantly on the top of the Aiguille, and gradually creeping down towards us, loosening on its way the masses of ice with which the upper rocks were covered. The result was, that we were assailed by an intermittent, but annoying, fire of lumps of ice, some of which were sufficiently large to require dodging, while, occasionally, an entire icicle shot past us with a whiz. Two hours passed, and, looking back, we saw with dismay that, instead of being on the top of the Aiguille, as we had hoped, we were scarcely half-way up, while the state of affairs higher up was equally bad with that we had found below.

At this period of the day, I, certainly, and, I believe, Almer also, had almost given up all hope of reaching the summit of Mont Blanc. We both felt that, unless we wished to sleep at the Grands Mulets, for which we had made no preparations, we should have in all probability to abandon our expedition at the Dôme du Goûté, and strike down from there to the Grand Plateau, and so reach Chamouni by night-fall. But these gloomy anticipations by no means caused us to relax our exertions. On the contrary, we worked away steadily, only pausing now and then to take a suck at some of the beautifully clear icicles with which the rocks were fringed. Throughout there was not one single foot of easy climbing, but some places were so specially bad that we had the greatest difficulty in passing. Upon these occasions, Almer always went to the full length of his tether, while I fixed myself as I best could, and made ready to bear a jerk, if called upon, until he was firm, when I, in my turn, followed. Once or twice our rope was not sufficiently long to allow of this operation being satisfactorily performed, when, of course, something had to be risked, and we were both simultaneously in positions, where one slipping, could scarcely have failed to drag down the other. There was not much fear of Almer performing such a manœuvre, and I exerted myself to do my best. My Dauphiné experience stood me in good stead, and enabled me to grapple with the difficulties with more confidence than I had ever before experienced in such a position. The work was far too exciting to be tedious, and the hours slipped by almost unnoticed, as we clambered, crawled, and wriggled from one slippery ledge to another, looking out anxiously the whole time for the first glimpse of the little wooden cabin on the summit. We had been compelled by the necessities of the ground to bear away so much to the right that I was half afraid we might be beaten close to the top, and have to find a passage diagonally along the face of the Aiguille, in order to reach it. Our delight, therefore, was unbounded, when we suddenly caught sight of the little building, standing out in the brilliant sunshine, immediately over our heads. The sight animated us with fresh energy, and, with a yell of triumph, we attacked the last steep cliffs that lay between us and it. The struggle was severe but short, and at 10.10. a.m. we lifted ourselves with a final effort over the brow of the cliffs, and stood upon the summit of the Aiguille du Goûté, after four hours of most severe climbing. We turned to give a last look down the way we had come, and, as we did so, Almer said, "Not for a thousand francs, would I go down there myself alone, and nothing should induce me to take a Herr down." Of course, he meant in the then condition of things, which, I fancy, does not occur once in twenty years.

In spite of the brilliant sunshine, there was a bitterly cold but not very violent wind blowing, which made us very glad, so soon as we had looked round at the view, to take shelter behind the cabin, while we proceeded to recruit exhausted nature. The view which we rather summarily disposed of was most striking, and we could scarcely have seen it under more favourable atmospheric conditions; the sky was perfectly cloudless, and there was nothing to mar the distinctness of the panorama. The valley of Chamouni was at our feet, but the village is not visible from the cabin itself. To see it or be seen from it, it is necessary to climb a snow slope in front of the hut. But the most picturesque part of the view, is that towards the rich mountainous district that lies to the west of the Geneva road, in the direction of Annecy, where the scenery must be charming, although the mountains are comparatively insignificant. The condition of the cabin was such as to render the idea of sleeping, or rather passing a night in it, highly exhilarating. Outside it was surrounded by a framework of gigantic icicles, stretching from the eaves of the roof right down to the ground, many of them as big round as a man's arm and as clear as glass, so that the effect in the bright sunshine was most beautiful. Inside we could not see, as the door was closed, and blocked, in addition, by an immense pile of snow; but my last year's experience enabled me to form a doubtless pretty accurate idea of the state of things within.

As the bread and butter and red wine passed into our interiors, our spirits rose, and we agreed that, having come so far on our way, and overcome difficulties greater than any we were likely to encounter further on, it would never do to abandon our original intention of going on to the summit of Mont Blanc. It was true that we were two hours later than we had hoped to be, but we should undoubtedly have time to get down to the Grands Mulets, where we should be able to exist through the night, though not very comfortably. All Almer's pride was roused, and, as he said, had we known the condition of the Aiguille, we should not have started, but, having done so, " *wie mussen auf den Mont Blanc gehen.*" I was quite as eager as himself, feeling that I might never have another chance of attacking the mountain, and, also, not being at all desirous to enter Chamouni for a second time a beaten man, and have to listen to condolences, of which the burden would be the folly of attempting such an expedition without a Chamouni guide, so at 10.40 a.m. we started over the snow-fields in the direction of the Dôme du Goûté.

Looking up from Chamouni, there appears to be a considerable depression between the Aiguille and Dôme, but this is an optical delusion, caused by the way in which the ridge between those two points circles round, the real depression being very insignificant. At so late an hour, on so bright a day we had expected to find the snow thoroughly softened, and a great impediment to rapid progress, but we were agreeably disappointed. The névé was completely covered in a remarkable way with an upper coating of what had all the appearance of frozen rain. I should have thought rain never fell at such an elevation ; but, from whatever cause the effect may have arisen, this frozen surface bore our weight, and did not allow us to sink in at all. So far as the ground was tolerably level, this state of things was all very well, and helped us materially ; but, when the slope became steeper, we should have preferred it yielding rather more under the feet. It was not steep enough for us to cut steps, but too steep and hard for us to get on comfortably without doing so, and the ascent was, in consequence, very toilsome, so much so, that we found it necessary to halt for a few seconds, at intervals of about ten minutes, in order to take breath. These halts, be it understood, were not in any way caused by rarefaction of the air, or any peculiar condition of the atmosphere, but simply by ordinary fatigue, the natural result of our previous exertions and present labours. We were astonished to see how very soon we left the Aiguille de Bionnassay below us. I always imagined this to be the highest of all the Aiguilles, but it cannot be much over 13,000 feet, considerably lower than the Verte and Jorasses. Our route was intersected by a few crevasses, which were dodged without difficulty or incident, except that Almer went through into one that was completely concealed by snow ; but I had the rope taut, and he recovered himself instantly. Exactly at noon we reached the top of the Dôme du Goûté, the height of which, according to the new French survey, is 4331 metres, or 14,210 English feet, that is to say, 1680 feet higher than the Aiguille du Goûté, and 1574 feet lower than Mont Blanc itself.

From here we looked down upon, and completely along, the arête connecting the Dôme with the Aiguille de Bionnassay, which is a perfect knife-edge of snow, varied by occasional patches of rock, and altogether one of the most forbidding I ever saw. I asked Almer whether he thought it would be possible to pass along it to the summit of the Aiguille, and he at first replied unhesitatingly in the negative, but, after carefully scanning it again, said that he thought it might be possible to traverse it, but that the attempt would be a "dummheit," in which he would be very sorry to join. The summit is an exquisitely sharp snow-point, from this side one of the loveliest peaks in the Alps, and if it ever *is* reached, must be approached by the horrible arête above described. I saw the Col de Miage side last year, and from that direction the peak appears quite inaccessible.*

From the top of the Dôme, a few feet of positive descent, which was most grateful but too short, led us down into a hollow at the foot of a patch of steep rocks, which are well seen from Chamouni, and form the next step in the ascent. We reached their base and scrambled up them, finding a copious sprinkling of snow on them, but we kept rather too much to the left, and so found ourselves, on getting to the top, overlooking the plateau beyond, but cut off from it by a precipitous wall, some thirty or forty feet in height. The error was soon rectified by bearing a way to the right, until we found an easy descent down a gentle slope of snow on to the smooth plain below. It was at this point that last year, with Morshead and some other friends, I had been driven back by violent wind and general bad weather, and forced to "execute a strategic movement" down to the Grand Plateau, a mortifying failure which I had feared at the time never to have an opportunity of revenging. We were now at the foot of the steep slope of snow or ice which leads up to the curious projection on the ridge, to which the name of Bosse du Dromadaire properly

---

* See note, page 133. The ascent there mentioned was *not* effected by the arête here described, but by the one which runs northwards towards the Mont Tricot.

belongs, although the name is generally applied to any point on the arête, which extends from the hollow in which we were standing to the top of Mont Blanc. There was a little soft snow at the foot of the slope, which we hoped would continue all the way up, but as we advanced it became thinner, until in the end we had to deal with the same curious hard frozen crust we had had ever since leaving the Aiguille. Almer was compelled to cut or punch steps here, so that our progress was rather slow, but rapid by comparison with what it would have been had the slope been ice, as it sometimes is. Still the angle was considerable, and a good deal of care necessary in placing the feet, as a glissade would have been, to say the least, unpleasant. The slope was broad at the bottom, and gradually narrowed as we mounted, until on reaching the top we found ourselves on a true arête, along which we evidently had to keep, until we were on the summit of the mountain itself, which was seen in front, slightly to the left, in apparent but most deceptive proximity, and no very great height above us.

The arête is rather narrow, but its passage presents not the slightest difficulty to a person blessed with an ordinarily good head, though, of course, it is not a place to lark on. There was a rather violent and intensely cold wind blowing, to the full force of which we were exposed, and, to prevent my ungloved left hand being frost-bitten, I was compelled to keep it in my pocket, which I certainly could not have done if our route had not been so free from difficulty. The views all along were delicious. On our left we looked across the Grand Plateau and Corridor to the range of the Aiguille du Midi, Mont Blanc du Tacul, and the Monts Maudits, behind which the Aiguille Verte towered, certainly the most elegant summit in the district. We looked at it with especial interest, knowing that Reilly and Whymper were preparing a grand attack on its hitherto impregnable buttresses, but we did not think the appearance of the peak boded well for their success, as it was covered with so much snow, that we could not help suspecting that its rocks, reported very hard at the best of times, would be found so glazed with ice as to be altogether inaccessible.* Beyond the limits of what may be called the Mont Blanc district, our eyes were greeted by range upon range of the Bernese and Valaisan Alps, but most of them so dwarfed as not to be individually distinguishable. On our right, a very long and steep snow slope fell to a considerable field of névé, which, lower down, was split into several branches by ridges of rock, rising from the still lower level of the Southern Miage Glacier. Between the point where the névé curled abruptly over and the surface of the Glacier de Miage we could see nothing, but we knew that the intervening space was occupied by three extensive tributary glaciers, falling to the main stream below, very steep and broken, separated from each other by the aforesaid ridges of rock. We had carefully examined these glaciers last year while crossing the Col de Miage, and had then come to the conclusion that it would probably be not impossible to get up one at least of them, although the enterprise would be one of great difficulty, and no small danger from avalanches. But from below we had been unable to see what lay between their upper parts and the ridge of the Bosse, and had imagined that, even if we could ascend to the highest point visible, we should be then brought to a full stop. Almer agreed with me, however, that in a snowy year, and with the snow in good order, it might be possible to ascend the slope down which we now looked, if once a way were found to the field of névé at its base, and that it would be well worth while for some one, in a favourable season, to make a very early start from the châlets of Miage, and see what could be done in this direction. The great Glacier de Miage lay extended at full length below us, and we could trace the whole of our last year's route over the Col de Miage, the summit of which was now more than 4000 feet beneath us.

---

* No serious attack was made on the Aiguille Verte in 1864; but in the following year the peak was ascended, first by Mr. Whymper, and later by other parties, from the direction of the Jardin.

I was greatly surprised at the immense length of the arête of the Bosse. I had always imagined that, so soon as the first hump was passed, the summit was quickly won, but never was there a greater mistake. Point after point was scaled, each of which in succession we imagined to be the highest, but the result in every instance was a sore disappointment and trial of our patience. The general angle was very trifling after the first steep slope was surmounted, but there came an occasional steep bit where the axe was required. The whole route, however, is singularly little toilsome, and, but for the intense cold of the wind, we should have been in a contented frame of mind. Almer still led vigorously onwards, but I was lapsing into an apathetic state at the absence of any sign of an early result to our labours, when, after passing one of the deceptive snow eminences, he suddenly exclaimed, "Dort ist die Spitze." My torpor instantly vanished, as I looked along the level ridge and saw a slight protuberance at its further extremity. We hurriedly pressed along the small intervening distance, and, at 3.5 p.m., two proud and happy men grasped each other's hands on the summit of Mont Blanc.

We had been rather more than thirteen hours from the Bellevue, of which twelve hours had been actual walking, but, under ordinary circumstances, the distance might be accomplished in certainly two hours less time, as we were detained quite that on the Aiguille du Goûté. The sky was still cloudless, and the atmosphere retained the marvellous clearness by which it had been characterised all day. We, therefore, saw the view under such favourable circumstances as fall to the lot of few, yet I turned away convinced that the panorama is inferior in interest to almost all that I have seen in the Alps. Its vastness must always be impressive, but it is this very quality which robs it of charm. The Bernese, Pennine, Graian, and Dauphiné Alps were around us, yet, in all those mighty ranges, there was not one single group, except, perhaps, that of Monte Rosa, which arrested the eye in its search for something on which to fix itself. All are completely dwarfed and reduced to insignificance, even those in comparative proximity. The great peaks of the Grand Paradis and Grivola, amongst the Graians, were with difficulty picked out from the common throng, while the Aiguille de Trélatête and the Aiguille du Glacier, still nearer at hand, were absolutely undistinguishable. The summit of Mont Blanc is a long ridge, which drops on the south to a great plateau of névé, extending as far as the brow of the precipices impending over the Allée Blanche. At the further side of this rises the Mont Broglia, which, from it, is probably accessible without much difficulty, and would be worth the attention of any one starting in the morning from the cabin on the Aiguille du Goûté. Even if time had not pressed, the bitterly cold wind would have prevented a long halt. Accordingly, at 3.10 p.m. we left the summit, on which, since the first ascent of Jacques Balmat and Dr. Paccard, I believe so small a company had never stood, and commenced the descent towards Chamouni, the indefatigable Almer still leading with as much energy as if we had not already done a fairly hard day's work.

The final dome of the mountain, or " Calotte," as it is ordinarily termed, is both long and steep, and here we found the peculiar condition of the snow before alluded to a positive impediment to progress. It was almost impossible to preserve our footing without cutting steps, a most cruel expenditure of time, and, in spite of every precaution, I once fairly lost my legs, but was, of course, soon stopped in my glissade. At the base of the Calotte is a small plateau, and, crossing this, we bore rather to the right, and found ourselves looking down upon a broad snow-trough, on the other side of which rose the Monts Maudits. This snow-trough was the so-called Corridor, and we were looking down the famous Mur de la Côte, by which alone it could be reached. I had been prepared to find in this famous wall, the ancient bugbear of all who ascended Mont Blanc, an ordinary steep slope, but I was not prepared to find its descent so simple a piece of business as it proved to be. We descended right along the edge overhanging the Glacier de Brenva, and, although I had *not* expected a "fathomless abyss," I *had* expected in this direction a very considerable precipice, down which it would not be expedient to cast *too* admiring glances. But I was completely astounded to see the trifling depth at which the upper névé of the Brenva Glacier appeared to lie below the Mur, and was at once led firmly to believe what I had before doubted, viz., the accessibility of Mont Blanc from that side, if the head of the glacier can only be reached from Courmayeur.* I can understand the ascent or descent of the Mur being a rather long business when it is ice instead of hard snow, as we found it, but I cannot imagine that any one, at all accustomed to mountain work, could experience the slightest feeling of nervousness when engaged in either operation. But Almer is not the man to neglect a precaution, or allow his watchful care of his "Herrschaft" to sleep, even in straightforward places. Turning his face to the slope, he kicked the steps for himself, and then improved them with his axe for me, while I followed in the usual way, face in front, but keeping close up to him, so that as fast as each step was ready, I lowered myself into it. In this way we descended with great regularity and steadiness, though, of course, not very rapidly, until the foot of the Mur was gained. We dropped over a small bergschrund, and at 4.20 landed at the head of the Corridor, on the Col above the Glacier de Brenva, between the summit of Mont Blanc and the Monts Maudits.

We had hoped here to be in shelter, and able to take some much-needed food, but the wind pursued us in the most inveterate way, and, sweeping up the Corridor, annoyed us almost as much as it had done higher up, so that the cold was still too severe for us to be able to halt in comfort, and we, therefore, postponed our meal to a more propitious moment. Hurrying along the level surface of the Corridor, we soon reached the brow of the abrupt descent on to the

---

* In the following year, with Messrs. F. and H. Walker and G. S. Matthews, I had the pleasure of demonstrating the correctness of this opinion. *See* Appendix.

Grand Plateau, which lay extended at our feet, and here, for the first time during the day, we hesitated as to the correct line of route, Almer having, I believe, only once gone over the ground before. We first steered to the extreme left, and progressed a short way down the slope, until it curled over in front in an ominous way, betokening either ice-cliffs or rocks below. We went down as far as possible, and Almer craned over to try and make out what lay beneath, but he could see nothing, so we retreated, feeling tolerably sure that there at least was not the right way. We now worked to the right, and shortly turned down again, but, as before, were soon arrested by a precipice, and had to retrace our steps. Half measures were evidently of no avail, so we now bore well away to the right, until we were so close under the Monts Maudits that we could go no further, when we once again turned our steps downwards, and this time with a more favourable result. The snow-slope, down which we passed diagonally to the left, was certainly steeper than the Mur de la Côte, but equally free from difficulty, as the footing was very good, and there was not a sign of the great crevasse which is usually found near the bottom, and forms one of the recognised difficulties of the ascent from Chamouni. We were soon on the Grand Plateau, and at once saw that we had hit upon the proper line of descent, the Corridor being upheld on the left by a wall of rocks, and in the centre by ice-cliffs.

Advancing across the Plateau until we had passed some avalanche débris, the presence of which showed that the aforesaid ice-cliffs were not very firm in their position, we then halted, at 5.0 p.m., to take the first refreshment we had had since leaving the Aiguille du Goûté seven hours before. The scene from this point struck me as being the finest on the Chamouni side of the mountain, and the vast level field of spotless névé, surrounded on all sides save one (towards the Grands Mulets) by huge cliffs of ice and snow, seen under a cloudless sky on a glorious evening,

L 2

has remained impressed on my mind as one of the most sublime spectacles I have ever witnessed in the Alps. Indeed, in the European Alps I fancy there is no other site where the *ice* scenery is on so grand a scale; certainly there is nothing in the Zermatt district to compare with it, not even the great plateau at the head of the Monte Rosa Glacier. The wind had now fallen, and the temperature was agreeable, so that I could have sat, silently admiring the glories around me for a long time; but we were reminded that our work was not yet done, and of the elevation at which we still were, by seeing the top of the Aiguille du Midi, itself 12,822 feet in height, considerably below us.

Accordingly, at 5.25, after a moderate repast, we resumed our passage of the plateau, bearing towards the base of the Dôme du Goûté, but working gently downwards, so as not to lose ground unnecessarily. So soon as we were well across, we turned sharp to the right, and commenced the descent of the first great snow-steps between the Plateau and the Grands Mulets, which were just visible a long way below us. Last year I had been able to get over this portion of the route very rapidly in a series of glissades, and I had naturally been looking forward to a repetition of the operation; but, although at a much earlier period of the season, the glacier was now in a very different condition from what it had then been. The slopes were intersected by numerous huge chasms, which we had before found either altogether closed or securely covered with snow, and these necessitated such a constant winding about and dodging, that we had never a clear run for any considerable distance. Upon one occasion we were considerably bothered by a monstrous gulf running almost across the glacier, and we finally had to pass along its upper edge from one end to the other before we could find a way over. In addition, our progress was now materially impeded by an enemy who had been singularly complaisant to us during the day—soft snow; and I must say that what we now underwent from this source completely banished from our recollections our previous unexampled good fortune. At every step we went in almost up to our middles, and the fact of Almer going first saved me very little, as he simply made deep holes, into which I sunk still deeper, principally owing to the width of the steps apart, which was so great that a sort of spring was required to get from one to the other. But, even had they been made shorter, the result would, perhaps, not have been very different, and time was so precious that Almer naturally and properly did his best to cover as much ground as possible at every stride. In spite, however, of all difficulties, we progressed rapidly, and by 6.30 were abreast of the rocks of the Grands Mulets, the cabin on which did not look sufficiently tempting to invite a visit, so that we passed on without halting.

We looked anxiously out for the tracks of the party of guides who were reported to have been up to the Mulets, and soon hit upon them, but they had melted away in so many places, that, on the whole, they did not serve us much. Fortunately, the glacier was in such remarkably good order, that we had no difficulty in finding our way. The passage of the junction of the Glacier du Tacconay with that of Les Bossons, ordinarily so complicated, was perfectly easy and straightforward in consequence of the enormous quantity of snow. We had occasionally to retrace our steps, but never went far astray, and, as the snow was not so soft as it had been higher up, this part of the day's work was rapid and pleasant, and we were soon on the Glacier des Bossons proper, where we congratulated ourselves on having left behind us the last point where difficulty was to be apprehended. The ice scenery on the Bossons was as fine as usual, the glacier being split into towers and pinnacles of the most fantastic shapes, through which we wound without trouble, keeping a sharp look-out for a clear pool of water, with which, when found, we took our revenge for our enforced abstinence since leaving the Bellevue. Approaching the right bank of the glacier, just under a couloir of the Aiguille du Midi, which is in the habit of playfully sending down showers of stones, we were fairly puzzled how to get off the ice, an operation which could not possibly be performed at the point we had struck. We could not dawdle where we were, as, to judge from the state of the ice, which was thickly dotted with stones, the couloir appeared to have been in a particularly lively humour, so we diverged a little towards the centre of the glacier, and managed to stumble upon the missing track, which led us through the labyrinth, and landed us at 7.30 p.m. on terra firma.

The light was failing fast, and it was of such consequence for us to traverse the very rough ground over which the track passes until it reaches the châlet at the "Pierre Pointue," before it was quite dark, that we did not even halt to take off the rope, but hurried on, just as we were, as rapidly as possible. In broad daylight the track is not a pleasant one—passing along the side of a precipitous ravine—and in the dusk it was specially repulsive. Nevertheless, I managed to get along pretty well, with the exception of making the trifling mistake of jumping into, instead of over, a torrent, and we walked, slipped, and stumbled along, until, on rounding a sharp corner, we caught sight of the welcome châlet, and at 8.20 knocked at its closed door. Our summons was soon answered by a solitary young woman, who, seeing two strangers at such an hour, naturally enquired where we came from. Had we answered "from Heaven," or its antipodes, it would not have created more astonishment than did our simple reply of "from Mont Blanc." She was, at first, apparently stupified with amazement, and then broke out into a torrent of "Mon Dieu's," &c., which was only checked by our demand for wine, which we did not in the least want, and merely ordered for the good of the house. When we were ready to start again, the young woman very good-naturedly offered us a lantern, which we at first declined, but, seeing the darkness of the night, subsequently accepted. It was lit, we wished our friend good night, and at 8.30 set off in high spirits along the mule path, which was said to run uninterruptedly to Chamouni.

We soon entered the forest clothing the side of the mountain, through which the path descends by rapid zig-zags, and were immediately involved in the most inky blackness, which the lantern scarcely penetrated at all with its feeble rays. The path itself is not bad, but, as Almer facetiously observed, would have been better if it had not been three-fourths mud and the remaining fourth water, the result being that every now and then we went in with a squash almost up to our knees. In due course we reached a point where last year I had missed the path, and, in default, had taken a steep short cut down a grass slope, which had answered equally well. We now again lost the path, but, as the short cut was not available in the dark, were compelled to discover it again, which we did, after some trouble, and again progressed rapidly. By 9.30 we guessed that we were not far from the bottom of the forest, and were beginning to indulge in all sorts of delicious anticipations, of which champagne, a hot supper, and a comfortable bed formed the principal items, when the track which we had been following became very vague, and finally died away altogether, while, at the same time, our lantern, which had already shown signs of indisposition, threatened a total collapse, and became almost useless. We pushed on in our former direction, but, finding that it appeared to be leading us away from Chamouni, we halted, undecided what to do, and, after a few minutes' consideration, turned in hopes of finding the lost track,—a fatal error, to which I impute all our subsequent misfortunes, as, had we pushed steadily on, I believe we should have extricated ourself before we got confused. We never even got back into our original vague track, and the dismal fact gradually dawned upon us that we were completely lost, and that our comfortable beds were likely to be represented by the hard earth, and our hot supper by the scanty remains of our provisions. We did not, however, despair, but hunted about vigorously for some sort of a path, and were occasionally deluded into following what, by the flickering light of our lantern, looked like the tracks of human feet, which only led us deeper into the darkness of the wood, without bringing us nearer our goal. Once my hopes were raised by our coming to what I knew was the torrent from the Cascade du Dard, which had to be crossed somewhere. But it was impossible to do so at the point we had struck, and the bank was so steep and overgrown with brushwood that we could not force a passage along it in either direction, at least in such darkness as that by which we were encompassed. We endeavoured to keep as near the course of the stream as possible, but were driven further and further away from it by the nature of the ground, and never came upon it again. Every now and then we stood still and shouted at the tops of our voices, in the faint hope of being, without knowing it, in the vicinity of human beings or habitations; but our cries were unanswered, and my thoughts became more and more devoted to the finding a convenient spot for a bivouac, the necessity of which, however, Almer was still loth to admit. I was anxious for him to leave me in the wood, where I was in no fear of molestation from man or beast, and endeavour to force his way out alone; but he would not hear of such a thing, and it was at last settled that we should together make a final desperate effort to extricate ourselves, by keeping straight on in the direction where we supposed the valley to be, turning neither to the right nor left. But it was just this straight course that we were unable to preserve. We were perpetually compelled to abandon it until we found ourselves wandering, as I believed, in a circle as hopelessly as ever.

Looking at my watch, I found that it was 11.30 p.m., so I suggested that, having been on foot for $21\frac{1}{2}$ hours, we might as well pass the brief remainder of the night in a recumbent position, instead of continuing our manœuvres of the last two hours till daylight, with, probably, no better result than had attended them hitherto. Almer agreed, so we sat ourselves down under a clump of trees, where the ground was sufficiently open for us to lie at full length. Personally, the feeling of annoyance and irritation which had possessed me at the commencement of our wanderings had long since vanished, and my predominant feeling was now one of intense amusement at the idea of our being thus baffled, within a stone's throw, so to speak, of our destination; but poor Almer almost cried with vexation, and for a long time refused to be comforted. He insisted that our misfortune was all his fault, an absurd idea, of which I did my best to dispossess him; by emitting small jokes, digging him in the ribs, and otherwise assuming an air of excessive cheerfulness, which I was far from feeling, I succeeded in somewhat restoring his equanimity, and he at last appeared to appreciate the absurdity of the situation. We made a frugal supper off some very dry prunes, and then buttoned up our coats, tied our hats over our ears, and stretched ourselves side by side on the hard earth to " woo the drowsy god," who soon responded to Almer's appeals, but was for a long time not equally obliging to me. However, he relented at last, and I lapsed into a state of oblivion.

Sunday, 3rd July.—Although the night was fine and not really cold, yet the total absence of any covering after so much bodily exertion made me very chilly, and I woke several times with a shiver, and each time experienced a feeling of disappointment that there were yet no signs of day. At length, at 2.40 a.m. we woke for good, and, finding that there was sufficient light, shook ourselves preparatory to resuming our labours. Almer went a few paces forward to look about him, and suddenly emitted a howl, which made me jump and join him. He pointed with his finger, and there, not a hundred yards from the spot where we had thrown ourselves after two hours' fruitless search, was the broad path for which we had hunted, so that had we persevered for two minutes longer we could scarcely have failed to hit upon it. We scarcely knew whether to be most annoyed or amused at the discovery, but the latter feeling finally prevailed, and we laughed till the forest echoed with our mirth. There was no further delay, and at 2.50 we started along the perfectly level track, which brought us at 3.15 to the door of the Hotel Royal at Chamouni, where it seemed at first as if we should have to remain some time, as my vigorous pulls at the bell were unanswered. But I had no fancy for a second bivouac on the door-step, so made my way round to the side-door, leading into the garden, by clattering at which I at last succeeded in attracting the attention of the porter, who speedily admitted us within the hospitable walls. I immediately went off to bed, not seeing any particular fun in keeping watch until the other inmates were on the move, but Almer did nothing of the sort, considering that such a course would be an admission of fatigue, of which he was determined the natives should not have an excuse for accusing him.

My slumbers were none the less sound for the pre-liminary snooze I had had in the forest, and I slept more or less continuously till 10.15, when, knowing that every-body would be safe in church, I got up, dressed, and went downstairs, when I was immediately rushed at by my two old friends, the black-bearded manager of the Hotel and the head waiter. One caught hold of my right hand, and the other of my left, and, between them, they simultane-ously worked the pump-handle motion with such effect that I was at last obliged to cry for mercy. The first hearty greetings over, I heard with no small satisfaction that, my note having been received, a careful look-out had been kept all day, and we had been seen on the summit, so that there was no opportunity for cavillers to cast doubts upon our success. We had again been seen near the Grands Mulets, and a large party of the villagers had gone out as far as Les Pelerins to meet us, and had remained there till past eleven o'clock, unable to account for our non-arrival, as our lantern had been seen in the upper part of the forest. They were also said to have lit a large fire, and shouted to guide us, but we neither saw the one nor heard the sound of the other. After church Whymper came in, much to my satisfaction, as we were the only two persons with mountaineering proclivities in the house, the

other visitors being either very mild, enquiring whether
"I had not found the mountain very difficult, and been
very much afraid," or else highly offensive, evidently looking upon us as unclean beasts, with whom contact was to
be avoided, because our garments and general appearance
were not strictly "en rêgle." Almer was invisible all day,
but I was told that he had been seen in the morning surrounded by an admiring throng, with whom he was unable
to communicate, and who, therefore, had to be contented
with staring at him, as if he had been some extraordinary
animal. The ascent certainly created great excitement in
the place, partly on account of the unusual manner in
which it had been accomplished, and partly because it was
the first of the year. In their delight at the mountain
thus, as it were, being proclaimed open, the good people
forgot the severe blow which had been dealt at their
principal sources of profit, and even looked with friendly
eyes on Almer, who, under other circumstances, would
have been certainly scouted as an audacious and obnoxious
interloper. Personally, I never before appreciated the
exquisite misery of being a (temporarily) distinguished
character. It was bad enough to be stared and pointed at
whenever I chanced to set foot out of doors, but my horror
may be imagined when at the Table d'Hôte I was forced
to take the head of the table, to the exclusion of all the
"potent, grave, and reverend Signors" present, a bouquet
being placed in front of my plate, and my napkin arranged
in a wonderful way, that must have taken some hours to
manage. After dinner there was more firing of cannon in
honour of the event, and after that I was left in peace
for the remainder of the evening. All day the weather
had been rather unsettled, and in the evening a thunder-
cloud swept up the valley, and perched itself on the Brevent,
threatening to burst right over us, but, although there were
some claps of thunder and heavy rain-fall, the main body
of the storm passed on, working round towards the Col du
Géant, on the Italian side of which, as we afterwards
heard, it raged with great violence.

Monday, 4th July.—I got up at 8.0 this morning, and found a fine but rather blowy day after the rain, which, however, we both passed in a state of delicious idleness. I could not have done anything even had I been inclined, as my boots were hors de combat, and under repair; but, after a fortnight of incessant hard and rough work, a short interval of absolute repose was almost essential, and, at any rate, very welcome. As usual on a Monday, there was a general clear-out of all the people in the Hotel, and we were left pretty much to ourselves, but, what with reading, writing, and the consumption of strawberries and cream, did not find the time heavy on our hands. Early in the afternoon Reilly arrived from Courmayeur over the Col du Géant, the ice-fall of which he had found in a ludicrously easy condition. He was stopping at the "Londres," but came over to dine with us, and it was arranged that we should all three sleep to-morrow at the Châlets of Les Ognons, with a view of attacking the virgin Aiguille d'Argentière on the following day. The Aiguille was supposed to be accessible from the Col between it and the Chardonnet, leading down to Orsières, a very convenient thing for me, as I was bound to that place en route to Evolèna, where I hoped to meet Morshead on Saturday, the 9th instant.

Tuesday, 5th July.—Two parties started for Mont Blanc this morning under a cloudless sky, but there was a violent wind raging in the upper regions, which, I thought, might bother them unless it subsided before the morrow. I had enough to do arranging my baggage, all of which I sent off by post to Zermatt, where I calculated that it would arrive a day or so before I did myself. I kept next to nothing with me, experience having by this time taught me how little is really required when on the march. We dined early, with Reilly, at the "Londres," and then finished our preparations, which, with the packing and arranging the provisions, took so much time, that it was 2.55 p.m. before we bade farewell to Chamouni, and even then we left our three men, Croz, Couttet Baguette, whom Reilly had engaged, and Almer, to follow us.

As far as the little village of Les Tines, our route lay along the good but rather dusty Char road, but, on reaching that place at 3.45, we turned off to the right into the fields, in order to strike the path leading up to the Chapeau. But there were no signs of our men, so we threw ourselves down under a shady clump of trees to await their appearance. They were soon seen coming along the road, but turned into the little "auberge," and there remained. It was very hot, and our position was a pleasant one, so we sat still, and allowed ourselves to be cross-examined and inspected by a small female child, who was waylaying unlucky tourists from the Chapeau with the usual collection of crystals. She first expressed a desire to act as our guide up to the Chapeau, where we were not going, and then offered us each of her crystals separately, at a price ten times its value, but, finding us inexorable, proceeded to pass her observations on our personal appearance. She was specially enamoured of Reilly's legs, which, it must be confessed, in knickerbockers and most gorgeous stockings, presented a highly fascinating appearance, and then expressed her opinion that I was older than Whymper, an erroneous conclusion to which she came after a careful comparison of the relative amount of stubble—which she was pleased to dignify by the appellation of "barbe"—visible on our respective chins. In spite of the amusement thus afforded, our patience was at last exhausted, so, making use of our small friend to carry a message to the guides to the effect that we were going, we resumed our way at 4.15.

This move had the desired effect, as they quickly followed us, and the united party was soon busy, laboriously toiling up the steep but excellent mule path, carried in zig-zags along the hill side. The exertion on a broiling afternoon so soon after dinner was rather severe, so our progress was not very rapid, and our momentary halts "to admire the scenery" were numerous. It would, indeed, have been a pity to hurry over such a charming path. It wound through a luxuriant pine-wood, gaps in which here and there disclosed lovely peeps of the great sea of séracs of the Glacier des Bois, backed in the far distance by a portion of the grand wall of the Jorasses, and nearer at hand by the wonderful-pointed crags of the Charmoz, and Aiguille de Blaitière. Slightly above the first steep ascent, we diverged from the Chapeau route, leaving it on our right, and bore well away to the left, along a track the comparative roughness of which showed that we had again left the ordinary routes of tourists. Nothing could have been more agreeable than our onward walk through the forest. The way had ceased to be steep, and we had perspired away the effect of our dinners, so we wandered along, getting good views of the long valley below, until we finally emerged at 5.35 on to an open expanse of pastures, in the centre of which appeared the exceedingly-dirty châlets of La Pendant. We should get no milk higher up, so determined to have a good draught while we could, and gave the necessary directions to the herdsmen, who were as filthy-looking specimens of their class as I ever saw. Bowls of cream soon made their appearance, and the contents disappeared with a rapidity that to the uninitiated would have been alarming, the guides appearing to have quite as keen a perception of the merits of the liquid as ourselves. The situation of the châlets is charming, commanding a fine view of the valley below, and the bold craggy range of the Aiguilles Rouges on the opposite side, but the accommodation appeared to be most wretched, and we congratulated ourselves that our quarters lay higher up. At 5.45 we started off again, and, although we did not appear to be rising much, the increasing scantiness of the woods and roughness of the ground showed that our elevation was increasing. We still followed the same direction along the side of the hill, gradually working round the base of the Aiguille Verte, and passing under the end of two small glaciers, those of La Pendant and Les Ognons, which come down from one of the buttresses of that peak. They both appeared to have diminished much of late years, scarcely

anything being visible but a narrow tongue of ice, surrounded by vast tracks of moraine and débris. After crossing the remarkably-dirty torrent from the Glacier des
Ognons, we came at 6.40 p.m. upon our destined night-
quarters, the lower châlets of Les Ognons, situated on
rising ground a short distance from the left bank of the
Glacier d'Argentière.

There was some talk about going on to the higher châlet
further on, but, as the place was understood to be an awful
den, it was considered that the saving of half-an-hour's time
in the morning would be dearly bought at the cost of a
probably sleepless night, so we very wisely resolved to
remain where we were. The view of the valley is, of course.
not materially different from that from La Pendant, but in
other directions there are several important objects visible,
which are not seen from the lower station. First and foremost, immediately over our heads, towered the Aiguille
Verte, looking accessible with the greatest ease from our
position. But this apparent accessibility is a delusion and
a snare, the châlets being so directly under the mountain
that it is impossible from them to grasp its real form and
height, and, in fact, there is not the slightest chance of
attacking the peak with success from this direction. Looking across the Glacier d'Argentière, the steep and rugged
range that forms its right bank was visible from above the
village of Argentière to the Aiguille of the same name. The
appearance of the Aiguille d'Argentière is from hence most
disappointing; indeed, any one not specially on the look-out
for it, would certainly pass unnoticed the ungraceful tooth
projecting from the ridge, which is all that apparently
represents one of the most considerable of the famous
Chamouni Aiguilles. The nearer peak of the Chardonnet,
on the other hand, though lower than its neighbour, is a
superb object, a grand, towering mass of cliff, which, on this
side at least, offers little encouragement to a climber.

There were two châlets, the smaller one apparently
being the dwelling-house, and the larger building opposite,
the stable for the cows; but both were as yet unoccupied,

and in the cow-house, on an upper shelf, we found a quantity of good straw, which was at once thrown down on to the floor, and joyfully hailed as a luxurious couch by Reilly and myself, Whymper and the guides expressing their preference for the other châlet, where they could make themselves comfortable round the fire. It was a most glorious evening, and the sunset one of the finest I ever saw; the rocks of the Chardonnet absolutely glowed, as though they had been red hot, and the snowy summit of the Verte was illumined with the most exquisite crimson tinge, but, so soon as the sun was gone, the air became cold, and we were glad to retreat under cover, and get round the blazing fire that the guides had lit. A certain amount of caution was necessary in moving about the châlet, as close to the door was a large hole, full of water, into which, I believe, each one of the party in succession, unwarned by the example of his predecessor, managed to plunge his foot, of course, much to the satisfaction of the previous, equally with the future, victims. After supper and a brew of hot wine and water, Reilly and I retired to our straw, attended by Almer, who, having packed us up all right, left us to our meditations, which, in my case, were not long.

Wednesday, 6th July.—We were so exceedingly warm and comfortable that, when at 1.20 a.m. some one put his objectionable head into our den, and insinuated that it was time to get up, we scouted the notion, and insisted that it was a good deal too early. However, when 2.0 o'clock came, the fatal moment could be no longer postponed, so we roused up, shook ourselves, and went into the adjoining châlet, whose occupants had not, I think, fared quite so luxuriously as we had, and were, therefore, less loth to move. There was a good fire, but, as usual, breakfast was a far colder and less cheerful meal than supper had been. Few men can be jolly when their slumbers have been cut short at such an hour of the morning, besides which, tea without milk, with the tea leaves floating about in it, is at the best of times not an exhilarating beverage. Then no butter had been brought, and the bread was not

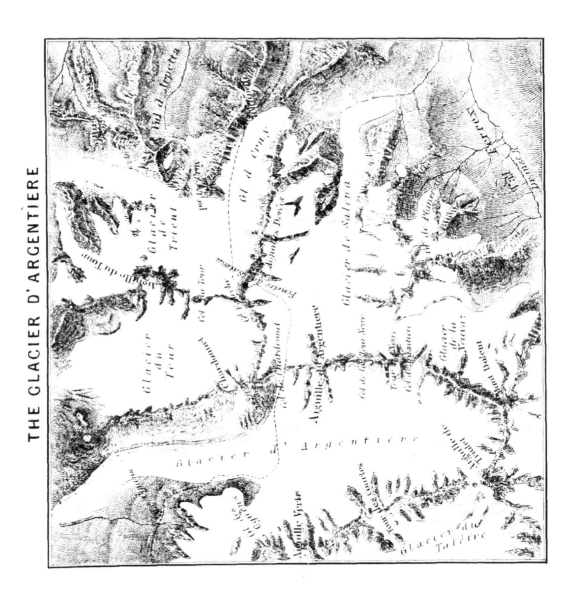

THE GLACIER D'ARGENTIÈRE

particularly fresh, so that on the whole I was rather glad when the apology for breakfast was over, the baggage arranged, and all ready for a start, which we managed to effect with unusual rapidity at 2.50 a.m.

Picking our way over steepish slopes of grass and stones, the latter predominating unpleasantly, we passed the upper châlet of Les Ognons, a miserable den, skirted some slopes of débris mingled with snow, the passage of which, disagreeable enough as it was, would have been worse in the dark, and at 3.55 found ourselves at the side of the Glacier d'Argentière. Although we were at a point above the final ice-fall, which is so well seen from the village of Argentière, yet the glacier was still too steep and broken for us to take to it with advantage, and our route, therefore, still lay for some distance along the moraine at the side. The piece of walking which now ensued was essentially unpleasant. Sometimes we were on the moraine, scrambling over huge blocks whose equilibrium was in a most uncertain state, while at others we were able to keep in the hollow between the moraine and mountain side, along the still unmelted remains of the winter avalanches from the precipices of the Aiguille Verte. But by 4.25 we had risen above what I suppose must be called the central ice-fall, though it is scarcely worthy of the name, and were standing at the entrance of the great upper basin of the glacier. The scene from this point was extraordinarily fine, and would alone render the passage of the Col du Chardonnet a far more interesting route to Orsières than that of the Col du Tour.

Looking south, we saw straight up the whole length of the glacier, which is remarkable, first for the unusual directness of its course, and secondly, for the singularly slight inclination of its bed. It is, indeed, an almost level field of névé, nearly free from crevasses, and hemmed in on three sides by precipitous walls of cliff, that on the east being broken by several considerable bays, filled by steep lateral glaciers. The very head of the glacier is closed by a tremendous wall, extending from the Mont Dolent on the east to the Aiguille de Triolet on the west. The

M

Mont Dolent is one of the most beautiful snow-peaks I ever saw, and rises steeply from the general level of the ridge to a perfect point. From this side it is quite inaccessible, but it was subsequently ascended by Whymper and Reilly from the Col Ferrex, without very serious difficulty, and they report the view from it to be even superior to what might be expected from its height of 12,566 feet. The great wall connecting it with the Aiguille de Triolet is seamed with snow couloirs, of great length and steepness, all hopelessly inaccessible in appearance,* which may also be said of the Aiguille de Triolet, a superb tower of rock, rising to a height of 12,727 feet, far more massive but less graceful in form than the better-known Aiguille du Dru. The line of precipices extending northwards from the Aiguille de Triolet to the Aiguille Verte, which forms the left bank of the Argentière Glacier, and separates it from the basin of the Glacier de Talèfre, is of the same character as that above described, but loftier and even more forbidding in appearance. It rises about midway between the two Aiguilles into a very beautiful, sharp snow-peak, the highest point of the Tour des Courtes, but otherwise preserves along its whole course a tolerably uniform elevation. It has always been a dream of the Chamouni guides in general, and of old Auguste Simond in particular, to find a passage somewhere over this ridge from the Glacier de Talèfre to that of Argentière, but, although it is possible without much difficulty to scale the ridge from the former glacier, close under the Aiguille de Triolet, no one has yet been rash enough to attempt a descent of the crags on the east side, nor is any traveller likely to waste time in such a foolhardy expedition, as the pass, if effected, would be of no use for any practical purpose. North of the Verte the general level of the ridge is much lower, and a considerable lateral glacier comes down towards the main stream, over which and the Glacier des Grandes Montets on the other side lies an

---

* In 1865, Mr. Whymper made a pass over this tremendous wall, ascending from the Italian Val Ferrex by the Glacier du Mont Dolent. The descent of the couloir down to the Argentière Glacier took him seven hours.

easy pass to the Chapeau and Montanvert. The parallel range that extends from the Mont Dolent to and beyond the Chardonnet, and comprises the fine peaks of the Tour Noire and Aiguille d'Argentière, is broken by spurs, running down from those peaks, which enclose considerable lateral glaciers, all more or less steep and crevassed, but all practicable without much difficulty. The consequence is, that three passes have been made in this direction to the glaciers descending into the Swiss Val Ferrex,—the Col d'Argentière to the La Neuvaz Glacier, between the Mont Dolent and the Tour Noire,—the Col de la Tour Noire, between the Tour Noire and the Aiguille d'Argentière,—and the Col du Chardonnet, between the Aiguille d'Argentière and the Chardonnet,—both communicating with the head of the Glacier de Salèna, though the first-named pass of the two is never likely to be a frequented route. Immediately north of the Chardonnet, the ridge re-assumes its usually forbidding aspect, and there are no signs of the pass which Professor Forbes was informed many years ago existed in this quarter from the head of the Glacier du Tour.

We were now immediately opposite the foot of the lateral glacier, leading up to the depression between the Aiguille d'Argentière and the Chardonnet, from which we supposed the former peak to be accessible, and whither we were, therefore, bound. Our first step was to cross the glacier towards the Chardonnet, making for a point just to the south of the spur coming down from that peak, which forms the right bank of the lateral glacier, whose left bank is protected by a similar spur from the Argentière. This operation was quickly performed, and by 4.35 we were on the other side, and halted a few moments to contemplate the wonderful precipices of the Verte which towered up magnificently on the side of the glacier we had just quitted. The lateral glacier, in its final plunge towards the main stream of the Argentière, is considerably broken up into séracs which stretch pretty well from one side to the other, and, when Reilly first made the passage last year, were found rather troublesome. But they were now almost covered with snow, and would have presented no serious difficulty even had we been compelled to make an attack "en face." This, however, was rendered unnecessary by the presence, close under the moraine from the Chardonnet, of a long slope of snow, which offered a steep but easy way through the broken part of the glacier on to the smooth snow-fields above. The ascent was sufficiently rapid, and the snow rather hard, but by a series of short zig-zags we mounted without much trouble, and in an incredibly short space of time, had left the Glacier d'Argentière a considerable depth below us, the séracs behind us, and, striking into the centre of the glacier, had the pleasure of seeing nothing but straightforward snow-slopes between us and the Col. On our left were the splendid crags of the Chardonnet, which we carefully examined in hopes of discovering a practicable line of ascent to the summit; but the rocks are hopelessly steep and smooth, while the few couloirs by which they are marked, are most impracticable-looking, and not likely to be of much use in an attack. On our right rose the great mass of the Aiguille d'Argentière,—in spite of its superior height, not so striking an object as its neighbour, but far more accessible in appearance. A broad couloir, or rather slope of névé, ran from the glacier we were traversing, very far up into the recesses of the mountain, and, indeed, seemed to strike the arête at a point not far below the summit. Its appearance was so tempting that a question was raised as to the propriety of changing our line of march and seeing what could be made of it, but we were all so persuaded that an equally easy, and probably more interesting, route would be found from the Col, that we adhered to our original plan. The snow was very hard and in the best possible order, and we progressed rapidly, as far as the foot of the final slope, which was rather steeper than lower down, and could not, therefore, be carried at a run, but it did not delay us long, and at 6.5 a.m. we reached the Col.

We cast a hasty glance up at the arête leading towards the Aiguille, the aspect of which slightly startled us, but, before we could take a thorough good look at it, we were compelled to find some shelter from the violent and piercing cold north-west wind that was blowing. Scrambling up the rocks of the Chardonnet, we found a tolerably-sheltered position, and settled ourselves to study carefully the appearance of our enemy. A very short inspection revealed the painful fact that we were undeniably "sold," and that, in calculating so surely on the accessibility of the Aiguille from the Col, we had reckoned without our host. Instead of an ordinary arête, as we had expected, of good rock succeeded by snow, we found the lower and most considerable portion to consist of a steep ridge of splintered, rocky pinnacles, the interstices of which were filled with snow and ice, completely cutting us off from the evidently practicable part higher up. The guides, as usual, did not like to confess that the thing was from its very nature impracticable, so took refuge in the orthodox platitudes about the quantity of snow being the cause of the difficulty; but I am certain that the total absence of snow would make no material difference in the accessibility of this lower portion of the arête. Of course, our thoughts now reverted to the slope of névé which we had observed on our way up, and by which we had little doubt it would be possible to get on to the upper part of the arête, but the idea of toiling up it in such a bitterly cold wind as was raging was the reverse of agreeable. The height of the Aiguille d'Argentière is 12,836 feet, and the Col du Chardonnet cannot be more than 10,800, so that, allowing for the distance to be first descended, we should have some 2000 feet of almost continuous step-cutting, on a slope exposed from its position to the full force of the wind, before even reaching the arête. We were sitting in comparative shelter, but could form a tolerable judgment of the violence of the wind from its effect as it blew across the eastern face of the Aiguille. The snow was streaming away in clouds, while, occasionally, thin slabs of ice were forced away from the surface of the slopes, and whisked through the air. The guides looked blue (by anticipation) at the notion of what their sensations would be while cutting the steps, but, of course, would not express their candid opinion as to the propriety of the proceeding. However, at last Almer plucked up courage, and admitted that for his part he thought the attempt would be an unjustifiable piece of folly; the other men concurred, and it became tacitly understood that for to-day the Aiguille d'Argentière was to be let alone. I must confess to having been sorely disappointed, though I by no means regretted the decision, but our previous unlimited confidence only made the total collapse of our plan more aggravating.

As each party had plenty of time before it we were in no hurry to leave our refuge, and sat contemplating the spotless fields of névé at the head of the Salèna Glacier at our feet, the towering mass of the Grand Combin in the middle distance, and more remote, but not so much so as to be hazy, the grand forms of the Weisshorn and Dent Blanche. The sky was perfectly cloudless, a state of things which rendered us only more savage at the wind, which prevented our taking full advantage of so glorious a day. I was at last so thoroughly chilled, that a move was thought advisable; so a fair and equitable division was made of the provisions, Almer and I said good-bye to Reilly, Whymper, and Croz, and at 7.15 a.m., having roped ourselves together, we commenced the descent towards the Glacier de Salèna. (I may as well mention here that, after all, the other party did try the Aiguille, but were beaten by cold when near the top of the couloir below the arête; however, a second attempt, made a week later, was more fortunate, as, on that occasion, they succeeded in reaching the highest point without serious difficulty). A steep snow-slope fell away from our feet to the glacier below, but, keeping close under the rocks of the Chardonnet, we crept cautiously down the upper portion of the slope, until, finding the snow sufficiently soft to give good footing, we quickened our pace, and at 7.35 dropped over a small bergschrund on to the level field of névé beneath.

The head of the Glacier de Salèna is divided into two

bays by a buttress of the Aiguille d'Argentière, and at the lower extremity of this buttress, and for some distance beyond, the width of the main stream from bank to bank is very great. But, in its descending course towards the valley, the glacier is squeezed through a steep and remarkably narrow gorge, with the natural result of producing one of the longest and most dislocated ice-falls in the Alps. It is quite possible, as shown in 1863 by George and Macdonald, to force a passage straight down this, but it is most unprofitable, and the necessity can be avoided by a rough and tiresome scramble along the rocks on the right bank. But we had no desire to encounter either the difficulties of the one course or the unpleasantness of the other, so determined to make for the Fenêtre de Salèna, a narrow gap in the ridge, forming the left bank of the glacier, and descend to Orsières by the Glacier d'Orny. Our route was now both easy and pleasant. We had on our left the wall of cliffs extending from the Chardonnet to the Grand Fourche, which supports the head of the Glacier du Tour; this wall is of no great height, and is marked by several broadish snow couloirs, not very steep, down any of which a pass might be effected direct from the Tour to the Salèna Glacier, avoiding the détour usually made to the head of the Glacier de Trient. One of these couloirs, indeed, led up to such a well-marked gap, that we half thought it was the Fenêtre, but finally concluded that the latter must be lower down, so continued our march until at 8.0 we reached the mouth of a sort of bay, with a snow slope at its head rising to a gap just under the Grande Fourche, through which we knew our way must lie.

From this point the general view of the head of the Salèna Glacier is particularly good, and we were able to study the great wall of ice and rock at the head of the southern arm, between the Aiguille d'Argentière and the Tour Noire, the descent of which last year occupied George and Macdonald, with Almer and Melchior, six hours. The wall is very steep, and certainly not the

place one would choose in cold blood either to ascend
or descend, but its appearance was less formidable than
I had expected, as the bergschrund was almost invisible,
and the whole wall was well coated with snow. Indeed,
Almer, who from his previous experience was certainly
qualified to give an opinion, insisted that we could now
accomplish the ascent in two hours at the longest without
much trouble. The ridge, running east from the Tour
Noire, and forming the barriers between the Glaciers of
Salèna and La Neuvaz, appeared to me to be far more
impracticable than its neighbour, showing a line of tremendous ice-cliffs, lower but steeper than those at the
very head of the glacier. Were it possible to scale them
the traveller would find himself on the Col, at the north-
western angle of the La Neuvaz Glacier, which looks so
tempting from the Val Ferrex, and is mistaken by the
uninitiated for the Col d'Argentière. The Aiguille d'Argentière appeared in its true proportions for the first time,
and we were able to form some idea of the immense length
of the arête leading up to it from the Col du Chardonnet,
and also of the utterly impracticable character of its lower
portion. The Chardonnet itself on this side offers no
chance of a successful attack, and, unless it is more accessible from the head of the Glacier du Tour, its summit is
likely long to remain unscaled.* But the most singular
feature of the scene was the line of cliffs by which the
lateral glacier leading to the Fenêtre is encircled, and
which, running eastward from it, constitute the left bank
of the main glacier. The crags are wonderfully shattered
and broken into most fantastic pinnacles, but their great
peculiarity is their colour, the rocks being of a decided
yellow tinge, rendering the name of "Les Aiguilles Dorées,"
given them by Professor Forbes, very appropriate.

Turning sharp to the left, we left the great glacier behind us, and, advancing up gently rising slopes of snow,
soon reached the base of the final one leading to the Col.

---

* The Chardonnet was climbed in 1865 by Mr. Fowler from the side of the
Argentière Glacier.

This was steep but not long, and, climbing carefully over
a patch of bare rock near the top, we stood at 8.25 in
the narrow cleft of the ridge, well-called by Mr. Wills the
"Fenêtre" de Salèna, and found ourselves at the edge of
the great plateau of névé, forming the common source of
the Glaciers of Trient and Orny. We sat down on the
south side of the Col just below the ridge, out of the wind,
to take a last look at the grand basin of the Salèna. We
were much struck by the fine appearance presented by the
Tour Noire, which, from here, really shows something of its
actual height of 12,609 feet, or 43 feet more than its neighbour, the Mont Dolent. The ascent of the final peak would
be a tough piece of work, but, probably, not impracticable
by the ridge connecting it with the Aiguille d'Argentière.

At 8.40 we stepped once more over the ridge, and struck
across the snow-fields towards the head of the Glacier
d'Orny. Nothing can be conceived more beautiful than
this broad expanse of névé, as it lay glistening in the sun,
under a sky whose deep blue was undimmed by even a
solitary cloud, and even Almer was in ecstacies of delight.
Immediately on our left was the low snow ridge, extending
from the Grande Fourche to the Aiguille du Tour, over
which goes the ordinary route of the Col du Tour, while, in
front, we looked away to the Alps of the Oberland, the
sight of which, in such comparative proximity, reminded
us that for the last hour and a half we had been in our
beloved Switzerland, a thought which raised still higher
Almer's already, for him, boisterous spirits. The snow was
in the same perfect order as it had been throughout the
whole excursion, and we were, consequently, able to make
rapid progress, soon reaching the point on the other side
of the plateau where the Glacier d'Orny begins to fall
towards the valley. We here again opened out a superb
view of the Combin and the Weisshorn, while beyond
but slightly to the right of the latter appeared two very
lofty sharp peaks, soaring into the air, which a very short
inspection enabled us to identify as the Dom and Täschhorn.
We kept down the centre of the glacier, avoiding without

difficulty the few half-concealed crevasses that lay in our way, until the inclination became rather steeper, when we bore away to the left bank, and at 9.30 a.m. got off the ice on to the moraine at the side. Descending along the moraine and patches of snow on either side of it, we came at 9.40 to the little Chapelle d'Orny, a ruined and roofless hovel, adorned with a few crucifixes and a dilapidated doll to do duty as an image of the Virgin, and perched on an eminence above a tiny green lake, in whose waters islets of snow were still floating about. Once every year a grand pilgrimage is made by the population of the Val Ferrex to this desolate spot, to the great damage, I should think, of their shoes, and consequent benefit of the cobblers, by whom the arrangement is probably promoted.

As Orsières was still 6000 feet below us we did not stop, but hurried on over the faint track which here first showed itself. The descent is one of the most abrupt in the Alps, passing through a mere ravine which was once entirely filled by the glacier, whose traces, in the shape of enormous old grass-grown moraines, are evident to the most inexperienced eye. The track, though rough and wearisome enough, is far better defined than any one would expect in such a situation, where there is not the usual Alp to which it is required to give access, and the Chapelle must, I suppose, be thanked for this. Throughout the descent, Orsières is in sight, always apparently at the same depth below, a very tantalising spectacle to an impatient and foot-sore traveller. As we went along, I derived a fresh consolation for the failure of our attack on the Aiguille d'Argentière in the reflection that, had we carried out our original plan, we should probably have had to traverse this obnoxious path in the dark, a contingency not to be contemplated without a shudder. During the first portion of the way the Combin is in view, and serves to distract the attention from the objectionable character of the route, but, so soon as it sinks out of sight, there is nothing interesting in the walk. For the first time this year I was rather foot-sore, and succeeded in establishing a raw on one of my toes, which did not serve to increase my equanimity, and I was sincerely glad when we abandoned the path, and struck straight down the steep and stony bed of a dry torrent, which landed us in the Val Ferrex, close to the village of Som-la-Proz, whence a broad mule path brought us to the Hotel des Alpes at Orsières, exactly at noon, or in seven hours and three quarters' actual walking from Les Ognons.

I had not the slightest intention of passing the remainder of the day at Orsières, but made up my mind to catch the afternoon train from Martigny to Sion, and get on as far as Sierre by evening. Having ascertained from the landlord the time required to reach Martigny, I ordered some lunch, pending the preparation of the Char, and, in its consumption, effaced the recollection of the grind of the last two hours. At 12.55 we started in plenty of time, as I supposed, until the horrible recollection flashed across me that my watch was still regulated by French time, which is half an hour slower than the Swiss, by which, of course, the trains run. There was, however, the chance that the train might be late, and I urged the driver to push on as fast as possible, but he was deaf to my objurgations, seldom getting out of the conventional jog-trot pace, and the consequence was that, after a hot and sleepy drive through rather uninteresting scenery, we drove up to the station at Martigny at 3.0 p.m., just as the train was rolling out of it.

There was nothing for it but to wait for the night train, so I went to the Hotel Grandmaison and spent a rather dreary afternoon, there being very few people in the house, and those far from agreeable or sociable. I, therefore, passed the time in meditating on what should be my next move, having left Chamouni without any fixed idea as to how I would pass the time before Saturday. I was half inclined to run over the Gemmi to Kandersteg, and have a shy at the Balmhorn, the highest peak of the Altels group (since ascended by the Walkers); but I had also a strong desire to take a look at the great Glacier de Moiry, at the head of the western arm of the Val d'Anniviers, from which direction it seemed probable (on the map) that

the fine peak of the Grand Cornier, 13,021 feet in height,
might be scaled, and after much consideration I determined
on the latter plan, which was highly approved of by Almer.
Dinner, though on the whole not a lively meal, was productive of some amusement, as I sat between two snobs,
who with an authoritative air favoured me with a great deal
of good advice as to the precautions to be adopted if I contemplated crossing the difficult and dangerous pass of the
Tête Noire.   I took it all in silently, and was rewarded for
my forbearance by the expression of their countenances,
when it happened to leak out through a gentleman opposite who had seen me at Chamouni that I had been up
Mont Blanc last Saturday.   I never was more glad than
when it was time to go to the Station, which I found occupied by a large school, consisting principally of jolly
English boys, with whom I got into conversation.   Nice
fellows as they were, I wished them anywhere else on hearing that they were going to sleep at the Hotel de la Poste
at Sion, whither I also was bound.   The train left at 9.45,
and landed me at Sion at 10.45 p.m.   I immediately
rushed off to the hotel, and was so fortunate as to secure
the last remaining bed (the school having secured the
others by telegraph), an acquisition of which I very soon
took possession.

Thursday, 7th July.—I was called at 5.0, and at 6.0 a.m.
we started for Sierre in a one-horse Char, well satisfied
with our hostelry.   I believe that the "Lion d'Or" is the
crack inn at Sion, but I can answer for the excellence of
the accommodation and civility of the landlord of the
"Poste."   The valley of the Rhone, though rich and fertile,
is a part of Switzerland which a mountaineer always does
his best to avoid, or, if unable to circumvent altogether,
escapes from as rapidly and as soon as possible.   The heat
generally makes even driving unpleasant, but at this early
hour of the morning the air was fresh and our journey
agreeable, so that I carried away more pleasant impressions
of the valley than the ordinary ones of dust and weariness.
We rattled merrily along, and at 7.35 reached the Hotel

Baur, a fine new house, standing by itself just the other side of the town of Sierre. It is, I believe, largely frequented by Germans *en pension*, but, otherwise, I can't imagine so large a house in such a hot position being remunerative to its proprietor. While Almer was filling the wine flask, and making the other preparations necessary for a two days' flight from the haunts of tourists and civilization, I took a second breakfast, which I by no means wanted, for the good of the house, and listened to the ravings of the landlord on the beauties of the Val d'Anniviers, whither we were bound. At 8.15 all was ready, and we set off along the broad road of the Simplon which had to be followed for a short distance. As it was, we turned off too soon, and did not discover our mistake till we were brought up by the rapid stream of the Rhone, without a bridge across it. However, a short cut across the fields brought us back again into the road, which we finally quitted at 8.45, and, crossing the river, commenced a rapid ascent up the hillside on the opposite bank, in order to reach the entrance of the Val d'Anniviers. The gorge through which the Navisanche, which drains the valley, flows to join the Rhone, is of immense depth and very narrow, so that the path is carried by a long succession of zig-zags to a great height above the valley of the Rhone, of which it commands an admirable view, before it turns the corner and fairly enters the Val d'Anniviers. Thenceforward the rise is very gradual, and the path smooth, broad, and for the most part well constructed, far better, indeed, than that of the adjoining but, in my opinion, much less beautiful valley of St. Nicholas. Improvements, too, are still being carried out, as we passed gangs of men working away busily at the road. I had formed high expectations of the scenery of the Val d'Anniviers, and the reality far exceeded my ideal. Nothing is wanting to complete the effect, and rocks, wood, and water combine to form a perfect picture. The valley is far more picturesque than the valley of Zermatt, not being so narrow, so that all the lower slopes are dotted with fields and châlets, which form a charming foreground to the pine-clad hills behind. In the distance, at the extreme head of the valley, our eyes were regaled by a view of the broad expanse of the Moming Glacier, backed by the towering pinnacle of the Rothhorn, the dark obelisk of Lo Besso, and the sharp peak of the Gabelhorn. The Rothhorn we scrutinized with especial interest, as we hoped to meet Winkworth at Zinal on the 16th, to make an attack on its precipitous cliffs, and also try a pass to Zermatt between it and the Weisshorn. The path wound along at a great height above the stream, which was quite invisible, but was heard roaring in its course at the bottom of a deep and savage ravine, a mere cleft in the bed of the valley. It made long dips into lateral gorges, where the overhanging rocks were pierced by well-constructed galleries, and at the head of one of these, in a delightfully shady nook, was placed a seat and a trough with a beautiful clear spring flowing into it, presenting a combination which it was impossible to resist, so we sat down and refreshed ourselves for ten minutes. We were very loth to move again, but necessity compelled, and we sauntered leisurely along until at 11.30 we came to the village of Vissoie, the principal place of the valley, where, in order to economise our provisions, we determined to try and get something to eat.

We went first to the curé's house, but he was "not at home," so we were directed to the abode of one Mons. Georges Genoux, a peasant of the better class, who shewed us into a room, the windows of which, to judge from the musty odour by which our noses were saluted, must have been hermetically sealed for years. We soon effected an improvement in this particular, and our host set before us some excellent bread and butter, an omelette, and a bottle of genuine Vin du Glacier, as clear as crystal, and of no inconsiderable strength, far different from the nasty stuff sold at hotels under that name. All wines are to me more or less indifferent, but I really enjoyed this, and Almer smacked his lips over it with an expression of profound satisfaction quite pleasant to witness. While we were refreshing exhausted nature, a pleasant-looking, lively young

native, named Jean Martin, came in and entered into conversation with us. Hearing what our plan for the morrow was, he was most anxious to be taken with us, and showed a certificate from the Rev. Sedley Taylor to the effect that last year he had been on several expeditions with that gentleman. Almer was not at all anxious to have a second man, but suggested that if he would come for a moderate sum we might as well take him. There was not much difficulty on this score, as his demands were limited to the modest sum of five francs, so he was told to go and get himself ready with all speed. He made his appearance in due course, armed for the fray, and at 12.40 we left Vissoie, Mons. Genoux impressing upon me that his house was not an inn, but that he was always glad to furnish travellers passing up or down the valley with such rough accommodation as was in his power.

The path up the main arm of the valley to Zinal still keeps high up above the right bank of the stream, but we at once turned downwards, and made a rapid descent to a wooden bridge which carried us over to the left bank, along which lay our route. As we were descending, we met the curé coming up, and stopped to exchange greetings with him. The only thing remarkable about his reverence was his nose, the purple hue of which betokened that its owner's stores of Vin du Glacier were extensive, and his visits to such stores by no means unfrequent. After crossing the stream, the ascent was for some distance very steep, and the path by no means so good as it had been on the other side, but the view of the Moming Glacier, Weisshorn, and Rothhorn, which opened out as we advanced, was a more than sufficient recompense for the roughness of the way. The actual summit of the Weisshorn was in a cloud, but the great wall of rock which it presents on this side was well seen, while the final pinnacle of the Rothhorn was perfectly clear. We were rather too far off to see anything decisive, but what we could make out did not encourage us to hope for much success in an attack on that peak from that quarter, while the pass looked scarcely more promising.

We gradually worked round into the Val Moiry, as the western branch of the Val d'Anniviers is called, and at 1.55 p.m. passed through the first village, the dirty hamlet of Gremenz, situated just above the junction of the two branches. There did not appear to be a soul in the place, male or female, old or young, the whole population, I suppose, being engaged with cows on the mountains. The lower part of the valley is very fine, a narrowish gorge, densely wooded, through which the path mounts steadily, though never very rapidly. There appears to have been a landslip in days of yore, as the ground is strewn with various sized boulders, most of them grass-covered, and overgrown with trees. Higher up, the valley contracts still more, and the stream forces its way with difficulty through a narrow cleft, which the path avoids by a steep ascent, that brings it out into a long, rather desolate glen, where, for the first time, we came in sight of the end of the great Glacier de Moiry in front. We met several parties of peasants going down the valley, who gave us alarming reports of the illness of the cows at the Alp, which made us fear that our evening meal would be without the greatest of mountain luxuries, fresh milk and cream. The glen at last opened out into a rather extensive plain, in the middle of which were seen two groups of châlets, one on either side of the stream. At 3.50 p.m. we arrived at those on the left bank, near the foot of the Col du Torrent, where we found the herdsmen, who gave us the welcome news that, out of the 150 cows there assembled, not more than half were afflicted with the mouth disease, which appears so prevalent in all parts of the Alps this year.

The master of the châlets, a weather-beaten old fellow, received us most hospitably, and showed us a long shelf, running along the wall of one of the huts, covered with straw, where they all slept, and where, he said, there was plenty of room for us, if we could put up with such poor accommodation, an offer which we, not being fastidious, thankfully accepted. The Moiry Glacier, or rather its lower portion, was full in view, and above it considerable ice-fall, which I at first thought belonged to the main glacier, but, on adjusting the map and compass, it was evident that it merely belonged to an affluent of the main stream that comes down between the peaks called on the Federal map "Zatalana" and the Couronne de Bréonna. The three peaks of the Zatalana form a fine group, of which a snow-peak in the centre appears from the Alp to be the highest, but it is not really so, the most elevated point being a rocky peak, the most distant of the three. The old herdsman assured me that there was a pass up this lateral glacier to the Alp at the foot of the Ferpècle Glacier in the Val d'Erin, which he himself had crossed, and that it was difficult on this side, but easy on the other. He also said that "he had been on to the upper plateau of the Moiry Glacier; that he was uncertain about the accessibility of the Grand Cornier from that quarter, but that the head of the glacier was connected by undulating fields of névé with another considerable glacier running down towards Abricolla from the ridge between the Grand Cornier and Dent Blanche; that we should be able easily to get on to that ridge, and that from it he believed the peak to be practicable." This did not quite correspond with the map, which represented the Moiry Glacier to be cut off from its neighbour by a ridge of rocks; but the old man spoke as if he knew what he was talking about, and we thought that for once the map might be wrong.

The châlets are at a height of 7054 feet, and the air soon became chilly, so that we retired into the cheese-making apartment, and, sitting round the blazing fire, over which the huge cauldron, filled with milk, was simmering, made ourselves comfortable, watching the operations of the herdsmen. Our worthy hosts seemed determined that we should not starve, and plied us with milk, cream, séracs, curds and whey, and other châlet luxuries, to such an extent that our mouths were never empty, and I began to be somewhat alarmed at the possible effect upon our interiors of such unwonted indulgence. The old chief routed out a sheet of an "Illustrated London News" of

1862, containing some pictures of articles in the Exhibition, and wanted me to explain to him what they all were, a rather difficult task, as my German is not first-rate; but the old fellow was satisfied, and carefully folded up and put away his treasure. After sunset we retired to roost, and I flattered myself that I was going to be very comfortable in the straw, but, very soon after taking up my position, I became painfully conscious that, putting the other men out of the question, I was not alone. Now the bites of fleas at the time do not annoy me, but the sensation of being crawled over, or of an active steeple-chase being carried on about one's body, is unpleasant, and, what with this circumstance and the heat of the atmosphere, it was some time before I fell asleep.

Friday, 8th July.—My slumbers were very disturbed, and I was scarcely sorry when at 2.45 a.m. Almer announced that it was time to get up. The traces of my agile tormentors were very thick about my body, and, judging from the size of the bites, the breed must have been a particularly fine one. On going into the adjoining châlet, we found a blazing fire, which was very welcome, as the air was not too warm, and a quantity of boiled milk ready for our breakfast, of which, however, I could take but little, feeling rather bilious, and altogether out of sorts. On asking the old herdsman what we had to pay (for the three, be it understood), he replied, after a little hesitation, " half a franc," or about 4½d. English. I was so taken aback that for a few moments I could find no words to express my ideas on the subject; but, on being convinced that I had not misunderstood the reply, endeavoured to persuade him to name a higher price, but in vain, and I only succeeded in forcing two francs upon our excellent host by threatening to throw them down on the grass and leave them there, the amount being, after all, scarcely the actual value of what we had eaten and drunk, not to mention our night's lodging and the trouble we had given. Finally, at 3.55 a.m., we managed to make a start, under a parting shower of good wishes from all the men, on as glorious a

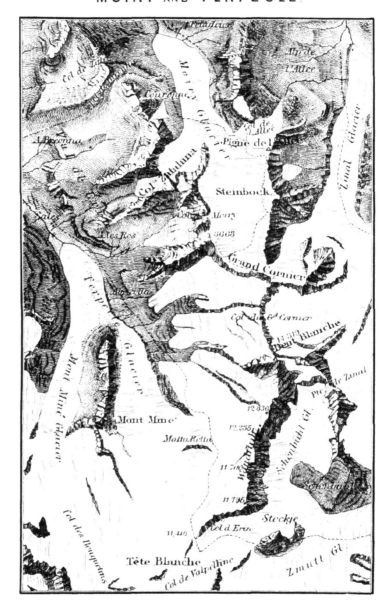

morning as could have been desired, the heavens being cloudless and the air calm.

Crossing to the right bank of the stream, immediately above the châlets, we followed a tolerable track over rough pastures, towards the foot of the glacier which was in full view in front. At 4.40 we were abreast of it, and were sorely tempted to take at once to it, as, above the final steep bank of ice, stretching completely across the valley from one side to the other like a great rampart, there was an uninterrupted stretch of smooth ice for a long distance. But as the "Gazon" along the right bank appeared to offer a way almost as easy, while the glacier might after all turn out less smooth and straightforward than we supposed, it was determined after consideration to exercise that discretion which is said to be the better part of valour, and stick to "terra firma" as long as possible. We were now able for the first time to get a view up the main Glacier de Moiry, which is a noble ice-stream, comparable to any other in the Alps, and bearing a strong resemblance in its physical features to the Glacier of the Rhone. Between the Pigne de l'Allée on the east, and a spur running down from the highest peak of the Zatalana on the west, is a tremendous ice-fall of great height and very steep. The lower part of this extends completely from one side of the glacier to the other, but higher up, under the Pigne de l'Allée, is a belt of smooth ice, which, we had no doubt, would give access to the field of névé above the fall. Below this great cascade of séracs, the ice is as compact and level as above it is steep and dislocated. Indeed, I never saw an ice-fall confined within such plainly defined limits, or terminate so abruptly. We bore away to the left, and, passing the wretched châlets of Fétadour, the highest buildings in the valley, where later on in the year the cows are driven up for a short period, I should imagine to the mutual dissatisfaction of themselves and their keepers, the pastures being poor and the accommodation limited, we had an agreeable walk over almost level ground. But at length the grass died away, the hill-side sloped more steeply towards the glacier, and we were reduced to a narrow tract between the two, covered with stones, varied by patches of fast-melting snow.

As we were picking our way over this wilderness, we suddenly came upon an uncommon scene which caused us to halt abruptly. Within fifty yards of us, by the side of a big rock lay a chamois—dead, and by its side stood a second, young but tolerably well-grown, so absorbed in contemplation of the body of its dam that our approach was unobserved. We held our breath, and cautiously crept towards the group. When the little creature at last perceived us it manifested no alarm, and still stuck close to the body of the other, but, as we approached, looked about, as though undecided what to do, appreciating its danger, but loth to abandon its useless watch. Almer and Martin were in an agony of excitement, and we all thought that the animal would allow us to surround and seize it, but, as we came closer, its natural antipathy to man prevailed, and, just as we were on the point of making a rush to secure the prize, it darted away up the rocks, and, although no great height up, was soon out of our reach. We examined the dam, which appeared to have died quite recently from natural causes, no sign of a wound or external injury being discoverable. It was a fine beast, and Martin gnashed his teeth with vexation at being unable to bring down its offspring. It seemed probable, however, that after the first alarm the little one might return to its post, so Almer and I hid ourselves, while Martin crouched underneath the rock, with the dead animal over his shoulders. But our stratagem was unsuccessful, as, although the beast came down a short distance, it sniffed mischief in the air, and remained out of reach, so that our patience was at length exhausted, and we went on our way. Personally, I was not sorry for the result, as, had we caught the creature, we must have killed it with our axes, an operation in which I should have been sorry to assist. Martin shouldered the body of the old one, but, finding it heavy, hid it away in a snow-filled cleft in the rocks, intending to recover it another day. Seeing this, Almer communicated to me his private impression that our friend was "a pig," and meant to sell the carcass to the inn people at Zinal for the use of unsuspecting travellers, an idea which made me resolve to be cautious what I ate on my eventual arrival at that place.

The ground rapidly steepened, and we soon found ourselves engaged in a rough scramble up and along rocks and shaly slopes, with an occasional patch of hard avalanche snow, where steps had to be cut. The way was by no means difficult, but our progress was very slow in consequence of numerous halts, caused by alarms of chamois, when Almer and Martin would persist in standing for five minutes at a time with their eyes immovably fixed on some patch of rocks, where they persuaded themselves that they saw those tantalising animals. For the sake of peace I always pretended to share the delusion, but on one occasion there was really no mistake about the matter, as there, perched on the very top of the rocks on our left, cut out against the sky line, were three magnificent beasts, posed in the conventional attitude always seen in wood carvings, but so rarely in actual life. Under ordinary circumstances these delays would have been very aggravating, but the various combinations of milk in which I had indulged last night had had their not altogether unexpected effect, and I was so very unwell that I was glad of any excuse for resting on our toilsome ascent. By 6.30 we had risen to a great height, and, finding a convenient nook in the rocks, halted for breakfast, in the hope that a meal would restore me to my usual state of salubrity. I did feel better for the time, but the good effect was only transient. At 7.0 we were off again, and, having climbed rather too high up the rocks, were obliged to make a considerable descent, in order to get round a projecting spur. This was accomplished without difficulty, but entailed another steep ascent, which brought us at 7.30 a.m. to a point above the worst part of the ice-fall, where we could take to the glacier. On our right we looked across the ice-fall to the group of the Zatalana, and the lateral glacier at their base, which is rather steep and much crevassed, and closed at its head by a lofty ice-wall, cut off from the névé below by a well-marked bergschrund. The pass in this direction to the foot of the Ferpècle Glacier would be undoubtedly difficult, but practicable. It has never, I believe, been crossed by a traveller, but is well worthy attention as a high level route from the Val Moiry to the Val d'Erin. On our left the glacier ran up in a bay, rising in a series of very gentle snow-slopes to the ridge, or rather broad " grat," north of the Pigne de l'Allèe, over which lies a pass, used occasionally by the natives, to the Alp de l'Allée, and so to Zinal, from which place the head of the Glacier de Moiry can, therefore, be gained, with the same facility as by the route I adopted. My object in following the course I did was to see the western arm of the Val d'Anniviers, and, principally, to examine the whole length of the Moiry Glacier from its very end.

By this time my malady had so increased, that I began to fear that for the first time in my life I should have to abandon an expedition from sheer physical inability to put one leg in front of the other. I felt as weak as a rat, and certainly should have succumbed then and there, had not Almer almost forced me, very much against my inclination, to swallow a cup of the thin red wine we had with us. I did not put much faith in the remedy, but it worked wonders, and completely quieted the raging demon within me, who thenceforward troubled me no more, but I had been taught a lesson which I did not soon forget, of the advisability of moderation at châlets.

The snow was perfectly hard, but it was thought prudent to put on the rope, which was quickly done, and we then, under Almer's lead, started across the bay before mentioned, steering to the right towards the main glacier, in order to pass round a long spur from the Pigne de l'Allée. The passage was easy enough, the snow scarcely yielding under our feet, but there were signs of crevasses, which showed that the rope was not a needless precaution. The

end of the spur round which we passed showed as bare
rock, crowned with ice-cliffs, which, judging from the débris
that lay scattered over our route, are not always so quiet
and innocuous as we found them. Once round the spur,
we struck straight up to the left, in order to get on to
the ridge above the Zinal Glacier, from which we rather
expected to get a view. This was not the most direct line of
march for the head of the glacier, but Almer thought that,
once on the ridge, we should find the walking easier than
if we made straight running for our goal. The slopes were
rather too steep for comfortable walking, but the ever
thoughtful Almer made gashes in the snow as he went
along, which, slight as they were, were sufficient to give
good footing and yet cost him very little labour, so that
we progressed rapidly, and at 8.15 got on to the ridge,
and looked down upon the lower part of the Zinal Glacier,
and across to the great wall of cliff extending from the
Weisshorn through the Schallhorn, Rothhorn, and Trifthorn, to the Gabelhorn.

Of the magnificence of this glorious array of peaks and
glaciers no words of mine can pretend to give an idea.
The Weisshorn, as it is the loftiest, is also the most massive
of the great peaks visible, but the Rothhorn is an even
more remarkable object, its final pinnacle towering defiantly into the air abruptly from its supporting ridges,
in a manner that I have rarely seen parallelled. At the
base of the ridge, connecting these two peaks, lay the
broad expanse of the Moming Glacier, terminating above
the Arpitetta Alp, in a great ice-fall. There were two well-
marked depressions in the wall above it, one between the
Weisshorn and Schallhorn, the other between the latter
peak and the Rothhorn, both the reverse of promising in
appearance, though we thought not impracticable. We
could not see so much as we had hoped of the ascent to
the second gap nearest to the Rothhorn, in consequence
of the glacier in that direction being to a great extent
masked by the remarkable peak of Lo Besso, and its
ramifications on the right bank of the Zinal Glacier. On

our left was the Pigne de l'Allée, rising but slightly from the ridge on which we were standing, while, on our right, the same ridge gradually rose to a snow point, which, though higher, was scarcely better marked. This was called by Martin the "Steinbock," and is, I believe, though I don't feel quite certain on the subject, the point marked on the Federal map 3484 mètres, or 11,432 feet.

For a short distance we kept right along the top of the ridge above the precipices overhanging the Zinal Glacier, but were at last obliged to bear down to the right, in order to get round the shoulder of the snow-peak aforementioned. The descent was not very considerable, and we were soon round the corner, when, for the first time, we came in sight of the immediate object of our ambition, the Grand Cornier itself, which rose in a steep cone from the head of the glacier to a height of about 1700 feet above us. Somehow or other we had never anticipated any very serious difficulty in reaching the summit, and the effect produced upon us, as we carefully studied the appearance of the peak, was, therefore, greater, the result being, that Almer and myself gradually and independently arrived at the painful conviction that from the head of the Moiry Glacier the summit was altogether inaccessible. Almer first expressed this in words; "Unless," said he, "we can find a way along the base of the actual peak to the other side, we shall not get to the top," a decisive opinion which carried more weight, as coming from one who, like all his class, shirks giving a candid opinion on such a subject, especially when that opinion must be unfavourable to the object in view. The nearer we approached, the less doubt was there about the matter, and, when at 9.10 a.m. we once more stood on the ridge above the Zinal Glacier, at the northern foot of the mountain, our first glance was downwards, to see what chance there was of our being able to get on to the arête which, running east from the summit, forms the right bank of a steep tributary of the Zinal Glacier. But the rocks at our feet fell sheer down towards the head of this tributary glacier, while the angle between the two arêtes of the Cornier was occupied by a slope, or rather wall of pure ice, of such steepness that, *even* if we could have got on to it, we could *not* have traversed it. We had imagined, from the Federal map, that the two ridges which form the southern and eastern boundaries of the Moiry Glacier, diverged from the very summit of the Cornier, and that, by one or other of them, or by the slope between the two, we should be able to get at the highest point. But, in this case, the map does not show its usual minute accuracy, for the two arêtes in question spring, not from the summit of the mountain, but from a point to the north of it, which is connected with the final peak by a jagged arête of rock, broken into teeth precisely like the blade of a saw. A steep ice-slope stretched from our feet to the top of this first point, and so far we could have probably got with some difficulty and much labour, but, the point attained, our progress would have been abruptly checked, as the arête was plainly quite impassable. I saw, therefore, no object in subjecting Almer to a useless fatigue, so, by way of doing something, we turned to the left along the ridge, and walked up to the top of the "Steinbock," which was close to, and very slightly higher than, our previous position. By 9.20 we were on its highest point, and our natural annoyance at missing the larger game was quickly forgotten in the contemplation of a view which for grandeur and interest is without a parallel in my Alpine experience. I have seen many more extensive prospects, but extent is but a single and by no means the most important feature of a panorama, and I cannot call to mind having been on any other point (the Gornergrat *not* excepted) from which I have had so perfect a view of so many elevated summits within a reasonable distance.

Looking across the Zinal Glacier, we saw two distinct lines of peaks. In front, the great chain which circles round from the Diablons to the Gabelhorn and Dent Blanche, seen to even more perfection than from below the Pigne de l'Allée, and behind, through gaps in the range of cliffs connecting those peaks, the towering forms of the Dom and Täschhorn, the Rimpfischhorn, (which stood out remarkably well exactly above the depression of the Triftjoch), the Strahlhorn, the Nord End and Höchste Spitze of Monte Rosa, and the Lyskamm. The Matterhorn and Dent d'Erin were completely hidden by the huge mass of the Dent Blanche, but, with those exceptions and the Zwillinge and Breithorn, every peak of consequence in the neighbourhood of Zermatt was seen to perfection. Looking south, to the right of the Dent Blanche, across the upper plateau of the Moiry Glacier, we saw straight up the whole length of the great glaciers of Ferpècle and Mont Miné, to a sea of unknown Italian peaks far beyond. Our attention was particularly drawn to the range of the Dents des Bertol on the left bank of the Mont Miné Glacier, which shows at least two very fine isolated peaks, well worthy the attention of mountaineers. But what principally struck us in this quarter was, that a very direct pass might be made from Zermatt to the foot of the Arolla Glacier by mounting to the Col d'Erin, and thence striking straight across the great field of névé that lies above the Mont Miné to a broad depression in the ridge, overlooking, I imagine, the Glacier de Bertol on the Arolla side, by which the descent could most probably be effected. On the Mont Miné side there would be no difficulty at all, indeed; I never saw so natural a pass, or one so well marked.* Beyond the crowd of considerable peaks that occupy the space between the Val d'Erin and the Val de Bagnes, the Grand Combin rose conspicuous, while, still more remote, Mont Blanc showed himself, pre-eminent over all the lesser summits. Towards the Oberland, the Bietschhorn was the only high peak visible, but the great level expanse of glacier that crowns the cliffs in the neighbourhood of the Wildstrubel was well seen.

---

* Mr. H. Walker and I succeeded in effecting this pass, from Zermatt, in 1865, in twelve hours' very slow walking.

We were in a most admirable position for studying the northern and southern arêtes of the Rothhorn which fall respectively towards the Schallhorn and Trifthorn. Both appeared to be exceedingly steep and serrated, offering not the slightest chance of a successful attack. Curiously enough the arête that runs up to the summit from Lo Besso, by which the ascent was subsequently effected by Messrs. Stephen and Grove, did not attract our attention at all, probably because it was so immediately in front of us that its lower portion was masked by the lofty peak of Lo Besso itself. Along the left bank of Moiry Glacier there was only one considerable summit, south of the highest point of the Zatalana, that marked on the Federal map 3663 mètres, or 12,018 feet. The connecting ridge showed no well-marked depression, though its general elevation above the glacier was trifling; but, later on in the year, Messrs. Hornby and Philpott made a pass over it from the Val d'Erin, ascending by a glacier above the Alp des Ros, below Abricola.

The sky was cloudless, the temperature agreeable, and we should have much liked to make a long halt, but we were anxious to descend to Abricolla and Evolèna by the glacier which is represented on the map as running down from the western face of the Cornier and the ridge at the head of the Moiry Glacier, so at 9.30 we quitted our perch. I may mention that my estimate of the merits of the view was fully endorsed by Almer, who ranked it as the finest that even he had ever seen. Nor was this a mere passing impression, for upon every subsequent occasion when we were favoured with a good view, he always brought forward that from the "Steinbock" as being superior. Running down the gentle slope on to the upper plateau of the glacier, we struck straight across for a point considerably to the south of the 3663 mètres peak. It was difficult to say when the highest part of the plateau was crossed, as at the head of the glacier there is no boundary ridge, but, as we were gradually descending, our progress was suddenly arrested by a series of enormous chasms right across our path.

We threaded a way carefully between them, Martin manifesting by his nervous clutch of the rope that he did not quite relish the position. But we were almost immediately brought to a full stop by the termination of the gentle slope we had been following, on the brink of a line of perpendicular ice-cliffs, which there was no possibility of descending. We were not much disconcerted by this check, as, on turning round and looking towards the Cornier, we saw that, to all appearance, under the face of that peak the Moiry Glacier was connected with that on to which we wished to descend by undulating fields of névé, exactly as described by the old herdsmen at the Alp. We, accordingly, turned to the left in that direction, and were trotting cheerfully along, unsuspicious of evil, when the névé we were traversing curled slightly over and came to an abrupt termination on the top of a wall of cliffs, at the base of which, a long way below, we had the pleasure of seeing the lower glacier, stretching in a succession of gentle but rather crevassed snow-slopes towards Abricolla. The apparent connection between the two glaciers is, therefore, an optical delusion of the grossest character, the line of crags being continuous from the Cornier along the whole length of the head of the Moiry glacier, which is, in fact, supported by them. The state of affairs required consideration, so at 10.5 we took up our position on the highest rocks, and, while refreshing the inward man, held a consultation as to what was best to be done.

We by no means despaired of finding a practicable descent down the rocks, so, after hunger was appeased, Almer and Martin started off to see what they could discover, leaving me comfortably settled to study the Dent Blanche, which was close at hand, and the Dent d'Erin, which was much more distant. The Dent Blanche from here shows as a perfectly symmetrical pyramid of rock, with scarcely any snow upon it. What principally struck me was its solidity and compactness. Unlike most mountains which are formed by a number of ridges, converging to a point, with extensive ravines between them, the faces of this glorious peak appeared perfectly smooth, with corners as sharp and well-defined as the corners of a house, and with none of the usual straggling arêtes. The Dent d'Erin, too, is a superb object, towering up a worthy rival to the Matterhorn, and, as I looked at its precipitous cliffs, I am afraid I felt horribly envious of Macdonald for his successful attack on the fortress last year. I satisfied myself that from the glacier at our feet the ridge connecting the Grand Cornier with the Dent Blanche might be gained without difficulty, and that from the ridge the former peak was probably accessible, so that Abricolla is apparently the proper basis for an attack.* At 11.0 the men returned and reported that, after descending a considerable distance, they had been compelled to abandon the attempt to force a passage, the rocks being perfectly smooth and absolutely overhanging the glacier at their base, so that a cat could not have found any footing. So far as they could see right and left, the character of the rocks was the same, but Almer suggested that another effort should be made in the same direction we had first tried unsuccessfully, but rather more to the right, as close as possible under peak 3663. We, accordingly, turned towards the desired point, and were again very soon checked by the threatening appearance of the ice. The rope was, therefore, unfastened, and the two men started off with it to see what could be done, while I took my ease on the slopes above. I was rather below the summit-level of the glacier and, consequently, quite sheltered from the wind, so that I had the full benefit of the sun's rays, which were shooting down with great power. The heat was intense, and, our change of position not having opened out any new object of interest in the panorama, the meditations in which I at first indulged were terminated by my falling asleep. I was awoke with a start by the arrival of the two explorers

---

* The Grand Cornier was ascended from Zinal in 1865 by Mr. Whymper. He mounted by the eastern arête, and did not think the summit accessible from any other direction.

exactly at noon, with the unwelcome, but scarcely unexpected, intelligence that it was not possible to descend. They had succeeded in getting on to the rocks, but found them of the same impracticable character as before. A person starting from Abricolla, and able to examine the cliffs which support the Moiry Glacier from below, might, perhaps, find a vulnerable point at which to effect the ascent, but all our attempts to find this vulnerable point from above signally failed ; nor is greater success likely to reward future comers, at least without a preliminary examination of the ground. I thought that Martin looked rather scared, and Almer afterwards communicated to me that he had chosen the favourable moment when they were standing in steps cut in an almost perpendicular wall of ice, to slip, and had only been held up by a prodigious effort of strength and skill on Almer's part.

Of course, the unexpected failure of our plans was annoying, but it was unavoidable, and the time spent could not be looked upon as thrown away, as, next to showing that there *is* a pass at a particular point, the establishment of the contrary truth is certainly most important. We had no choice but to execute a retreat down the glacier, and we, therefore, set off at 12.10 p.m., with the intention, however, of turning off towards the supposed pass between the peaks of the Zatalana, and so reaching Evolèna. Mounting again to the highest point of the glacier, we followed our morning's route, except that we kept away from the ridge above the Zinal Glacier, and preserved a tolerably direct course without difficulty or incident, until at 12.55 we were once more abreast of the spur running down from the Pigne de l'Allée. It now struck us that the shortest way to get at the lateral glacier up which our desired pass lay would be to cross to the left bank of the main glacier, whence a short descent would bring us down on to the tributary. The only obstacle to this course was the great ice-fall, across which a way would have to be found before the opposite side could be reached. Almer, however, thought that we were above the most dislocated part of the fall, and that we should be able to force a passage without much difficulty, so, turning sharp to the left, we agreed to make the attempt. For a short distance all went well, and we congratulated ourselves on the apparent success of our manœuvre; but, as we advanced the way became more and more intricate, and the difficulty of keeping the desired direction greater. I could scarcely refrain from roaring with laughter at the expression of intense misery on Martin's countenance when he realized the nature of the work we were undertaking. Nor was the state of his feelings betrayed by his visage only, for his legs actually trembled with nervousness, and, in case of accident, he would have been worse than useless. Still we persevered, creeping along slippery ridges of ice, and once descending right into the bowels of a huge chasm, until we found ourselves fairly brought to a stand-still at a point beyond which it seemed that we could not advance in any direction, neither up nor down nor straightforward. We were surrounded by enormous ice-cliffs and masses of toppling séracs, the passage of which, if possible at all, would have involved an expenditure of time that we could ill afford, and an amount of risk that we should have been scarcely justified in running. After a careful scrutiny, Almer positively refused, in terms more emphatic than I have often heard him use, to push the attempt any further, so we turned tail, and, carefully retracing our steps, were soon well out of the labyrinth. We struck across the bay leading to the Col de l'Allée, for the point at which we had first taken to the ice in the morning, but, on reaching it, instead of getting on to the rocks, we kept to the left, and descended in a few minutes to the level glacier below the ice-fall, in a succession of delightful glissades over snow slopes of just the proper steepness and consistency.

We were parched with thirst, and the heat was something fearful, so that, finding some large stones close by a pool of clear water, we sat ourselves down to rest and refresh. The ice-fall was, of course, seen to perfection, and we discovered what a fearful hash we should have made had we persevered in our attempt to cross it. We should never have reached the other side, or, if we could have done so, our last state would have been worse than the first, as we should have been just as far as ever from the lateral glacier leading to the Zatalana pass. Not that we were much better off, as it was, for we were now so far below the foot of the glacier that the idea of tramping up its whole length before even reaching the foot of the ice-wall, which might give trouble, was most distasteful to all of us, and we finally agreed to change our plans, and make for Evolèna by one of several gaps which were visible in the ridge, forming the left bank of the lower portion of the Moiry Glacier. A reference to the map showed that the Col de Zate, a little north of the Col de Breonna, offered the most direct route to Evolèna, and we, accordingly, resolved upon that line of march.

At 2.30 we resumed our way across the glacier which was perfectly level and uncrevassed, but of considerable width, and covered to a depth of about two feet with soft snow, into which we sank at every step. The walking was most laborious, and we were sincerely delighted when at 3.0 we got off the ice, and flattered ourselves that our labours for the day were practically over. But we were most miserably deceived, as the piece of work that ensued was without exception the most wearisome and difficult of its kind I ever had the misfortune to go through. Our route lay along the side of a steep slope, covered with débris, stones, and scattered masses of rock. Had the ground been clear, the walking would have been rough, and nothing more, but the whole slope was masked by a layer of deep snow, thoroughly softened by the sun, effectually concealing what lay beneath. The consequence was that we were in a state of blissful ignorance as to whether we were treading on an insecure rock, firm ground, or, as was more common, nothing at all, in which case we were immersed with a jerk, up to our middles, and sometimes almost up to our necks, in a cavity between two rocks, while, occasionally, to vary the amusement, the hole was, perhaps, only big enough to let one leg in, rubbing off a goodly portion of the skin in the operation.

Passing underneath a small glacier leading up to a gap in the ridge, 9886 feet in height, immediately south of the Couronne de Bréonna, we steered for a point high up on a projecting spur from that peak, and, having with infinite labour and trouble reached it, found ourselves near the head of a broad glen, giving access to two passes, one close at hand, under the Couronne—the Col de Bréonna, the other at the northern corner of the glen, separated from us by a considerable expanse of snow—the Col de Zate. We were so sick of the snow-wading that without hesitation we turned towards the nearest pass, and, after a short plod through the snow, stood at 4.15 in the gap of the Col de Bréonna, 9574 feet in height, considering its elevation, one of the least steep passes I ever crossed, the final ascent being very gentle.

The view was not very extensive, but comprised the ice-falls of the Ferpècle and Mont Miné Glaciers, and straight opposite, near the head of the Combe d'Arolla, or western arm of the Val d'Erin, an exceedingly lofty and bold rocky peak, which we supposed to be the Pigno d'Arolla, 12,473 feet. An easy descent over slopes of shale and stones, nearly bare of snow, led us down into a dreary glen, enclosed on the south and east by the bold precipices of the Couronne de Bréonna, but otherwise of the most uninteresting character. We soon hit upon a faint track, which brought us over almost level ground to the châlets on the Bréonna Alp at 5.15. The châlets are well situated on the brow of the steep descent into the Val d'Erin, and were occupied, but we were unable to get any milk in consequence of the afternoon supply not having yet been brought in. The herdsmen, however, gave us information as to the best line of route to reach Evolèna, furnished with which we hurried on, but contrived, when not far above the valley, to get out of the proper track, and take to one which kept much too high up along the hill-side. Moreover, it was exceedingly rough, being composed of mud, stones, and watercourses in about equal proportions. It tried our temper severely, and crowned its iniquities by suddenly coming to an untimely

o

end, leaving us to find our way down to the main road as best we could. A rough scramble, however, led us into a tolerable track at a lower level, which in due course formed a junction with the regular mule-path down the valley, and that once gained, our troubles were over. On our way we met a native, who informed us that four tourists had arrived during the day, and answered, in reply to my enquiry as to whether they were English, that he did not think so, as they had walked in, singing republican songs, a response which, I think said a good deal for his sagacity. We arrived at the Hotel de la Dent Blanche at Evolèna at 6.35 p.m., and the four tourists resolved themselves into four Parisians, the noisiest and most unpleasant individuals I ever encountered, who, with a quiet German, were the only other visitors in the house. I was served with a tolerable dinner after a long delay, and took myself off to bed soon after I had done justice to it, there being no inducement to prolong the evening.

Saturday, 9th July.—The idea did not occur to me at the time, but I have never ceased regretting that I did not make an early start this morning for Abricolla, and attack the Grand Cornier from there, instead of lying in bed till 9.30 a.m., and passing the whole of a fine day in slippers and idleness. When I at last made my way down to breakfast, I found that I had the place to myself, the Parisians having gone off at an early hour for the Col d'Erin, and the German on a botanizing expedition. Martin had returned to Zinal, and Almer was invisible. I should have been rather hard-up for amusement, had I not luckily found in the salon a volume of " Adam Bede," armed with which I sallied forth, and took up a position in the woods on the other, or left, side of the stream, where I remained till 3.0 p.m., reading and contemplating the Dent Blanche, which was well seen. At that hour I descended from my perch, and, returning to the hotel, found to my infinite joy, that Morshead and Perren had arrived from Zermatt over the Col d'Erin, Gaskell having been left at Zermatt. We had, of course, ample topics of conversation, and the time till dinner passed most agreeably in discussing our mutual adventures since leaving Paris. Circumstances, and especially very bad weather, with which, unlike myself, he had been persecuted, had prevented Morshead accomplishing much glacier work, but he had traversed an immense extent of country, and shown Gaskell some of the least frequented districts of the Alps.

As we were sitting outside the inn after dinner, we saw a party of men coming down the valley, who turned out to be the four Parisians and their guides, who, having reached the top of the Col d'Erin, had funked the descent on to the Zmutt Glacier. Their guides had in vain attempted to persuade them to go on, pointing out Morshead's fresh traces, on seeing which, they merely replied "Nous ne sommes pas des Anglais," and toiled through the soft snow again all the way back to Evolèna. We could not restrain our mirth, and Perren, after listening to the head man of the four discoursing on the subject of the perils they had undergone, said to their faces, with more point than politeness, "Mais, Monsieur, vous êtes fous!" I never saw men look so small, and their behaviour was very different from that of last night, no republican songs, no jocosity with the waitress over their supper, in fact, not a word, until they finally retired to bed with their tails between their legs.

Sunday, 10th July.—I am ashamed to confess that it was again very late before we descended to breakfast, but, so soon as that meal was over, we summoned the guides, and held a council of war as to our future proceedings. Our plan was to go up in the afternoon to Abricolla, and to-morrow ascend the Dent Blanche, making a desperate push to get over the Col d'Erin to Zermatt the same evening. There were two impediments to the realisation of this admirable project. First and foremost the appearance of the weather was very threatening, and we utterly failed in our attempts to persuade ourselves that it would certainly be fine. And, secondly, the little inn at Abricolla had been accidently burnt down about ten days before, and there was no accommodation of any sort in the still unoccupied châlets adjoining. Towards removing the first impediment *we* could, of course, do nothing, but the second was soon got over by the appearance of the proprietor of the defunct inn, who announced that de had two beds "bien propres" in the châlets at the foot of the Ferpèclo Glacier, which, with other articles, he would transport on a mule to one of the châlets at the higher station, an offer which we at once jumped at, but told him that we would dispense with the coverings of the beds and their probable inhabitants, and content ourselves with the mattrasses. We dined at 1.0 p.m. with the intention of getting off at 2.0, but there were more than the usual delays, and it was 3.5 before we managed to effect a start, after baffling a gross attempt at extortion on the part of the landlord. He calmly charged in the bill for our provisions three francs each for two skinney chickens, which had been sent up as the final course of our dinner (for the whole of which we were only charged three francs a head), and which we had ordered to be put aside to take with us, our appetites not being at the time sufficiently keen for us to demolish them. Otherwise the charges were not unreasonable, the bedroom accommodation being very comfortable, and the " cuisine" as good as can be expected in such an out of the way and comparatively unfrequented spot.

The scenery of the Val d'Erin above Evolèna, though pleasing, is not remarkable, the only high peak visible being the Dent Blanche, and that not seen to great advantage. At 3.55 we passed through the hamlet of Haudères, at the junction of the two branches of the valley, leading respectively to the Glaciers of Ferpècle and Arolla, over which latter goes the pass of the Col Collon to the Valpelline and Aosta, a route far less frequented than that of the Col d'Erin, which, after having for many years been considered one of the most difficult, is now recognised as one of the easiest of the high glacier passes. Above Haudères, the path becomes rapidly steeper

and the valley much narrower, being, in many places
reduced to a mere ravine, through which the torrent
thunders along at a tremendous pace. We did not keep
to the mule-path, but followed divers bye-ways known
to Perren, which, doubtless, shortened the road somewhat, but were rougher and more laborious than the
regular track. We were much struck by the appearance
of the forests through which we passed. The trees all appeared to be dying by inches, gradually fading away,
so that there was scarcely a single one with a healthy,
vigorous aspect. As we advanced the weather became
worse, until at 5.0 p.m., just as we reached the châlets
of Sales, close to the foot of the Ferpècle Glacier, down
came the rain and drove us in for shelter. We must have
waited anyhow, as our native, of course, had nothing
ready, and it took some time to arrange and pack on the
mule's back the two beds ("bien propres") and other
articles that had to be taken up with us. The natives
were very civil, and gave us unlimited milk, while a pack
of children surrounded us, watching our every movement
with an interest and apparent amusement quite refreshing. Although, like their parents and dwelling-place, sadly
dirty, they were the prettiest and most rosy-faced children
I have ever seen in the Alps, but dressed exactly like
miniature old men and women, according to the custom
of the country.

By 5.50 the rain had ceased, and the mule being ready,
we set off again, our cortège being further increased by a
small boy, laden with a pail of milk, who was also to accompany the mule down again. We at once began a rapid
ascent, in order to get above the Ferpècle Glacier, the lower
end of which showed itself close in front in the shape of a
very steep and lofty bank of ice, seamed by longitudinal
crevasses, but tolerably free from moraine. From the
path there was a very good view of the great ice-falls of
both branches, the Ferpècle proper and the Mont Miné,
and it was curious to observe how, even below the junction
at the foot of the rocks of the Mont Miné, the two streams,

though forced to flow side by side, declined to coalesce, and remained to the very end distinct, yet united. The path, though exceedingly rough, was good enough for bipeds, but there were some places where I blessed my stars that I was not a quadruped, especially a laden one. Our animal, however, managed very well, and displayed especial dexterity in the passage of several swollen torrents that lay in our way, where the streams were rapid and the footing, for both man and beast, decidedly bad. We remained at a great elevation above the glacier, the ice-fall of which was a superb object, of considerable width and very steep and broken; in spite of the absence of sun, the glacier was by no means quiescent, and we saw several pinnacles topple over, and heard the crash of many more. Nothing could be more barren and dreary than the ground over which we passed. There was neither tree nor shrub to relieve the desolation, and we were by no means sorry when at 7.10 p.m. we reached Abricolla, our destination for the night.

Not that the aspect of the place was particularly exhilarating, the most conspicuous object being the ruined inn, which was completely gutted, the charred walls being alone left standing. Nor were the surrounding châlets much more inviting as sleeping quarters. The most decent one was in a rather dilapidated state as regarded the roof, while the wind whistled cheerfully through the ample chinks in the walls, and the floor was sodden with melted snow, which could not have long disappeared. However, we had to make the best of it, so the traps were deposited, the mule sent away, and the men set to work to light a fire with wood brought up for the purpose, and generally make things as comfortable as circumstances permitted. Shortly after our arrival the weather showed signs of improvement, and allowed us to get an almost cloudless view of the Dent Blanche, which rises majestically immediately behind the châlets, a vision which raised our hopes, and sent us into supper feeling more sanguine than we had been all day. Some excellent chocolate was brewed, and, after its consumption, Morshead and I retired to one of

the mattrasses "bien propres," and, covered with my plaid,
composed ourselves for slumber. It was not long before
we began to entertain doubts as to what the interpretation
of the word "propre" might be in the Val d'Erin, and the
painful conviction at last forced itself on our minds that it
must mean "unlimited fleas," at any rate, the gambols
and displays of entomological agility that went on about
our bodies were rather remarkable, but, though, doubtless,
agreeable and exciting to the actors, were the reverse of
pleasant to the passive victims. Shortly after we lay
down, the wind got up. The ominous moaning which was
first all that was audible, deepened to a roar, until a furious
hurricane was raging, and our refuge shook under the tremendous blasts that surged against its walls, and occasionally threatened to sweep it away bodily. We felt that
things must improve materially before morning if we were
to do anything, as the passage of the arête of the Dent
Blanche was not to be thought of in such a wind. We
could not help fearing that the mountain was making
ready its batteries to baffle our enterprise, and that altogether, our prospects were decidedly shady. Bodily and
mental discomfort, therefore, combined to keep us awake,
and I lay for a long time listening to the cracking of the
fire and the snoring of one or other of the guides, until I
at last fell asleep, and for the time forgot our anxieties.

Monday, 11th July.—During intervals of wakefulness, the
roaring of the storm without was painfully audible, so that
when we roused ourselves at 1.20 a.m., and went to the
door to reconnoitre, we were not surprised to find the appearance of the weather as unpromising as it well could be.
The sky was altogether obscured, and the valley below was
filled with heavy clouds, while the wind, although it had
somewhat subsided, blew in fitful gusts of great violence.
In anticipation of a start, the fire had been made up, and
some chocolate prepared, which we, therefore, drank, and
then stood at the entrance of the châlet, hesitating what to
do, until the question was summarily settled by the rain
beginning to come down heavily, when, of course, we had

no choice but to remain where we were for the present. Our mattrass was under a part of the roof that was anything but water-tight, so it was moved to a more eligible position, and we again delivered ourselves over to our tormentors, who took their revenge for their enforced temporary abstinence, by a series of attacks of the most voracious character. However, the move had made me more sleepy than I had before been, and I got two hours and-a-half of sound and unbroken slumber till 4.15, when we once more got up, and found a dull, cloudy morning, which might or might not improve. The rain had temporarily ceased, but the wind was still uncomfortably high. The Dent Blanche was out of the question, and, as we had no wish either to vegetate all day at Abricolla, or descend to Evolèna and return in the evening for a second night of persecution, and possible similar discomforture in the morning, we determined to leave the peak for more fortunate adventures, and cross at once to Zermatt by the Col d'Erin. This course was the more advisable, as, after the considerable amount of fresh snow that had fallen in the night, we felt that the long arête of the mountain, difficult enough at the best of times, would, probably, be found almost impracticable. Accordingly, after discussing some hot wine and the usual bread-and-butter, we paid the native for our accommodation, adding as may be easily believed, an extra franc or two in consideration of the mattrasses having been found so *bien propre*, and, bestowing a parting benediction on the fleas, took our departure at 4.50 a.m. in a state of mind the reverse of jovial, the guides being quite as much " in the dumps " as we were, Almer especially, having been most anxious to effect the conquest of the Dent whose summit is almost a virgin one·* Picking our way over gentle slopes of rough herbage, débris, and stones, varied by occasional patches of snow, and succeeded in due course by a nasty

---

* The first ascent was made in 1862 by Messrs. Kennedy and Wigram; the second in 1864 by Mr. Finlaison; and the third in 1865 by Mr. Whymper.

moraine, we came at 5.40 to the edge of an extensive
glacier, which falls away in easy slopes from the ridge of
the Wandfluh on our left, towards the Ferpècle Glacier
below, which, however, it does not quite touch. Across
this lay our route towards a point on the opposite side,
where it merges in the great field of névé which supplies the main stream of the Ferpècle. Nothing can be
imagined more superb than the great central ice-fall of
the Ferpècle Glacier, as seen from this part of the route.
Its breadth is very great, and, for dislocation, it will
bear comparison with any in the Alps. Rumour has it
that, upon one occasion, when Mons. Seiler of Zermatt
was crossing the Col d'Erin, he missed his way in a fog,
and got entangled in this labyrinth of séracs, but history
does not say how on earth he ever got out again. That
he did so, however, his pleasant presence at the Monte
Rosa Hotel testifies. The slopes were for some distance
rather steep and crevassed, and the walking would have
been laborious, if we had not had the benefit of the steps
made by the four Parisians on Saturday. As we utilised the
results of their fruitless toils, we felt more amiably disposed
towards them than before, but could not help laughing at
the idea of what they must have undergone, mentally and
bodily, while they plodded back late in the afternoon over
the thoroughly softened snow-fields. The depth of the
steps was pretty good evidence of what the poor misguided
creatures must have suffered, but they saved us a good deal
of trouble, and we were able to get along quicker than we
could otherwise have done. Just above the head of the ice-
fall, a long wall of rocks showed itself through the névé,
between which and a spur from the Wandfluh we had to
pass. This is known as the Motta Rotta, though the name
is not admitted on the map, and so soon as we were abreast
of it, the steepest part of the way on this side was done,
the snow slopes giving place to a broad expanse of névé
which stretched away in front for an almost illimitable distance.

The weather, by no means perfect, had cleared sufficiently

to enable us to get a view of the surrounding scenery, though the tops of the neighbouring mountains were still invisible. The greater part of the arête of the Dent Blanche, extending from the very summit of the mountain to the Col d'Erin, which, in fact, passes over its lowest point, where it begins to rise again towards the Tête Blanche, was well seen, and we paid particular attention to it as we passed along right underneath its base. The arête is of immense length, but, for a long distance, not very steep, the total rise along five-sixths of the length being no greater than that along the remaining sixth to the summit, or, respectively, 1418 and 1483 feet. But it is fearfully narrow, appearing in many places to be a mere knife-edge of rock, and broken by a succession of natural stonemen, which alone must be almost insuperable obstacles to progress along it. One of these, certainly, is reported by all who have ever reached so high a point to be quite impassable, and, to turn it, it is necessary to get down on to and skirt the slope below, an operation involving considerable danger, except when the snow is in an unusually perfect condition. Altogether, I never saw an uglier-looking place, and, unless the actual difficulties are very much less than they appear from a distance, the ascent must be one of the most formidable in the Alps.

While making our observation, we pushed on steadily towards the slight depression in the edge of the snow-field, which marked the position of the pass, but without apparently diminishing the distance between us and it. In cloudless weather, of course, the route might be more interesting, but under the most favourable circumstances this portion of the way cannot be otherwise than monotonous, the absence of difficulty being complete, and the extent of snow to be traversed very great. Perren pounded along doggedly, and we followed in his steps in a somewhat apathetic frame of mind, wondering for how long the amusement was going to last, and steadfastly refraining from looking forward to the desired point, until at 7.45 a.m., or in rather less than three hours from Abricolla, our specu-

lations were cut short, and our hearts rejoiced by our
arrival at the Col, 11,418 feet in height. We fixed ourselves in a nook in the rocks, and prepared to feed, and
contemplate so much of the view as was vouchsafed to us,
which was not much. At our feet was the upper névé of
the Zmutt Glacier,—to the north of it a deep bay filled by
the Schonbühl Glacier, running far back into the recesses
of the Dent Blanche, which was tolerably clear,—and to
the south the immense wall of cliffs forming the bases of
the Dent d'Erin and the glorious Matterhorn, whose summits were still enveloped in mists. The same may be said
of the Gabelhorn and its neighbours, and the greater part
of the Monte Rosa chain, but the long, serpentine Findelen
Glacier, and the peaks of the Strahlhorn and Rympfischhorn at its head, were entirely uncovered and seen to great
advantage. Towards the Oberland, the weather was rather
better, and gave us cause to hope that the improvement
would later extend to our own district. We had a good view
of the snowy groups of the Diablerets, Wildhorn, and Wildstrubel, the great glacier plateau, out of which the latter
peak rises, being especially striking.

Below the Col d'Erin the precipitous face of the Wandfluh does not exceed 200 feet in height, and is masked by
an exceedingly steep slope of snow, cut off by the usual
bergschrund from the smooth snow-fields below. It was
this, to the uninitiated, rather formidable-looking curtain,
which had excited the fears of the luckless Parisians, and
sent them in hot haste back to Evolèna, and down it we,
at 8.5, started to find a passage. Following the course
adopted by Morshead and Perren in ascending on Saturday,
we bore away for a short distance to the right along the
exposed face of the rocks, the men being rather afraid of
avalanches on the upper part of the slope, which was
steepest immediately below the Col. The ledges along
which we had to descend were very narrow and rather
slippery with snow, so that care was undoubtedly necessary in passing them, but there was no serious difficulty,
and getting off them, on to the slope below, at a point where

it was less steep than elsewhere, we worked rapidly down to the bergschrund, the dimensions of which were insignificant, and dropped over it on to the plateau beneath. A broad expanse of rather crevassed névé lay between us, and the low point of black rock, which marked the summit of the Stockje, or buttress, which supports the northern arm of the Zmutt Glacier, and raises it to a considerable height above the southern, or Tiefenmatten branch, under the cliffs of the Dent d'Erin. Across this Perren led us at a tremendous pace, notwithstanding the extreme softness of the snow, into which we sank at every step above our knees. The length of his strides was something enormous, indeed, he went bounding along with an agility I should not have given his somewhat unwieldly frame credit for, and which was worthy of a chamois, an animal of which for the time he might be considered a rather corpulent representative. It is rather curious that the concealed crevasses, by which the whole plateau is more or less undermined, are most numerous and complicated quite close to the rocks of the Stockje, and that the greatest care is necessary just when all danger might be considered over. As it was, when we were within ten yards of the rocks, every one of the party in succession went through into a chasm, of course, with no evil result, all being roped together, but a party ascending from Zermatt, ignorant of this peculiarity, might very easily neglect to get into harness before stepping on to the snow, and come to serious grief in consequence.

At 8.50 we got on to the rocks, which fall away steeply towards the lower glacier, and halted for five minutes to take off the rope, the further use of which could be dispensed with. The rocks are very shaly and easy, and we descended them rapidly until we were not far above the lower glacier which, although quite practicable, appeared to be more crevassed than usual, and induced us not to follow the usual plan of getting off the rocks at their western end, but to keep along the face of the cliffs to their opposite extremity. There was not the slightest difficulty in this operation, but the slope was steep, there were some rather awkward steps, and the glacier was below ready to receive all waifs and strays, so that a certain amount of care was necessary to avoid a bad slip. At 9.30 we got down into a curious hollow, filled with old avalanche snow, between the base of the rocks and the moraine of the glacier, and, passing along this, above a little lake, filled with exceedingly dirty water, we emerged at 10.40 on to the smooth ice, and had a long stretch of almost level glacier before us. In spite of the easy and straightforward character of the way, we did not find the walking over the Zmutt Glacier by any means agreeable, the ice being very hummocky, and, in many places, slushy, so that we were often plunged in a mixture of snow and water above our ankles, to the damage both of our boots and our tempers. Clouds, too, still enveloped the upper portions of the Matterhorn and Dent d'Erin, but the Gabelhorn, on the opposite side of the glacier, was quite clear, and stood up exceedingly well. The height of this peak, 13,364 feet (now, since the ascent of the Rothhorn, the only considerable summit near Zermatt that remains unscaled, the Matterhorn, of course, excepted), renders it well worthy of attack, but its conquest will be no easy task. From Zermatt itself I don't think there is much chance of success, nor is the appearance of the mountain from Zinal more promising. But, if ever I was to make an attempt myself, I should probably fix on that place as my basis of operations.* We kept straight down the centre of the glacier, much lower down than the point where it is usual to quit it, having hit upon a narrow strip of clear ice, in the middle of the enormous expanse of moraine, which offered us a tolerably smooth pathway. But, after a hard struggle, the ice succumbed to the moraine and disappeared,

---

* Subsequent observations made me change my opinion on this point. In 1865 Mr. H. Walker and I, starting from Zermatt, made the first ascent of the Gabelhorn. We ascended the southern branch of the Trift Glacier, and the wall at its head, to the north-eastern arête of the mountain, which we followed to the summit. The next day the late Lord F. Douglas climbed the peak from Zinal, with much greater difficulty than *we* had experienced, and descended by our route.

whereupon we bore away, over the mass of stones of all sizes and hues, towards the right bank of the glacier, which we reached at 10.40 a.m.

A rough track, passing for a short distance beneath a considerable glacier which hangs from the side of the Matterhorn, and occasionally discharges masses of ice over the edge of the cliffs on which it terminates, led us by 11.0 to the dirty and unoccupied châlets of Zmutt, situated a little below the foot of the glacier. We were here overtaken by a violent rain-storm, which wetted us thoroughly, but it appeared to be a final spiteful effort on the part of the weather, which thenceforward steadily improved, until there was scarcely a cloud visible in the sky. There is not a more delightful walk near Zermatt than that through the gorge of the Zmuttbach, down which Morshead now led us at a tremendous pace. The path passes through luxuriant woods along the right bank of the stream, then crosses by a wooden bridge over a wonderful ravine, a mere cleft in the rocks, to the left bank, whence it traverses open meadows, until it falls into the path leading to the Gorner Glacier. At 12.5 p.m. we entered the Monte Rosa Hotel at Zermatt, having accomplished the distance from Abricolla in six hours and three-quarters' actual walking—not bad work, considering that we had not exerted ourselves to travel fast.

In the salle-à-manger we were rejoiced to find Miss Walker, who, with her father, had last week effected the ascent of the Grand Combin, and traversed the high level route from St. Pierre to Zermatt. I was very sorry to hear that Horace Walker was "hors de combat." The weakness in his knee, which had first troubled him when we were descending from the Col des Encombres, had become much worse later, and, after struggling up the Combin, he had been compelled to retreat for medical advice to Vevey, where he still remained. Morshead and I held a council as to how we should employ our time till Friday, when we intended to cross from Randa to the Turtman Thal by the Bies and Turtman Glaciers. Our original intention had

THE SAAS GRAT

been to do the Weisshorn, but, owing to the immense quantity of snow, an attack on that mountain would be a mere fruitless expenditure of time, without prospect of success, so we gave it up, and determined to devote the morrow to the ascent of the Rympfischhorn. I had long had a strong desire to ascend this peak, which was conquered by the Rev. Leslie Stephen in 1859, but had never been visited since,—a neglect quite unaccountable, as its position is most favourable for a panoramic view, and it is one of the few summits accessible from the village of Zermatt itself, without the necessity of going up to the Riffel. Morshead readily acquiesced in my suggestion, as Gaskell was going up Monte Rosa with some friends he had found at the Mont Cervin Hotel, and, when Mr. Walker came in from an expedition up the Gorner Glacier, he and his daughter were persuaded to join us, an arrangement which was not only most agreeable to us, but highly advantageous, as we should have the services of Melchior, who had made the ascent with Stephen. An afternoon at Zermatt is always agreeable, and the hours before dinner flew rapidly by. Afterwards we did not keep late hours the weather giving us every reason to believe that we should have no excuse for shirking an early start in the morning.

Tuesday, 12th July.—We were called at 1.0 a.m., with the pleasing announcement of a fine morning, and, after the usual solemn and dreary meal, called by courtesy breakfast, started at 2.15, attended by Almer, Melchior, and his cousin Jacob Anderegg, a fine, handsome, fair man, with a profusion of beard, and apparently as strong as a horse. Perren was not with us, having to accompany Gaskell and his party up Monte Rosa. Miss Walker was mounted on a mule, which she intended to take as far as the path was sufficiently good, very wisely wishing to avoid unnecessary fatigue before the commencement of the real work of the day. We were, therefore, rather an imposing procession, or should have been had it not been so dark that we could scarcely see each other, the single lantern necessarily being carried in front, so as to show the way for the mule. Crossing the bridge leading to Winkelmatten and the Riffel, we turned up to the left into the pine-woods through which the path to the Findelen Glacier and Adler Pass is carried, as along it as far as the Stelli See lay our route. The darkness, bad enough below, was here, of course, intensified, but the mule climbed along the steep track as rapidly as though it had been broad daylight, performing in the effort a series of gymnastics, during the execution of which I should have strongly objected to be on his back. I had always imagined that a man could go up hill faster than a laden mule, but was for ever cured of the delusion by the performances of our animal, who cleared the ground at a pace which would have soon left us far behind had not he been compelled to halt occasionally at the foot of a bit steeper than usual, to gather himself together for the effort necessary to carry him to the top. We were rather uneasy about the weather, the appearance of which had changed for the worse since we were called, the sky being now partially obscured by clouds, which emitted occasional flashes of lightning, threatening an impending storm.

Once out of the wood and fairly in the gorge of the Findelenbach, our way was easy and pleasant enough, a level and good path conducting us to the châlets on the Eggen Alp, the occupants of which were still buried in slumber, and, therefore, for the moment, objects of envy to us poor wandering mortals. There was by this time daylight enough for us to be able to study the grand view of the Matterhorn behind us. From this direction it appears to almost greater advantage than from any other point, and now displayed itself to us with more snow on its rugged flanks than I ever before saw, a vision which quite confirmed the wisdom of our decision, not to waste time on the Weisshorn. We soon passed the end of the Findelen Glacier, which terminates in a remarkably smooth and pure convex slope of ice, whose appearance gives no hint of the dislocation to which it has been subject higher up. Our route lay along a wild sort of glen between the modern and active moraine of the glacier, on the right, and an old grassy-grown one, a relic of former days, on the left, below the slopes of the Unter Rothhorn. A part of this mountain appears, ages ago, to have fallen from the main mass, and has covered the scanty grass-slopes with a sea of ruin, blocks of stone of all shapes and sizes lying scattered about in the wildest confusion. The walking, however, for us was very pleasant, but the antics of the mule were remarkable, and it must have been an equal relief to the animal and its rider, when, after passing some wretched hovels on the Flüh Alp, its labours were brought to an end by Miss Walker dismounting.

We were now, at 5.5, not far from the point where travellers, bound for the Adler Pass, take to the moraine of the Findelen Glacier, and began to mount in earnest, striking up the slopes to the left, in order to get on the long ridge of the Rympfischwänge, as the rocky spur is called which runs west from the Rympfischhorn, and separates the basin of the Findelen Glacier from that of the glaciers which drain towards the Täsch Alp. A stiff ascent over stunted grass brought us to a tract covered with boulders and masses of rock, apparently fallen from the higher part of the ridge, a style of ground at getting over which I am a shocking bad hand, my extremely short sight impeding me horribly. It requires a quick eye to look a-head and seize at a glance the most eligible route over such a chaos of shattered blocks as that which we had to traverse, and, in consequence of my inability to do this, I dropped gradually behind the rest of the party, and often found myself in a regular maze, extrication from which required a series of gymnastics of a startling character. In spite of their size, the position of some of these rocks was by no means stable, and, when the foot was placed upon some of them, they manifested a decided inclination to tilt up summarily, and deposit the luckless intruder on his proboscis. I quite envied the facility with which Morshead, with unerring judgment, hopped from one sharp-edged mass to the other, a manœuvre which requires a confident eye as well as a sure foot, as the result of a slip would be an ugly, and probably

P

disabling, fall. However, by 6.0 we had got through the worst of it, and, finding a convenient arrangement of stones, halted for breakfast, which certain internal sensations suggested must be about due. Our fears for the weather were by this time dissipated, the clouds had vanished, and the aspect of the sky betokened a brilliant day, and, as we hoped, a renewed series of successful expeditions. There was, therefore, nothing to mar our enjoyment, as we sat munching the bread-and-butter of peace and contentment, and gazing at the long snowy ridge of the Stockhorn and Hochthäligrat, the prolongations of the promontory of the Riffelberg, and the spotless fields of névé at the head of the Findelen Glacier. At 6.30 we resumed our way over stones of a slightly less obnoxious character than below, varied by patches of snow, which, although still fairly hard, required some diplomacy in passing, as they occasionally manifested a tendency to let one through with a jerk into the holes formed by the stones that lay underneath. One consolation was, this state of things did not last long, and at 6.55 we got on to the crest of the ridge, between the shattered peak of the Flühhorn on the left, and the point marked on the Federal map 3258 mètres, or 10,679 feet, on the right. A slope of snow led us up to the top of this latter point, whence a short descent over shaly rocks was necessary to get down on to the snow-fields below, which stretched away, without interruption, to the base of a sort of mamelon of rocks, seamed by snow couloirs, immediately in front of the final peak of the Rympfischhorn. The latter showed itself in the shape of two parallel towers of steep, black rock, linked together by a broad curtain of snow, and so inaccessible in appearance that we were rather sceptical at Melchior's assurances that the ascent would not be found a very serious matter.

Nothing could be more straightforward than our route appeared to be as far as the foot of the aforesaid mamelon, along the slopes of the Rympfischwänge. On the south, the snow-fields come to an abrupt termination on the top of the precipices which overhang the Findelen Glacier, but on the north they send down the extensive Längenfluh Glacier, which falls in a succession of gentle but rather crevassed, slopes towards the Täsch Alp, which might be reached by it without, so far as we could see, any serious difficulty, so that the ascent of the Rympfischhorn might probably be effected from Randa in about the same time as from Zermatt. No words can give the faintest conception of the magnificence of the views which opened out on either side of us as we advanced. On our left we looked across the grand expanse of the Täsch Glaciers to the graceful snow-point of the Allaleinhorn, the unwieldy mass of the Alphubel, and the towering forms of the Dom and Täschhorn, the latter, as usual forming many points of view, appearing to hold the supremacy over his loftier, but slightly more distant, brother. On our right, was the whole chain of Monte Rosa, from the Cima di Jazi to the Breithorn, a superb line of snow-peaks and broken glacier, sparkling in the rays of the sun, and more dazzling even than usual from the extraordinary amount of snow with which, the glaciers were enveloped. The Breithorn, Zwillinge, and Lyskamm were magnificent objects, but the grand feature of the view in this direction was Monte Rosa itself, which fully maintained its claim to respect as the second summit in the European Alps. I never before fully appreciated the real height and proportions of this mountain, which from most points of view, and notably that from which it is most generally seen—the Gornergrat,—is a comparatively insignificant and unattractive object, while, from our present position, it towered up wonderfully. This was, no doubt, partly owing to the fact that between us and it the ridge of the Stockhorn intervened as a foreground, and served as a scale by which to measure the altitude of the main mass, but the great effect was produced in consequence of our gradually rising above and overlooking the ridge that runs from the Monte Moro to the Cima di Jazi, so that the eastern face of the mountain from the Signal Küppe to the Nord End was exposed. In fact we got the Monte Moro view, but from a far more elevated and favourable point.

The full glory of the scene was not displayed from the point where we first got on to the ridge, but, walking along it towards the Rympfischhorn, we opened out a view of the precipices above the Macugnaga Glacier, simultaneously with the ordinary one of the snow-slopes that fall towards the Gorner Glacier, the combination producing an effect such as I have rarely seen surpassed. Nor, looking back towards the west, was the prospect less interesting than in other directions.   On the opposite side of the Zermatt valley, the Weisshorn, white with snow, towered a worthy rival, and in elevation superior, to its neighbour—the Dom, but it is even more graceful in form than the latter, while it is decidedly the harder nut to crack.   The Rothhorn and Gabelhorn both looked well, but very inaccessible, the arêtes of the former being particularly steep and serrated. As I have before said, I don't think there is much prospect of attacking the Gabelhorn with success from Zermatt, but, if the attempt were made, the line of march must be by the southern arm of the Trift Glacier.   From the ridge at the head of the glacier, an arête undoubtedly runs up to the very summit, whether practicable or not is another question, but the great difficulty would be to scale the precipices leading up to that ridge, which appeared to be of considerable height and fearfully steep.   Of the latter quality we should have hesitated to judge at so considerable a distance, but a careful survey with the glass revealed the suggestive fact that the line of crags was unrelieved by a single snow couloir, which it probably would have been, were it possible for snow to lie at all.   As our eyes wandered on to the grand spear-like form of the Dent Blanche, now clear enough, I am afraid we were animated by an unchristian spirit, as we reflected on the total collapse of our meditated assault on that most objectionable summit.   On the other side of the long Zmutt Glacier, which was seen to its very source under the Tête Blanche, rose the Matterhorn, but, wonderful and singular as the form of that marvellous peak is from every point of view, it never, in my opinion, shows to such advantage from a great elevation, as it does from

comparatively low points, such as the Stelli See and Riffelberg. In fact, when seen as one amongst many summits,
it loses its distinctive character.

The snow along the slopes of the Rympfischwänge was
in superb order, hard and crunching pleasantly under the
boot. The angle of ascent was generally inconsiderable,
and, wherever the inclination happened to be rather greater,
Almer and Jacob went a-head, making gashes in the snow
so as to facilitate our progress. Under these favourable
circumstances we advanced steadily, though without hurrying, until at 8.45 we reached the foot of the mamelon in
advance of the main peak, and halted to refresh ourselves
before commencing the serious part of the day's work. I
cannot imagine a more delightful excursion for ladies, able
to walk tolerably, than that as far as this point, taking a
mule as far as the Stelli See. The passage of the "clappey"
below the Rympfischwänge is certainly rough and toilsome,
but otherwise there is not the slightest difficulty, and I
know no walk in the Alps commanding such a long continuance of gorgeous views. Up to the present time we
had not been obliged to put on the rope, not a single crevasse having been encountered, but, when we were again
preparing for a start, it was thought advisable to get into
harness, as a precaution against a possible slip on the steep
ascent before us. This was, perhaps, not strictly necessary,
but I always, myself, like to make all sure, when a party
must anyhow keep together, and the fast walker must, therefore, accommodate his pace to that of his weaker brethren,
as no delay is thereby caused, and the increased security
(real or imaginary) actually facilitates progress. All our
traps and provisions, with the exception of a bottle of champagne, were deposited on the snow, and at 9.15 we started
to carry what might be looked upon as the first line of
the defences of the mountain.

A series of short zig-zags, up a very steep slope of snow
in good condition, brought us to the foot of the rocks, which
were plentifully interspersed with snow couloirs. We
climbed sometimes by one, sometimes by the other, in

along tolerably quickly; the first point was reached and passed, the ridge beyond was traversed along its crest with nothing to hold on by, and at 11.10 a.m. we stepped with a howl on to the summit of the Rympfischhorn, 13,791 feet in height.

There was not much room for our large party on the highest point, and we all had to stand in attitudes, more or less uncomfortable, up to our knees in snow, and keep a sharp look-out not to take an unwary step over the highly alluring precipices which surrounded us on all sides. The view was most superb, the sky being fairly clear in every direction except towards Italy, where, as usual, nothing was visible. The Monte Rosa chain was pretty much as we had seen it all the way up, but in the opposite quarter we now looked across the spotless expanse of the great Fee Glaciers to the grand wall of the Mischabel, which shut out a considerable portion of the Bernese Oberland. Scarcely less imposing than the ranges of the Mischabel and Weisshorn was that of the Weissmies and Fletschhorn on the right side of the Saas Thal, between it and the Simplon, while away to the west the eye wandered over a sea of summits, over which Mont Blanc and the Combin towered supreme. The cairn raised by Stephen's party in 1859 was still in existence, but in a rather dilapidated state, and there were no materials at hand wherewith to repair it. Melchior was especially delighted at seeing this evidence of his previous presence on the summit, which, before our ascent, had not been again visited. This being the anniversary of the day on which I made my first appearance in this wicked world and howling wilderness, a bottle of champagne had been brought up to celebrate the event, and this we now proceeded to open. Now, in my humble opinion, champagne is a most admirable thing anywhere except on the top of a high mountain, where it is a decided mistake, as half the contents of the bottle invariably escapes before a glass can be got ready, while the remainder appears in the shape of froth, bubbles, "et præterea nihil." The present case was no exception to the rule. We *did* get nothing but froth, and Mr. Walker was favoured with most of that, not, however, in the manner he would have preferred, as, in the act of pouring out, it was blown all over his garments, and not down his throat. No provisions had been brought up, fortunately, as we could not possibly have eaten them, all our energies being required to maintain our equilibrium in the hurricane that was raging, which I verily believe would have carried a loaf of bread forcibly over to the more frequented pinnacle of Monte Rosa, on the opposite side of the Görner Glacier.

By 11.30 we had had enough of it, and, having with some difficulty disentangled the rope from the awful jumble into which we had contrived to get it during our halt, turned to descend in the same order as before. I must confess to having been by no means happy on the first part of the arête, as the wind, blowing so violently in our faces, rendered it difficult for me to keep my eyes open, and otherwise had such a bewildering effect, that I scarcely knew where to put my feet. I had, too, another special source of misery, in that I was animated with a strong desire to blow my nose, and was totally unable to gratify that desire, my handkerchief being securely stowed in an inner pocket of my coat (which was buttoned up), where I could not at the moment have got at it to save my life. On the whole, therefore, I was not sorry when we turned off the arête and took to the firm rocks again, down which we scrambled cautiously, but soon reached the head of the couloir, and, commencing its descent, were at once comparatively sheltered from the wind. The few steps near the top which had been found unpleasant coming up, were worse going down, but, so soon as they were passed, our difficulties were at an end, we glissaded down the lower part of the couloir on to the plateau beneath, rapidly descending the easy rocks and snow-slopes of the mamelon, and at 12.30 p.m. reached the spot at its base where we had left our traps, and where we now halted to lunch.

Morshead and I were anxious to get down to Zermatt in time to dine before the Table d'Hôte, as we intended to go

on to Randa in the evening, with the view of ascending the
Dom to-morrow, and, knowing this, the Walkers most kindly
insisted on our not waiting for them, but making the best
of our way down with Almer.   As an early arrival was
really of importance to us, we agreed to the course proposed, and at 1.0 p.m. wished them good-bye for the present,
and started across the gently sloping snow-fields we had
ascended in the morning.   But the snow was now in a vastly
different condition from what it had then been, and at every
step we sank deep into it; nevertheless, Almer led at a
pace I have rarely seen equalled over such ground, and at
1.30 we stood on the top of the rocky point from which we
had before taken to the snow, having traversed in half-an-
hour what in the morning, when we also went fast, had
taken more than thrice that time.   Having taken off the
rope, we resumed our descent towards the Findelen Glacier,
but found our morning's route over the upper tract of stones
and snow so troublesome, that we determined to try and
evade the still more objectionable "clappey" lower down,
and, accordingly, bore away rather to the left, without trying
to descend much.   Our manœuvre was rewarded with success, as we found a stretch of comparatively clear ground,
which, though steep, was luxurious as compared with the
stones, and, moreover, introduced us to a slope of snow,
long and steep enough for a glissade.   Down it we went
double quick, but there were stones beneath, rendering the
snowy surface weak in places.   At one of these, Morshead,
who was first, went through, making a hole which I vainly
tried to avoid, and catching my foot in it, of course, pitched
forward, and finished the glissade spread-eagle fashion,
prone on my stomach, head foremost, in an attitude more
entertaining to the lookers on than elegant or agreeable.
However, no harm was done, and by 2.30 we were close to
the moraine of the Findelen glacier, whence a few minutes'
rough walking over the tail of the "clappey," which we
had otherwise circumvented, brought us to the point where
we had commenced to ascend in the morning.   Our troubles
were now over, and we had a pleasant walk onwards, but

were especially struck by the different impression which the path made on us by daylight from what it had in darkness or semi-darkness; then it had seemed rather good than otherwise,—now, we pronounced it simply atrocious. At 3.25 we reached the châlets on the Eggen Alp, where we found a large and lively party, come up from Zermatt "to see the glacier." We made tender enquiries from the châlet people after "Niedl," and were informed that there was none, but, venturing to doubt this, brought our powers of blandishment to bear, and finally elicited a jug nearly full, to the unmitigated astonishment of our friends, who had totally failed to get anything but milk. Resuming our way at 3.30, we pushed on rapidly, our movements being quickened by the appearance of the weather, which threatened a change; indeed, a sharp shower came on before we got into the forest. Hurrying down the steep track, we emerged from this, ran across the meadows, and at 4.15 p.m. arrived at the Monte Rosa Hotel, after an absence of exactly fourteen hours, and one of the most agreeable and enjoyable expeditions I ever made.

Dinner was ordered, appeared in due course, and was quickly eaten, but we might have saved our hurry, as, by the time we had done, the weather looked so bad that we did not know what to do. The idea of walking down to Randa at night, merely to have the pleasure of walking back again in the morning, was not particularly attractive, but there appeared to be no alternative unless we gave up the expedition altogether, when Morshead was suddenly seized with an idea worthy of himself. "Why," said he, "should we go to Randa? Let us sleep the sleep of innocence here, and if, the weather is fine in the morning, start from here. We shall only have to start two hours earlier than we otherwise should." This was certainly the simplest way out of the difficulty, and upon this plan we ultimately determined. The Monte Rosa party arrived in the evening, having been prevented by the wind from reaching the summit. Of course, we had the privilege of chaffing them unmercifully, but I can quite believe that they felt the violence of the hurricane even more than we did.

Wednesday, 13th July.—At half-an-hour after midnight
Almer called us, the weather being clear, and to all appearance promising a fine day, so we tumbled up,—very loth to
move, it must be confessed,—dressed, and went down into
the salle-à-manger, where we found breakfast ready, and
the unfortunate waiter, who, almost single-handed, has to
attend to all the wants of visitors, tranquilly slumbering in
a chair.   While we were feeding, Peter Perren came in
with a rather blank expression of countenance, and announced that he was very unwell and did not feel equal to
accompanying us. Our impression was, that, having crossed
the Col d'Erin on Monday, and passed yesterday in a futile
attempt on Monte Rosa, he was rather knocked up, and did
not feel inclined to spend the third day in toiling up the
steep slopes of the Dom.   However, of course, as he
pleaded illness, we could not insist on his company, so, as
a second man was considered necessary by Almer, we engaged young Peter Taugwald, who happened to be opportunely on the spot, and at 1.30 a.m. set off.

The night was very dark, though the sky was spangled
with stars, and we should have been better pleased had the
temperature of the air been a good deal lower than it was,
the atmosphere being uncomfortably warm and oppressive.
I was unpleasantly reminded of the morning last year on
which I started for the same expedition, upon which occasion, in spite of early promise, I had been enveloped in fog
and snow on the upper part of the mountain, but I kept my
misgivings and reminiscences to myself, and we tramped
silently along the broad path leading to Randa, hoping for
the best.   Having reached the summit last year, my only
object in repeating the expedition was to see the view, which
had then been entirely blotted out, but which is considered
by all who have seen it to be the very finest in the Alps.
Morshead had never been up, but he agreed with me that
the moment it became evident that we should have no view
we should abandon the attempt, and not go on merely for
the sake of getting to the top.   An excellent new path has
recently been made from Randa to Zermatt, and just above

Täsch the old track has been entirely carried away by the ravages of the Visp. In the darkness we missed the point where the old and new routes diverge, and were within an ace of walking into the river, above which the track breaks off abruptly, a catastrophe which would have made a summary end of our wanderings. At 3.30, when we reached Randa, which was as silent as the grave, it was daylight, so we woke up for the first time, shook ourselves, and prepared to begin the day's work in earnest. Passing through the village and the meadows beyond, we crossed the furious torrent of the Randaierbach, which takes its origin in the snows of the Graben or Festi Glacier, many thousand feet above, and plunged into the forest which covers the steep side of the valley. I had so vivid a recollection of the discomfort attending the ascent through this forest last year in the dark, that, when Morshead proposed to make Zermatt our starting point on the present occasion, it had at once struck me that one of the principal recommendations of such a plan was, that this portion of the route would be traversed by daylight. Our experience amply confirmed this view, for, punishing as the work was, it was luxurious compared with what I had before undergone, and would have been positively agreeable if Almer had not led at a pace with which I found it difficult to keep up, and which soon reduced me to a state of dissolution. I don't suppose that, of its kind, there is a steeper bit of climbing in the Alps than that of these slopes above Randa, up which we now positively raced, although the ground was in places so very precipitous that we had to haul ourselves up by the roots and branches of the trees. There was at first a faint track, but this soon died away, leaving us to select the line of route which seemed best in our eyes, though, in very truth, "bad was the best." As the trees became scantier and gradually thinned away, the ascent became less steep, but even more laborious and difficult, lying over huge broken masses of rock, over and between which it was not easy to pick a way. As usual on such ground, I was especially ill at ease, and was sincerely glad when at 5.15 we came to a tract of comparatively open country, which might, perhaps, be considered the top of the first step in the ascent.

We were now exactly opposite the Bies Glacier on the other side of the valley, and, consequently, in a most favourable position for a thorough examination of it, with a view to determining the most promising route for our contemplated expedition on Friday. The central portion of the glacier itself looked the reverse of tempting, if not altogether impracticable, but we thought that we should be able to circumvent the enemy by taking to the rocks on the left bank, which, though formidably steep, we had little doubt would offer some sort of way to the upper plateau of névé. There is scarcely a finer object in the Alps than the Weisshorn, seen from this point. The whole mountain is visible at once, from summit to base, and the elevation is sufficiently great to allow the observer to form an idea of the true proportions of this, the most graceful, as it is one of the most difficult of access, of the higher summits. As regarded our own expedition, I was vexed, though scarcely surprised, to see that we had perpetrated precisely the same error as last year, in keeping too far to the north, and ascending higher than was necessary. After crossing the Randaierbach, we ought to have stuck as close as possible to the course of that stream, and not allowed ourselves to be seduced into following stray paths through the heart of the forest, whereby we not only lost time, but incurred a quite unnecessary amount of labour. We now bore away to the right, making a slight descent, and then skirted the rapid slopes of rock and turf mingled which lie at the base of the line of cliffs which support the tails of the Graben and Hohberg Glaciers, and formed the next obstacle that we had to overcome. Although the ground is steep, the footing is not bad, and we climbed along with great care, gradually working round the foot of the cliffs which, at all points save one, are quite inaccessible,—at least no way has yet been found up them. Personally, I infinitely prefer rocks, however steep, to the disgusting style of ground we had to traverse, where tufts of slippery grass were the only supports for the foot, while there was little or nothing to hold on by, and the results of a bad slip would have been a roll for a longer distance than would have been agreeable. When almost under the end of the Graben Glacier, whose final ice-blocks were just visible peering over the rocks above, we again struck straight up, and, having mounted above the top of a ravine which bites deep into the hill-side, turned once more to the left, and, after a rather awkward scramble, approached the base of the gully by which alone it is possible to scale the cliffs. This, from below, looks by no means prepossessing, but, in point of fact, only the last few feet of it offer any serious difficulty; there, however, the gully contracts to an exceedingly narrow "cheminée," and the rocks absolutely overhang. I had all along looked forward to this place to afford a test whether my mountaineering powers had or had not improved since last year, when I was hauled up more like a bale of goods than anything else, and arrived at the top feet foremost, in a most undignified manner. Almer's opinion on the subject was shown by his observing that he did not think we need put on the rope, and, after he had scrambled up, when it came to my turn, I was delighted to find that I managed to overcome the difficulty with comparative ease, with the help of a good grip from him as I appeared at the top. The gymnastics necessary to carry out the operation were, however, sufficiently remarkable, and I was by no means sorry that the effort required was but a short one.

It was consoling to think that the steepest part of the ascent was now over, and the most serious difficulty to be encountered left behind, and, on the strength of the reflection, we proposed to stop and breakfast. Almer, however, suggested that we should defer the meal until we reached a certain spring which he remembered to have seen higher up, and we readily acquiesced. Our route lay over a desert of loose stones, succeeded by banks of shale, until at 6.30 we came to the expected spring, and established ourselves as comfortably as possible. Two causes, however, combined to defeat our efforts, one physical, the other mental. In the first place, a fierce wind swept across the mountain side and chilled us to the bone. Secondly, our minds were grievously disquieted at the aspect of the weather, which had been getting steadily worse ever since we left Randa. The Matterhorn, Gabelhorn, and Weisshorn were enveloped in dense clouds, and over the former especially a most furious storm was evidently raging; still, on our side of the valley all was yet clear, and we solaced ourselves with the rather feeble hope that the attractive power of the three above-named mountains might retain the bad weather where it was. The spring is a very excellent one, and is noteworthy as being the only one to be found on the mountain, but under the melancholy circumstances we could neither appreciate it nor our bread-and-butter as they deserved, and so at 7.0, bringing our meal to a conclusion, we resumed our way in a somewhat doleful frame of mind. Dreary slopes of shale, interspersed with patches of snow, led us in due course to the moraine on the right bank of the Graben Glacier, at a short distance above its termination. We did not take to it at once, but kept to the hard slopes of old avalanche snow alongside, which appeared to offer a smoother and pleasanter way. We were at last, however, driven on to it, and, after picking a way amongst the dirty crevasses by which its continuity is broken, found ourselves at 8.10 fairly on the main glacier, and halted for a few minutes to put on the rope.

This was rendered advisable by the state of the ice, which for some distance was steep, and much broken,—very much more so, it struck me, than we had found it last year. A good deal of dodging and some step-cutting were necessary before we left the worst crevasses behind us, but we finally worked our way on to the comparatively level and quite easy plain of ice above. The great mass of the Dom was now straight in front of us, still quite free from clouds, but a glance behind revealed the painful truth that the storm was rapidly drifting over in our direction. Indeed, we had gone a very short distance when the clouds swooped down on us, enveloping everything in a dense fog; it began to snow violently, and the wind, which had moderated, commenced to blow again with increased force. To carry out our virtuous resolutions, we ought instantly to have turned tail and fled, but we could not bring ourselves to do so, and, as Almer, when appealed to, for a wonder, gave an unhesitating, decisive answer to the effect that he believed that, in spite of the bad weather, we *could* get to the top, we determined to persevere to the latest possible moment. In fact, the idea of having undergone the grind up from Randa, and then turning, without result, just when the greatest difficulties of the route had been overcome, was repugnant to all of us, while Almer was animated with a laudable ambition to have the power of boasting that he had passed the Col d'Erin and ascended the Rympfischhorn and Dom in three successive days. Fortune seemed at first inclined to smile on our boldness, as the storm lulled perceptibly, the wind blowing with rather less violence, and the fog becoming less dense, so that we were just able to make out the forms of the surrounding peaks. We steered for the ridge at the head of the glacier, making for the point at its north-eastern angle, which is marked on the Federal map 3757 mètres, or 12,327 English feet, but found the snow in such bad condition that our onward progress was rather slow. Hoping to improve matters, we made for the rocks on our left, and found a broad, sloping shelf near their base, along which we were able to advance without difficulty, and with much greater speed and less labour than over the snow. This led us to the base of the wall which hems in the head of the glacier, up which a broad snow couloir offered a natural route, of which we promptly availed ourselves. The angle was considerable, but the snow was in sufficiently good condition, and we mounted rapidly, until it became necessary to get on to the rocks on the right, which were steep and broken, and required more care to avoid a slip. A stiff scramble brought us to the crest of the ridge at 9.20, or only twenty minutes. later than I had been on the same spot last year, starting from Randa, so that, happen what might, we had proved conclusively that it is by no means essential to make that place the starting point for the expedition.

We were now standing on the main ridge of the mountain, which stretched away on our right towards the summit, while at our feet lay the Hohberg Glacier, whose snows take their origin on the north-western face of the peak, and occupy the angle between it and the ridge of the Nadelgrat, whose highest point, the Nadelhorn, the third peak of the Mischabel group, was exactly opposite our position, though, alas! quite invisible. The summit can be gained with equal ease either by the arête or the glacier; the former, probably, offers a rather shorter, more interesting, and less laborious route, but is not recommendable in bad or windy weather, being very much exposed, while the glacier is comparatively sheltered. There was, therefore, no question as to which we should adopt on the present occasion, the real point at issue being whether we should adopt either, as it became painfully evident that, during the lull on which we had been congratulating ourselves, the storm had been gathering itself up for an outburst, to which all that had yet passed would be like child's play. Almer, however, was still in favour of an advance, and, as his word was, of course, law with us, we set about finding a line of descent on to the Hohberg Glacier, which was not far below, but separated from us by a very precipitous wall of rock and ice. Advancing towards the Dom for a short distance, we turned down, but found the descent quite impracticable at the point selected, so retraced our steps along the ridge, until a spot was found where a second attempt could be made. This was more successful, as, clambering carefully down some ledges of shaly rock, succeeded by a steep bank of snow, we jumped over a small bergschrund, partially choked, and landed on the glacier. We struck straight across underneath some overhanging cliffs of névé, which appeared in a most uncertain state of equilibrum, and are evidently in the habit of coming down occasionally with a run, the glacier being covered in all directions with scattered blocks and débris. Taugwald, who was leading, hurried over this rather dangerous bit of ground as fast as possible, but the crevassed state of the glacier rendered it impracticable to travel as rapidly as was desirable. The chasms were numerous and complicated, and a great deal of step-cutting and pulling with the rope was required to force a passage. One or two places were particularly nasty, and, just as we were past the worst bit, the storm that had been threatening burst upon us with a fury, such as I have rarely experienced. The wind roared and screamed so that we could not hear one another speak, while the snow fell thick and fast, obliterating everything from view, and completely blinding us. The cold, too, was most intense, but Almer's cry was still "Vorwärts! vorwärts!" So on we struggled up the steep snow slopes, Morshead, myself, and Taugwald becoming at every step more doubtful as to the prudence of proceeding. Taugwald's opinion was not worth much, but its nature was sufficiently evidenced by the feeble and spiritless manner in which he wielded his axe and trod the steps. His blows were those of a man who felt that he was expending strength in what was a hopeless task. At length an icy gust of more than ordinary violence, which seemed to drive all the breath out of our bodies, caused us to halt and reflect upon the possible results of further persistence. The appearance of the party was rather curious, every one being so completely covered with snow, that he was scarcely distinguishable from the slopes on which we were standing, Morshead, who was blessed with a beard, presenting a particularly remarkable aspect. Amidst the roaring of the storm it was not easy to interchange ideas, and to stand still long was to be frozen, so, when even the undaunted Almer admitted that the battle had turned against us, and that in such weather we could not reach the top, there was no further discussion, and at 10.0. a.m. we turned tail, and fled precipitately.

I believed at the time, and believe still, that the attempt was pushed to the verge of rashness, and that, had we persevered for a quarter-of-an-hour longer, the expedition would have resulted in a serious disaster. The quantity of snow that was falling was proved by the fact that the deep steps which we had made coming up were already entirely obliterated, and that the rocks below the Col, which we reached again at 10.20, were completely covered. The descent of the wall down to the Graben Glacier was rapidly effected by the snow couloir, and at 10.30 we took up our position in a sheltered nook in the rocks on the right bank, and prepared to recruit exhausted nature. While we were engaged in this agreeable and necessary operation, the clouds over the Weisshorn and Rothhorn partially lifted, and enabled us to get a tolerable view of the ridge connecting those peaks at the head of the Schallenberg Glacier. This was important, as I proposed making a pass from Zinal to Zermatt in that direction, and it was desirable to ascertain for what point on the ridge it would be best to make. Two Cols were visible, one between the Rothhorn and Schallhorn, the other between the Schallhorn and Weisshorn. The descent from the former would lie over the main branch of the Schallenberg Glacier, and appeared preferable to that from the latter, which would be down a very steep and broken secondary glacier, under the Weisshorn. Both were undoubtedly practicable, but Almer and I agreed that, supposing the difficulties of either to be equal on the Zinal side, we would select the gap between the Rothhorn and Schallhorn.

In spite of a gradual clearance of the weather in other quarters, over the Dom the clouds remained thick and impenetrable, and were driven along by the wind at a pace which indicated that it would be hard indeed for any one to stand up against it. At 11.0 we took our departure, and, hurrying over the Graben Glacier, cautiously picked our way through the crevasses, and at 11.45 got on to the moraine, and took off the rope. Instead of following our morning's route, we kept along the moraine for a considerable distance, finding the walking easier than we had expected, and did not quit it till we were not far above the end of the glacier, when we struck away to " terra firma,"

and, taking another pull at our friendly spring, reached in
due course the top of the Cheminée. The descent of this
was decidedly more awkward than the ascent had been,
the gully below falling away so rapidly that it was not
easy to keep one's footing on landing in it from above.
Almer, however, went down first to receive waifs and strays,
and we followed without accident. To Morshead the thing
was a mere "bagatelle," but I must plead guilty to having
been sincerely glad when we had left the difficulty behind,
and were scudding down the steep slopes below. On reaching the base of the cliffs, we carefully eschewed the sea of
stones we had toiled over on the way up, and instead kept
straight down near the torrent, a shorter and easier course.
But, on getting into the forest, we unfortunately came upon
what looked like a path, and were inveigled into following
it. It led us right into the middle of the wood, and finally
resolved itself into an old watercourse, and came to an untimely end, leaving us to recover the proper direction after
a most irritating waste of time. We at last hit upon a track
which really led us "out of the wood," when we quickly
gained the bank of the torrent, tumbled across it, ran
through the meadows, and, at 2.35 p.m., entered the little
Hotel du Dom, at Randa.

We ordered up a bottle of lemonade, and consumed it
with enormous satisfaction and much smacking of the lips,
until, arriving at the bottom of the bottle, we discovered
the bodies of some two dozen blue-bottle flies, in various
stages of decomposition, when our feelings were by no
means so pleasurable. At 3.0 we went on our way, and
had a pleasant walk to Zermatt, which we reached at 4.45
p.m., and entered, it must be confessed, with our tails
rather between our legs; not that our failure had been
discreditable, but the feeling of being beaten is never
pleasant. Gaskell and Perren had gone up to the Riffel,
in hopes of a fine day to-morrow for Monte Rosa, but, when
we went to bed, although the weather was not absolutely
bad, their chances of success appeared rather doubtful.

Thursday, 14th July.—I woke at an early hour this

morning, and, on getting out of bed to inspect the weather, found the sky obscured by clouds, and the aspect of things generally unpromising for the Monte Rosa party, so, congratulating myself that I had no expedition on hand, I turned in again and "took it out" in sleep till 9.30 a.m., when I woke once more to the unexpected presence of a fine day. Nevertheless, Gaskell and Perren arrived early from the Riffel, not having been able to start for Monte Rosa in the morning, and having been, consequently, obliged to finally abandon the idea of making the ascent. The result of this was, that it was settled that Gaskell should cross the Bies Glacier with us to morrow, which he otherwise would not have been able to do, an arrangement by which he gained an expedition very much more exciting and interesting than the ascent of Monte Rosa. The day was spent in luxurious ease and idleness, only broken by the completion of the various little arrangements rendered necessary by a "change of base;" but by the evening we had had enough of it, and sat down to dinner, before the Table d'Hôte, glad that we were soon again to be on the move. After dinner Seiler brought in two bottles of sherry, which he insisted on drinking with us. His civility, indeed, and anxiety to please were so marked, that we quite forgave him certain little offences which he had perpetrated last year. We subsequently heard that our expressions of discontent had worked round to him, and were the cause of the present demonstration. However, in every respect there was a vast improvement this year, and we had good reason to be satisfied with our treatment and charges, in which latter a tendency to extortion, which we had observed, was no longer perceptible.

At 6.35 p.m. we left Zermatt, and had an agreeable walk down to Randa, which we reached at 8.20, and were rejoiced to find the Hotel du Dom free of tourists, so that we had the field to ourselves. Before retiring for the night, we took a long and anxious survey of the Bies Glacier, over which our morrow's journey lay, though, of course, it was too dark for us to make out much of our intended route.

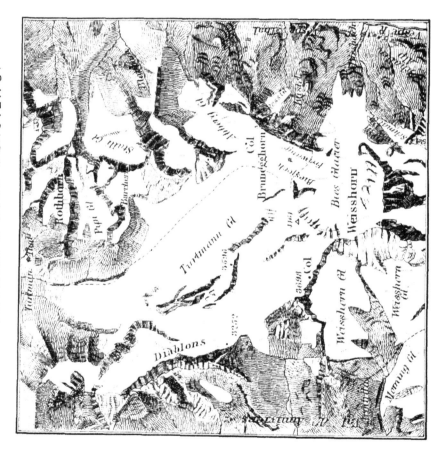

THE TURTMAN & BIES GLACIERS.

As is well known, the declivity on which this glacier hangs is one of the steepest in the Alps, and the natural result is, that from the point where it springs from its reservoir of névé under the Weisshorn, to its termination above the valley, it is a continuous ice-fall of the most hopeless and forbidding character. The idea of making a direct pass to the Turtman Thal in this direction seems to have occurred to no one till 1862, when Franz Andermatten, of Saas, with two French gentlemen, ascended the great Turtman Glacier to the Col between the Brunegghorn and the second peak of the Weisshorn, and descended to Randa, an exploit which no one had since attempted to repeat. From the visitors' book at the Inn, we found that they had taken seven hours to reach the Col, and nine hours to get down to Randa, a sufficient commentary on the difficulties of the route. Perren, however, gathered from some hunters, at Randa, that they had not descended by the glacier, or by the rocks immediately to the left of it, but had kept far to the north, and made their way down by a series of couloirs under the Brunegghorn. We, therefore, determined to try and find a more direct course, and mount either by the glacier itself, or, if that should prove impracticable, by the rocks alongside, taking particular care to avoid being driven towards the Brunegghorn. Almer was very confident we could get up in a good deal less than nine hours, but an early start was none the less advisable, so we went to roost without much delay.

Friday, 15th July.—When Almer called us at 1.45 a.m., my first operation was to thrust my head out of window to see how we were likely to fare as regarded the weather, and the result was encouraging, as, looking up the valley, from which quarter bad weather was to be anticipated, if at all, the sky was clear, and there was nothing to indicate mischief brewing. But, by the time we had finished breakfast, an extraordinary change had occurred. The valley was entirely filled with clouds, which lay so low that the tail of the Bies Glacier was completely hidden, and the general appearance of the weather was as bad as it could possibly

be. Still it was not raining, so at 3.5 a.m. we started, in
rather a melancholy state of mind, and with dire forbodings
of defeat and discomforture. The passage we were about
to attempt had been one of the pet items of my programme
on which I had specially set my heart, and I could not contemplate with equanimity the idea of failure, or having to
abandon so long-cherished a plan. Having crossed the
swollen stream of the Visp by a bridge immediately opposite the village, we found ourselves at the foot of the
long fan-shaped slope of débris which stretches from the
very foot of the Bies Glacier down to the bank of the river,
widening in its downward course until at the bottom its
width is very great. This is all brought down by the torrent,
or rather torrents, from the glacier, which in winter, by this
evidence of their violence, must be furious streams, but in
summer are nothing but tiny rivulets, which meander promiscuously amongst the ruin around, until they lose themselves in the Visp. We were on the wrong side of this slope,
and had to cross it, so as to get on to the left bank of the
torrents, and the piece of walking which was necessary in
order to accomplish this operation reminded me strongly
of Dauphiné in general, and the Vallon des Etançons in
particular. There was a slight sheep-track, but it was
almost lost amongst the chaos of stones, of all shapes and
sizes, through which it led, and over which, in the still uncertain light, it was difficult to pick a way without coming
down on one's nose. I have never in the Swiss Alps seen
such an extent of débris produced from such a cause. Not
an atom of vegetation is visible, every shrub or tree having
been swept away by the ravages of the torrents. These
were easily crossed, and, so soon as we were close under the
cliffs on the left side of the gorge, we turned up towards the
foot of the glacier, which was at a far greater height above
us than would have been supposed from below, keeping
along the base of the cliffs, whose top was marked by a
clump of three solitary trees, which, standing out against
the sky, had a curious effect, as though they had been deserted by their wiser companions, and left there by mistake.

The ascent was very rapid, and the sheep-track was of the vaguest possible character, requiring the use of hands almost as much as feet, and occasionally disappearing altogether for a hundred yards or so. We should, probably, have thought more of the objectionable nature of the way, had we not been absorbed in contemplating the weather, which drove us half mad by the way in which it changed alternately for the better and worse, until our good genius finally prevailed, the clouds became thinner, patches of blue extended themselves over the sky, and, when we at last caught sight of the snowy pyramid of the Weisshorn, curiously foreshortened, rising, apparently, to a height of a very few feet above the top of the ice-fall of the glacier, we dismissed further anxiety on the subject, and went on our way rejoicing in the expectation of a glorious day, which was not destined to be disappointed. Deeper and deeper did we penetrate into the gorge, but, though the climb was cruelly steep, the end of the glacier still kept its distance in front. It was evident from the very first that it would be impossible to get on to the ice at its foot, and that we should have to make more or less of a détour over the slopes on our right in order to circumvent the final fall. Accordingly, when we were about on a level with the lowest point of the extraordinary tongue of ice in which the norther arm of the glacier terminates, we bore away to the right, and, turning again towards the valley, retraced our steps, as it were, for a short distance at a higher level, and thus, describing a gigantic zig-zag, landed at last on a tract of open ground above the cliffs which had seemed so high above Randa, and looking down upon the three weird and solitary trees beneath which we had passed. Just before attaining this spot, we passed the unfortunate sheep who are condemned to pick up a precarious existence on these almost barren slopes, and for whose benefit the path we had followed is maintained. Bad as it is, it is better than none, and we felt duly grateful to the wretched animals, the authors of the convenience. Here, however, it came to an end, but the comparatively easy character of the ground made its absence a matter of indifference, and, turning our backs once more upon the valley, we pursued our course up gentle slopes of broken ground, until at 5.5 we found a tempting spring, which struck us as an eligible position for a short halt to look about.

The most conspicuous feature in the view was the magnificent chain of the Mischabel, which, exactly opposite to us on the other side of the valley of Zermatt, was seen to extraordinary advantage. I have never been quite able to determine which presents the most glorious spectacle,— the Dom and Täschhorn from our present position, or the Weisshorn from an exactly corresponding point on the slopes of the Dom. I am, however, inclined to give the preference to our present view, the number of peaks and glaciers visible being greater than from the opposite slopes, although no summit in elegance of form is comparable to the single peak of the Weisshorn. The resemblance between the Dom and Täschhorn is most remarkable, and even as regards height, any one ignorant of the truth would find it hard to award the crown of supremacy. They are, indeed, worthy rivals, but notwithstanding that the Täschhorn in elevation must yield, though but slightly, to his brother, he can boast of being by far the most difficult of access. We were able to trace very step of the route up the latter, and clearly made out the exact point where we had been obliged to halt on Wednesday. The Kiem, Graben, and Hohberg Glaciers were set before us from end to end, and were very attractive objects all terminating in a most abrupt manner on the brow of steep cliffs. The Hohberg Glacier is much the most dislocated of the three, its final ice-fall being one of the longest and most hopelessly broken I have ever seen. The Nadelhorn, which rises from its right bank to a height of 14,203 feet, is a very fine peak, but less massive than its two neighbours. There is no chance of attacking it with success from the side of Randa, but I believe it has been once ascended from Saas, at which place it was long considered the true Dom. The only glacier of the range that was not well seen was the great Ried Glacier, which, flowing from a great field of névé, between the Balfrin, Ulrichshorn, and Nadelhorn, takes a north-west direction and terminates above St. Nicholas. It was, consequently, masked to a great extent by an intervening spur, but we saw enough to allow us to form some idea of its size and steepness. Not the least interesting part of the view to us was the steep side of the valley below the Graben Glacier, up which I had twice so painfully toiled, and which looked almost perpendicular, causing Gaskell to pour forth heart-felt thanksgivings that he had not been doomed to take part in our futile expedition of Wednesday. It may be as well to observe that the point from which this superb view of one of the loftiest, though generally invisible, Swiss ranges, is to be obtained, is only two hours' distant from Randa, that is to say, is within the compass of an easy afternoon's walk, which would also include a near view of the end of the Bies Glacier, in itself sufficiently curious.

At 5.20 we got on the march again and struck up rather to the right, in order to get round a bold, rocky peak, which, with its buttress, was now between us and the Bies Glacier, and completely hid it from us. The ground was steep but no ways difficult, and we pushed on rapidly, passing many admirable sites for a bivouac, which might be turned to account by any one wishing to attack the Weisshorn from this side, or desiring to get on to the upper plateau of the Bies Glacier at an earlier hour than is possible, starting from Randa. The slopes, at first composed of stones and the usual poor soil, gradually gave place to smooth rock and patches of snow, which increased in extent, until, after resuming our proper direction to the left, we once more entered the basin of the glacier, and at 6.40 got on to the moraine at a point just below the central ice-fall, but high above the end of the glacier. Between the moraine and the cliffs, forming the left side of the basin, was a broad tract of open ground, which must once have been covered by the now shrunken glacier, but in these degenerate days shows nothing but slopes of shale and the débris of avalanches fallen from the cliffs above. At the western end of this dreary expanse a wall of rocks rose abruptly to a sort of shelf, above which a tremendous line of precipices towered, running north and south, and supporting what looked like a wall of snow of considerable height.   This wall of snow we knew to be the edge of the great field of névé which supplies the Bies Glacier, and on to which we were desirous of finding a way; but this way was not visible at first sight, so we took up our position on the moraine to breakfast, and at the same time make a thorough reconnaissance of the ground.   Our desire was, if possible, to ascend by the glacier, so we set about examining what prospect of success there was in that direction.

The field of névé before referred to has only one outlet— towards the east, but even on that side it is almost enclosed by a line of precipices, which, originating on either side from the Brunegghorn and a spur of the Weisshorn, leave only a comparatively narrow opening through which the glacier can find its way to the valley.   Just at the point of greatest compression, the fall in the ground is most rapid, and, as might be expected, the result is a most fearful dislocation in the ice, which continues without interruption, though less marked in some places than in others, until the glacier comes to an end.   We were now looking at the steepest and most shattered part of the fall, which, although narrow as compared with the reservoir from which it springs, is wide enough to present a superb spectacle, as its confused maze of icy cliffs and pinnacles sparkled in the morning sun.   The forcing a passage through this wonderful labyrinth, if practicable at all, would evidently be a work of no small difficulty and danger, and, before deciding on the feasibility of such a course, we turned our attention to the rocks on its left bank, to see what sort of an alternative route they offered.   It is notoriously difficult to form from a distance any reliable opinion of the character of rocks, but of the steepness of the upper line of cliffs at which we were looking there could be no doubt.   It was an absolute wall, seamed here and there with snow couloirs, of whose practicability it was impossible to judge.   The lower tier of rocks, which would have to be scaled in order to reach the foot of the final precipice, was even more unpromising in appearance; for, although the rocks were less steep, they were very smooth, having, probably, at some period or other been covered by the glacier, and would offer serious difficulties before the shelf that stretched from their top to the base of the upper tier could be gained. On the whole, after mature consideration, Almer and Perren decided that, in the first instance, it would be best to attack the glacier, though the latter seemed by no means sanguine of success, either on the ice or the rocks. From our position, we got a most admirable view of the peaks of the Saasgrat, south of the Täschhorn (amongst which our latest conquest, the Rympfischhorn, showed by far the most imposing front, though really slightly inferior in height to the nearer summit of the Alphubel), and also of the whole range of Monte Rosa as far as the Breithorn, in which the Lyskamm was, perhaps, the finest object. What with breakfasting, deciding on our further line of march, and contemplating the view, our halt was rather a prolonged one, and it was not till 7.25 that, having put on the rope, we started, under Perren's lead.

Descending a little, over banks of shale and snow, we skirted the amphitheatre that lay between us and the glacier, and, passing close under the base of the lower rocks, very soon reached the edge of the ice. So far our work had been of the most straightforward and easy character, and our advance had been unopposed, but henceforward, the onset was to be desperate. So far as we could judge, the central portion of the glacier offered the least unpromising line of attack, so we turned in that direction, and forthwith encountered our first obstacle in the shape of a broad steep slope of hard ice, which had to be crossed and could not be circumvented. Perren began cutting steps across, and we were about one-fourth of the way over, when whir-r-r-r-r! down came a stone, about as big as a cocoanut, right in front of us, taking a leap over the top of the slope and then ricochetting away to help to swell the

moraine below. The enemy's batteries had opened on us,
and we paused for a moment to see whether the first shot
was the precursor of a volley, but the supply of ammunition,
fortunately for us, was defective, and we continued our way
unmolested by the larger artillery, though raked by a constant and irritating musketry-fire of small stones, which
came down at the rate of nineteen to the dozen. It was
decidedly not a place to linger in longer than was necessary,
so Perren contented himself with merely chipping notches
in the ice sufficient to give foothold, at the longest possible
intervals, by help of which we quickly made our way on to
the glacier proper, and turned upwards. We were out of
danger from the stones, which we now with equanimity saw
shooting down the slope on our right, but the walking in
which we were engaged was by no means easy. The glacier
was so steep that every step had to be cut, and was, moreover, at regular intervals, intersected by broad crevasses,
running transverse to our course. We were not ascending
an ice-fall, in the general acceptation of the term, but a slope,
whose continuity was broken by a series of chasms, ranged
in parallel lines one above the other. These were all, without exception, choked with snow, and so offered no serious
impediment to our progress, only ordinary care being required to pass them, but in a less favourable season the
state of affairs might be very different. The great ice-fall
was on our left, and we must soon take to it; but, as we
contemplated its steepness and dislocation, the length of
time which, judging from our present rate of progress over
much less difficult ground, its ascent would require, and the
risk from avalanches, to which during the greater portion
of the way we should be exposed, we became momentarily
more doubtful of the wisdom of adhering to our original
plan. Almer, after anxiously scanning the icy battlements
above us, suggested at last that the ascent of the glacier
might take too much time, and that, perhaps, we had better
try and find a way up the rocks, which were now on our
right, but separated from us by the upper portion of the
ice-slope which we had traversed lower down.

However void of results in other respects, by our manœuvre we had turned and got above the lower rocks, and were on a level with the sort of shelf at the foot of the final line of cliffs, which did not look more accessible than they had from below. Still we determined to take to them, but, in order to get at their base, had to cross the slope before mentioned, an operation which would evidently involve for a short time an amount of risk far greater than any to be encountered if we adhered to the glacier. This slope, we now saw, took its origin at the foot of a tolerably lofty spur of rocks, projecting from the main line of crags, supporting a shelf of glacier, fearfully broken, terminating in tremendous ice-cliffs. It was clear that these masses of ice must periodically be forced over the edge of the rocks and swept down the slope, which probably owes its origin and nourishment to such falls, and from the threatening position of some of the pinnacles of ice, it seemed probable that an avalanche on a grand scale might come down at any moment and carry everything away before it. The danger was of the character which a guide most strongly objects to incur, as his skill and courage can avail nothing in the event of a fall really occurring; but in the present case the risk must be run, or we must abandon the expedition. Between such alternatives there was no hesitation, so we turned off to the right, and commenced passing the slope, on which débris was lying pretty thickly. We almost ran across, in spite of the insecurity of the footing, and thought the rocks on the other side never would be reached. In point of fact, however, the passage, long as it seemed, did not occupy more than ten minutes, but they were ten of the most exciting minutes I ever passed, and I must confess to an unbounded feeling of relief, when at 8.20 we got on to the rocks, and, being then in safety, halted to take breath after our effort. We had scarcely been half a minute on the rocks, and were still panting with our exertions, when our attention was drawn to a cracking noise in the broken glacier beneath which we had passed, which seemed to indicate that something remarkable was about to happen.

We had hardly time to look up, when an enormous tower of ice, the dimensions of which I cannot estimate, became loosened from the contiguous mass, tottered for a moment on the brow of the precipice, and then, heeling over slowly and reluctantly, dashed with a thundering crash on to the slope below, and rolled, in a thousand pieces of various sizes, right across our late path. Before we had time to recover from the astonishment caused by this sight, a second and even larger mass burst the bonds which restrained it, and, following its predecessor, swept down with a resistless violence which nothing could have withstood. We were standing at a distance of about two hundred yards from the base of the precipice, which was, perhaps, five hundred feet in height, over which the fall occurred, and I don't suppose it ever before fell to the lot of any one to witness two avalanches on such a scale in such proximity. It was simply the most wonderful sight of the kind I have ever seen in the Alps, and impressed us the more at the time, as we reflected that we had escaped "by the skin of our teeth" from a still nearer acquaintance, which would scarcely have been so agreeable. As regarded the success of our expedition, it was fortunate that the falls occurred after and not before we had crossed the slope, as, in the latter case, I feel sure that neither of the guides would have allowed us to risk the passage.

After a halt of five minutes, we started up the rocks, which were at first very shaly, so that we went up two feet and down one at every step, but this formation did not last long, and we were soon at the foot of the great wall supporting the upper névé of the Bies Glacier, which is named on the Federal map "Freiwänge." The look of this tremendous barrier was most formidable, but well away to the right was a couloir, which appeared to offer a more or less difficult route to the top. To get at this, however, a considerable détour would be necessary, which we did not fancy, and, moreover, we had an idea that the Frenchmen must have descended somewhere in that direction, and had no desire to follow in their steps. Almer, after taking a good

look at the rocks, expressed his opinion that we could get
straight up, keeping tolerably near to the side of the glacier,
and, as that was undoubtedly the most direct course, we determined on it, and committed ourselves to his able guidance.
Above the bank of shale a steep slope of soft snow abutted
against the face of the cliffs, and offered a means of reaching what appeared to be their most accessible point.   Up
this we zig-zagged, but, on gaining the top, found that the
warmth of the rock had caused the snow to melt, leaving a
narrow and treacherous edge, separated from the crags by
a profound chasm.   This, though rather broad, would have
been easily crossed, had the snow on our side not been so
insecure, threatening to fall away under our weight, and
had the rocks beyond been better; but they were steep and
smooth, and made more slippery by a small fall of water
which inconsiderately chose this as its line of descent.
How Almer contrived, unaided, to get across, I know not,
but he did manage, and, scrambling up a few feet, established himself securely, and pulled us over one after the
other.   Thenceforward we were fairly committed to the
climb, which speedily resolved itself into one of the most
thoroughly break-neck pieces of scrambling I ever took, surpassing in difficulty even the well-remembered rocks of the
Pic des Ecrins.   It soon became evident that our rope was
much too short, so we effected a junction between mine,
which was 100 feet long, and Morshead's, which was 70 feet,
and brought the whole into play, Almer going a-head with
a space of 50 feet between him and myself, while Morshead,
Perren, and Gaskell followed, at intervals of about 40 feet.
We were not ascending a couloir, but mounting along an
exceedingly narrow and broken ledge on the face of the
precipice, which occasionally died away altogether, leaving
us to find a way up the smooth wall as best we could.
While Almer climbed we remained steady, until he found
a position where he could make himself "fest," and help
me up by the rope.   This rarely happened until he had
gone the full length of his tether, and the rope was so
taut that necessity compelled him to hold on by his eye-

R

lids, while I advanced a few steps. The same game went on below; while Almer was climbing and I was steady, Morshead scrambled up towards me, Perren holding hard, and a similar manœuvre was carried out by the latter and Gaskell. Perren has the reputation of being a courageous man, but on the present occasion he was undeniably nervous, and was unable to render much assistance to Gaskell, his reply, when appealed to now and then to advance or retreat a few steps, as the case might be, being, " Monsieur! je ne puis pas, je suis dans un mauvais endroit," an undoubted fact, but one which was equally true of the rest of the party. However, Gaskell fortunately got on very well, and, indeed, we were all compelled to rely almost exclusively upon ourselves individually, the rope round our waists, though it was doubtless a security, giving us but little real assistance, every man's hands being so engaged in holding on, that they had little leisure to lend a friendly pull at the connecting cord.

We were for the most part quite invisible one to the other; Morshead could not see me, and from the time we began to climb in earnest, until we reached the top of the rocks, I scarcely caught a glimpse of Almer, a state of things which added materially to our difficulties, as, except verbally, it was impossible for him to give us any directions as to the exact track we were to follow. The slowness of his progress, however, from point to point, prepared us for the difficulties we in turn had to overcome, and the emphatic "Nein! nein!!" with which he generally responded to my occasional enquiries as to whether I should advance before all his rope was paid out, sufficiently betokened the insecurity of his position. It generally happened that we were detained longest at the most awkward points. Once especially, I was kept a long time in a most objectionable position, hanging on till my arms ached, with my legs wide apart, while a small stream of snow-water was flowing over me, and finally wetted me to the skin. During the whole time we gradually bore to the left, that is to say, towards the glacier from which, though we could not see it, we were never very far distant, and we had the satisfaction of hearing our friends, the avalanches, tumbling away in grand style. I shall make no attempt to describe particular difficult points, the probable nature of which can be easily guessed by any one who has climbed, or even seen, a really steep wall of rocks; suffice it to say that I never was on a place where the climbing was so continuously bad, and where the level bits on which we could conveniently "rest and be thankful" were so few. But, in spite of the arduous nature of the ascent, we thoroughly enjoyed it. The very magnitude of the difficulties to be overcome had an exhilarating effect, and, as we were all in peculiarly good trim, we went at our work, confident in our ability to bring it to a successful conclusion. At length, a howl from Almer indicated that he was near the top, and immediately his voice was heard confirming the fact, and urging us to come on as fast as we liked, as he was in a secure position, and able to hold us all up if necessary. He forthwith began pulling at the rope with such vigour that I had to moderate his ardour, as I painfully worked my way to where I supposed him to be. As usual, the last steps were peculiarly bad; but, after rounding a specially unpleasant corner, which would have been convenient for a person of suicidal disposition, I came upon our gallant leader's outstretched hand, its owner being comfortably moored in a narrow cleft, from which I really think "all the king's horses and all the king's men" could not have drawn him against his will. In order to facilitate the ascent of the others, I passed behind him and cast off the rope, scrambling up the few remaining feet of rock, kicked steps in the short steep bank of snow above, and found myself standing at the edge of an almost level, spotless field of névé, the upper plateau of the Bies Glacier, on which, at 10.30, we were all assembled.

We had fulfilled our threat of keeping a direct course, as we had landed close to the southern extremity of the Freiwänge, to the end of which ran Almer to reconnoitre the glacier that we had circumvented. He was of opinion that we could have mounted by the ice, and, I rather gathered from his tone, with less actual difficulty than by the route we had followed.* I think that it would be almost impossible to *descend* by the way we had mounted; certainly the idea would never occur to any one looking from above, as I never saw a more frightful-looking place, the ledges along which we had climbed being quite undistinguishable, and a smooth wall of rock appearing to sink to an untold depth. I may mention here, that we met Franz Andermatten subsequently at Zermatt, and that he would not believe it possible for us to have scaled the cliffs at the point we did, and at the same time told us that he had passed much further north, nearer the Brunegghorn. The Col was still invisible, hidden by a low spur from the last-named peak, but we knew that our difficulties were over, and, gathering up our rope, started across the plateau, the snow on which, in spite of the blazing sun, was in good order, rounded the aforesaid spur, and instantly came in sight of our goal to the right of us. Only a few gentle slopes intervened between us and it, which were quickly traversed, a small patch of shaly rocks was scaled, and at 10.55 a.m. we gained the Col of the Biesjoch, and looked down upon the head of the great Turtman Glacier, which was separated from us by a short, but very steep, ice-wall.

The view from the Col was scarcely so extensive as we had expected from its height of 11,645 feet, the most interesting part of the Oberland being largely shut out by the group of which the Ausser Barrhorn is the highest point, while, in the opposite direction, everything west of the Breithorn was concealed by the great mass of the Weisshorn. The latter mountain, however, was a most superb object, seen in close proximity, on the other side

---

* In 1866, Mr. Walker's party crossed the Biesjoch and reached the Col entirely by the glacier, without any difficulty, or even the necessity of being roped together. But this must be considered an exceptional piece of good fortune, to be imputed to the incessant bad weather of that season, and consequent mass of snow.

of the broad "cirque" of névé, at whose northern edge we
were standing. We were in the most favourable position
for examining the whole length of the eastern arête, by
which the ascent has always been made, but the slopes
below it presented a marked contrast to the appearance
they offer on the side of the Schallenberg Glacier. On
that side they are cut away in formidable precipices of
bare rock, but towards the Bies Glacier not a rock is visible,
slopes covered with névé, of great length and steepness,
stretching uninterruptedly from the crest of the ridge
down to the glacier. Almer declared that it would be
possible to go straight up the side of the mountain by
these slopes, and hit the arête at a point close to the
summit, and we agreed with him, but in some places there
would be risk from avalanches, where the slope is broken
into séracs, and the difficulty of reaching the upper plateau
of the Bies Glacier will always be a great impediment to
the adoption of this route. As, however, it would only be
practicable in a *very* snowy year, such as 1864, when the
ordinary route from the Schallenberg Glacier is impassable,
the rocks being more or less covered with snow, it would,
in such a season, be worth any one's while to pass the
night in some of the eligible holes, which are to be found
about two hours up from Randa, and make the attempt
from this side, descending to the Turtman Thal. The
northern arête, that falls towards the peak, marked in the
Federal map 4161 mètres, or 13,653 feet, looked most unpromising, nor do I think the cliffs that fall from it to the
glacier could be scaled at any point; were it possible to
do so, a grand pass would be made to Zinal, as the ridge
was gained by William Mathews from that place in 1859
without the slightest difficulty by the upper Turtman
Glacier. The 4161 mètres' peak itself is a very fine snow
summit which might be reached from our Col without
much actual difficulty, but the ascent might be long and
laborious, as the snow slopes and final arête are steep, and
might require a good deal of step-cutting. The view of the
Mischabelhörner and Saasgrat was even more glorious than

from below, and the chain of Monte Rosa as far as the Breithorn was also well seen, but the nearer portion of the view was undoubtedly the most interesting.

We took up our position on the rocks just below the Col, on the south side, and for some time devoted our attention to luncheon, but at 11.20 Almer and Perren started off to cut the steps down the wall leading to the Turtman Glacier, leaving us to take our ease during the operation. The sky was cloudless, and the heat intense, far more so than I ever remember to have felt it at so great an elevation, and we soon became rather torpid. Indeed, from the suspicious eagerness with which every one subsequently accused every one else of having been asleep and snored, I am afraid there is little doubt but that we all took, at least, our forty winks. The men did not return till 12.45, having found the ice bare of snow and very hard, obliging the steps to be made very good and large. They swallowed some wine, and then, at 12.55 p.m., we left our perch, after a halt, so far as we three were concerned, of two hours.

Immediately below the Col it was quite impossible to get down, as the ice fell perpendicularly in a sheer wall, and was cut off from the névé below by a great bergschrund, so we had to bear to the left, along the face of the slope forming the base of the nameless peak 4161 mètres. I have never seen harder ice, and I could quite understand the amount of time which the cutting of the ninety steps we had to traverse had taken. I thought that they had been made almost unnecessarily large, but, if so, it was an error on the right side, and, therefore, not to be complained of. When we were at last able to turn downwards, although the slope was exceedingly steep, we soon found sufficient snow to give footing, and, working cautiously down it, we reached the bottom, passed the bergschrund, which was choked, without difficulty, and were then on the upper névé of the eastern arm of the Turtman Glacier. On our left was a long spur coming down from peak 4161 mètres, and on our right the glacier ran up into a broad bay, at the head of which was an undeniable Col, over which we felt sure that there must be a passage (since effected by Messrs. Hornby and Philpott) to Randa or St. Nicholas, descending by the Abberg Glacier, which may be a shorter route than the Biesjoch, but can scarcely be so exciting or interesting. In front of us the glacier stretched away in superb fields of névé, almost level, and perfectly free from crevasses, over which our progress was easy and rapid, the snow being in much better order than we had any right to expect at such an hour on such a day. We kept, generally, near the right bank, although in all directions the glacier appeared to be equally free from difficulty, and our way was perfectly devoid of incident and rather uninteresting, until we approached the end of the long spur before mentioned, and began to get a view up the western arm of the glacier between it and the Diablons. I had expected to see slopes of névé steeper, but similar in character to those which we were traversing, and was immensely astonished to discover instead a tremendous ice-fall, stretching completely across from the dividing ridge to the Diablons. We had always understood that there was an easy pass to Zinal in this direction, and this formidable barrier was, therefore, totally unexpected. It seemed to us, indeed, very doubtful whether a pass could be made at all, as Almer could discover no way of circumventing the ice-fall, which is very lofty, steep, and broken. The odd part of the whole thing is, that, subsequently, Mr. Hornby's party, mounting from Zinal, *did* pass from the western to the eastern arm of the glacier without the least trouble, without cutting a step, without even seeing much of an ice-fall at all, and in a very short space of time, having accomplished the distance between the Col, situated at the point above Zinal, marked 3252 mètres on the map, and the head of the Abberg Glacier, in not much more than two hours. It is certain, to my mind, that the Federal map is not perfectly accurate in its delineation of the head of the Turtman Glacier, and especially of the ridge between the two branches of the glacier, which, in my opinion, as also in that of Mr. Hornby, is made considerably too long. The Diablons looked particularly well and very steep, but it is a regular impostor, being accessible, with great ease, from Zinal, at which place it holds a position corresponding to that of the Mettelhorn at Zermatt. We were particularly struck with the colour of the rocks on the right bank of the glacier close to which we were. They were almost white, and I have always regretted that I did not secure a piece of the stone for more learned persons than myself to examine.

The snow at last became rather slushy, so that it was a relief when we passed on to the bare ice of the glacier proper, below the névé, over which we were able to put on a spurt, Almer capering away in rare style. At 2.10 we came to a point where the glacier curled over rather steeply, and produced, in consequence, a mild ice-fall, through which we might have descended without much trouble, but the "gazon" on the right looked tempting, so we made for it. We had to cross the lateral moraine, which, owing to the nature of the rocks above referred to, was the cleanest I ever saw, and presented a marked contrast to the great medial moraine, which takes its origin in the ridge dividing the glacier, and is an uncommonly dirty gentleman. The appearance of the western or Diablons' branch below the great ice-fall was most remarkable. It seemed extraordinarily smooth and uncrevassed, and arranged in most curious folds, looking like a cigar split in half, and placed with the convex side uppermost, the comparison, of course, not holding good as regards colour. The moraine, just above the point where we were, was in a most excited state, and sent down showers of stones to the lower level, so that we scrambled across as quickly as possible, and were not sorry to find ourselves again on firm ground, where we halted for ten minutes to take off the rope. We feared, at first, that we had, after all, made a mistake in quitting the glacier, as below where we were standing there was an abrupt fall in the ground; but we soon discovered a rather steep, but practicable, gully between the moraine and the cliffs, which took us, without any difficulty, to the comparatively smooth ground below. The glacier below the fall looked so level and easy, that it was irresistibly tempting; so, instead of keeping along the grass-slopes, which would have given rather rough walking, we turned down them, and at 2.40 again got on to the ice. Nothing could have been easier than our route, until we neared the end of the glacier, when it began to be rather cut up by crevasses; so, after picking our way amongst them for a short distance, we gave it up, and, making for the right bank, got on to the "gazon" once more, at 3.10.

A very faint track soon presented itself, along which we hurried, until we had fairly left the glacier behind us, which at its termination is completely covered from one side to the other with moraine, and found ourselves at the head of the Turtman Thal. The track very soon died away, leaving us in doubt which side of the torrent we ought to keep to, but, as we knew that the Graben Alp, whither we were bound, was on the right bank, and I was under the impression that, when I had ascended the valley in 1861, I had throughout kept to that bank, we determined to adopt the same course now. At 3.30 we came to the first spring, and, as we had not tasted a drop of water for more than ten hours, a short halt to indulge was, of course, unavoidable. The tap was delicious, but at 3.45 we tore ourselves away, and resumed our old direction. We were getting more and more uncertain as to our proper course, when the question was suddenly settled by our coming to the brow of a cliff, which entirely prevented further progress along the right bank. Accordingly, we retraced our steps a little, and then, striking down to the side of the stream, found an opportune bridge, which took us across to the left bank, close to a group of châlets, still unoccupied. Our troubles, such as they were, were now over, and we had a most delightful walk down the valley, which, though the least visited, is, I think, in itself the most charming of all the great southern tributaries of the Valais, and totally different in character from its two neighbours of St. Nicholas and Anniviers. Though the general scenery is more savage, yet the Alps are greener and more extensive, and the forests, notwithstanding that sad inroads have been made upon them, still clothe the sides of the valley with a dense belt of vegetation, but the comparative inferiority of the glacier scenery at its head, although the Turtman Glacier is one of the largest in the Alps, will sufficiently account for the paucity of visitors, few of whom care really to explore the numerous fine points of view within easy reach of Graben. After a pleasant ramble over extensive pastures, we again crossed to the right bank of the stream, and, at 4.30, came to the châlets of Blummatt, where we found the cows, and got some milk, the consumption of which occupied till 4.45. The path onwards was rather vague, but, such as it was, we pushed on rapidly over it, and at 5.15 p.m. reached our haven, the little Hotel du Weisshorn, on the Graben Alp, the passage from Randa having occupied fourteen hours and a quarter, but only eleven hours and a half actual walking, so that we had "wiped the eyes" of the Frenchmen considerably.

The position of the inn is most charming,—on a verdant Alp, on which a large number of cows were grazing, at an elevation of more than 6000 feet. Though not very large, it is very comfortable, the bedrooms being models of cleanliness, and the "cuisine" would shame many more pretentious establishments. We had the place to ourselves, and, I suppose, in consequence of no one having been expected, it was some time before our dinner was ready; but, when it did finally appear, it turned out most excellent, and we did full justice to its merits. The evening was lovely, the sky being absolutely cloudless, but after the sun was down we soon retired, as our day's work had been sufficiently long and fatiguing, and the idea of bed was pleasant to us all.

Saturday, 16th July.—At 4.0 a.m. we tore ourselves from our couches and prepared for the labours of the day, Morshead and Gaskell being bound down the valley to Turtman, en route to Vevey and Chamouni, while I had to find my way over to the Val d'Anniviers and Zinal. Of course, I ought to have gone up and explored the western arm of the glacier, and tried to make a pass over it, but, truth to tell, I was lazy, and more inclined, for once in a way, to tread the footpaths of civilization, than to make a path for myself, so I determined that Almer and myself would go over the Pas de Bœuf, and, if we felt so disposed when the time came, wander up the Bella Tola en route. Breakfast was as creditable a meal as last night's dinner had been, but was soon finished, and, at 5.30 a.m., after bidding farewell to Morshead and Gaskell, with mutual regrets that our pleasant week's ramble could not be prolonged, Almer and I started on our solitary way.

The former had obtained information as to our route from some of the herdsmen, but, as the event proved, it wanted the essential element of correctness, and, as we had unfortunately no map to verify it, might have been dispensed with to advantage. Crossing the stream immediately opposite the inn, we forthwith entered the forest on the opposite side of the valley, which we found full of cows, on their way up to the higher pastures. There could not have been less than two hundred animals, magnificent beasts, and the sight was most picturesque, but, as they occupied the path to our exclusion, we were glad to part company, so put on a spurt until we had passed ahead of them. The path through the wood, though steep, was good and pleasant to traverse, and we were almost sorry when we finally emerged from amongst the trees on to the open pastures above, on which are situated the châlets of Z'Meiden, whither our horned friends and their keepers were bound. We had already risen to a considerable height above the valley, and overcome the steepest part of the ascent, the Col being in full view at the head of a dreary glen, which stretched away in front for a long distance. Looking back across the valley, we commanded a view of several precisely similar glens, leading up to depressions in the ridge, over one of which goes the pass of the Jungjoch to St. Nicholas. To our right the eastern arm of the Turtman Glacier could be traced from the Bies pass at its head to the moraine at its foot, while away to our left, but much more distant, on the further side of the valley of the Rhone, the noble peak of the Bietschhorn, the guardian of the Lötschen Thal, was seen to singular advantage, and to the west of it the remarkable level field of névé, which covers the ridge of the Petersgrat. The glen along which lay our route was not remarkable, but was dominated on the left by a curious detached rocky peak, which, though of no great elevation, looked so utterly inaccessible, that we were astonished to discover a stone man, evidently raised by hands, on the top of it. Indeed, the number of these isolated pinnacles is one of the great features of the scenery of the country between the Turtman Thal and the Val d'Anniviers. They are almost without exception crowned with cairns, probably erected by the herdsmen in the châlets on either side in their idle hours, as no traveller would take the trouble to scramble up them. We kept generally towards the left side of the glen, following a path which, though vague in places, was always easily distinguishable, and whose direction was pointed out by a line of stonemen, placed on the several eminences which were passed in succession. At 7.15 we came upon a rather extensive lake, which, in spite of the tolerably advanced period of the season, was filled with masses of snow and ice floating about, and was a very picturesque object. Thenceforward our way lay over gentle slopes of shale, varied by large patches of snow, until we reached the foot of the last ridge. This was bare of snow, and the path was carried up it in a succession of long, well-defined zigzags, which brought us to the Col at 7.40, or in little more than two hours from Graben.

Supposing that we were on the Pas de Bœuf, we expected to see the Bella Tola immediately above us to the north, but our astonishment was great when we discovered it, in the expected direction certainly, but so very distant that it was plain we had made a mistake. In point of fact, we had come to the Z'Meiden Pass instead of the Pas de Bœuf, which is the next depression in the ridge to the north of the one we were standing in, and separated from it by several rocky peaks. To get at the Bella Tola from our position, we should have to make a long détour over the shoulders of divers hillocks and dreary slopes of shale, an amusement for which we had no particular fancy, so we resolved to abandon the idea. Still, though the view from the Col was very good, I was anxious to see something more, especially towards the Oberland, so I suggested to Almer that we should try and get to the top of the nearest of the before-mentioned rocky peaks to the north of us. He thought the idea a good one, so at 8.0 we turned along the ridge towards it. The ridge was wonderfully shattered, and covered with loose blocks of stone, which a very slight touch sufficed to set in motion, but there was not the slightest difficulty in passing along it, and, skirting an outlying point, which appeared in a most fragile state and likely very soon to contribute its quotum to the sea of ruin on either side, we soon stood at the foot of our peak. This appeared so very steep, that we began to think we had reckoned without our host, and should not get up after all, so Almer went a-head to reconnoitre. He did succeed, with some difficulty, in scrambling up the worst bit, and, having effected a lodgment, called upon me to follow. When I got to the foot of the cheminée, he threw down the rope, and with its help I was soon by his side. The climb which ensued was rather stiff, but it was not long, and at 8.30 we were comfortably seated on the summit, which must be about 500 feet higher than the Col, of whose elevation I am ignorant.

As we had expected, there were loftier points to the north of us, but we had attained our object, and opened out a view in every direction of great extent and interest, though, of course, inferior to what is to be had from the Bella Tola. The sky was perfectly clear in every quarter, except towards the Oberland, where ominously heavy banks of clouds concealed a good deal of what would have otherwise been visible; but we were vouchsafed a clear view of what I was most anxious to see, the peaks and glaciers at the head of the Lötschen Thal. Our attention was princi-

pally directed to the well-marked depression between the
Tschingelhorn and the Lauterbrunnen Briethorn, to which
the name Wetter-lücke is given in the Federal map, and
through which, it is alleged, a pass led in former days, by
a very direct route, from the Lötschen Thal to Lauterbrunnen, but it has long been considered impracticable. As
we hoped to make an attempt upon this deserted route, we
carefully examined the glacier on the south side, and saw,
as we had expected, that there would, at least, be no serious
difficulty in reaching the Col from that side. Our programme also included a possible attack on the still unas-
cended Breithorn, en route, but what we could see of the
arête, running down to the Col, was not encouraging, as it
appeared to be long, steep, and, worst of all, very serrated.
In other directions the view was still more interesting.
Looking over the range on the other side of the Turtman
Thal, the superb mass of the Fletschhorn, above the
valley of Saas, was very striking, while, nearer at hand,
the towering forms of the Dom and Taschhorn were even
more imposing. At the head of the Turtman Thal, the
great glacier was exposed to us in its whole length. The
Biesjoch was, of course, conspicuous, and through my glass
we could plainly distinguish our steps on the ice-wall below
the Col, and on the lower part of the glacier where the snow
had been soft. We looked straight up the ice-fall of the
western branch underneath the Diablons, but could not see
so much of the field of névé which supplies it as we could
have wished, it being enclosed to a great extent by several
ridges radiating from the Weisshorn. Still we saw enough
to confirm me in my opinion that the map, in this part of
the chain, is not strictly accurate, the ice-fall especially
being laid down on far too minute a scale. The peak
4161 mètres is a fine double-headed summit, but is reduced
to comparative insignificance by the proximity of its mighty
neighbour, the Weisshorn, of whose superb appearance I
can give not the faintest idea; but, had we seen nothing else,
the view of this glorious peak would alone have repaid us
for our climb. To the right of it was the Rothhorn, which,

though less massive, and a thousand feet lower, is an even more wonderful object, owing to the startling abruptness with which its final pinnacle shoots into the air. I never saw anything so sharp or so utterly inaccessible in appearance, and the result of a careful inspection on the part of Almer and myself was, that we determined, unless from the Arpitetta Alp, or en route for Zermatt, we should discover a probable way up, not to have anything to say to it, and, anyhow, not to waste time in attempts from the Zermatt side, which we felt sure must be futile. It was not without a pang that we looked at the noble form of the Dent Blanche and the sharp peak of the Cornier, but our equanimity was restored as our eyes wandered to the snow-point of the Steinbock and the great billowy fields of névé at the head of the Moiry Glacier, and we thought of the unparalleled view with which we had been blessed from those heights. Amongst the confused group of mountains, occupying the district between the head of the western arm of the Val d'Erin and the Val de Bagnes, the long ridge, whose highest points at either end are the Mont Blanc du Cheillon and the Ruinette, was very well seen, and suggested the thought that neither of those summits, though in the heart of a most interesting district, have yet been scaled.* The valley of the Rhone could be traced nearly throughout its entire length, from the glacier at its head to the town of Martigny, and is certainly a pleasant object to look down upon, though not agreeable to traverse.

Having built a cairn upon our peak, which Almer facetiously observed ought to be christened under the decidedly euphonious title of "Moore Spitze" (an honour which I respectfully declined), we took our departure at 9.0, after half-an-hour of unmitigated enjoyment. The first part of the way down required care, but the steepest bit was soon left behind, and we quickly reached the base of the dilapidated outlying peak, having passed which, we struck down the side of the ridge on our right, and, descending

---

* The Ruinette was ascended by Mr. Whymper in 1865.

without difficulty, by 9.35 were fairly in the lateral glen,
whose waters drain down past St. Luc to the Navisanche
in the Val d'Anniviers.   Looking back from here, the
appearance of the ridge we had just passed was very
remarkable.   It is broken in the most wonderful way
by a succession of natural stonemen, and sharp teeth
of rock of the most fantastic forms, especially along that
portion south of the Z'Meiden Pass.   In fact, the whole
thing is gradually crumbling away, and, I suppose, every
year sees some change in the form of the ridge and its
excrescences.   It is not unreasonable to suppose that the
numerous isolated towers of rock, which are curious features
in the scenery, owe their origin to the slow progress of destruction which has been going on for years, and will, in
time, bring them, also, level with the ground.   We at first
followed a faint track over the usual shaly ground, but, as
that bore gradually to the right, in the direction of St. Luc,
which was out of our way, we very soon abandoned it, and
struck away to the left, a line of march which shortly brought
us to some châlets and a herdsman.   Our hopes of milk
were disappointed, the cows, as usual, being ill, but, in
default, we got information as to the shortest way to Zinal,
which was, perhaps, more valuable.   In accordance with
the directions received, we descended rapidly over good
pastures, always working to the left, until, after crossing a
small stream, close to quite a village of châlets, we found
ourselves at the entrance of a broad lateral glen, which
opens out between the Tounot and a spur from the Roc de
Budri, to the north of the Pas de Forcletta.   We might
have ascended this, and, crossing the low ridge at its head,
fallen into the track from the Forcletta, and so reached
Zinal, but, although a shorter route in point of distance
than the one we actually followed, it would, probably, have
required as much, if not more time, owing to the rougher
character of the ground.

As it was, we crossed the mouth of this glen, and immediately hit upon a good path, carried high up along the
side of the hill, between it and the main Val d'Anniviers,

at 10.35. The views of the valley below, and of the little village of St. Luc on the opposite side of the glen which we had descended, were charming, and we wandered on leisurely in a high state of satisfaction. Our path wound round the hill-side, until we were fairly in the Val d'Anniviers, and looked down from a great height upon the main track below, and the dark clusters of densely-packed houses that marked the several hamlets through which it passes on its way to Zinal. The day was now exceedingly hot, so that the shelter of the woods was very pleasant, and we loitered along, looking for no difficulty, and expecting shortly to descend upon Ayer. Suddenly our path, after passing a group of châlets and a crucifix, came to an abrupt and unlooked-for termination, leaving us in a state of uncertainty what course to pursue. By striking straight down we might, of course, sooner or later fall into the main path, but the side of the valley was steep, and the path a long way below, so Almer was against this plan, and recommended in preference that we should keep along the slopes at our present level, unless forced down by the lay of the land, in hopes of eventually stumbling upon another track leading in the direction of Ayer. The adoption of this course involved a horribly rough piece of walking, over steep grass slopes and through the thin woods with which the side of the hill was here clothed; this, disagreeable at any time, was specially so in the condition of my boots, which, I feared, would hardly hold out till I got to Zermatt. However, after a long "hiatus," we did, as Almer had expected, fall into a rough track, which finally resolved itself into a good path, and led us down, by a rapid descent through splendid woods, to the large village of Ayer, the first in the eastern arm of the valley.

Expecting to descend from the Bella Tolla to St. Luc, where there is a good inn, we had rather foolishly not supplied ourselves with provisions, and were, in consequence, now, at 12.20 p.m., perfectly ravenous. Ayer at first sight appeared deserted, but we at last discovered a native who showed us the house of one Monsieur Epinay, where we were told we could get something to eat. Monsieur Epinay was represented by a corpulent old lady, who, after some delay, evidently to make the place presentable, ushered us into a large room, which must have been shut up for years. Bread, butter, cheese, and some tolerable red wine, were the sole resources of the establishment, but we were not inclined to be dainty, and made a hearty meal on the materials at our disposal. Then, having presented the venerable female in possession with a sum which drew down blessings innumerable on my head, at 1.0 we went on our way, with the vacuum in our interiors considerably reduced. The walk onwards up the valley was very pleasant, the scenery becoming more wild and savage at every step, and the path not being at all steep. Nevertheless, we were neither of us sorry when at 2.20 p.m. we reached the scattered châlets constituting the village of Zinal, and the little "Restaurant des Alpes," which is the title borne by the particular house which has been fitted up as an inn. Winkworth, to my surprise, had not arrived, so, after a party of Germans had taken their departure, I had the place to myself, which, considering its size, was an advantage. Though even more unpretentious than the inn at Gruben, it is as scrupulously clean, and the "cuisine" is even better, if I may judge from the dinner with which I was served in the evening, the discussion of which, and a subsequent stroll a little way up the valley, sent me to bed at an early hour, in a state of great internal satisfaction.

Sunday, 17th July.—I was awoke in the night by a violent storm of thunder, lightning, rain, and wind, so that it was an agreeable surprise, when I finally roused up at about 8.0 a.m. to find a fine bright day and an almost cloudless sky. There were no signs of Winkworth, and I found time hang rather heavily on my hands, but a catechism of French history, which was the only book in the place, afforded me some amusement. I learnt from it some curious facts of which I had previously been ignorant, amongst other things that, at the battle of Talavera, during the Peninsular War, an army of English and Spaniards, 90,000 strong, had been totally defeated by 26,000 Frenchmen. Although Zinal is the point of departure for some of the grandest excursions in the Alps, there is not much to be seen from the place itself, the lower portion of the glacier, which is in comparative proximity, being so covered with moraine that it is scarcely distinguishable from the slopes on either side. The most prominent peaks visible are the Diablons, immediately opposite the inn, and Lo Besso above the right bank of the glacier. The latter is a remarkable object, a fine obelisk of black rock with a double summit. The highest, or northern, point, which rises to a height of 12,057 feet, has never been scaled, but the southern and contiguous point, which is only sixteen feet lower, has been reached by some hunters from Zinal, who have raised a cross upon it, which, with a glass, can be clearly seen from the valley.

Of the difficulties likely to be encountered in the attempt to reach some point on the long ridge connecting the Weisshorn and Rothhorn, I could get no reliable information from the natives. The general impression appeared to be that it was not possible to get up, but as no one, apparently, had ever tried so to do, public opinion was not worth much. Mr. Ball, in 1859, first suggested the possibility of effecting a passage between Zinal and Zermatt in this direction, but no one took up the idea, and so, while passes of every variety of difficulty and degree of uselessness were being made in other parts of the Alps, the ridge at the head of the Moming Glacier remained unscaled and unattempted.

The reputation of utter inaccessibility attaching to this portion of the chain may account for this neglect, added to the fact that it was scarcely probable that any route would be found either shorter or grander than the two established passes of the Triftjoch and the Col Durand. I had mentioned my project to Melchior at Zermatt, but had not received much encouragement from him. On the contrary, he expressed himself in the strongest terms against the plan, assuring me that he had carefully examined the place, and that we might take his word for it, it was not possible to get up,—we might risk our lives, but we should never be able to cross any point of the ridge between the Rothhorn and Weisshorn. I was, therefore, by no means sanguine of success, but consoled myself with the reflection that even the best guide is liable to be deceived in the nature of a place which he has not actually tried. Shortly after noon Whymper and Croz arrived, and their appearance was the more welcome from being rather unexpected, as, although I had asked Whymper to join me on the contemplated expedition, it had been doubtful whether he would be able to "come to time." He brought news which sufficiently accounted for Winkworth's absence, viz., that he was ill at Zermatt—a most unfortunate contre-temps, as I knew how anxious he had been to make the proposed passage. On looking at my boots, I was horrified to find only one nail in one and three or four in the other, and inquiry elicited the alarming fact that there were none suitable for the purpose to be had in Zinal. It was really a serious matter, as we might come to places where the safety of the whole party might depend upon the sureness of foot of each individual member of it. Almer, however, made vigorous search, and succeeded in finding enough to raise the number in each boot to six, a mean allowance, certainly, but they were arranged so as to be as effective as possible. We dined early, the "pièce de résistance" being some chamois, about which I had my suspicions when I heard that it had been brought in by my friend Jean Martin, but that worthy assured me that the one we had found *dead* on the Moiry Glacier had been devoured by foxes, and that he had *killed* the one we were eating only yesterday. However this may have been, I cannot honestly say that it was either tender or palatable.

We meant to have got off by 2.30, but there was a long delay in getting the bill, and it was, consequently, 3.25 p.m. before we actually started for the Arpitetta Alp, where we were to pass the night. We soon crossed to the left bank of the stream, and made for the foot of the Zinal Glacier. It is necessary to adopt this course, as the cliffs below the Alp, which is above the right bank of the stream, are inaccessible "en face," and, in order to turn them, the gorge through which the drainage from the Moming Glacier pours must be ascended. At 4.20 we came to the foot of the Zinal Glacier, and, after following the track along its left bank for a few minutes, struck down to the moraine which stretched right across to the other side. In the ticklish state of my boots, I had looked forward to the passage of this with perfect horror, and it was, therefore, an agreeable disappointment to find a rough, but well-defined, path over the piles of débris. This is kept up for the convenience of the cows on the Alp, but must require almost daily repair, as the motion of the glacier must unavoidably damage it. Anyhow it provided us with an easy route to the right bank, on reaching which, we at once commenced a steep climb along the gorge above mentioned. As we mounted, the view of the Zinal Glacier increased in grandeur at every step. The Dent Blanche was concealed by clouds, but the Grand Cornier, Steinbock, and Pigne de l'Allée were clear, and showed a line of precipices that was most imposing. At 5.10 we reached a group of clean and tempting-looking châlets, which were, however, unoccupied, and we, therefore, inferred that the cows had gone up higher, and prepared to follow them. We, somehow, managed to get out of the track, but kept along the hill-side, rising very gradually, the Moming Glacier opening out broadly and grandly in front of us as we advanced, backed by the wonderful cliffs of the Weisshorn, Schallhorn, Rothhorn, and Lo Besso. The tops of the peaks were in the clouds, but we saw enough to lead us to believe that the scene presented by the amphitheatre which we were entering, has few equals in the Alps. From all accounts, that which is to be had from the Belvedere in the Macugnaga Glacier *is* superior, but the cliffs of Monte Rosa, though more colossal, are not so precipitous as those of the Weisshorn.

The Moming Glacier is perfectly different in character from that of Zinal; the latter is a long, sinuous ice-stream, while the former is of immense breadth, but has comparatively little length, terminating in a steep tongue of ice, which dies away in the midst of a track of débris, that indicates its much greater extent at some former period. In the ridge at its head, connecting the Rothhorn and Weisshorn, three depressions were visible. One, the lowest, is at the point marked on the Federal map 3751 mètres, or 12,307 feet, between the Weisshorn and Schallhorn, at the head of the arm of the glacier which comes down between those peaks, and is called on the map Glacier du Weisshorn. This glacier is separated from the true Moming Glacier by a spur from the Schallhorn, but the two unite at the base of that spur, or at least are only divided by a moraine, common to both. There was no doubt as to the practibility of this Col, the other side of which we had seen from the Dom. On this side it was approached by a very long and steep slope of ice, with occasional patches of rock cropping out, but more or less step-cutting was evidently all that would be required to surmount it. We wished, however, to descend on to the main arm of the Schallenberg Glacier, which would not be feasible in this direction, so we determined not to adopt it, except as a last resource. The two remaining gaps were between the Schallhorn and Rothhorn, one at the point marked 3867 mètres, or 12,688 feet, the other very slightly to the south of it, and rather higher. Practically these two gaps are one and the same thing, the intervening distance being trifling, while both must be approached by the same route. The upper part of the wall, between the Schallhorn and Rothhorn, beneath them, is formed by an exceedingly steep slope of snow or ice, intersected by a considerable bergschrund, and looked so straightforward, that we began to think the pass would, after all, turn out a humbug. It was not till we had advanced some distance that we realised the nature and extent of the difficulties which would have to be overcome before the base of the aforesaid slope could be reached, and, when we did so, our previous confidence vanished, and was replaced by serious doubts whether the pass was practicable at all. The upper portion of the Moming Glacier occupies an immense bay under the ridge which connects

THE MOMING GLACIER.

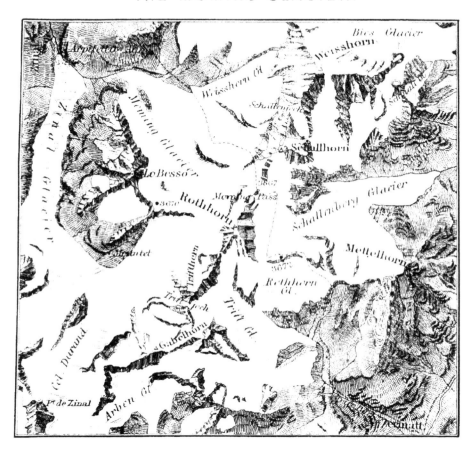

the Rothhorn with Lo Besso. In the centre, this sea of ice
is raised above the lower glacier by a long and lofty ridge
of rocks, running approximately east and west. Between
the western end of this supporting ridge and the peak of
Lo Besso, the upper glacier finds its way in a very broad
and shattered ice-fall to the lower level, but between the
eastern extremity of the ridge and the rocks of the Schallhorn the space is very confined, and the glacier is forced
through in a precipitous wall of ice-cliffs and séracs of the
most forbidding character. This wall is of great height,
and lies immediately under the snow-slope leading up to
the two gaps, through one of which we wished to pass. To
get, therefore, to the foot of the final slope, we must adopt
one of four plans; either we must ascend the great ice-fall
under Lo Besso, and pass along the whole length of the
base of the ridge joining that peak to the Rothhorn, or we
must find a way up the supporting ridge of rocks, whose
presence was the cause of the difficulty, or attack the wall
of séracs, or else find a way up the rocks of the Schallhorn
on the right of it. The fatal objection to the first plan was,
that, putting aside the difficulties of the way, which would
be great, the détour required would be so enormous that a
whole day would probably be spent in the effort to reach
the Col. A careful survey of the supporting rocks revealed
a broadish snow couloir, by which we at first thought we
might be able to circumvent the enemy, but examination
through the glass showed it to be of such length and steepness, and so furrowed by stone channels, that its ascent
would be practically impossible, without incurring an unjustifiable amount of risk. The second plan was, therefore, disposed of, and the only alternatives left were the
ascent of the séracs or of the rocks of the Schallhorn, and
of the practicability of either route it was impossible to
form any trustworthy opinion without nearer approach.

While engaged in reconnoitring, we wound steadily round
the hill-side, but without seeing any sign of the expected
châlets, although we were well above the end of the Moming
Glacier. There could be little doubt that we were too low

down, so we struck straight up to the left, and, after a stiff pull, fell into the path which we had contrived to miss after leaving the lower châlets. This soon brought us in sight of the cows, which were scattered thickly over the pastures, which are the highest on the Arpitetta Alp. We looked anxiously out for the châlets, but none were visible, until at 6.5 p.m. we stumbled upon a low hovel, built against the side of the hill, from which it was scarcely distinguishable. At the door stood a filthy native, from whom we elicited the horrible fact that we were looking at our quarters for the night, there being no other building on this part of the Alp. There was no alternative, so we entered what, externally and internally, was nothing but an exaggerated pigstye, of a specially filthy character. To make matters worse, shortly after our arrival a violent shower of rain came on, accompanied by heavy thunder, and the weather assumed a threatening aspect, which was not calculated to elevate our spirits, rather depressed at the prospect of an uncomfortable night. After a long delay, we managed to get some milk, and then set about brewing some chocolate for supper. The result was satisfactory, and under other circumstances we should have been tolerably jolly, but the appearance of the weather became momentarily worse, and acted as a most efficient damper.

The height of our den was scarcely sufficient to allow of standing upright, while the floor was a sea of filth, into which we sank above our ankles. In one corner was a rough platform of stones, raised a few inches above the general level, covered with some sheepskins, apparently in an advanced state of decomposition, which was pointed out as our couch for the night. After a long delay, a brew of chocolate was prepared, and we then retired. To take off boots was impossible, so, rolling myself up in my plaid, I assumed my allotted place on the sheepskins, persuading myself, as really proved to be the case, that their appearance was the worst thing against them. Whymper, however, could not bring himself to trust to their tender mercies, and, I believe, sat all night on a stone, meditating on the immortality of the soul, and kindred topics. I had just settled myself, and was listening to the contest going on amongst the animals outside for the sheltered positions under the walls of the hut, and beginning to think myself not so badly off after all, when my complacency was disturbed by the receipt, exactly in my eye, of a heavy drop of rain—a convincing proof that, whatever might be the merits of the roof, watertightness was not one of them. Having, after several trials, taken up a more secure position, I was again dropping off, when there was a sudden irruption into the cabin of at least a dozen men, women, and children. Where they came from heaven knows, and I should be sorry to say where we wished them. Seating themselves with the previous occupants round the fire, they forthwith commenced an animated discussion, which lasted, with very slight intermission, throughout the night. What the seductive topic was we could not accurately discover, but, from the excited and prominent part taken in the conversation by the female portion of the community, I inferred that it was some local scandal of a peculiarly piquant and agreeable character. There was some consolation in the reflection that the women of the Val d'Anniviers are not superior to the weaknesses of their sex in *less* enlightened parts of the world, but the thought, soothing as it was, failed to act as an antidote to the incessant cackling, and I slept but little.

Monday, 18*th July.*—About 1.0 a.m. there was a movement amongst the guides to see what was the aspect of the weather, and, as I had expected from the ominous pattering on the roof of our refuge, the report was unfavourable; a thick fog enveloped everything in its clammy folds, and heavy rain was falling, so that it was obviously impossible to start. Whymper had throughout abjured the sheepskins, but I quickly composed myself afresh, and was rewarded by a good, long sleep, which lasted unbroken till 4.30, when I finally awoke to the consciousness of a dull, miserable day. In spite of their unprepossessing appearance, I must do the sheepskins the justice to admit that they really made a not uncomfortable couch, and, so far as my experience goes, were not infested with fleas to the extent that might have been expected; some there were, undoubtedly, but nothing to seriously complain of. When I went to the door of our stye, the appearance of things was not encouraging; the rain had certainly ceased, and the fog in our immediate neighbourhood had lifted, the Col being clear, but the sky was encumbered with heavy masses of clouds, which concealed every high peak, and completely shut out the Zinal Glacier from view. It certainly was not a day on which to try a new and difficult pass, but the idea of vegetating for twenty-four hours in the foul den in which we were, was too fearful to be seriously entertained, while I could not help feeling that, if we once went down to Zinal, it was a great chance whether we should toil up again for another miserable night, possibly to encounter a second disappointment in the morning. Still, I could not bring myself to contemplate the total abandonment of the expedition, which, like the Biesjoch, had been one on which I had specially set my heart, so we sat for some little time in a dubious and melancholy state, uncertain what to do. I was becoming more and more disconsolate, and inclined to pack up my traps and beat a retreat to England, when the fact dawned upon us that the weather was not getting any worse, and the guides seemed to think that we might at least make a start, as, even if ultimately compelled to return, we should have killed time, and most probably discovered the best line of march. So it was finally determined, and we forthwith set about breakfast. Some wine was heated, with which we warmed the cockles of our hearts, with the result, in my case, of seeing things from a less blue point of view. We paid the chief herdsman the very moderate sum which he demanded for our accommodation, and then started on our way at 5.40 a.m., amidst most encouraging assurances from all the people on the Alp, that we need not distress ourselves about the weather, as it was not possible to get up at the point for which we were aiming.

It must be admitted that a party rarely started on a considerable expedition under less encouraging auspices, and I think that none of us entertained much confidence of success, as we walked in silence over the barren slopes that intervened between us and the ice. We had to pass below the end of the considerable glacier, flowing in a southerly direction from the base of the ridge which circles round from the Weisshorn to the point marked on the Federal map 3698 mètres, or 12,132 feet, and forms the southern boundary of the western branch of the Turtman Glacier. I cannot help thinking that there must be a pass at some point over this ridge, which would afford a route of amazing grandeur from Gruben to the Arpitetta Alp, but, both now and during the remainder of the day, the weather prevented me from seeing more than the lower end of the glacier, which terminates in a broken, but not very steep, ice-fall, on the higher portion of the slopes we were traversing. The elevation of the châlet at which we had slept cannot be much under 8500 feet, so that we were spared the "grind" usual before beginning the day's work, and, after an easy walk along the side of very gentle slopes of grass and stones, at 6.15 got on to the moraine of the Glacier du Weisshorn. We struck straight across this, leaving the route we ought to follow, if we wished to get at the Col between the Weisshorn and Schallhorn, on the left. This was subsequently adopted by Messrs. Hornby and Philpott, who crossed the pass with Almer and Christian Lauener, and christened it by the appropriate name of Schallenjoch. The moraine was of enormous extent, but in due course we emerged on to a narrow strip of clear ice, which was rendered unusually slippery by the quantity of rain that had fallen, and was by no means agreeable walking in the almost nailless state of my boots. Making our way across this strip, which has a hard struggle for existence with the immense masses of débris which border and press upon it on either side, we were very soon encountered by the moraine which draws its supplies from the spur of the Schallhorn, forming the division between the Weisshorn and Moming

Glaciers. This, though less extensive, is steeper than its
neighbour on the other side, and, on cresting its summit,
we found a considerable drop beyond, between us and the
true Moming Glacier. Scrambling down and disturbing
the stones considerably in the operation, we were in a few
minutes once more on clear ice, which, though equally level
and uncrevassed, was less slippery than before, and, therefore, more pleasant to walk over. Keeping close under the
moraine, we steered tolerably straight up the glacier towards
the Schallhorn, until at 7.20 we came to a point, close to a
dirty little tarn in the ice, where we halted to put on the
rope, and decide upon the course which it would be best
to follow.

We were now nearly opposite the eastern end of the ridge
of rocks which supports the upper part of the glacier, and
had to determine whether it would be better to attack the
great wall of séracs between it and the Schallhorn, or endeavour to force a passage up the rocks of the latter peak,
on the right side of the wall. Almer was in favour of the
latter course, rightly supposing, from the immense mass of
débris at the foot of the séracs, that the ice-cliffs were in the
habit of coming down with a run. Indeed, I have rarely, if
ever, seen a greater extent of avalanche débris; it stretched,
in the usual fan-shaped form, from the foot of the wall
down on to the level glacier, a broad slope which, at its
termination, could not have had a width of less than half-
a-mile. The whole of this space was completely covered
with ice-blocks of various sizes, the apparently fresh condition of which showed that falls occurred daily, and might
be expected at any moment. The danger was so very
palpable, that I must confess to having been astonished
when Croz objected to take to the rocks, and advocated a
direct attack on the wall, on which he appeared to think
there was a vulnerable point, close under the eastern end
of the ridge before mentioned. The inconvenience of our
guides being mutually ignorant of each other's language
was here specially apparent, as, had they been able to
communicate direct, I don't think that Croz would have

proposed the line he did. As it was, I was the sole medium of discussion between the two, and, my knowledge of German being the reverse of extensive, I probably failed to understand the exact route by which Almer proposed to approach the rocks, and, consequently, to explain it to Croz with sufficient clearness. I pointed out to Almer the line of march which Croz wished to adopt, and, though evidently disapproving of it, he manifested his usual utter abnegation of self, did not insist on the superior merits of his own plan, and begged of us to do whatever Croz thought best. My own opinion, and I believe Whymper's also, was in favour of making for the rocks, whose principal difficulty seemed likely to be near the bottom where we should have to get on to them, but Croz adhered so strongly to his original choice, that we gave in, against our better judgments, and at 7.30 started, Croz leading, followed by Whymper, myself, and Almer.

We struck straight across the glacier, on which a good deal of snow was lying, and picked our way amongst the few crevasses by which the regularity of its generally-level surface was occasionally broken, and approached a long slope of snow on its opposite side. The snow on this slope was rather soft, and the inclination considerable, so that zig-zags were required; but we mounted rapidly, and soon rose to a great height, gradually nearing the ice-cliffs which we were going to attack. But, at every step we rose, I became more convinced that we had made a great mistake in choosing such a line of march, and that sooner or later we should have to manœuvre to get on to the rocks. The wall above us was, in appearance, one of the most hopelessly impracticable places I ever saw, broken into cliffs and pinnacles of ice, many of which heeled over towards the slope below at any conceivable angle, and evidently could not long maintain their equilibrium. Almer kept up a subdued growling behind me expressive of dissatisfaction, but nothing was said, as it was better, for many reasons, that Croz should find out his mistake himself, a result which, judging from the irresolute manner in which he

looked first to the right and then to the left, glancing occasionally round at us as if to see what we thought about it,
could not long be delayed.   No man likes to admit himself
wrong, even if the error be merely an excusable one of
judgment, still less to admit that a rival is right; but our
leader at length stopped, and suggested that it might, after
all, be wiser to take to the rocks of the Schallhorn.   We
readily concurred, but the operation, which at the proper
time would have been simple enough, was now attended
with an amount of danger so great, that, had it been
possible to succeed by persevering in our previous course, we
should have done so, in preference to incurring it.   We
were very near the top of the long, fan-shaped slope of
débris, whose foot we ought to have skirted, but along
whose side we had mounted.   It was now, therefore, between us and the Schallhorn, and, to get at the desired
point on the rocks, we must cross it from one side to the
other.   But at its head rose an almost perpendicular wall
of ice of considerable height, crowned by an enormous mass
of broken séracs, in a most frightfully insecure position,
which would clearly be the next contributors to the collection of débris.   We knew that a similar formation extended
upwards to the base of the final slope below the Col, and
that the upper and invisible masses were as likely to
pay a sudden visit to the depths below as those that were
before our eyes.   Beneath this delightful arrangement for
the manufacture of avalanches at the shortest notice we
must pass, and we could see only too plainly that the
operation would be by no means a short one, and that we
should be very fortunate if we got over without accident.
However, the thing had to be done, so, abandoning our
smooth slope of snow, we turned to the left and commenced
the passage.

After our recent experience on the Bies Glacier, Almer
and I, possibly, were more impressed with the nature and
imminence of the danger than Whymper and Croz, but,
great as had been our peril on that occasion, I believe that
it was still greater now.   Then, had the fall occurred while

we were in the line of fire, I think that we might have had a chance, though a poor one, of escape from fatal injury, but on the present occasion nothing could have saved us, as we were so close under the cliffs, that, in the event of a fall, we must have been instantaneously crushed and swept away. Again, on the Bies Glacier the angle of the slope was not too great to allow of rapid movement, and we had the satisfaction of feeling that we *were* exerting ourselves to get out of danger; but here that consolation was denied to us, as the slope was inclined at an angle of at least 48°, and the blocks of ice were, in consequence, jammed together into a compact mass, in which nearly every step of the way had to be cut with the axe. At intervals, too, the surface was scored by deep grooves, which had been scooped out by falling blocks of more than average dimensions. The passage of these channels was the most anxious and difficult part of the business, as in them the footing was specially precarious, the débris having been carried away, and smooth ice left exposed, while, in the event of a fresh fall occurring, the chances were, of course, in favour of the weightiest and most deadly missiles selecting the convenient routes marked out by their predecessors. One enormous tower of ice impended right over our path, apparently in the act of falling, and on this we kept our eyes fixed, speculating whether the inevitable catastrophe would or would not be delayed until we reached the rocks. I never in my life heard a positive oath come from Almer's mouth, but the language in which he kept up a running commentary, more to himself than to me, as we went along, was stronger than I should have given him credit for using. His prominent feeling seemed to be one of *indignation* that we should be in such a position, and self-reproach at being a party to the proceeding, while the emphatic way in which at intervals he exclaimed "Schnell! schnell!!" oblivious that it was all Hebrew to Croz, sufficiently betokened his alarm. I am not ashamed to confess that, during the whole time, my heart was in my mouth, and I never felt relieved from such a load of care as when at 8.40, after, I suppose, a passage of about twenty minutes, we got on to the rocks and were in safety.

We immediately commenced the ascent of the cliffs which rose precipitously above our heads, but for how far we could not see, as they disappeared in the mist by which everything around was enshrouded. From the very beginning the work was hard, and we had to bring all our energies into play to overcome the difficulties that were encountered in rapid succession. The rocks were exceedingly steep and very smooth, being arranged in large slabs, which afforded by no means more hold than was agreeable. Some awkwardly long strides were necessary in places to get from one point of vantage to another, but there was one consolation to be derived from the formation of the crags, viz., that the rock was firm and good, there was, consequently, no danger from falling stones, and we could rely upon every point that we grasped, however small it might be, holding securely and not giving under our weight. We worked for some little time along and up the side of the precipice which overhangs the ice-fall beneath which we had passed with so much danger, and the regularity of our way was occasionally interrupted by narrow snow couloirs, running across our path, down towards it. The passage of these gullies was, as a rule, the most critical part of the climb, as on either side the rocks were almost invariably covered with a thin coating of ice, in which it was almost impossible to cut a secure step. On these occasions, hands, feet, and eyelids were brought into play, but, in spite of every precaution, thanks to the state of my boots, I lost my footing in one specially bad step, and was fairly on my back, held up only by the rope. Fortunately the others held their ground, and Almer soon hauled me up to my former position; but without the rope, which some people profess to think should only be used on a crevassed névé, my fate would have been no doubtful one. I could not have recovered myself, and nothing could have saved me from instant destruction. Severe as the climbing undoubtedly was, it was not so difficult as it had been on the Biesjoch, and, in decent weather, the whole thing would have been most enjoyable; but that was denied us, the elements appearing determined to do their very best to baffle us, or at least render our progress as uncomfortable as possible.

As we rose higher, it became desirable to see something of what lay above us, in order that we might know how to steer, as we had no ambition to find ourselves by mistake on the top of the Schallhorn, but it was snowing hard, and the mist was thicker than ever; so, as it was not very cold, we halted at 9.35 on a convenient ledge, and determined to breakfast, in hopes that by the time we had finished there might be a partial clearance. As we sat we looked down upon the Moming Glacier at our feet, or rather upon the mist which concealed it from view, and which did not appear inclined to disperse. However, it all of a sudden became less dense, and disclosed immediately on our left an enormous pinnacle of ice, towering like an uplifted hand to an apparent height of several hundred feet above our heads. As this fantastic monster loomed mysteriously through the haze which concealed its base, and, doubtless, magnified its real proportions, it presented an appearance that was quite unearthly, and made a greater impression upon me than anything else of the kind I have ever seen. We had scarcely turned our eyes from this fascinating vision towards the glacier, which was now visible below, when we saw one of the immense masses of ice, underneath which we had crept in fear and trembling, lurch over, totter for a moment, as if struggling against the resistless pressure which was urging it on, and then fall with a crash, straight down upon the slope we had traversed. I suppose that the height of the mass that fell must have been at least as great as that of the Monument near London Bridge, but the sight was not nearly so impressive as that of the falls we had seen on the Bies Glacier, in consequence of our greater distance from the scene of action. We were, however, able to judge of the resistless violence with which the avalanche swept downwards, and of the certain results to

T

ourselves had the catastrophe taken place a little earlier, by its effect on the portion of the slope which it traversed in its course—every atom of the old débris was swept away, and a broad band of smooth ice left in its place.

The mist was now sufficiently thin for us to see our way in front, so at 10.10 we set off again, Almer and myself taking the places of Croz and Whymper as leaders. We were at the top of the first line of crags, which were connected with a higher range by a steep slope of snow, which, a little higher up, narrowed to an arête, the slopes on either side falling rapidly. Right along the crest of this arête we went without difficulty, the snow being soft and the footing good. Towards the top it widened out again, and we should have liked to strike away to the right and cross the slope diagonally, so as to cut off a corner and get on to the snow plateau below the final ridge, at a point more immediately under the Col than would be possible if we preserved our present route. But the soft snow was lying on hard ice, and was in a most dangerous condition, so that we could not have traversed it without imminent risk of damaging its coherence and creating an avalanche, which would carry us double quick down the ice-fall that we had with so much labour dodged. The attempt was, therefore, not made, and we, in due course, again took to the rocks, which were more than ever glazed with ice, and gave us an opportunity for some very pretty scrambling, but they were not long, and at 10.35 we left the last one behind us, and stood at the foot of the final ridge. We were on a narrow plateau, or rather shelf, of snow, which lies at the base of the ice-slope running from the Schallhorn to the Rothhorn, sweeps round and under the latter peak and the ridge connecting it with Lo Besso, gradually widening in its course until it expands into an extensive bay of névé, that falls to the lower Moming Glacier under Lo Besso. We were a good deal to the north of both the gaps in the ridge above us, but resolved to steer for the most distant one, nearer to the Rothhorn, although it was higher than its neighbour. We came to this determination in consequence of the slope below the lower Col appearing to be very much steeper and more bare of snow than that leading to the other, so that, in spite of the superior height of the latter, less time would probably be consumed in reaching it. For the present, our way was delightfully easy, and we plodded along over the level corridor of snow, passing above the head of the ice-fall we had circumvented, looking out for a favourable point at which to pass the bergschrund, which, as was to be expected, ran along the base of the final slope. After passing underneath the lower gap, which is the point marked on the map, 3867 mètres, or 12,688 feet, we turned up to the "schrund," and crossed it, without much difficulty, at 11.15. The slope above was formidably steep, probably 50°, but would have been soon ascended had the snow been in good condition. But it was in the worst possible order, there being a hard upper crust which had to be kicked through to get footing, and, underneath, nearly two feet of soft, powdery snow, without the slightest cohesion, in which, so soon as the foot was through the upper crust, we floundered about hopelessly. I found, at last, that the best plan was to go down on my hands and knees, with only the tips of my toes in the steps, resting upon the hard crust, which bore my weight securely, and so climbing, as if we were going up a ladder, we mounted steadily behind Almer, until at 11.50 a.m. our efforts were crowned with success, and the Moming Pass was won.

The pass must be about 70 feet higher than the neighbouring depression, or 12,800 feet in height, and the view from it in fine weather cannot be otherwise than superb, but I cannot speak from personal experience, as we saw absolutely nothing, mists enveloping everything, so that many interesting questions in connection with the Weisshorn and Rothhorn had to remain unsolved. The same fatality attended Mr. Hornby's party when they passed the Schallenjoch, so that two of the grandest and most difficult passes in the Alps have been effected without their conquerors seeing anything of the scenery through which they lead. The next problem to be solved was the descent on to the Schallenberg Glacier; and, as there was no prospect of any serious improvement in the weather, we turned our minds to the solution of it, without a moment's delay. It was not easy to discover what lay between us and the glacier, for, at the point at which we had hit the ridge, an immense snow cornice impended over it, and it was impossible to venture far enough on to this to get a look down. However, advancing along the ridge towards the Rothhorn for a few yards, we found a point where the breadth of this overhanging fringe was not so great, and the guides, having cut away a portion of it, disclosed a wall of snow, which, so far as we could judge through the fog, though exceedingly steep, was of no great height, that is to say, not more than a hundred feet. Anyhow, Croz led the way through the hole in the cornice, and we followed, Almer bringing up the rear. The descent was more formidable in appearance than reality, the snow being soft but good, and, floundering down, we were soon on the comparatively-level surface beneath.

We had no very distinct notion as to what was the nature of the ground between us and the lower portion of the glacier, and the fog was too thick for us to see much. I had seen from the Dom that the central ice-fall was long and broken, but we must be still far above that, and neither Almer nor myself had any recollection of what was above it. For a short distance beyond the foot of the final slope, the snow stretched gently downwards, and we pushed on quickly, bearing rather to the right, until the inclination became more rapid, and our progress was arrested by an enormous chasm. This was turned with some trouble, and proved to be the beginning of difficulties, as we forthwith found ourselves involved in one of the most formidable ice-falls I ever encountered, not a jumble of séracs, like the fall of the Glacier du Géant, but a great wall, broken into ice-cliffs, and intersected by " schrunds " of the most forbidding character, It bore a strong resemblance to the descent below the Col de la Pilatte on to the glacier of the same name, but was very much steeper and altogether more difficult, which is saying a good deal. Most fortunate was it that we had as guides two of the first ice-men in the Alps, to whom ignorance of the ground was a matter of very trifling consequence, as, with incompetent or second-rate men, I doubt whether we ever should have extricated ourselves from such a labyrinth. As it was, Croz, who led, was in his element, and certainly selected his way with marvellous sagacity, while Almer had an equally honorable and, perhaps, more responsible post in the rear, which he kept with his usual steadiness. I should despair of giving, in words, any idea of the exciting and critical positions in which we were placed for more than an hour and a half, but one particular passage has impressed itself on my mind as one of the most nervous I ever made. We had to pass along a crest of ice, a mere knife-edge, with on our left a broad crevasse, whose bottom was lost in blue haze, and on our right, at an angle of 70°, or more, a slope falling to a similar gulf below. A person of suicidal turn of mind might thus have chosen between a "tremendous header" on one side, and a roll, followed by a plunge, on the other. Croz, as he went along the edge, chipped small notches in the ice, in which we placed our feet, with the toes well turned out, doing all we knew to preserve our balance. While stepping from one of these precarious footholds to another, I staggered for a moment. I had not really lost my footing; but the agonised tone in which Almer, who was behind me, on seeing me waver, exclaimed, "Schlüpfen Sie nicht, Herr!" gave us an even livelier impression than we already had of the insecurity of the position. On the side of the cliffs there was little or no snow, and nearly every step had to be cut. To save time, the holes were not made by any means too large, and more than once, when we were cutting down towards small crevasses which had to be leaped, our gallant leader lost his footing, and shot over before he had intended, of course taking care not to perform such a manœuvre in places where there was serious risk. One huge chasm, whose upper edge was far above the lower one, could neither be leaped nor turned, and threatened to prove an insuperable barrier. But Croz showed himself equal to the emergency. Held up by the rest of the party, he cut a series of holes for the hands and feet down and along the almost perpendicular wall of ice, forming the upper side of the "schrund." Along this slippery staircase, we crept, with our faces to the wall and a fringe of icicles over our heads, until a point was reached where the width of the chasm was not too great for us to drop across. Before we had done, we got quite accustomed to taking flying leaps over the "schrunds," though there was no jump on so grand and nervous a scale as that on the Col de la Pilatte, which remains without a parallel in my experience. To make a long story short; after a most desperate and exciting struggle, and as bad a piece of ice-work as it is possible to imagine, we emerged on to the true upper plateau of the glacier, close to a short, but lofty, wall of rocks, which were crowned by ice-cliffs, the neighbours of those with which we had been contending. We passed close to their base, utterly regardless of the avalanche débris which was scattered about in profusion, and, so soon as we were out of danger from this source, at 1.35 p.m. sat down in the snow to refresh and look about us.

It was again snowing fast, but the fog had lifted, so that we were able to see some distance a-head, and determine upon our further proceedings. I had always intended to get to Zermatt, if practicable, by crossing some point on the ridge which runs from the Rothhorn to the Mettelhorn, forming the right bank of the Schallenberg Glacier, and separating it from the basin of the Rothhorn and Trift Glaciers; but, at what point the passage could be effected, I had no idea, and to this ridge we, therefore, now turned our attention. Close under, and to the west of the Mettelhorn, whose summit was visible considerably below our position, were several well-defined gaps, led up to by steepish snow slopes, which would evidently give access to the ravine of the Trift; but to get at the base of these slopes we should have to force a way through the central ice-fall of the glacier, the aspect of which, as seen below, was suggestive of considerable trouble and difficulty, while from the foot of the fall, the ascent to either of the gaps would be by no means short. It was, therefore, with no small satisfaction that we saw that, from the very spot where we were sitting, the névé ran up in a broad bay, almost due south, to a particularly well-marked depression in the ridge of the Rothhorn, which appeared to be intended as the natural exit from the upper part of the Schallenberg Glacier. The slopes leading up to this depression were so gentle, and its appearance generally was so irresistibly tempting, that with one consent we resolved to turn our steps in that direction, never doubting that we should find some sort of a descent on to the Rothhorn Glacier, and thence to the level of the Trift. For the first time during the day, the snow was accompanied by a bitterly cold wind, which chilled us to the bone, and made us all very glad to move, at 2.5, in the direction of the gap, which we hoped was to rescue us from our difficulties. The snow was in very good order, and nothing could have been easier than our progress, as we skirted the base of the magnificent precipices of the Rothhorn, which, in clear weather, must be one of the grandest features of the pass, judging only from the imperfect view which was vouchsafed to us. As we progressed, the slopes became slightly steeper, but there was not the least difficulty, and at 2.50 we stood on the crest of the ridge, when a view of the greatest magnificence burst upon us, and was the more effective from having been totally unexpected. Towards Zermatt the sky was perfectly clear, and there, free from a speck of cloud, stood the great range of peaks from Monte Rosa to the Matterhorn, with the long line of glaciers between them, while at our feet was the Trift Glacier, leading up to the Triftjoch, over which the fine peak of the Gabelhorn shewed to great advantage.

The ridge on which we were standing was several yards in width, and covered with snow. We hurried across it, but the snow curled suddenly over, and we were brought to a full stop on the brow of a precipice, falling sheer to the

Rothhorn Glacier, from which we were thus completely cut off. This hitch was as alarming as it was unexpected ; but Croz and Almer, after some discussion, started off in different directions to try and find a practicable descent, leaving Whymper and myself to ruminate on the highest rocks. We were, I believe, at a point just to the west of that to which a height of 3672 mètres, or 12,049 feet, is given on the Federal map, which I do not think is quite minutely accurate in its delineation of this ridge. Looking east along the ridge, our eyes at once fell upon a broad opening in it from which the Rothhorn Glacier fell away in easy slopes, and it was evident that, if we could only get at that opening, our escape was secured, but to pass along the south side of the ridge was impossible, and the arête between us and the desired point did not look promising. We ought from our position to have seen something of the Rothhorn, which must have been in immediate proximity on our right, but it was still enveloped in clouds, so that the last chance of discovering a route to the summit was lost. After considerable delay, the guides returned and reported the descent of the rocks quite impracticable, so there was nothing for it but to retrace our steps, and endeavour to get at the other and more promising gap by skirting the slopes on the north side of the ridge above the Schallenberg Glacier. Accordingly, at 3.30 we turned, and, after descending in our steps for a short distance, struck up to the right, and commenced working round the steep slopes of snow which masked this side of the ridge. There was no difficulty beyond what arose from the steepness of the slope, which, further on, appeared to increase so considerably that it was doubtful whether we should be able to pass ; so the two men cast off the rope, and went up the slope to see what sort of going the arête would offer, leaving us to shiver, a violent squall of wind and snow having chosen this inopportune moment to vent its fury. Fortunately it was not long, and as it passed away, we got our first and only view of the Weisshorn, which showed its precipitous crags above the northern and smaller arm of the Schallenberg Glacier, perfectly white with snow. Almer soon returned, and announced "All well;" so we went up in his steps, and got on to the arête, which, although very narrow, was easy enough to traverse, and led us, at 4.15, after a considerable descent, to the wished-for gap, where Croz was waiting our arrival.

It is probable that at some former period the Rothhorn and Trift Glaciers formed one and the same sea of ice, but the Rothhorn Glacier has now shrunk considerably, and terminates on the brow of steep cliffs at a great height above its far more extensive neighbour. The only point we were now in doubt about was, whereabouts we should be likely to find these cliffs most accessible; and, all being in an equally blissful state of ignorance on the subject, we trusted to luck, and struck well away to the left from the Col, descending very gradually. The glacier proved even easier than we had expected, with very few crevasses, and those generally covered with snow, so that we ran, trotted, and finally glissaded along at a great pace until at 4.50 we got off the ice on the extreme left, just above a stony ravine, which we hoped would give us access to the grass slopes below. I have omitted to mention that, while on the arête above the Rothhorn Glacier, on looking back at our pass, we made a rather important discovery, viz., that, by keeping well to the left from the foot of the first steep snow slope, we should have avoided almost all the difficulties that we had encountered in descending to the upper plateau of the Schallenberg Glacier, as in that direction there appeared to be a tolerably connected slope of névé, by which we could have evaded the ice-fall.* At the point where we quitted the ice, there was a small stream of clear water which could not be passed without a halt, so down we sat, and as we drank, reflected with considerable complacency on what we

---

* Mr. and Miss Walker, who crossed the pass with M. Anderegg in 1865, found no difficulty in descending to the upper plateau of the Schallenberg Glacier. From it, instead of following my route, they kept down the glacier until below the lower ice-fall, when they struck up to the right, and passed through one of the depressions under the Mettelhorn, spoken of at page 278. They were of opinion, however, that my route was the best.

had accomplished. We had made what, though by no means the shortest, is beyond question the most direct pass that can *possibly be made* between Zinal and Zermatt, seeing that a straight line drawn on the map from one place to the other traverses the two ridges respectively connecting the Schallhorn and Rothhorn, and the Rothhorn and Mettelhorn, at the exact points to *a hair's breadth,* at which we effected the passages. On the other hand, however, Croz told Whymper that he considered the pass the most dangerous he had ever crossed, and there can be no doubt that it is far more difficult than the Triftjoch or the Col de la Dent Blanche.

At 5.5 we terminated our debauch, and continued the descent down the ravine, which was steep and very rough, considerable care being required to avoid knocking the stones down upon the heads and legs of those members of the party who were in front. But there was no difficulty, and we soon reached the rough grass slopes which extended downwards towards the foot of the Trift Glacier. These were very nearly level, and the walking over them was pleasant enough, until at 5.40, after bearing well to the right, we were close to, but a very little below, the termination of the glacier. We now turned to the left, into the gorge of the Triftbach, and, thenceforward, followed the usual route from the Triftjoch, keeping, however, along the slopes on the left bank of the torrent, instead of taking to the old and now rarely-used way along the right bank, where there is at least one "mauvais pas." I cannot conscientiously say that our path was a pleasant one, but bad as it was, when we eventually lost it, as, of course, we did, we wished for it back again. The ravine through which the torrent flows is a mere cleft in the rocks, and at the beginning of a day would be considered curious, but the thought of Zermatt absorbed us, to the exclusion of all other topics. Fortunately, we stumbled upon the track again, on the brink of the final descent into the valley, which is very steep, and to a luckless individual with boots worn perfectly smooth, as mine were, most disagreeable.

Still, all things must come to an end, and at 7.20 p.m. we walked into the Monte Rosa Hotel at Zermatt, just in time to escape a violent storm of rain. The passage from the Arpitetta Alp had occupied exactly twelve hours' actual walking, but, of these, one hour at least had from various causes been wasted.

I found a letter from Winkworth to the effect that he had been taken ill, and obliged to return to England, an event which involved the total overthrow of all my plans, as I could not, single-handed, accomplish the expeditions which we had proposed doing together. I went to bed quite uncertain what to do, but thought the matter over before I fell asleep, and finally determined to go on the morrow to the Bell Alp above Brieg, ascend the Aletschhorn from there, and cross to the Lötschen Thal by a pass which was understood to exist over the Jägi and Distel Glaciers, and thence try to get by the Wetter-lücke to Lauterbrunnen and Grindelwald, at which latter place I had little doubt but that I should stumble upon some one who would join me in a few expeditions wherewith to wind up my campaign.

Tuesday, 19th July.—I got up at 6.0 a.m., as I had a good many packing and other arrangements to make, and we had quite as much before us as could be conveniently accomplished during the day. All my traps were sent off to Grindelwald, and at 8.5 a.m., after saying good-bye to Whymper, Almer and I started for Visp, accompanied by Jean Baptiste Croz, and another Chamouni man, who were also going down the valley, en route home. We reached Randa at 9.45, and halted till 10.0,—came to St. Nicholas at 11.45, where five minutes were spent in conversation with Reilly, who was on his way to join Whymper at Zermatt,—passed through Stalden at 1.35, and arrived at the Hotel de la Poste, at Visp, at 2.50 p.m., rather footsore, in less than six and a half hours' actual walking from Zermatt. I had insisted upon travelling fast, as I knew that a long delay for dinner at Visp was unavoidable, nor was I deceived, for it was 4.30 before we started again, in a one-horse char, which, after a pleasant drive, dropped us at

5.25 p.m. at Näters, a large village on the right bank of the
Rhone, slightly above Brieg. We had now an ascent of
more than 5200 feet before us in order to reach our destination for the night, the Aletschbord Inn on the Lusgen
Alp, or, as it is more generally called, Bell Alp, though most
improperly, as the latter name is given on the map to a
position a good deal lower down. The idea was not very
fascinating, but Almer started off instantly at a tremendous
pace, his energies, somewhat damped by the quick walk
down from Zermatt, having been completely restored at
Visp, where he had encountered a Bernese friend, who had
stood him some champagne, a liquor to which, though no
toper, he is naturally partial. The path, which mounts
very steeply from Näters into a lateral valley between the
Gredetsch Thal at the base of the Gross Nesthorn, and the
gorge of the Massa, down which pours the drainage from
the Aletsch Glacier, is very stony but well made, and leads
for some distance through luxuriant groves of cherry and
other trees. Nothing could well exceed the picturesqueness
of the scenery as we advanced; right and left towered
splintered crags, broken by an extraordinary number of
ravines, and thickly overgrown with pine-trees, presenting
so charming an "ensemble," that I forgot my fatigue in
admiration. We left, on our right, one specially curious
gorge, called on the map Tiefethal, which I should have
much liked to see nearer at hand. It appeared to be a cleft
not many yards wide, with absolutely perpendicular walls
of rock, rising on either side to a height of many hundred
feet. After crossing to the left bank of the torrent, we
came at 6.50 to the hamlet of Blatten, through which we
were passing, when a voice hailed us to know if we wanted
a guide to the Aletschhorn. Now, as we did require such a
commodity, we stopped and entered into negociations with
the owner of the voice, who proved to be a tall, decent-
looking man, by name Anton Eggel, who had been one of
the guides upon each of the two occasions that the Aletschhorn had been ascended from this side. I finally engaged
him to go with us as far as Lauterbrunnen, and he went

off to make his arrangements.   These took some time, and
it was not till 7.20 that we were on the move again, when
my opinion of our new recruit was not increased on seeing
that he was armed only with a very frail-looking alpenstock.
We went up at a most tremendous pace, along a delightful
path through woods and over pastures, but it soon became
too dark for us to see much, and also began to rain violently,
the only effect of which was to make us quicken our already
rapid pace.   Under Eggel's guidance we left the path,
and took a short cut over very steep ground, without incident, until, on cresting a rise in the hill, we suddenly
looked down upon the sinuous form of the Aletsch Glacier,
which, seen under the light of a watery full moon, struggling
in vain to pierce the clouds, had a most startling and sepulchral appearance.   We reached the inn at 8.35 p.m., in
two hours' and three quarters cruelly fast walking from
Näters, and glad enough we were to find ourselves under
the shelter of its hospitable roof, being pretty nearly wet
through.   The weather did not promise well for the Aletschhorn in the morning, and I went to bed without much fear
of being aroused at an unearthly hour of the night.

Wednesday, 20th July.—Heavy rain and thick fog had it
all their own way at the hour we ought to have started, nor,
when I got up at 8.30, were matters much better, but, as the
morning wore on, the clouds vanished, and the day turned
out gloriously fine.   Almer had found a cobbler, to whom
he had given my boots to patch up, but enforced idleness
in such a position as that of this most charming inn was
not a matter of regret.   The situation of the Eggischhorn
Hotel is not comparable to that of the Aletschbord, but the
latter is not well placed for the ascent of most of the great
Bernese peaks, so that there can be little or no rivalry between the two, and each must be visited on its own account.
As I lay on the grass slopes, in a state of bliss, I looked
straight up the Aletsch Glacier for many miles.   Beyond
the upper Valais was range upon range of unknown peaks
and glaciers, while, looking south, the enormous mass of
the Fletschörner, the noble chain of the Mischabel, the

obelisk of the Matterhorn, and the Weisshorn, the most beautiful summit in the Alps, presented an array on which the eye never wearied of feasting. In the same direction, at our feet, the roofs of Brieg sparkled in the sunshine, and reminded us of the dust and heat from which we in our eyrie were free. The evening was one of the finest I ever remember in the Alps, and the sunset on the Dom and Weisshorn, a thing to be dreamed of, so unearthly beautiful was it, so that, altogether, we went to bed under most favourable auspices for the morrow.

Thursday, 21st July.—After a day of idleness, I was not very tired, and the moonbeams which streamed into my room, rendering it as light as day, effectually prevented me from falling asleep for some time. When I did at length drop off, my slumbers were not very sound, so that, on the whole, I was sincerely glad when Almer called me at 12.30 a.m. He had slept as little as myself, and we both regretted that we had not started several hours earlier, so as to have been very near the top of the mountain by sunrise. However, that most brilliant idea not having occurred to us till it was too late to carry it into effect, we hurried over breakfast, and at 1.40 started on our way.

Our design was not only to make the ascent of the Aletschhorn, but to combine with it the passage to the Lötschen Thal, over the Jägi Glacier and Birch Grat, between the Kippel Breithorn and the Schienhorn, a tour which we had little doubt of being able to accomplish, as, from the account in the visitor's book by Mr. Tuckett, who had crossed the pass for the first time, the reverse way, about a week before, the time required for the latter appeared to be comparatively short. On going out into the open air, the view that greeted us of the superb masses of the Saas Grat and Fletschörner, seen under the light of a moon of most dazzling brilliancy, was beyond expression lovely, while the broad stream of the Aletsch Glacier, in our immediate proximity, stretching upwards as far as the Marjelen See, a river of ice, rippled only here and there by a few crevasses, was even more fascinating in appearance.

THE ALETSCHORN.

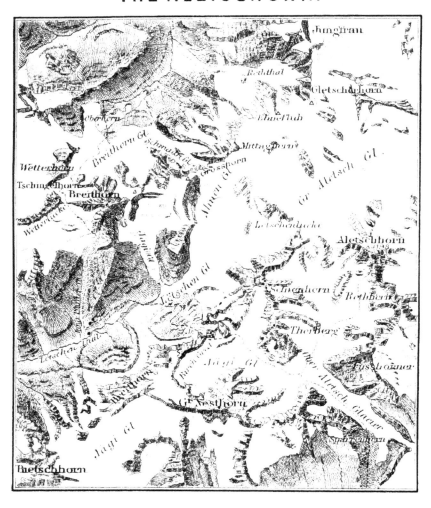

Turning our steps in the direction of this latter, we followed a good, but rough, path, along the lower slopes of the Lusgengrat above the glacier, which took us rapidly down until we were nearly on a level with the ice. We were walking with our backs to the moon, and the long shadows, which we consequently cast in front of us, bothered us considerably, and in one or two places, where the path had been carried away by avalanches, and not yet repaired, nearly threw us on our noses. The Ober Aletsch Glacier, into whose upper regions we were about to penetrate, falls towards the Great Aletsch, slightly above the Lusgen Alp, in a steep, but very narrow, ice-fall, whose insignificant appearance by no means prepares the traveller for the great extent of the snow-fields which it drains. The ice-fall itself is probably not impracticable, but the ascent would be long, laborious, and uninteresting, and is fortunately unnecessary, as the lower slopes of the Sparrenhorn, on its right bank, afford an easy route by which to flank the enemy. Up these slopes we turned in due course, and, mounting rapidly, were soon on a smooth stretch of avalanche snow between the rocks on the left, and the moraine of the glacier on the right, over which we tramped in luxurious ease, until it died away, and the moraine itself had to be taken to. It was just 3.20, and the day was beginning to break over the distant mountains at the head of the Binnen Thal, and in the neighbourhood of the Gries Glacier; the colour of the sky in that direction was something perfectly wonderful, and the gradation of tints such as no pen could describe, nor pencil reproduce. We followed the moraine for a short distance, until the glacier on our right seemed to promise a more agreeable road, when Almer and I proposed getting on to it. We here had a first specimen of the quality of our friend Eggel, who objected to our proposal on the ground that the ice was crevassed, but, as we had the evidence of our eyes to the contrary, we disregarded his protest, and scrambled down on to the glacier, which was as level and easy to traverse as the Unteraar Glacier below the Abschwung. Pushing on rapidly over the smooth ice, at 4.0 a.m. we were abreast of a broad opening in the left bank of the glacier, through which a second stream of at least equal width to that which we had been traversing, was seen stretching upwards to the base of a noble peak, which rose symmetrically from its head in a wall of crags, tapering away to a point.

The peak was the object of our ambition, the Aletschhorn itself, the second summit in the Oberland, and the glacier was the northern branch of the Jägi Glacier, that name being also applied on the map to the still more extensive ice-field, which rose gradually westward from our stand-point to the low ridge of the Birchgrat, between the Kippel Breithorn and the Scheinhorn. This latter is the natural source of the Ober Aletsch Glacier, that name, for some inconceivable reason, being only given on the map to the comparatively short length of ice between the junction of the two arms above mentioned and the main stream of the Great Aletsch. To avoid confusion, I shall hereafter speak of the glacier following from the Birchgrat in its entire length, as the Beich Firn, applying the name Ober Aletsch to that which comes down from the Aletschhorn, and is as distinct from its neighbour as the Lauteraar is from the Finsteraar, or the Talèfre from the Glacier du Géant. The stupidity, originally displayed by the Swiss engineers in their nomenclature of the Oberland peaks and glaciers, is conspicuous in this part of the district, where there are no less than four Jägi Glaciers in close proximity to each other, though perfectly distinct, and two Breithorns face to face on opposite sides of the Lötschen Thal.* The Aletschhorn, of course, absorbed the largest share of our regards, but on our left, at the head of a small steep, lateral, glacier, rose an almost equally beautiful, though less cle-

---

* Since this was written, the nomenclature of this and other parts of the Bernese chain, depicted in Sheet 18 of the Carte Dufour, has been revised by the Swiss Authorities. The name "Jägi" is now no longer applied to either of the two glaciers here described. The name "Ober Aletsch" has been extended to the ice-field under the Aletschhorn, while to the still more extensive reservoir below the Birch (or Beich) Grat, the appellation Beich Firn has been given. The two Breithorns still remain.

vated summit, the Gross Nesthorn, a bold, rocky peak, 12,534 feet in height, whose southern face looks down upon the Gredetsch Thal, a small valley, which drains into the Rhone between Visp and Brieg. We turned sharp to the right, towards the point of junction of the Ober Aletsch Glacier with the Beich Firn, and at 4.10 came to a big stone, near the right bank of the former, which was selected as a suitable spot whereon to deposit our traps, to await our return from the attack on the peak which was looking down upon us so defiantly.

From where we first caught sight of the mountain, its appearance was suggestive of considerable difficulties, but, from our friendly stone, we saw that, right and left from the 'actual summit, arêtes fell to well-marked depressions in the ridge at the head of the glacier, which were led up to by slopes of névé, steep, but evidently practicable, so that serious difficulty was only to be anticipated, if at all, between them and the summit. So far as inaccessibility goes, the peak is, therefore, a gigantic impostor, and at 4.20 we started to express personally to the offender our opinion on the subject. The "cirque" of névé at the head of the Ober Aletsch Glacier is divided into two bays, of nearly equal dimensions, by a spur which runs straight down from the face of the Aletschhorn. On either side the névé is steep, and falls towards the level glacier below in a rather dislocated condition. The western bay, however, runs up to a very well-marked depression, just under the Aletschhorn, in the ridge, which circles round from that peak to the Schienhorn,—a depression which could be reached without the slightest difficulty, and must be close to the Col of the Lötschen-lücke, which it cannot much exceed in height. This would, probably, afford an interesting route from the Bell Alp to the Eggischhorn (or Faulberg), or vice versâ, for persons wishing to see a little of the glaciers in the neighbourhood of both those stations without ascending any of the higher peaks. The eastern bay is steeper and more crevassed than its neighbour, and is shut in at its head by the line of cliffs running from the

Aletschhorn to the Fusshörner, but at one spot these cliffs are masked by a broad couloir, or slope of snow, leading up to the crest of the ridge, close to a prominent point projecting from it, and to reach this point was now our object. We pushed rapidly up the glacier, striking diagonally across from the right towards the left bank, and crossing in the operation the considerable moraine which draws its supplies from the spur mentioned above. The snow could not have been in better order, and we were soon near the head of the glacier, which, up to the foot of the ice-fall, is as level as a billiard table. The direct course would have been to keep straight on in the direction of the peak, but the slopes were too steep and broken to render this advisable, even if it were possible, and in lieu thereof, after passing the last spur of the Fusshörner, we turned up to the right, where slopes of snow promised to lead us by a considerable détour to a point above the final plunge. The hardness of the snow was here rather a nuisance, as the inclination was sufficiently great to make the walking difficult without step-cutting, an expenditure of time and labour we were loth to incur. So we struggled on as best we could, occasionally losing our footing, but always managing to avoid a roll down the ground we had already passed, a manœuvre, the most serious result of which would have been the time lost in a second ascent. The labour, however, was severe, and it was a welcome relief when, after winding about amongst a few crevasses, we came to a more level stretch of snow, in the middle of which, close under the crags, was a small patch of moraine, whose appearance was irresistibly suggestive of breakfast. It was 5.20, so that that meal was certainly due, and we, therefore, established ourselves in comfortable attitudes to pay our "devoirs" to the solids. Nature refreshed, the rope was for the first time put on, and at 5.50 we resumed our exertions.

From our halting-place, the Dom and Matterhorn had been the only distant peaks visible, but now, as we gradually progressed up the steep snow-slopes, the form of the Weisshorn came into view over the elevated ridge which runs

.east from the Gross Nesthorn. Seen from any point, this
glorious mountain has, for grace of outline, no rival in the
Alps, but, accustomed as I was to the sight of it from all
quarters, I was quite unprepared for the ravishing beauty
of its appearance as witnessed from these slopes above the
Ober Aletsch Glacier. I can call to mind no object which
has left on me such an impression of perfect loveliness, the
effect being intensified by some peculiar condition of the
atmosphere, imparting a mellow tint to the distant snows,
and softening the outlines, so that the mountain had an unsubstantial aspect, and scarcely seemed to belong to earth.
Every succeeding step in the ascent was now productive of
a fresh enjoyment, as peak after peak of the great Pennine
chain opened out, until every summit, from the Dom to Mont
Blanc, stood out clear in the southern sky. This gradual
unfolding of the panorama must be lost by those who make
the ascent by the ordinary route of the Mittel Aletsch
Glacier, which is one amongst many reasons why the Bell
Alp should be preferred to the Eggischhorn as the starting point for the expedition. For some time we kept
close under the crags on our right, which are very precipitous, making long zig-zags up the slopes, the snow on
which was generally in good condition, but let us through
into the soft substratum once or twice. But at last we
bore well away to the left, towards the centre of the
glacier, the most broken part of which we had left below
us, and commenced winding about amongst the few huge
crevasses which intersected the slopes that intervened between us and a sort of plateau at the foot of the broad
couloir leading up to the crest of the ridge. The first of
these crevasses was almost worthy to be called a bergschrund, so steep was the slope above it, and Almer's first
effort to get across was a failure, as the bridge gave way
with him, whereat Eggel looked rather uncomfortable, and
muttered something about "acht zu nehmen," which seemed
to indicate that he had had little experience of the virtues
of a rope on such a place. Of course, the obstacle was
soon surmounted, but a good deal of winding about was

necessary before we stood at the base of the final slope,
close to the right of a patch of rocks running down from
the ridge in front, by which the ascent might also be made
when the slope happens to be in bad order, The angle of
this was, I should think, about 40°, and some avalanche
débris on the lower portion of it appeared to hint that,
late in the day, some of the snow above was in the habit
of coming down with a run, but at this early hour of the
morning there was no fear of such a catastrophe, and
Almer, accordingly, started a-head, kicking the steps at a
great pace. We had all along travelled fast, but Almer now
surpassed himself, and worked away with such energy and
rapidity, that Eggel could not repress his astonishment
at his apparent insensibility to fatigue. The slope was
generally snow, but occasional patches of ice cropped out
here and there, requiring footsteps of the coal-scuttle order,
but these were, fortunately, few and far between, and, although the distance was greater than it had appeared from
below, we got on to the ridge at 7.30, just to the end of the
small projecting tooth of rock which is visible from the
Eggischhorn, as the first point on the arête to the south-
west of the summit.

As we emerged on to this ridge, an exclamation of
astonishment burst from us at the magnificence of the
prospect which was suddenly unrolled before our eyes.
An instant before our view had been limited to the wall
up which we were toiling, but now we looked across the
whole extent of the vast waste of snow and ice, from which
rise the giants of the Oberland. Ten minutes were spent
in looking about us, but we deferred careful examination of the glorious objects around us until we should be
on the summit, which was now in full view to our left, but
separated from us by a long arête, up which we started at
7.40. This arête is neither very steep nor very difficult;
indeed, Eggel declared that, in the two previous ascents
(by Germans), the passage had only occupied three-quarters
of an hour, and had been effected without even using the
rope, the rocks being particularly good, but upon the present

occasion the rocks were in many places covered with snow, and one or two steps were, in consequence, rendered undeniably awkward. The arête is exceedingly narrow, but, so long as it was possible to keep right along the top, we got on well enough. Teeth, however, projecting from the ridge, made this sometimes impracticable, and then we were obliged to pass below them, along the exceedingly steep slopes of rock, masked by rather soft snow, above the Ober Aletsch Glacier. I must confess to not having liked some of these détours at all. Not that there was any difficulty in the operation, but the snow seemed to me to be by no means in a safe condition, and very likely to give way under our weight, in which case we should have landed on the glacier below—rapidly, it is true, but, I am afraid, in a general state of smash, that would have debarred us from ever boasting of the speed with which we had effected the movement. It was impossible to avoid the danger by keeping below the other side of the ridge as, on that side, the cliffs fell to the Mittel Aletsch Gletscher in a sheer precipice, so smooth, that a cat could not have found footing on it. Altogether, this part of the route gave us some very pretty scrambling, and (from a climbing point of view) relieved the ascent from the dulness and monotony which had previously characterised it. The length of the arête was greater than I had expected, and the summit was seldom visible until we were close to it, one point after another, as usual, presenting itself as the genuine article; but these imposters were at last left behind, and at 8.50 a.m. we stood upon the true summit of the Aletschhorn, 13,803 feet in height.

The summit is (or was upon this occasion) a snowy ridge some half-dozen yards in length, of which the end furthest from the point first reached is the highest, and on this was planted an alpenstock, left by some former visitor, of which I forthwith cut off the end as a memento, in the absence of any available pieces of rock. It would have been scarcely possible to have had more favourable conditions for enjoying the wonderful view that was extended around us, as, although over the plain of Switzerland there were some clouds, yet, in every other direction, from the mountains of the Engadine to and beyond Mont Blanc, the sky was perfectly clear. I suppose there is no other summit in the Alps so well placed for a view of the great Pennine chain as the Aletschhorn, its position being extremely central, and the intervening distance not too great for easy identification and careful examination of the long line of peaks and glaciers. The Weisshorn, Dom, Fletschhörner, Matterhorn, Dent Blanche, Grand Combin, and Mont Blanc, of course, towered supreme above their neighbours, but we picked out many old friends amongst the common throng, associated with pleasant memories, and amongst these Almer did not fail to point out, with his usual rhapsody, the point of the Steinbock and the great swelling snow fields of the Moiry Glacier. So, also, did we retrace a large portion of our way down from the Biesjoch and up to the Moming Pass, Eggel being favoured by Almer with some reminiscences of those memorable expeditions, which made his hair almost stand on end with astonishment. The peaks of the Oberland itself were, after all, the most attractive in my eyes, and of these, the Bietschhorn and Gross Nesthorn, close at hand, though by no means the most elevated, were certainly amongst the grandest, the former especially, towering abruptly from the ridge above the Lötschen Thal in a wonderful way. Scarcely less striking were the two subordinate groups of the Balmhorn, Altels, and Rinderhorn, and the Blumlis Alp and Doldenhorn, separated from each other by the broad snow trough of the Tschingel Glacier. The Balmhorn was particularly fine, and presented his precipitous face to us, overhanging the Lötschen Pass and Gastern Thal. I had once thought of attempting the ascent of this peak, which is a few feet higher than the Blumlis Alp, and we now again discussed which would probably be the best line of attack, in happy ignorance that the problem no longer remained to be solved, and that the Walkers, at that very moment, were calmly studying the panorama from the hitherto virgin summit.

At last, turning round towards the north, we had before us all our old friends, the sharp pinnacle of the Jungfrau, looking scarcely lower than our own position, connected by the low ridge of the Jungfraujoch with the rounded, but noble, form of the Mönch, which may almost be looked upon as Almer's peculiar property, he having assisted on every ascent yet made. Then came the black crags of the Eiger, the huge mass of the Schreckhorn, and, over its shoulder, the sharp pyramid of the Wetterhorn, then the long ridge of the Vieschergrat, leading up to our old conquest, the Gross Viescherhorn, and, lastly, the monarch of the district, the Finsteraarhorn, a worthy ruler over such a court of noble vassals. Although the fact had been frequently forced upon our notice, yet I never quite appreciated the enormous quantity of snow which was lying this year in the high Alps until the present time, when I was able to see at a glance how changed even familiar objects were by their unaccustomed mantle. This was especially manifest in the neighbourhood of the Trugberg Glacier, the ice-fall of which was almost entirely concealed, while the rocks on its right bank, where George and I passed a night in 1862, were almost undistinguishable, and would certainly now have afforded quarters even less comfortable than we had then found, which is saying a good deal. The long range of the Grindelwald Viescherhörner, too, which ordinarily shows a wall of rock above the Trugberg Glacier, was now masked by steep slopes of snow, through which the rocks only cropped out here and there, but what chiefly interested and disgusted Almer and myself was the sight of the tremendous cliffs of the Schreckhorn, perfectly white with snow. Now we had looked forward to the ascent of this, to my mind the most attractive of all the Oberland mountains, as the finale and crowning "course" of my campaign, never doubting but that by the end of July the rocks would be in a sufficiently good condition, and our disappointment at finding them in a state which would evidently render the ascent for the time quite impracticable, was as bitter as it was unexpected. However, notwithstanding Almer's authoritative dictum, "Mit so viel Schnee, wir kommen nicht auf dem Schreckhorn," I was very loth to abandon my long-cherished plan, and continued to nourish a secret hope that all might yet be well.*

In spite of a bright sun, the wind was not too warm, and by 9.5 a.m. we had had enough of it, so, after a parting look round, we took our departure down the arête by which we had mounted, but, had we not been bound for the Lötschen Thal, we could have easily gone down to the Eggischhorn by the regular route, as was afterwards done by Hornby's party. The descent required as much care as the ascent, and the snow was in an even more ticklish state, but it occupied less time, and at 9.45 we reached the Col on the ridge, where we remained for eating purposes till 10.15, and then resumed our downward journey. We glissaded down the lower portion of the final slope, and then had a long and fatiguing grind down the crevassed slopes beneath, the snow being thoroughly softened and letting us in at nearly every step. Indeed, I found it, as a rule, more advantageous to avoid the steps of the leader and strike out an independent course to the right or left, by which manœuvre I was often able to slide or slip along for yards at a time, without the otherwise inevitable plunge. Almer did the whole of the work, as Eggel, after going a-head in a spiritless way for less than ten minutes, declared that he was too tired to do any more, whereupon he was sent to the rear, and remained there for the rest of the day. The crevasses on the lower slopes were more insecure than they had been in the early morning, and a certain amount of dodging was required before we were fairly down on the level glacier. The snow here was in a worse condition than ever, and we had a most irritating walk, our tempers not being materially improved by finding ourselves upon several

---

* It has since been shown that snow, far from impeding, facilitates the ascent of the Schreckhorn. In the season of 1866, when the quantity of snow was enormous, several ascents of the mountain were made without any serious difficulty being experienced, and in far shorter time than had been required in previous years.

occasions suddenly plunged above our knees into some glacier brook, whose waters were completely hidden by the snowy covering. At 11.45 we rejoined our baggage on the big stone, and from there might have reached the Bell Alp in two hours more, so that the ascent of the Aletsch-horn from that side is not a formidable expedition, either as regards difficulties or the time required for it.

The heat was most intense, and the thought of the plod over the smooth snow fields of the Beich Firn before we could reach the Col was not a pleasant one. However, every moment lost would increase our ultimate labour, so at 12.15 we shouldered our respective packs, and turned towards the moraine on the right bank of the Ober Aletsch Glacier, under the Thorberg, as the long promontory is called, which projects from the Schienhorn, and separates the two glaciers. The snow between the interstices of the moraine let us through up to our waists, and it was with gloomy anticipations that we rounded the last spurs of the Thorberg, and emerged on to the main glacier, which stretched away for a long distance in front, covered with snow, which could almost be seen melting under the burning sun. We were about to strike into the middle of this cauldron, when Almer's eye was attracted by an almost imperceptible difference between the colour of the snow under the cliffs on the left bank and of that in the middle of the glacier. "There" said he, "I think we shall have avalanche snow, let us try;" and, changing our direction accordingly, we found that he was right. The winter avalanches from the Thorberg had not yet entirely melted, and the particles being welded more closely together than on the regular névé, the surface was less sensible to the heat, and the result was, that, instead of floundering about hopelessly, as we had expected, we walked on very fast, scarcely sinking above our ankles. A plateau of névé, stretched right up to the ridge at the head of the glacier, for which we were making, but was separated from the lower level at which we were by a rather broad ice-fall, neither very steep nor very much broken, which was divided into two arms by a low shelf of rocks. I know scarcely anything more beautiful than the ice scenery by which we were surrounded, as we approached the base of this final ascent. We were standing in the centre of a vast "cirque," into which extensive glaciers streamed on all sides. In front was the double fall, just mentioned; on our right, a broad affluent came down from the Schienhorn; while, on our left, a great bay between the Gross Nesthorn and Kippel Breithorn was filled by a superb sea of séracs. Of the three peaks which thus looked down upon us, the Gross Nesthorn, though yielding in height to the Schienhorn, is incomparably the most imposing. Its ascent on this side would be difficult, but, Almer thought, practicable, though I felt rather doubtful on the point, the sides of the mountain being loaded with precipitous séracs and ice cliffs, which it would be equally difficult either to scale or avoid.* From the ridge of the Birchgrat above the central ice-falls, connecting the Kippel Breithorn and Schienhorn, a prominent double tooth of rock projected, the highest point of which is, doubtless, that marked on the Federal map 3120′, mètres, or 10,237 feet, and both to the north and south of it were very tempting-looking depressions. The question now was, which of these was the Col; and, as Eggel turned out to be profoundly ignorant on the subject, although when I engaged him he had professed to know all about it, Almer and I had to settle the matter for ourselves, and, after some discussion, determined to make for the southern gap, between 3120′ and the Breithorn. I may as well at once say that we were entirely wrong in our decision, the true course being to the north, a fact of which, later in the day, we were convinced, and which has received confirmation since, Mr. Tuckett having informed me that he (who made the passage from the Lötschen Thal, a week or so earlier), had passed at that point. Keeping to the north side of the "cirque," we struck across it to the foot of the

---

* The Gross Nesthorn was ascended in 1865 by Mr. George from this side without any difficulty at all.

.ice-fall, and at 1.20 reached the base of a steep, narrow slope of old snow, running up between a patch of moraine and some rocks, forming part of a spur of the Schienhorn. Over these rocks trickled some very dirty water, with which we quenched our burning thirst before tackling the snow slope, that promised to lead us on to the upper plateau. The slope was sufficiently steep, but Almer kicked the steps with his usual vigour, so that we were soon near the top, when, turning to the left, we scrambled across the moraine, which was chiefly composed of fine shale that slipped away under the foot, and then, after a few zigzags over good snow, we were fairly on the upper plateau which stretched away in gentle slopes of névé to the ridge of the Birchgrat. In consequence of our previous manœuvres, we were very much to the north of the point at which we proposed to pass the ridge, so now had to strike across the intervening snow fields diagonally, in the course of which operation we realized what we should have suffered lower down, had not Almer fortunately thought of keeping to the avalanche snow, out of our direct course, instead of making straight for the Col by the centre of the glacier,—the snow was, without exaggeration, up to our middles, and we almost waded through it. As we advanced, we opened out several depressions in the ridge north of point 3120′, which almost induced us to change our direction, but, from some reason or other, we were all persuaded that the real Col lay to the south; so the temptation was resisted, and we kept on our way, until at 2.20 we stood in the desired gap, and found ourselves looking down a precipitous couloir on to the Distel Glacier and the head of the Lötschen Thal.

"Ganz unmöglich," said Eggel, as he glanced down the "cheminée;" and I was almost inclined to agree with him. But the cautious Almer said nothing until he had carefully examined the enemy, and, when fully satisfied, at once set my doubts at rest, with the cheering dictum, "Schwerrig, aber es geht." That point settled, we sat ourselves down on the rocks to look about us, our principal anxiety being as to the locality of the cows in the Lötschen Thal, which, however, was soon relieved by our discovering them, precisely where we should have wished them to be, viz., at the Güggi Staffel Alp, just below the end of the Lötschen Glacier, and close to the entrance of the Inner Pfaffler Thal, up which our morrow's route would lie. The long snow plateau of the Petersgrat and the bold peak of the Tschingelhorn were straight in front of us, but the Wetterlücke and Lauterbrunnen Breithorn were concealed; the beautiful snow summit of the Kippel Breithorn, which rises to the south of the Col to a height of 12,452 feet, is certainly not accessible from it, as a lower point, itself by no means easy of access, intervenes. We had no means of determining the height of the Col, but, assuming the correctness of the figures placed on the Federal map against the rocky tooth to the north, it can scarcely exceed 10,000 feet. At 2.35 we commenced the descent down the rocks on the right side of the couloir, a course which was rendered necessary by the presence at its very head of a perpendicular and almost overhanging wall of snow, some fifteen feet in height, which effectually cut off access to the centre of the gully. The rocks were very steep, and so broken, that the greatest caution was required, and it was with considerable difficulty that we crept down a short distance, to a point from which we could get on to the snow which, as usual in such positions, occupied the middle of the channel. But this snow was only resting on ice, and Almer hesitated to take to it, as he feared that, in its half-melted condition, there was not enough to give footing, and that we might create an avalanche. However, further progress by the rocks was almost impossible, so he determined to run the risk. The three or four steps that were necessary, in order to get off the rocks, were the most nervous of the whole day, the rocks close above the snow being glazed with ice, while the hand-hold was "nil." Eggel and I, however, held hard until Almer was safe in the centre of the couloir, and had proclaimed the welcome fact that the snow was better than he had expected, when we followed in turn, holding on by our eye-lids. The couloir was only a few feet wide, and its inclination must have been at least 50°, but, once committed fairly to the work, we got on pretty well, the snow being thick over the ice and not so soft as we had supposed. Still the greatest care had to be exercised to avoid a slip, and we all went down with our faces to the snow, Almer kicking and treading down the steps, which we fished for in turn, holding on firmly to the step above until at least one foot was securely landed. Lower down, the slope was less steep, and we were able to adopt the usual and more agreeable style of progression, face forwards, until we gradually neared the bergschrund at the bottom,—the dimensions of this were insignificant, and at 3.25 we crossed it, without any difficulty, on to the névé of the small Distel Glacier.

During our descent furrows in the snow had caused us to suspect that we had adopted a route, which, though new to human beings, was not entirely unfrequented by missiles antagonistic to such intruders, but we were scarcely prepared for the enormous quantity of stones and avalanche débris, lying across the Distel Glacier, which had evidently travelled from the heights above by the same course as ourselves. This satisfied us that we had not selected the true col, as no man, *ascending* from the Lötschen Thal, would be mad enough to select such a line of march, after ocular proof of the peril attendant on the ascent; the less so, as the slopes, leading up to the ridge north of point 1320′, are from that side obviously the proper way, though at all points they are exceedingly steep. Our connection with the Distel Glacier, which flows steeply down to the foot of the Lötschen Glacier, was not long, as we simply crossed it, and at 3.30 got off the ice on to the slopes of the Birchflühen on its right bank, when a halt was made for ten minutes to take off the rope. Thenceforward our descent was rapid, the slopes, though steep, being very easy to traverse, and we scudded merrily along over stones, shale, and, finally, scanty herbage, admiring the beautiful glacier of Jägi which streamed down on the opposite side of the valley, from between the Lauterbrunnen Breithorn, and the fine peak of the Grosshorn. It would be quite possible to get on to the ridge connecting those peaks from the Lötschen Thal, but the practicability of a descent on the Lauterbrunnen side is something more than doubtful.* The necessities of the ground drove us gradually to the right, and, the final slopes being very abrupt, we had to make a considerable détour in that direction, before, at 4.15, we reached the level of the Lötschen Glacier which had next to be crossed.

The moraine which had first to be scrambled over was of considerable size, but the glacier itself was particularly smooth and easy, and, so far as we could see, continued so right up to the depression of the Lötschen-lücke at its head, the walk to which must be the very incarnation of dulness. The right bank of the glacier was soon reached, and we shortly hit upon a faint track, which gradually improved into a decent path, that led us over pleasant pastures to the highest châlets in the valley, those of the Güggi Staffel, at 5.0 p.m. Only women were in charge, who seemed by no means anxious to receive us, but at last consented on our solemn promise to pay for whatever we had, as to which they seemed strangely sceptical. The châlets themselves were well-built and clean, but the accommodation was not first-rate, there being no hay for our beds, and only a quantity of Alpine roses, scattered on the floor of our hostess's bedroom, of which, however, we were only too glad to avail ourselves. The evening was lovely, and, while Almer and Eggel set off to reconnoitre the Inner Pfaffler Thal, I lay on the Alp, studying our couloir, the appearance of which, from below, was positively appalling, so that I found it hard to believe the little actual difficulty we had encountered in its descent. While thus engaged, the sudden appearance of a hen suggested the possible presence of eggs, and an omelette for supper; so, when the men returned, inquiries were made with a favourable result, as a dozen eggs were produced, with which

---

* The pass was made by Mr. Hornby's party in 1866.

Almer concocted a capital omelette, after the demolition of which we retired for the night.

Friday, 22nd July.—My bed of roses was not free from the traditional thorns, and, on the whole, I should have preferred the prosaic straw to the more poetical material. Behind my head, moreover, was a ruminant and bilious cow, only separated from me by a thin partition, who took particular care that I should not be oblivious of his presence for more than a quarter of an hour at a time, so that altogether the night was not a luxurious one, and I was by no means sorry when Almer called me at 1.30 a.m. to commence the labours of another day. Some coffee was brewed, and our hostesses paid what they demanded for our accommodation, the sum being ludicrously small, after their doubts of our solvency last evening, and then, at 2.40 a.m., we started, the weather not presenting so favourable an appearance as we could have wished, and the moon, on whose light we had reckoned, being almost obscured by clouds.

The problem, the solution of which we were about to attempt, was a peculiarly interesting one. The depression of the Wetter-lücke between the Tschingelhorn and Breithorn is not only the natural line of communication on the map between the head of the valley of Lauterbrunnen and the Lötschen Thal, but it is the best marked Col across the chain of the Bernese Alps between the Jungfrau and the Gemmi. Seen from Mürren, Berne, or any point commanding a distant view of the range, it is, like the Jungfraujoch, "obtrusively and offensively a pass," but, also, like its loftier and more famous neighbour, nature has placed on the north side such serious impediments to access, that up to the time of our expedition, the pass remained untraversed, and its snows unprofaned by human feet. In Studer's "Hochalpen," indeed, mention is made of an alleged record of a passage at this point having been effected in the year 1783 by four miners of Lauterbrunnen, who crossed to the Valais for the purpose of attending the Catholic service, and returned the next day by the same route; and Mons. Studer adds

that the pass had since been abandoned in consequence
of the impassibility of the Breithorn Glacier. Now,
I must confess to being profoundly sceptical as to the
truth of the numerous stories current in Switzerland about
the existence of passes, in former years comparatively
easy of access, at points which are now either quite inaccessible, or only to be reached with great danger and difficulty. The abandonment of all these alleged passes is accounted for by the increase in the size of the glaciers, but
it is in no case stated whether this increase was gradual
or sudden, and it is certainly curious that, if true, there
should be no reliable record, official or otherwise, of a
physical change which must have been productive of such
serious inconvenience to the inhabitants of the valleys on
either side of the several chains. I cannot myself believe
in such an increase of the glaciers at any point within
anything like a reasonable period, as would have closed
routes formerly practicable, but it would be a cheering
thing to suppose such an event possible now-a-days, as,
without some such interposition to convert paths, now
traversed by mules and tourists, into places suitable for
the haunts of chamois and mountaineers in general, and
the Alpine Club in particular, the supply of novelties in
the high Alps will soon be exhausted. However, whether
the passage of the devout miners be mythical or not, certain it is, that no travellers, animated either by piety or
curiosity, had followed in their steps, the only recognised
route between the Lötschen Thal and Lauterbrunnen being
the circuitous one by the Tschingel Glacier and the ridge
of the Petersgrat, which, though by no means uninteresting,
is too free from difficulty to be quite satisfactory. We
hoped, therefore, to establish a route, which would be
shorter in point of distance, if not in point of time, and
would also have that spice of difficulty and uncertainty
about it, which gives a relish to the enjoyment of even the
finest scenery.

Leaving the châlets, we turned immediately up the steep
grass slopes behind them, in order to get over the shoulder

of the hill between us and the Inner Pfaffler Thal, the last
of the numerous short glens which drain down into the
Lötschen Thal. The researches of the men the night
before had resulted in discovering a faint track up these
slopes leading in the required direction, and upon this track
we soon hit, and followed it up, until we were brought to a
point overlooking the glen at a considerable depth below,
when it appeared to think that its mission was fulfilled,
and abruptly vanished, leaving us to adopt what further
route we thought best. This was awkward, but we had no
fancy to lose the height we had gained, so in the first place
we tried to keep along the hill-side at about the same level.
Difficulties, however, thickened round us, the slope of the
ground was very precipitous, and we were encountered by
smooth faces of rock, the passage of which, in the dark,
was neither easy nor safe. After a few minutes' scrambling,
therefore, we agreed that discretion was the better part of
valour, and determined to make our way down to the
torrent without further loss of time. This proved a task
of no great difficulty, and, working down through the scanty
forest on the hill-side, we were rewarded, when fairly in
the bed of the valley, by stumbling upon another track,
which was visible for a long way in front, winding along
the left bank of the stream.

The Inner Pfaffler Thal is an inexpressibly-dreary glen,
nearly bare of vegetation, and altogether uninteresting. It
is closed at the head by two glaciers, of which we first came
in sight of the one we were *not* going to traverse, that comes
down from the Tschingelhorn in a south-easterly direction,
and undoubtedly communicates directly with the Petersgrat,
which could be reached by it. The main glacier, however,
which flows due south from between the Tschingelhorn and
Breithorn, soon came into view. Both are of precisely the
same character, terminating at a considerable height above
the bottom of the valley on very steep rocks, which they
must once have covered entirely. The one first mentioned
descends rather lower than the other, but in either case
the final tongue of ice is insignificant, the névé scarcely

giving rise to any *glacier*, properly so called. The inclination of the valley is very gradual up to the foot of the rocks below the glacier, but, as these were evidently inaccessible " en face," we gradually bore away to our right, in which direction there seemed most chance of getting on to the upper névé without serious preliminary difficulties. The grass slopes were steep, but we mounted rapidly, and, at 4.40, after some tolerably stiff scrambling, and being once obliged to retrace our steps, we were high above the valley, and at the foot of a very steep and narrow couloir, which stretched invitingly upwards. We all agreed that by daylight it would be possible to reach this point from the châlets, as we had first tried, by keeping at a high level along the rocks and grass slopes, but in the dark it would not be easy to find the way, and not very wise to try to do so. The couloir was as steep as was agreeable, and the footing by no means too good, but Almer led us up at a great pace, showering down stones at the rate of nineteen to the dozen, some of which came in unpleasant proximity to our heads. I found, indeed, some difficulty in keeping up, as, on the lower slopes, I had had an awkward fall, and, in saving myself, damaged my right hand, which for the time was " hors de combat," no slight loss in a climb of the nature we were engaged in. However, we got to the top in due course, rather pumped, and, after a less fatiguing pull over the stone-covered slopes above, came, at 5.15, to the moraine on the extreme left bank of the glacier, close under the great southern back-bone of the Breithorn, and this was selected as an eligible place for breakfasting, in consequence of the presence of water close at hand.

We were already at a great height, indeed, not far below the level of the Col, as, looking across the lower part of the glacier, whose tail was now a long way beneath us, our eyes ranged over the level snow fields which extend along the base of the Tschingelhorn towards the Petersgrat, although we could not see the exact point where it is usual to cross that ridge. Looking down the Inner Pfaffler Thal, the magnificent peak of the Bietschhorn was straight in

front of us, rising precipitously from the very abrupt and
rugged ridge which forms the left flank of the Lötschen
Thal. The mountain was seen to perfection from base to
summit, and certainly vindicated its claim to consideration
as one of the most striking single summits in the Alps.
Less satisfactory was the prospect in other directions,
where heavy masses of cloud were gathering and drifting
up the valley towards us with ominous rapidity, suggesting the desirability of gaining the Col with as little
delay as possible, so as to get a look down on the Lauterbrunnen side before everything was obscured. We had
never expected serious difficulty on the south side of the
pass, but had been prepared for some trouble in getting on
to the glacier. This, however, the most doubtful part of
the first stage of the expedition, had been accomplished
with comparative ease, and at 5.50, having put on the
rope, we started again, expecting a short and easy run
over a level and uncrevassed glacier.

Crossing the moraine, a broad tract of avalanche débris
from the cliffs of the Breithorn first presented itself. This
did not appear to have fallen recently, and was traversed
without difficulty, and, on getting off it, we were rejoiced to
find that the snow on the glacier was in excellent order,
scarcely yielding at all under our weight. In consequence
of the détour necessary to approach the glacier, we were
now far to the right of the Col, which was hidden from us
by the intervening fields of névé. We, therefore, struck
well away to the left in its supposed direction, which was
indicated by the western arête of the Breithorn that falls
directly to it. We had intended, had the fates been propitious, to have made an attempt to ascend that mountain,
which has a height of 12,383 feet, from the Col, but the
threatening state of the weather necessitated the abandonment of the plan, there being no time to lose in accomplishing the main object of the expedition. Almer and
I, however, carefully examined the arête, and came to the
conclusion that, even under the most favourable circumstances, the ascent by it would probably be impractica-

ble, as it is very long and serrated, broken by enormous natural stonemen and deep and broad clefts, which would offer almost insurmountable obstacles to progress along it. As we passed right along the base of the peak, we had excellent opportunities for discovering a vulnerable point, if such existed, but we only saw one that seemed to offer any chance of success. This was in the angle between the western and south-western spurs, where a very long and steep snow couloir, broad at the bottom, but gradually narrowing in its upward course, ran very deep into the heart of the mountain, certainly in the direction of the summit, but, so far as we could see, not up to it, and what intervened we were unable to make out. Nevertheless, under other circumstances we should have gone up this couloir to see what was to be seen, as the mountain, though not one of the first order as regards height, is attractive from its boldness of form, and must command a most interesting view.* The glacier was at first particularly easy, and our route devoid of incident, but its inclination gradually steepened, and we were soon brought up at the edge of a magnificent chasm, some fifty feet in width and fringed with gigantic icicles in the most exquisite manner. Beautiful as the obstacle was, we could willingly have dispensed with its presence, as in either direction it ran for a considerable distance before it was hidden by a canopy of snow, and, even then, several trials were made before a point was found where the covering was sufficiently firm to allow us to cross. This was merely the first of similar difficulties, as we found ourselves entangled in a perfect maze of huge gulfs in the névé, few of which, indeed, gave any outward sign of their enormous extent, only a small crevice being, generally speaking, visible in the snow, which was found on examination to give access to a gulf, of the depth and dimensions of which it was difficult to form a just idea. The difficulty of finding a passage was, of course, some-

---

* The summit of the Breithorn was reached in 1865 from the Wetter-lücke by Herr von Fellenberg, and on the same day, a few minutes later, by Messrs. Hornby and Philpott. The ascent proved quite easy.

what lessened by this state of things, but even greater care had to be exercised than would have been necessary had the chasms been fully exposed to view. As it was, we were several times hard pushed to find a secure crossing, and upon more than one occasion the whole party at once was found to have been standing on the snowy roof of one of these "caves," when two of us, at least, were supposed to have been on firm ground. In short, I have been on very few places where, with so little actual difficulty, every step of the way has been so doubtful, and at a later period of the season, or in a year with less snow than 1864, a party trying the pass might find it impossible to traverse this curious névé without a ladder. The distance, too, was much greater than we had supposed, the appearance of the slopes from the valley below being very deceptive, while they are by no means so gentle as would be imagined; but Almer led with his usual courage and skill, and gradually picked his way amongst the hidden dangers, until we emerged from the labyrinth on to a comparative gentle and quite uncrevassed slope of snow, which stretched away towards the Col. While we were traversing this, the clouds, which had been steadily gathering, suddenly swooped down upon us, and completely blotted out the surrounding objects, so that we could not see five yards in any direction. The mist was of that peculiar milk-and-water colour which is most unfavourable for making out anything, and we really could scarcely distinguish the snow at our feet from the atmosphere around us. Still, we kept on our way in the supposed proper direction, knowing that, so long as the ground sloped upwards, we could not come to much harm, but the inclination became more and more slight, until at 7.15 a.m. we halted simultaneously, with an instinctive feeling that we were on the Col. Almer gave a shrill " Jodel," which, after a few seconds, was answered back by the cliffs of the Tschingelhorn, and our exact position was thus confirmed; so down we sat on the snow, and twiddled our thumbs, in the hopes of an eventual clearance.

To attempt the descent without seeing something of the

way was not to be thought of, as neither Almer nor myself
had the foggiest notion of the details of the Breithorn
Glacier, and we only knew for certain that it was so steep
and broken as to be reported impracticable. It was still
early in the day, and we could afford to sit, if necessary,
for a considerable number of hours. The air, too, was
remarkably warm, and there was a total absence of wind,
so that we might have been a good deal worse off. Half-
an-hour passed, and the state of affairs remained the same,
though the sun did make one desperate effort to force his
way through the dense mantle of mist, without, however,
the success he deserved. But at 8.0 we thought we might
as well creep down a little way, so set off, striking well
away to the left, towards where the Tschingelhorn was supposed to be, in which direction we had, for no particular
reason, taken it into our heads that the glacier would be
found least broken. The descent was very gentle, and we
had not gone many yards when the mist suddenly lifted,
disclosing to us our position, on the edge of a tremendous
crevasse running along the base of the Tschingelhorn, and,
at the same moment, the rain began to fall heavily. We
had, however, much to be thankful for, as the inconvenience
of getting wet through was trifling compared to what would
have been caused by a snow storm, or the continuance of
the fog, involving the possible descent of the whole party
into the beautiful, but frigid, bowels of a crevasse. The
chasm under the Tschingelhorn was about forty feet in
width, of great depth, and entirely unbridged, so that progress along the left side of the glacier was for the present impracticable, and we, therefore, struck well away to the right
in the direction of the Breithorn, descending very gradually.
The glacier here was not steep, but undermined by chasms
of a size which I have rarely seen paralleled. They were
mostly covered with snow, but snow so soft as to be quite
untrustworthy, stretching from one side to the other without
intermediate support. It soon became evident that our
rope must be re-arranged, so the surplus coils which had
been wound round Eggel were taken from him, and the

whole hundred feet brought into play, so that we had an interval of more than thirty feet between each person, Almer, of course, going in front, followed by myself, in the middle, and Eggel bringing up the rear, the countenance of the latter worthy expressing anything but satisfaction at the position in which he found himself.

Everything being thus arranged, Almer cautiously advanced, sounding vigorously with his axe at every step, and in many places turning aside, where I should have gone straight on, unsuspicious of danger. We all walked as if treading on eggs, and took particular care to keep to a hair's breadth in the footsteps of the leader, at the same time preserving the rope perfectly taut, not a very easy thing to do, with so great a length between each member of the party. So manœuvring, we passed several monsters with more or less trouble, and gradually described a gigantic zig-zag, until we were once more near the left side of the glacier, on the brow of the first great plunge which it makes towards the lower level, where, as was to be expected, the dislocation became very much more marked, and the covering of snow less general. Dodging about, we progressed pretty well, until we suddenly found ourselves on the brink of an enormous crevasse, running from the ridge of rocks, to which the name of Wetterhorn is given on the map, and which divides the upper portions of the Breithorn and Tschingel Glaciers, away to the right, until it merged in the chaos that reigned supreme in the centre of the glacier. At the point we had struck there was no bridge, but we turned along the upper edge to the right, never doubting but that we should either be able to turn the enemy, or find some sort of a way over; but we began to be slightly uneasy, when it appeared that the further we went in that direction, the wider became the obstacle, and the glacier generally more hopelessly impracticable. "Hier, es geht nicht," said Almer; and we, therefore, turned in our steps, and steered in the opposite quarter, towards the rocks of the Wetterhorn, casting the while anxious glances into the bowels of the chasm, in the vain hope of suddenly discovering a bridge; but at only one point was there even an apology for such a convenience, and there it was represented by a narrow strip of snow débris, which projected from either side of the crevasse a certain distance below the surface, and was evidently the relic of an avalanche. Where it merged in the walls of the chasm it seemed fixed with tolerable firmness, though at no point could it have been more than a foot and a half thick, but, in the centre, at the crown of the arch so to speak, it almost died away, leaving a mere patch of snow but a few inches deep. Almer looked at this for a few minutes, and then, turning away with a shake of the head, kept on his course towards the rocks, on reaching which a feeling of blank despair came over me. We were close to them, but completely cut off by a broad trench, caused by the melting away of the glacier; not that it much mattered, as, under any circumstances, it would have been impossible to traverse them, as their eastern face, which was towards us, proved to be a perfect wall. The end of the crevasse abutted against these cliffs, and yawned hopelessly in front of us, so, with despair at our hearts, we again turned in our steps, and I began to meditate upon the necessity of having to return to the Col, and make our way round the Tschingelhorn to the Petersgrat,—in the state of the weather, by no means a pleasant prospect. Almer, however, stood gazing fixedly at the débris, which, as before described, formed at one, and only one, point, a feeble connection between the two sides of the crevasse, and after an interval of profound meditation, announced his intention of trying to get across, and in spite of my adjurations to do nothing rash, adhered to his determination. Eggel and I, therefore, secured ourselves up to our middles in soft snow a short distance above, and, having satisfied ourselves of our ability to resist a sudden jerk, commenced slowly paying out Almer, who disappeared over the edge of the chasm, and was lost to view. The excitement of the next few minutes was intense, while we heard him busy with his axe, and I never experienced a more intense feeling of relief and joy than when our gallant leader emerged on to the opposite side of our baffled foe. It was now my turn, and, advancing to the edge, I let myself carefully down in Almer's steps, holding on by my axe, until I landed on the end of the débris, and commenced the passage. The width of the crevasse was about twenty feet, but of its depth I cannot speak, as the eye lost itself in a blue haze, and in such a position, I did not care to investigate the matter too closely. I never could have believed it possible that so frail a structure, as this bridge, would support a man's weight, and at one point in the centre, Almer's foot had actually gone through, but I effected the passage in safety, Almer drawing me in, as Eggel paid me out, until the further side was gained. Eggel then followed, and we resumed our descent through a labyrinth of which I shall give no description, but content myself with the bare statement, that turning some crevasses, cutting down and up others, and jumping the rest, we arrived at 9.20 on the central plateau of the glacier, having left the most serious difficulties behind us.

Bad as it was, the part of the glacier which we had traversed, was smooth and easy, compared with that more to the east under the Breithorn, where ice-cliffs were piled upon ice-cliffs in a way that I have never seen equalled. The lower ice-fall still remained to be passed, and we determined to attack this as near the centre as possible, in preference to seeking a way under the rocks of the Wetterhorn. The event proved the wisdom of our choice, as, though the fall was very steep and broken, we got through without serious difficulty, thanks to the snow which choked most of the huge crevasses, that later in the year might be very troublesome. Below the fall, we got on to a small patch of rocks, which divides the glacier into two branches, of which the western one, communicating with the Tschingel Glacier, is the smallest. We scrambled down on to the eastern, or main, arm, and followed it along the base of the rocks until 9.40, when we reached a point where it curled over in a long steep bank of ice without a particle of snow, towards the Oberhorn Alp. To have cut steps down this

would have taken hours, so Almer started off to try and
find a way by the western branch.   At 9.50, he returned,
having been successful in his search, so we again climbed
over the rocks, and found a steep and narrow gully between
them and the ice, down which we descended with some
difficulty, and much care to avoid dislodging the loose
stones.   It was a dirty piece of work, the rocks being
covered with grit, and very wet from the rain, and I was
well pleased, when, after working round to the right, we
were able to make our way on to the smooth and level
glacier, covered with easy moraine, at the foot of the steep
bank of ice we had thus circumvented.

At 10.30 we halted for a few minutes to take off the rope,
and then pushed on over the stone-covered glacier, which
gradually died away on the scanty pastures of the Oberhorn,
in the middle of which was an exquisite little lake of deep
but clear water.   In fine weather, the view from this point,
right down the long valley of Lauterbrunnen, and of the
great amphitheatre of peaks and glaciers which circles round
from the Jungfrau and Roththal to the Tschingel Glacier
and Gspaltenhorn, must, even judging from what was
vouchsafed to us, be one of almost unequalled magnificence,
and the spot is certainly worthy of more frequent visits
than it receives.   We wandered about a good deal before,
at 11.0, we hit upon the wretched "berg-hütte," which is
the highest hovel in the valley, and then lost a great deal
of time in hunting for the path downwards.   We tried to
get down to the right towards the fall of the Schmadribach,
which, springing straight out of the Schmadri Glacier,
gains the valley in three successive leaps. At last, however,
we found the track in exactly the opposite direction, viz.,
well to the left, and were again delayed in consequence of
our ignorance that it led across the terminal moraine of
the Tschingel Glacier, but, once over this waste of stones,
all our difficulties were over, and at 11.45 we halted for
lunch close to a good spring and a ruined hut.   At 12.15
we broke up in pouring rain, and, passing the Steinberg
Alp, instead of descending to Trachsellauinen, followed a

small path through luxuriant woods, which kept at a high
level along the slopes above the left side of the valley, and
commanded delicious views of it, and the great precipices
of the Jungfrau above the Roththal. We took it very easy,
and at 2.5 descended into the regular path down the valley,
close to the village of Stechelberg, at the entrance of
the remarkable ravine of the Sefinen Thal. Thence, a
walk along the char-road, at the base of the tremendous
cliffs below Mürren, which no amount of familiarity can
render less striking, brought us to the "Capricorn" at
Lauterbrunnen at 3.20 p.m. The passage had thus occupied ten hours and three quarters actual walking, but we
had lost nearly an hour in descending from the Oberhorn
in consequence of our ignorance of the ground.

Having paid and dismissed Eggel, who, though a poor
mountaineer, by no means particularly truthful, and inclined to be extortionate, had answered my purpose, Almer
and I started in a one-horse char for Grindelwald, at 4.20,
and, after a very pleasant drive, the rain holding off, arrived
at the "Adler," where we were warmly welcomed by Mons.
Bohren, the excellent landlord, at 6.35 p.m. Having given
over my boots to Almer for final and much-needed repairs,
I dismissed him to the bosom of his family, with an inti-
mation that, for the morrow he was absolutely free, as,
having been away from home for six weeks, he would
probably have a good deal to see to, and then turned my
own attention to dinner, newspapers, and bed.

Saturday, 23rd July.—I had the pleasure of making the
acquaintance this morning of Mr. C. Wigram, whom I succeeded in persuading to join me in an attack on the Eiger
on Monday, and in whose company a dull, but not rainy,
day was passed in most agreeable idleness. In the afternoon, an old friend, Mr. Whitwell, arrived over the Strahleck, with designs on the Wetterhorn, and in the evening,
to my equal astonishment and delight, I was patted on the
back by Horace Walker, who, with his father and sister, had
just arrived from Kandersteg, after doing the Balmhorn.
They also were intent upon the Eiger, so it was, of course,

arranged that we would make one party, unless Melchior and Almer should think we were too numerous, a point, the discussion of which was reserved for the morning.

Sunday, 24th July.—Melchior and Almer, having consented to the union of the two parties, were ordered to procure such other men as were considered necessary for our contemplated expedition. Wigram had with him one Johann von Aa, who had rashly abandoned the occupation of "voiturier" for that of guide, but he was considered incompetent for the Eiger, so was informed that his services would not be required on the morrow, upon hearing which, he very wisely resolved "to go back to his horses," and went accordingly. Peter and Hans Baumann, and Peter Schlegel were ultimately engaged for us, so that we were a party of five, with six guides, Jakob Anderegg being the sixth,—a strong force, but not stronger than the reputation of the mountain for difficulty and labour seemed to require. After an early dinner, we set off for the Wengern Alp, at 3.0 p.m., Miss Walker being mounted on a mule. It was a fine, but very hazy, day, without a breath of air, and the intense heat took it out of us considerably, so that the usual halt of ten minutes about half-way up, for a tremendous feed of strawberries and cream was particularly agreeable. As we opened out the view up the lower glacier of the Finsteraarhorn and Schreckhorn, the appearance of the latter peak was so tempting, that the thought of having to abandon my proposed attack on it was more than ever bitter, and Almer at last consented that the question should not be finally decided, until we saw in what state the rocks of the Eiger were, and that if they were pretty free from snow the attempt should be made.

At 5.50 p.m. we reached the Hotel Bellevue, on the top of the Wengern Alp, where, although I had not visited it since 1862, I was at once recognised, and greeted as an old friend with a heartiness that was really quite refreshing. A capital "heavy wet" was set before us, and, from the rapid manner in which the victuals disappeared, our early dinner and subsequent dessert did not appear to have had much effect on us. Afterwards we went out to look at the Eiger, which, from this point, is certainly one of the most hopelessly inaccessible-looking peaks in the Alps. The appearance of the rocks below the great sheet of snow or ice which covers the upper part of the mountain is positively frightful, and I could not bring myself to put the least faith in Almer's assurance that they were really not very bad. It was with no slight interest that I once more looked at the Güggi Glacier, through whose threatening séracs a party, of which I was a humble member, had in 1862 forced the passage of the Jungfraujoch, but the immense quantity of snow on the glacier made it difficult to retrace our route. The northern face of the Mönch, too, was greatly changed, and, Almer and I both thought, looked rather more practicable than when, with George, we had made an ineffectual effort to get to the summit of the mountain by it.* The appearance of the weather, though doubtful, was not bad, and we went early to bed, tolerably hopeful of a decent day for our morrow's exertions, which were expected to be severe.

Monday, 25th July.—We were called exactly at midnight, and, after a hurried breakfast, and the usual subsequent delays, started at 1.25 a.m. amidst fervent good wishes from the members of the establishment, who were all up to see us off. The morning, though by no means perfect, was tolerably fine, the sky being generally clear, and the moon, now on the wane, giving us sufficient light to allow us to dispense with a lantern, and pick our way over the grass slopes in the direction of the Eiger Glacier. Looking towards the valley of Grindelwald on our left, the three peaks of the Wetterhörner stood out wonderfully sharp and clear against the faintly-illuminated sky, while, nearer at hand, the grand forms of the Mönch, Jungfrau, and Silberhorn, not to mention the immediate object of our ambition, were still more imposing. One of the small flags which are

---

* The ascent of the Mönch from the Wengern Alp was accomplished in 1866 by Herr Von Fellenberg.

placed on the fence running along the crest of the Alp, was
secured, to be planted on the summit, in the event of our
reaching it, and we then walked on in silence, meditating
upon the tough job which, judging from our predecessors'
experience, was before us. The Eiger was first ascended
in 1858 by a Mr. Harington with Almer, the second ascent
was made in 1861 by Dr. Porges of Vienna, and the third
and only other by Messrs. Hardy and Liveing in 1862. The
time occupied in the first ascent was, according to Almer,
not excessive, but Dr. Porges had to pass the second night
half-way up the mountain, with the natural result of being
frost-bitten, and Messrs. Hardy and Liveing, having left
the inn at about 2.0 a.m., did not reach the summit till
4.30 p.m., nor the Wengern Alp again till 11.30 p.m. On
both these occasions, it was the enormous amount of step-
cutting required on the upper part of the mountain that
ran so into time, and we were, of course, liable to the same
thing, but we were not without hope that the exceptional
quantity of snow this year might stand us in good stead,
and enable us to get on rather faster than our predecessors.
Still, although a help on the ice, the snow would probably
impede us on the rocks, so that, taking the most sanguine
view of things, I did not expect to be back at the Wengern
Alp much before eight o'clock in the evening.

Advancing leisurely over the undulating slopes of broken
turf, we came at 2.15 to a tract of snow lying between the
Alp and the lateral moraine of the Eiger Glacier. Turning
sharp to the left along this, we had on our right the glacier,
and on our left the long spur which projects in a westerly
direction from the great mass of the Eiger, and is, in fact,
a prolongation of what may, perhaps, be called the western
arête of the mountain. The snow was hard and in good
condition, and we tramped along it contentedly enough for
some time, rising very gradually, but finally, when the
inclination became more rapid, took to a broad shelf of
rocks on our left in preference. These were shaly, and
particularly pleasant to traverse, but they lasted only too
short a time, and we were soon compelled to bear away

again to the right over the snow, which now rose very
steeply in front of us towards the base of the peak, running
up into a very narrow cleft in the rocks, for which we
steered. The slope was rather severe, and zig-zags were
the order of the day, but we mounted rapidly, and should
have been in a tolerably happy frame of mind had it not
been for the weather, which, as the day dawned, showed
unmistakable signs of an inclination to be vicious. Heavy
clouds were sweeping up from the plain, and the prospect
of failure and an ignominious retreat presented itself to our
minds with unpleasant distinctness. Still, we did not give
up all hope of, at least, being able to reach the summit,
though it was improbable that we should see anything when
we got there. But the latter consideration was quite a minor
one, and was insufficient to overcome that repugnance
to abandoning an undertaking once commenced which appears to be naturally inherent in the breasts of Britons,
male and female alike. Accordingly, we worked away
doggedly, and gradually screwed ourselves up into the
couloir, at the top of which there was barely room to turn.
A few gymnastics of a mild character were, however, all
that was required to get us out of the "cheminée," and
place us fairly on the rocks at 3.30. We were astonished
to hear the bleating of sheep on these crags, so far removed
from the track of men, and, on looking about us, discovered
nine or ten deluded animals, who, our men declared, had
wandered up inadvertently, and now, with the stupidity of
their race, were utterly unable to find their way down again;
so, as they would inevitably starve in their present position,
we resolved that, on our way down, time permitting, we
would endeavour to drive them back to the regions of grass
and civilization.

We now, however, turned our attention to the rocks,
which, to our unmitigated astonishment, proved to be perfectly easy, so that their hopelessly-impracticable appearance as seen from below, is a regular delusion. From the
nature of the stone, they are rather slippery and very
much shattered, but are broken into such an easy stair-

case, so to speak, that we were rarely obliged to use our hands. There was, indeed, no difficulty of any sort, and care had only to be taken not to knock down the loose masses of stone upon the heads of those members of the party who were in the rear. We, therefore, made good progress, and gradually bore away to the left, until we were close to the edge of the cliffs that form the northern face of the mountain, along the base of which goes the path from Grindelwald to the Wengern Alp. Of the thousands who annually pass under the shadow of this magnificent wall, which in height and steepness alike excels the corresponding face of the Wetterhorn, few can have failed to be impressed with its rugged and precipitous character. But grand and striking as is the view of the cliffs from below, no one who has not looked down them as we now did, can appreciate them properly. Except in Dauphiné, I have never seen so sheer and smooth a precipice, and it is rather remarkable (and fortunate) that, while the northern face of this great mass of rock is cut away so abruptly, in such an inaccessible manner, its western face should be so comparatively easy and practicable. As we climbed along the edge, a stone, dropped over on our left, would have fallen clear for several hundred feet before encountering any obstacle to its progress; but it must not be understood from this that our position was in the least degree nervous, for the nature of the ground on our right was such, that we were not compelled to keep nearer the edge than we liked, and we were very rarely *obliged* to cast our glances towards the depths below. So we pushed on, until at 4.20 we came to a small level platform, which it was agreed would be a better breakfast-place than any we were likely to find higher up, and a halt for that purpose was called accordingly. The weather remained in the same unsatisfactory state of armed neutrality, but, as it might have been openly hostile, and we were vouchsafed very fair views of the Mönch and Jungfrau, and the plain of Switzerland, we were thankful for small mercies, and were tolerably jovial over our bread and butter, while the avalanches, tumbling away merrily on the Güggi Glâcier, "discoursed sweet music," as an aid to digestion.   Jakob was particularly jocose, and he and I howled at each other, and endeavoured to see who could make the most fiendish noises for the longest time, until we were both nearly black in the face, and the amusement was suspended by our again getting on the move at 4.50.

So far the rocks had been free from snow or ice, but we now came upon patches of constantly increasing size, by which our progress was very much impeded, as every step had to be cut, and the footing, after all, was left very insecure.   The guides worked away vigorously, but were evidently uneasy at being thus delayed on a part of the mountain so far below that where the axe has usually to be used.   From this moment the question of the Schreckhorn was considered settled, as its rocks, to which those of the Eiger are a "bagatelle," would probably be so glazed as to render it impossible to gain the summit under a week at least.   "Well!" said Almer, "if this goes on, we shall arrive at the top about midnight;" and we certainly began to feel rather blank at the prospect before us, but, nevertheless, by no means wavered in our intention of *getting* to the top, and, accordingly, worked away, keeping, as before, more or less to the edge of the cliffs.   Suddenly we came upon a most remarkable object, in the shape of an isolated column of rock, standing completely apart from the face of the precipice, with which, of course, it was connected lower down, but at so great a depth that, looking down, we were unable to see the point whence it sprung.   On the very top of this extraordinary column was perched a perfectly separate block of rock, exactly like the "rocking stones" in various parts of England, very much broader at the top than at the bottom, so that it seemed as if a vigorous push, if we could have stretched across to it, would have sent it flying down to the pastures beneath, to the astonishment, and possible bodily harm, of the unsuspecting tourists passing to and from the Wengern Alp.   We at length reached a point where further progress straight up was

Y

impossible, and we had, therefore, to bear away well to the right, diagonally, across the face of the mountain, which was here pretty well covered with snow, lying at a steep angle below the base of the rocks. The guides stopped and held a consultation, the purport of which we could not at first catch; but it ultimately appeared that they did not like the passage before us at all, being apprehensive that the hard cake of snow, of no great thickness, would not support our weight, and would slip away, of necessity carrying us with it. The obvious idea now arose, whether it might not be possible to get along the rocks above the snow, and Melchior accordingly cast off the rope and began scrambling up them, to see what they were like; but they were hopelessly smooth and impracticable, so that Melchior, practised cragsman as he is, had the greatest possible difficulty in getting along them, and was compelled to return before he had climbed many yards. I believe that both Melchior and Almer were within an ace of turning back, on the ground that the risk to be run was too great, and I was beginning to use (mentally) language of the most unparliamentary character; but, after another short consultation, my objurgations were stopped by Almer leading off, evidently with great reluctance, in the desired direction. We were solemnly adjured to take heed to our steps, and hold on as much as possible by the rocks above us, never letting go until our feet were secure in the very treacherous holes, which were all that could be cut or knocked in the hard snow that covered the smooth rocks. Not that I think the hand-hold would have availed us much had the expected catastrophe actually come to pass, as Melchior subsequently told us he really thought it would, he having at one point distinctly heard the snow crack underneath us, an alarming circumstance as to which I am rather sceptical, and which certainly was not observed by the other members of the party,—fortunately, as it might have been too much for our equanimity. Still, this was undoubtedly the most critical part of the expedition, and we all breathed more freely when the most obviously dangerous bit was left behind, and the snow became deeper.

Peter Baumann here pointed us out the patch of rocks on which Dr. Porges and his party passed the night, and its appearance was not such as to animate us with a desire to follow his example. A more ineligible place for a bivouac could scarcely have been selected, as they must have found it difficult to sit down in secure positions, and the only recess at all convenient for the accommodation of a human body was selected as its line of fall by a stream of water, which must have been a companion more chilling than agreeable. Getting round the base of the rocks, of which this "Hotel Porges" formed a part, we were soon fairly on the great curtain of snow with which the upper part of the mountain is clothed, and here our fears were set at rest and our hearts rejoiced by the welcome discovery, after a very few steps, that we really had *snow* before us, and not, as is usual, *ice*. I don't mean to say that ice did not crop up here and there, but it was never for more than a few yards at a time, when, of course, steps had to be cut, whereas, generally, the leader was able to kick a secure step without very much trouble or labour. I carelessly omitted to note the time when we bade adieu to the rocks, but I looked at my watch at 7.30, at which hour we had been fairly on the snow for some time. The weather, which had hitherto been behaving tolerably, now changed its tone, the clouds were driven up around and above us, and it began to snow a little, but this outburst of spite did not last long, and the sky was soon once more comparatively serene. The slope up which we were climbing was steep, but not extraordinarily so—I should say about 40°, and, as we found it, was not materially different from the thousand and one slopes of a similar character to be found in the high Alps. We kept for some distance pretty straight up, passing several patches of rock, and, above them, bore away to the left again, until, at 8.15, we once more got on to the northern edge of the mountain, looking down, as before, but from a vastly-increased height, into the valley of Grindelwald, and here a second halt was made to refresh. With its usual provoking disregard to comfort, the wind, which had not hitherto troubled us, now made itself unpleasantly percepti- ble, and a bitterly cold, but, fortunately, not violent, breeze rendered our meal the reverse of comfortable. It seems, however, to be an established rule that when a halt of this sort is made at all, it shall not be cut shorter than half-an- hour, however adverse may be the atmospheric conditions; and it was, accordingly, not till 8.45 that we started on the final stage of our upward journey, all the provisions and other "impedimenta" being left to await our return.

Our course lay along the northern edge of the slope, whose inclination was somewhat smaller than it had been lower down, but, on the other hand, for some distance we were on a patch of hard ice, where steps had to be cut, and our progress was, consequently, impeded,—and this, too, during the only time of the day when the cold was at all severe. What we were traversing was in no sense of the word an arête, but merely the outer edge of a slope, which was certainly cut away in a tremendous precipice on our left, but, on our right, fell away very gently indeed, so that no gymnastics were required to get along, and we only had to keep our feet in the steps. The sky was now clearer than it had yet been, and we had delicious views in every direction, except where the summit of the Eiger itself inter- vened. The Mönch, whose arêtes looked fearfully sharp, the Jungfrau, and the beautiful peak of the Silberhorn were seen to great advantage, and, on the other side, the eye ranged over a vast extent of comparatively flat country, whose verdant and smiling appearance was the more striking, in contrast to the scene of desolation around us. As we over- topped the lofty ridge, connecting the Eiger with the Mönch, an old friend, especially dear to Almer and myself, came into view, the Gross Viescherhorn, which stood out imposingly; indeed, a friend of mine, residing not a hundred miles from the Colonial Office, who is in the habit of denying the claim of this mountain of 13,281 feet, to rank as one of the great Oberland peaks, is constrained to admit that its appearance from the Eiger *is* "objectionably" fine. We kept, generally, a pretty straighforward course, and the ice soon giving place again to snow, we made quick running, and so passed without trouble a spot which, when the mountain is in a different state, is considered by the guides the most difficult on the ascent. This is where a small patch of rocks rises out of the ice, round and beneath which it is necessary to pass, an operation which, when steps have to be cut, I can quite understand is rather a ticklish piece of business. Once round this obstacle, we looked straight up to a point which we supposed to be the summit of the mountain, but, on working up to it, this proved to be an optical delusion, as the real summit was further on. The intervening distance, however, was not great, but few more steps were required, and at 10.15 a.m. we reached the goal of our ambition, the top of the Eiger, 13,045 feet in height.

Bang! Bang!! went the guns at the Wengern Alp, as a sign that our progress had been watched, and our success perceived, but we had not been on the summit a minute, and had scarcely looked round us, when the envious mist swooped up, and summarily blotted out the landscape. Still, we had been able to get a glimpse of the Lower Grindelwald Glacier at our feet, at an immense depth below, the majestic cliffs of the Schreckhorn, the sharp peak of the Ochsenhorn, and the great field of névé on the top of the cliffs, connecting the latter with the Gross Viescherhorn, which forms the head of the southern Viesch Glacier, so that we might have been worse off. There was not too much room for our large party on the summit, which is cut away sharply in every direction, except that by which it is approached, but we arranged ourselves as securely as possible, and then proceeded to howl ourselves hoarse to express our exultation, while we waited for a possible clearance of the mist. The wind had again fallen, and the temperature was agreeable, but the clouds showed no disposition to break, so, having planted our flag on the very highest point, slightly below which was a pole, left, I suppose, by Mr. Hardy's party in 1862, we gave it up as a bad job, and turned to descend at 10.30.

We worked down with great care to the point where we had left our baggage, which was reached at 11.10, and thence continued the descent of the snow slope with an amount of precaution which, I must confess, I thought rather exaggerated. As a rule, the snow was in excellent condition, but, in places where we had found ice on the way up, the steps were sometimes damaged, and required renewing, which was done with his usual skill by Melchior, who throughout the day had Miss Walker in his particular charge. During the whole of the descent, my temper was sorely tried by Peter Schlegel, who was immediately behind me, and who, with the best intentions, at every step pulled at the rope so energetically that I had the greatest possible difficulty in getting on at all, and was several times jerked into a sitting position. Neither my objurgations, nor Almer's assurance that I was quite able to take care of myself, had the slightest effect upon him, and I was obliged to grin, or rather groan, and bear it. The passage along the face of the rocks, which had been considered so dangerous in the morning, appeared now to impress the guides less, though, in the softer state of the snow, the real risk was probably greater. Anyhow we passed without accident, and soon after halted at 12.35 for lunch. The position was a good one, Miss Walker in particular being lodged in a charming cleft, the weather had cleared again, and we, therefore, prolonged our halt till 1.15, when we broke up, and hurried down the remaining rocks, which were wet from the melting snow, and rather more slippery than during the ascent. On reaching their base, we stopped while Hans Baumann made a détour to try and rescue the unlucky sheep, which, after some trouble, and a delay of more than a quarter of an hour, he succeeded in driving down off the rocks on to the snow, along which they scampered double quick. We then descended the couloir, and at 2.15 stood at the top of the long, steep slope of snow, which stretched down to the Eiger glacier. This was irresistibly tempting for a glissade, so away we all went, and in a very few minutes reached the bottom of the slope which had taken nearly an hour to ascend. Hence, running over the easy rocks and smooth snow we got to the "gazon" at 2.40, and, after a rapid walk over the pastures, amidst the firing of guns at the hotel, which was commenced as soon as we appeared in sight, at 3.10 p.m. once more arrived at the Wengern Alp, where we were received with an amount of enthusiasm and hand-shaking that was quite overpowering.

The expedition had thus occupied thirteen hours and three quarters, inclusive of halts, then an unprecedentedly short time, but succeeding travellers, later in the year, have accomplished it considerably quicker. In an unfavourable season, however, the ascent might be most *laborious*, but, in our opinion, could never be really *difficult*, unless the ascent or descent of such an ice-wall as would then cover the upper part of the mountain, is considered of itself, and of necessity, a different operation, which I myself do not think the case, when the party is composed of experienced men. The astonishment amongst the people, collected at the inn, at a lady having performed such an unusual feat, was immense and entertaining. One foreigner came into the Salle, and, seeing us, announced, interrogatively, that "Mademoiselle" had gone to bed, and was profoundly amazed when we gave him to understand that "Mademoiselle" was at that moment more anxious for dinner than for bed, though the latter would doubtless be welcome in due time. Nothing could exceed the civility and anxiety to anticipate our wants, which were displayed by the good people of the inn, and the dinner, when it appeared, was of so enticing a character, that we all made, more or less, gluttons of ourselves, and, I in particular, sad to tell, was reduced to a perfectly apathetic condition, before the bowl of whipped cream, which wound-up our repast, was nearly emptied. The natural consequence was, that after dinner we were all *very* torpid, and took ourselves off early to bed.

Tuesday, 26th July.—A tremendous storm of wind and rain raged during the night, and, on getting up at 8.30 a.m., we found a dull, cheerless morning, and the mountains obscured by clouds, which momentarily threatened a down pour. After a capital breakfast, we started at 10.25, and had a not unpleasant, though dirty, walk to Grindelwald, where we arrived at 12.25 p.m., just as the rain began again. Whitwell had yesterday gone up to the Gleckstein cave, where it is usual to sleep before ascending the Wetterhorn, and, instead of being induced by the bad weather to come down again to the comforts of civilization, he very pluckily remained where he was, in hopes of being able to make the ascent to-morrow. My intention was (the Schreckhorn being impracticable) to go up to the Gleckstein to-morrow, and ascend the Wetterhorn on Thursday, descending to Rosenlaui, a route almost unknown, and, I believe, only once traversed by an Englishman, viz., Mr. Chapman, many years ago. The Walkers were going to start for Geneva early to-morrow morning, and Wigram could not be tempted to join me, so that my final expedition promised to be a solitary one. Almer, however, suggested that instead of sleeping at the Gleckstein, we should make the ascent to-morrow, starting from Grindelwald itself, a brilliant idea, which so fired Horace Walker's ambition, that, to my infinite delight, he consented to accompany me. The rain poured in torrents all the afternoon, but ceased towards evening, and the weather showed signs of clearing, but nevertheless, when we went to bed at 8.30, was still very doubtful, so that we were by no means sanguine of being able to start. The night was very warm, and we kicked about in our beds, sleepless and anxious, without once closing our eyes. It was, therefore, a great relief, when, at 11.0 p.m., Almer called us, in order that we might look at the weather, and determine what to do. The aspect of things was the reverse of promising, but, after some discussion, we made up our minds to start, and trust that matters would improve before we came to the beginning of our difficulties. We accordingly dressed, and went down to a breakfast at the somewhat unusual hour of 11.45, the service of which was superintended by Herr Bohren himself, who had kindly sat up in order to start us on our way.

Wednesday, 27th July.—Breakfast was soon over, and at

THE WETTERHÖRNER.

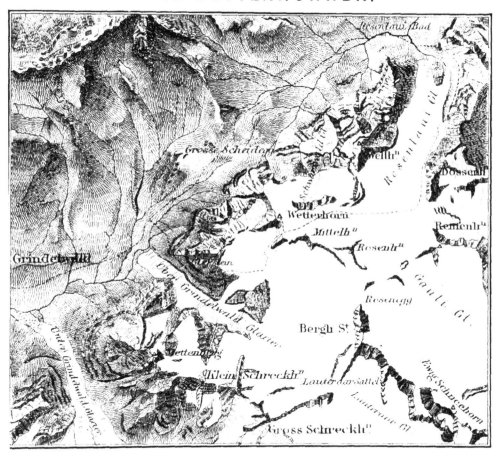

12.15 a.m., we started, with Rudolph Boss as a second guide. Had we been going to descend the usual way, Almer would not have required a second man, but, as it was probable that considerable difficulty would be encountered in forcing a passage down the Rosenlaui Glacier, he thought it advisable that the party should be reinforced. The night was very dark, and the weather had certainly not improved since we were called, so that we tramped along the path to the Scheideck in a rather disconsolate frame of mind, and with dire forebodings that our advance would come to an untimely end at the bottom of the mountain, instead of the top. The heavy rain had converted the path either into a running stream or a swamp, and the lantern, which Almer carried, turned out very useful in helping us to pick our way through the filth, which at the close of the day we should have utterly disregarded. Our progress was entirely without incident, and the ever varying appearance of the weather was almost our sole topic of conversation, save when some yelping cur rushed out from the châlets on our route, to make hostile demonstrations against the passers by at such an unwonted hour, thereby drawing down maledictions on his head.

Shortly after passing the châlet near the foot of the upper glacier, we turned off to the right, abandoning the path, and struck across the grass slopes towards the base of the mountain. These rapidly became steeper, and were mingled with patches of rock, where the footing was none too good, and where, without Almer's faultless local knowledge, we must have been brought to a full stop. After keeping for some little distance towards the left in the direction of the Scheideck, we turned to the right, and, having cut across a broad, steep slope of hard avalanche snow, got fairly on to the rocks at 2.15. The footing at every step became more difficult, and as, in addition to the natural blackness of the night, we were now enveloped in a dense fog, the lantern served us but little, and we were obliged to advance with the greatest caution. As worse walking lay before us, Almer thought it prudent that the

rope should be put on, so that, in the event of a false step
on the part of anyone, the luckless individual would have
some chance of escaping the fate which would otherwise
inevitably await him. A short halt was accordingly made
for this purpose, and we then commenced an operation
which is unique in my experience. The passage of the
"Enge," as this narrow goat-track, worn along the side of
the cliffs, is called, cannot at the best of times and in
broad daylight be particularly easy,—what it was in pitchy
darkness, and after heavy rain, which had made both the
rocks and tufts of grass, which were generally the sole support for the foot, extra slippery, may, perhaps, be imagined.
To see where the foot had to be placed was impossible, but
fortunately there was usually more or less to hold on by,
either a knob of rock or a shrub, clinging to which, we fished
with our feet, until the required ledge or hole was found. We
could not, of course, see what lay before us, and, as a general
rule, the wall along which we were climbing, seemed to sink
into vacancy, but Almer always let us know what he considered the worst places, by his emphatic admonition not
to let go with our hands until one foot, at least, was tolerably
secure. Looking back, I am always at a loss to conceive
how we managed to pass these places without accident, and
believe that the risk was really greater than we imagined at
the time, as I can scarcely fancy that the rope would
have afforded any real security in the event of a slip. Of
one thing I am sure, that few guides in the Alps, however
familiar they might be with the ground, would have consented to make this passage in the dark. Shortly after
turning the sharp angle of the mountain above the upper
glacier, a stone avalanche had destroyed the track, such as
it was, and we had to descend slightly and ascend again in
order to hit it afresh, losing some time in the operation.
Thenceforward, however, the walking was easier, and, as
daylight was coming on, we were able to quicken our pace,
which Almer gradually increased, until, in spite of our
good condition, we were streaming with perspiration, and
strongly inclined to put the drag on. The weather, too,

showed signs of improvement, and the fog lifted sufficiently to show us the shattered stream of the glacier below us on our right, and the cliffs of the Mettenberg beyond, but the Schreckhorn and the upper ice-fall of the glacier were still veiled. Our route lay generally over slopes of rough herbage and shale, but we came occasionally to places where the cliff went straight down for hundreds of feet, and the only means of passing were some slight notches, chipped in the face of the stone, just like the passage of Les Ponts, on the Chamouni Mer de Glace. Of course, these places would present no difficulty to anyone but the merest novice, but I must confess that I found it hard to believe Almer's statement, that sheep were in the habit of passing without assistance, and very rarely came to grief during the operation. Boss was sent a-head to the Gleckstein to prepare some hot wine-and-water, the thoughts of which consoled us during our labours, but it was by no means clear to the inexperienced eye, how we were ever to get to that haven of rest, which we knew to be situated high up above the apparently inaccessible cliffs, beneath which we were passing. The mystery, however, was soon solved by the opening out of a narrow ravine, which, though steep and stony, stretched invitingly upwards in the required direction. Turning our backs, accordingly, upon the glacier, we committed ourselves to the ascent of this opportune gully, which was quite free from difficulty, and led us in due course on to a broad expanse of comparatively open ground, above the precipices we had been so long skirting.

At 5.0 a.m. we came to the hotel of the district, the Gleckstein cave, formed by two overhanging rocks that have fallen together, in the very centre of this upland plain. The guides have hermetically sealed every chink and opening, except in front, facing the Schreckhorn, where a hole has been left just big enough to admit a human body. Walker and I wriggled through this, and found ourselves in a tolerably commodious cave, thickly lined with hay, and, considering the situation, offering by no means uncomfortable quarters. The "impedimenta" of Whitwell's party were lying about, but "the birds had flown," and we soon caught sight of them high up the mountain. The mists had hitherto clung obstinately to the higher peaks, but they now began rolling away, and disclosed to our astonished gaze the superb upper ice-fall of the glacier, backed by the grand crags of the Schreckhorn, whose shaggy sides were white with fresh snow. I do not remember ever to have seen a more gorgeous spectacle than the gradual unveiling of this magnificent mountain, which, imposing as it is from all points, is from nowhere visible to greater advantage than from the Gleckstein, whence it displays itself as one of the most massive and inaccessible-looking peaks in the Alps. As we sat, looking about east, the Berglistock, the ridge connecting it with the Schreckhorn, (over which goes the pass of the Lauteraarjoch to the Grimsel,) and that great peak itself, were in front of us, while, on our right, at a great depth below, was the lower portion of the upper Grindelwald Glacier, and, beyond it, the bold point of the Little Schreckhorn, and the Mettenberg. Behind us towered the naked crags of the Wetterhorn itself, and on our left was the long and precipitous ridge which circles round from that summit to the Berglistock, and out of which rise the other two peaks, which constitute the group of the Wetterhörner, viz., the Mittelhorn and Rosenhorn. Right along the base of this ridge lies an almost level strip of glacier, which terminates on the edge of the Gleckstein plateau, but, at its eastern extremity, under the Berglistock, merges in the upper snow fields of the Grindelwald Glacier, above the worst part of the ice-fall, which can thus be circumvented without serious difficulty.

The hot wine-and-water was most comforting, and combined with the assurance of a brilliant day to elevate our spirits considerably, so that at 5.40 we started off again in a state of profound contentment, and steered towards the rocks of the Wetterhorn, which now rose like a wall between us and the valley of Grindelwald. The ground was steep and stony, although considerable patches of poor grass were not wanting, but we got over it rapidly, and at 6.15 reached the edge of the strip of glacier before mentioned, where we were greeted by the footsteps of the party in advance. We had not been looking about us very much, and now, chancing to look round, were electrified by the vision of the wonderfully-sharp spear of the Eiger, standing all by itself, and soaring defiantly into the cloudless blue sky. I have rarely seen anything more beautiful, and it was with proud satisfaction we reflected that, only two days before, we had stood upon that lofty pinnacle, which now turned towards us its most inaccessible side. Shortly afterwards, the higher, but, from here, scarcely so striking, peak of the Mönch came into view, and then, as we gradually topped the long promontory of the Mettenberg, the great wall of the Grindelwald Viescherhörner, which, circling round from the Mönch to the Finsteraarhorn, forms the boundary between Cantons Berne and Valais. The Gross Viescherhorn, or highest peak of the group, rises out of this wall, but the most considerable of the other peaks form a long ridge, which juts out to the south, and separates the Trugberg Glacier from the névé of the Walliser Viescher Glacier. At the southern end of this ridge, immediately above the Grunhorn-lücke, is the Gross Grunhorn, the second summit of the range, only three feet lower than the Viescherhorn. From our present position, its appearance was most attractive, more so, indeed, than that of the nearer and higher point, and I cannot too strongly recommend it to the attention of climbers in search of novelty, feeling sure that its ascent would well repay the labour, while it would be by no means a particularly easy task.*

The glacier was very smooth and easy, and we were helped a little by the footsteps of the other party, though not to the degree we had expected, in consequence of their having been made very short, so much so, that we were at

---

* The Gross Grunhorn was ascended in 1865 from the Trugberg Glacier by Herr Von Fellenberg without much difficulty.

a loss to understand how Whitwell had managed to accommodate his legs to them. We steered tolerably straight across, towards the wall of rocks running from the Wetterhorn to the Rosenhorn, and at 6.50 struck them at a point considerably to the left of (i.e., nearer to the Wetterhorn than) the Col between that peak and the Mittelhorn, for which we had to make. We therefore turned our backs on the Wetterhorn, and commenced climbing along the face of the rocks in the direction of the Berglistock, the glacier we had quitted being on our right below us. The rocks for some distance presented no considerable difficulty, being neither very steep nor very rotten, and were varied by large patches of snow, which, at so early an hour in the morning, was in good condition, and safe to traverse, but, in the afternoon, when softened by the sun, would require a certain amount of care to prevent it slipping away. But, as we advanced, the rocks became steeper and more shaly, and were in many places glazed with ice, caused by the freezing at night of the water which had dripped down during the day from the snow above, so that the footing was very insecure, and, after a short time, the rope, which had been laid aside before reaching the Gleckstein, was again put on. After passing the base of a broad and steep snow couloir, which stretched upwards to the crest of the ridge, we got on to the rocky rib between it and a precisely similar couloir further on, and then commenced climbing in earnest towards the Col. At first there was no particular difficulty except what was caused by the shattered and insecure state of the rocks, and the general steepness of the ascent, but this agreeable state of things did not last long, and we were soon engaged in a very pretty piece of scrambling. This part of the route is described in Mr. Ball's "Guide to the Central Alps," as a "steep, but not difficult, slope of rocks." I can only say that anyone, venturing on it, relying upon the accuracy of this description, would be considerably astonished. This so-called slope is an exceedingly narrow edge of splintered rock, falling precipitously, on either hand, to the snow couloirs before mentioned, and, as regards difficulty, I thought at the time, and still think, that some parts of the climb were as awkward as anything I have ever done. Walker, I believe, was of the same opinion as myself, and several of my friends, first-rate mountaineers, have been similarly impressed. We kept sometimes on one side of the ridge, sometimes on the other, as seemed preferable, but the footing was always of the most precarious character, a marked peculiarity being, that the very narrow ledges, to which we were obliged to trust, sloped outwards, instead of, as usual, inwards, towards the face of the cliff, and the support given was, therefore, particularly slight. Nor did the hand-hold compensate for these deficiencies, for the very top of the ridge was so rotten, that but few of the rocky splinters were thoroughly trustworthy, and all were so sharp and jagged that it was painful to grasp them, and, as it was, we got our hands more mangled in the space of an hour, than during the previous six weeks. Two places were especially unpleasant. Once the rocks on either side were impracticable, and we had to pass along the actual crest of the ridge. This, however, was so narrow, and composed of stones in such an uncertain state of equilibrium, that the idea of walking upright across it was rather alarming. I, therefore, preferred straddling it, and so, with Almer's assistance, worked myself over, but Walker scorned such a proceeding, and managed to get over on his feet, much to my admiration. On another occasion we had to creep along the side of the cliffs, standing literally upon nothing, or, at least, upon mere points, which just held the toes of our boots. We were, however, able to pass our arms over the ridge, and so support ourselves, the danger, therefore, being more apparent than real, but, to a nervous person, the position would have been a trying one. Almer here encouraged us with the assurance that we were passing the worst bit, and he was right, for shortly afterwards matters improved, the rocks became less steep, and the ridge less narrow, and, finally, after two hours' rather exciting work, we landed, 8.55, at a point slightly above the actual snow Col, between the Wetterhorn and the rather higher summit of the Mittelhorn.

On our left a steep, but apparently not very lofty, curtain of snow ran up to the former peak, while, on our right, more gentle slopes offered an easy route to the summit of the Mittelhorn, which, however, stands further back from the Col than its neighbour. In front, a gentle slope of névé stretched down to the head of the Schwarzwald Glacier, which is cut off from the Glacier of Rosenlaui by a well-marked, though not very lofty, ridge, connecting the Wellhorn with the Mittelhorn. On the Schwarzwald side, the névé covers the side of this ridge, which, as we afterwards saw, on the Rosenlaui side shows at most points a face of bare rock. Just as we gained the Col, Whitwell's party were descending from the peak, and, while we were feeding, they joined us. A meeting on the glaciers is always pleasant, and the present case was no exception to the rule, as both parties were in high glee at having such a glorious day for the expedition, but the time for conversation was but too short, and our friends soon started on their downward journey to Grindelwald. At 9.25 we broke up from our halting-place, and turned to attack the snow curtain, which the early explorers had found so formidable an obstacle to reaching the summit of the mountain. Mr. Wills, however, found this hard ice, whereas it was now covered with snow, which, of course, considerably modified the amount of difficulty that was to be expected in the ascent, but we were scarcely prepared for the ludicrous ease with which this final stage of the journey was vanquished. The lower portion of the slope is certainly not steeper than 40°, and we got up it very fast, helped somewhat by Whitwell's steps, though not much, as they had trodden through the firm upper snow into the soft, powdery stuff underneath, in which we floundered about, so that making entirely new steps would not have occupied much more time. About half-way up, the slope thinned away in a curious manner to a narrow arête, overhanging the Schwarzwald Glacier, where a certain amount of care was necessary, but above this it widened out again considerably. This last ·bit was undeniably steep, probably 60°, but it was very short, and climbing precisely as if we were going up a ladder, we rapidly drew near the slight cornice which impended over the slope, passed through the gap in it, cut by our predecessors, and at 9.45 a.m., *in twenty minutes* from the Col, stood on the top of the Wetterhorn, and in an instant had the whole of north Switzerland at our feet. The ascent from Grindelwald had occupied eight hours and twenty minutes actual walking, and from the Gleckstein, three hours and thirty-five minutes, so that, starting from the latter, the expedition is reduced to one of very moderate compass.

The summit is a ridge, some yards in length, of which the end most distant from Grindelwald is the highest, though, seen from that place, it does not appear to be so. The snow slope on the north side is at first *not* particularly steep, but very soon curls over, and nothing else is visible until the eye encounters the pastures of the Scheideck. We had not the slightest difficulty in walking along the ridge at our ease, with our hands in our pockets, and were, indeed, a little disappointed at the total absence of any excuse for nervousness. Nothing could exceed the gorgeousness of the view, which was seen under the most favourable combination of conditions, a cloudless sky, absence of wind, and a really agreeable temperature, so that we were compensated for our comparative failure on the Eiger. It is hard to say which portion of the view was the most attractive, the broad expanse of smiling country on one side, or the grim array of the great Oberland giants on the other, but the combination of the two was perfect. Of the mountains, the Schreckhorn was beyond comparison the grandest, but the Eiger was not far behind, while the Mönch, Jungfrau, Silberhorn, and Viescherhörner were little inferior to their rivals. The Finsteraarhorn was just visible, peering over the shoulder of the Schreckhorn, but was seen to singularly little advantage, and more remote, the Rhone Glacier, and the numerous peaks near the Gadmenthal, formed not the

z

least interesting portion of the panorama. Of all the great Bernese peaks, the Wetterhorn is the lowest, only attaining a height of 12,149 feet, or 16 feet less than the Mittelhorn, and 42 feet more than the Rosenhorn, but it is by no means the least attractive to a climber, and, from whatever quarter seen, is one of the most imposing of the range. On the highest point was a pole, with a small black flag attached, which we removed to the Grindelwald end of the ridge in order that it might be visible from below, and then, after I had secured a piece of the flag as a relic, we turned to descend at 10.5, after only twenty minutes' halt, which we would have gladly prolonged had time admitted.

The first few steps of the descent were awkward, in consequence of the steepness of the slope, and, when ice is encountered and not snow, the difficulty might be considerable, but, as we found it, the worst bit was soon left behind, and, almost running down the lower part of the slope, we reached the Col again at 10.20. We had had some thoughts of also ascending the peak of the Mittelhorn, which could have been reached without the slightest difficulty, but it would have occupied some time, and the snow was already showing signs of getting unpleasantly soft, so, as we were all ignorant of the difficulties likely to be found on the descent to Rosenlaui, it was thought more prudent to be content with what we had done. Almer had traversed the route we were about to follow once, about the year 1855, with Mr. Chapman, but he had no recollections on the subject, except that they had not reached Rosenlaui till 9.0 o'clock at night, a fact which did not encourage us to waste any time on extra ascents.

At 10.30 we left the Col, which, as a distinct, though, of course, circuitous, pass to Rosenlaui, is certainly worthy of a name, and should, I suggest, be called Wetter-joch, and descended by a very gentle slope of snow on to the head of the Schwarzwald Glacier, which occupies an angle formed by the Wetterhorn, Mittelhorn, and Wellhorn. After the first descent, we kept up along the shoulder of the Mittelhorn, making for a depression in the ridge, connecting that peak with the Wellhorn. There were a few crevasses, and we had to cross an extensive patch of avalanche débris, caused by some hanging séracs above us, but it was all plain sailing, and we pounded steadily along through the fast-softening snow. It was extraordinary how soon the Wetter-horn assumed the remarkable pyramidal shape it presents from the neighbourhood of Rosenlaui; already, looking back, it appeared to terminate in an acute point, which is far from being the case. 'On our left was the broad open-ing between it and the Wellhorn, through which the névé of the Schwarzwald Glacier finds an exit, prior to taking its fearful plunge towards the pastures of the Scheideck. The tourists, passing the Scheideck, who look up at the tremendous precipices down which the glacier finds a way to the lower level, not in a continuous ice stream, but in a succession of avalanches, so that there is a vast hiatus between the upper and lower glaciers, are unconscious of the very existence of the secluded reservoir, from which the supplies, that contribute so materially to their gratifica-tion, are drawn. In front of us rose the singularly-fine peak of the Wellhorn, which is, I think, one of the few summits of the Alps that are utterly inaccessible. I never saw rocks so perfectly and hopelessly smooth, and it would be totally impossible for any human being to find hold for hand or foot on them, either on this side or that of the Rosenlaui Glacier. I have, indeed, seen nothing at all like them in any other part of the Alps, and mountaineers in general have much cause to be thankful that this is the case.* At 11.15 we reached the second Col under the Mittel-horn, and found ourselves looking down upon and across a most superb field of névé, surrounded by the peaks of the Tossenhorn, Renferhorn, Rosenhorn, Mittelhorn, and Well-horn. This great plateau, which is one of the most extensive I have ever seen, feeds two glaciers, that of Rosenlaui which flows in a northerly direction between the Wellhorn and

---

* The Wellhorn was ascended in 1866 by Herr von Fellenberg, I *believe*, from the direction of the Schwarzwald between Rosenlaui and the Gross Scheideck.

Tossenhorn, and the Gauli, that runs east from between the Tossenhorn and Rosenhorn into the Urbach Thal. There would not be the slightest difficulty in passing from the one glacier to the other at almost any point between the two latter peaks, and, I believe, that by far the *easiest* route for the ascent of the Wetterhorn, would be over the Gauli Glacier to the plateau, across it to our position, and thence to the Wetter-joch. I think that, under ordinary circumstances, the base of the peak could be reached in about six hours from the highest châlet in the Urbach Thal, where the accommodation is at least as good as at the Gleckstein cave, and there is scarcely a stretch of glacier in the Alps of such extent, so free from difficulty. At the point where we had struck the ridge, we looked down a low but precipitous cliff on to the névé, and a descent was impracticable, but, turning to the right towards the Mittelhorn, we soon found a slope of snow, which quickly landed us on the level surface beneath. Although we were all more or less ignorant of the ground, we had an idea that the descent of the Rosenlaui Glacier would be found least difficult along its right side under the fine, rocky peak of the Tossenhorn, and in that direction we accordingly steered.

I have rarely experienced more intense heat than during this passage of the plateau; it was positively scorching, and my face, which, as usual, was unprotected by either veil or mask, received a final " pickling," of most powerful character. At 11.45 we stood at the top of the great ice-fall of the glacier, which fell away from our feet towards the valley in a magnificent cascade of séracs, of great breadth and steepness, to force a passage through which would evidently be a work of no slight difficulty, and call for the exercise of all Almer's skill and discernment. At the very outset we were stopped by an immense crevasse, running almost across the glacier, without any visible bridge. To have turned it on the left would have led us exactly in the direction we did not wish to take, so we kept along it towards the Tossenhorn, and, when close under that peak, a point was found where the width of the chasm was more moderate, but the upper edge was much higher than the lower, and curled over towards it in an almost perpendicular bank of ice. Down this Almer proceeded to cut his way, while we (or rather Walker and Boss, for after a time I was cast loose, so as to give more rope) held him up; though short, it was the very steepest bit of ice-walking I ever did, and it was hard work to keep in the steps. Almer, however, got over all right, and we followed in turn, jumping from the last step, but the jump was a trifle, when *once* the last step was reached. The central portion of the glacier below us on our left seemed practicable, but we could not get at it immediately, and were obliged still to hug the Tossenhorn, and cut down a very steep slope of hard avalanche snow, which masked the face of the rocks, and was not altogether free from signs of being occasionally raked by falling stones. We were not molested, however, by any such missiles, and, working cautiously down it, were at last able to turn to the left, and attack the séracs, which were decidedly awkward, but under the convincing blows of Almer's axe, in time saw the propriety of yielding us a way of which we quickly availed ourselves, and at 12.30 emerged on to a comparatively-level bit of ice, where we halted for lunch. We were firmly persuaded that we had left our greatest difficulties behind us, and were, consequently, in high glee, expecting soon to reach the foot of the ascent to the Weitsattel pass, which was in close proximity to us, but presented a very different appearance from what it had, when I crossed it early in June last year; then it had been covered with snow, the rocks only projecting couloir fashion, while now it showed as an exceedingly ugly-looking wall of rocks, quite bare of snow. I have omitted to mention the extraordinary appearance of the three Wetterhörner, as seen from the edge of the plateau above the ice-fall; they stood up as three colossal, perfectly symmetrical pyramids of snow and rock, ranged in a line, and all apparently the same height, the real difference of

59 feet between the highest and lowest being, of course, imperceptible. At 12.50 we resumed our way, and were trotting merrily down the glacier, unsuspicious of evil, when we were suddenly stopped at the edge of a broad chasm, which we had not observed until we were close upon it. There was no bridge, and we had to make a long détour to the left before we could turn it, a manœuvre which took us quite away from the apparently easy line we had hoped to follow, and forced us right into the great ice-fall that occupied the central region of the glacier. This did not look promising, but we were unwilling to retrace our steps, so pushed on for some distance with ever increasing difficulty. One crevasse had to be leaped, and, as it was uncomfortably broad, and there was no drop, I did not much like it, but just managed to land on the further side. But at every step ultimate success in this direction became more hopeless, and, as we could not get out either on the right or left, we at last turned from the midst of one of the grandest bits of ice scenery I have ever seen, and rapidly retreated until we were again on the other side of the broad gulf which had first disturbed the even tenor of our way. We again took refuge on the side of the Tossenhorn, which was here again masked by a slope of avalanche snow, which stretched down for some distance above, and to the right of, the glacier proper, and would evidently lead us in the desired direction. It was, however, exceedingly steep, and intersected by a series of broad " bergschrunds," which yawned below the path we must follow in a most alarming manner. But it was a case of Hobson's choice, so at it we went, Almer having cautioned us to hold on hard with our axes, and look out. It was, indeed, a nasty place, the snow as hard as ice, and inclined at an angle of $50°$, while the crevasse below was of such a width that we could not possibly have shot over it in case of a slip, and even then there were others below to intercept us. But Almer worked away with such energy that we turned all these obstacles one after the other, and finally left them all above us, the slope stretching down below us unbroken, and, then,

curling over, so that we could not see what was lower down. *We* thought that it was all right, but Almer had his suspicions, and determined, rather against our inclination, to strike to the left and get once again on to the glacier, which now appeared to be more practicable. The ice was, indeed, still much broken, and it was not always easy to get along, but there was no serious difficulty, and we worked gradually down, until at 2.30 we landed on a patch of moraine near the foot of the Weitsattel Pass, and at once saw that, had we stuck to the slope of avalanche snow, we should have come to hopeless grief, as it terminated abruptly at the top of an utterly impracticable line of cliffs.

Our difficulties were not yet over, as the lower ice-fall still remained to be descended, and this, which last year I had found covered with snow and easy to ascend, was now hard ice, and most decidedly awkward, requiring a great deal of step-cutting, and the exercise of all Almer's skill. Nevertheless we did force a passage, until but a comparatively short bit intervened between us and the moraine, which would be the end of our troubles. But to get at this moraine we had to cut down a hard slope, underneath a most magnificent cavern of ice (like that usually found at the end of a glacier), perched in an extraordinary position on the top of a wall of rock, some two hundred feet in height, and over the smooth, slanting roof of this, stones of all sizes, loosened from the cliffs above, came shooting on to the moraine with a velocity and force quite amazing. There was scarcely any cessation in the fire, which completely raked our line of march; but there was no other route, so we took our chance, and, scrambling down as fast as we could, fortunately got over without accident on to the moraine, down which we skedaddled, until by 3.10 we were well out of reach of any stray shots. Down the rocks of the Engelhörner, on our right, trickled innumerable rills of snow water, and round many of these, a tiny "Iris" was playing, presenting a most fairy-like and charming appearance, to which at any other time we should have given more attention. Hurrying along the smooth snow, lying between the moraine and the rocks, we soon passed the eastern tongue of the glacier, which is separated by a pine-clad buttress from the western one, which only is seen from the valley and ordinarily visited by tourists, and shortly fell into a rough track, which zig-zagged steeply through the forest, until we emerged on to the exquisite little patch of open ground, below the end of the before-mentioned western tongue, where the usual cannon firing was going on for the edification of a party, who had come up to " see the glacier." This is one of the most charming sites in the Alps, but we did not pause, and, crossing the wonderful gorge, in the depths of which the torrent thunders along, followed the excellent path down to Rosenlaui, where we arrived, at 3.55 p.m., in thirteen hours forty minutes actual walking from Grindelwald.

Having celebrated our triumph in a bottle of champagne, we left Rosenlaui at 4.45, and, after a rather wearisome walk, and one halt for a quarter of an hour to eat strawberries and cream, reached the top of the Scheideck at 6.40. Here we found Peter Bohren, *slightly* the worse for liquor, and a party of German gentlemen, with whom we entered into conversation until 6.55, when we resumed our journey. It was nearly dark by the time we passed the upper glacier, but the evening was very fine, and the walk consequently pleasant enough, nevertheless, we were not sorry when, at 8.20 p.m., to the no small astonishment of the natives, we walked into the " Adler " at Grindelwald, and thus terminated one of the most glorious excursions I ever had the pleasure of making. We had fairly earned our dinner, and so Herr Bohren seemed to think, for we were served with a specially good one, after which we took ourselves off to bed in a very sleepy state.

Thursday, 28th July.—We were up at 5.0 a.m., and after a hearty farewell to Almer, started in a one-horse char at 6.50 for Neuhaus, where we arrived, after a pleasant drive, at 9.20. The steamer left at 9.45, and, during the voyage to Thun, which was reached at 11.0, we discovered that our exploit of yesterday was a general topic of conversation; indeed, I understand that it was some time before the natives in general got over their astonishment at the performance.   The train arrived at Berne at 12.40 p.m., and, having put up at the "Berner-hof," we went out to survey the town, which was new to me, and therefore most interesting.   We saw everything, not forgetting the bears, made ourselves horribly ill by eating unlimited cherries, &c., and in the evening, after dinner, went up to the café of the "Schinzli," on an eminence just outside the town, whence we got a final view, by a tolerably good sunset, of all our old mountain friends, and where we sat for a long time, devouring ices, and listening to the anything but melodious strains of a brass band.

Friday, 29th July.—Walker started at 8.15 a.m. to join his family at Geneva, while I lounged about till 2.5 p.m., when I left for Paris, *viâ* Biel, Neuchatel, and Pontarlier, The scenery of the Val Travers between Neuchatel and Pontarlier is exquisitely beautiful, and the descent from the Jura into France, and the sunset over the plain was one of the finest things, in its way, I have ever seen.   After quitting Dijon, there were only two persons in the carriage besides myself, so that I passed a comfortable night.

Saturday, 30th July.—I arrived in Paris at 5.10 a.m., and at 6.45 started again for Dieppe, which was reached at 10.15.   The boat left at 11.5, and we had a most beautiful passage, until we were within three-quarters of an hour of the English coast, when the sea got up, and most people were more or less unwell before we were landed at Newhaven, at 5.10 p.m.   The Brighton train started at 7.35, and deposited me at that place at 8.40 p.m., thus terminating the most successful and enjoyable of all my Alpine campaigns.

APPENDIX.

THE ASCENT OF MONT BLANC FROM THE GLACIER DE
LA BRENVA.

*From the "*ALPINE JOURNAL*," No. 16.*

THE attempts which have of late years been made to find
routes to the summit of Mont Blanc, which should rival in
popular favour the established ones from Chamouni and St.
Gervaise, have not been attended with very great success. It
is true that the route from the Col du Géant, over the Mont
Blanc du Tacul, first tried by Mr. Ramsay in 1854, has been
found practicable, and has been once or twice taken, but, notwithstanding the erection of a hut in a convenient position
behind the Aiguille du Midi, it has not and does not seem
likely to become popular. Expeditions made from the side of
the Col du Miage have had even less result. The Dôme du
Goûté has certainly been gained from the Col, and a party has
descended to the southern glacier of Miage, directly from the
Dôme du Goûté ; but the summit of Mont Blanc is three hours'
distant from the Dôme, and no one has yet reached it starting
from the Col de Miage, or is ever likely to do so, as, I think,
Messrs. Buxton, Macdonald, and Co. will agree, from the level
of the southern Miage Glacier. Probably most mountaineers
have, at some time or another, dreamed of finding a practicable
route from the south side of the mountain, but, as seen from the
valley, the Brenva Glacier, which would naturally suggest itself
as the line of march, does not look promising, and has besides
a general reputation of inaccessibility, which has deterred
explorers from seriously examining it. Nevertheless, in 1863,
a large party, of which I had the honour to be a humble member,
went to Courmayeur for the particular purpose of seeing what
could be done from that quarter. We were attended by Almer,
Perren, and Melchior, and, with them, held a grand council of

war on a little hill behind the village which commanded a view
of the entire face of the mountain above the Brenva Glacier.
But Perren and Melchior were dead against an attempt being
made at all, the latter going so far as to call the plan " Eine
miserable Dummheit "—" A wretched piece of folly," while
Almer, although less despondent than his companions, declined
to say that he thought success probable. As the balance
of opinion was altogether unfavourable, and there were circumstances which rendered the majority of the party unwilling
to risk a failure, the idea was abandoned, and we had the
mortification of seeing the Italian flag, which had been prepared
by the natives for our expedition, rolled up and put away, and
of ourselves sinking considerably in the estimation of the men
of Courmayeur.

Personally, I must confess to having entirely concurred in
Melchior's opinion, and the ascent of Mont Blanc from the
Brenva Glacier was summarily erased from my list of " pos-
sibilities" for future years. Indeed, I thought no more of it,
and my apathy on the subject would never have been dissipated, had it not been for something I saw, while descending
from the summit with Almer, in 1864. To all but the most
nervous travellers, the Mur de la Côte has long since ceased to
be a bugbear. But, even in these enlightened days, there are,
probably, few who have not been taught to believe that, however
the steepness of the slope of the Mur above the Corridor may
have been exaggerated by early writers, its face above the
Brenva Glacier is absolutely precipitous. Now, upon the
occasion in question, we were compelled by the state of the
snow to descend right along the edge overhanging the Italian
side, and great was my surprise, on looking down on that side
to see, instead of a precipice of great height, an ordinary slope
of by no means excessive steepness, stretching down to a gently-
inclined field of névé, lying at the depth of apparently not more
than 150 feet below. It did not appear to me that there would
be much difficulty in descending on to it from almost any point
of the Mur, or, indeed, that even a *roll* down would be attended
with very serious consequences. I at once concluded that the
névé upon which I was looking could be nothing but the head
of the Brenva Glacier, and succeeded in persuading myself that
there must be some way of reaching it from below, which had

escaped our observation in 1863, when the upper region of the glacier had appeared to be separated from the Mur by some 5000 feet of steep rocks, interspersed with hanging glaciers of an "avalanchy" character. To avoid topographical detail further on, I may as well at once explain what the real nature of the ground is. The upper part of Mont Blanc is popularly supposed to be entirely cut off from the southern valleys by a more or less vertical wall of rock, and in every map yet published, with the exception of the new French Survey, this wall is depicted as sweeping round the head of the Brenva Glacier to and beyond the Mont Maudit. The popular notion is not so very far wrong, but it so happens that, at one point, and one point only, there is a break in the continuity of the wall. From the actual summit of the mountain, a considerable glacier flows straight down into the Brenva without interruption, and it was the upper part of this which had attracted my attention, the head of the main glacier lying at least 3000 feet below. The Corridor and Mur de la Côte are on the left bank of this lateral glacier, whose right bank is formed by a great rocky spur, which projects at right angles to the main mass of Mont Blanc, far into the Brenva Glacier proper. This spur was our base of operations in the expedition which I am about to describe, and entirely masks the lower part of the tributary glacier, the existence of which would not be suspected from below. What I had seen impressed me so strongly with a conviction of the practicability of reaching the Corridor from Courmayeur, that I determined to make the attempt at the first opportunity. In drawing up, therefore, with Mr. Horace Walker the plan for our campaign of 1865, it was agreed that an expedition should be made to the head of the Brenva Glacier, and Mont Blanc either ascended from it, or the reason why it could not be done definitely ascertained.

Accordingly, on the afternoon of July 12th, after an abortive expedition up the Val Grisanche, Walker and I, with Jakob Anderegg, drove from Ivrogne to Courmayeur. We were joined there on the 13th, by Mr. George Mathews, and also received a fresh recruit in the person of Mr. Walker Senior, who brought with him a tower of strength, in the shape of Melchior Anderegg. In the course of the afternoon, we walked a little way outside the village, until we opened out a view of the side of the mountain above the glacier, and then sat ourselves down to reconnoitre. In 1863 the great difficulty had seemed to be to discover any route which should not be fatally exposed to avalanches. The same difficulty, of course, still existed; but, whereas we had then signally failed in finding any solution of it, five minutes' inspection now sufficed to reveal to us what we wanted. The rocky buttress, which has been spoken of as projecting from the side of the mountain towards the centre of the glacier, appeared to offer a route free from all risk of avalanches, and in other respects presenting a fair chance of being followed with success. There were three doubtful points in connection with it. First, whether it would be possible to get across the glacier to its base; second, whether the rocks by which we must climb to its crest would be found practicable; and third, whether, having followed the crest, and ascended the steep slopes of broken névé, in which it merged, as far as possible, we should be able to bear away to the right, so as to reach the Corridor. As regarded the first two points, the balance of opinion was decidedly favourable, and, as to the third, no judgment could be formed at all, as, from our position, nothing could be seen of what lay between the highest practicable point visible and the Corridor. Altogether, we returned to our hotel, well satisfied with what we had seen, and, having given orders for the engagement of two porters, and the preparation of unlimited provisions and general necessaries, proceeded to pass the rest of the day in such mild dissipation as the Café dell'Angelo gave facilities for. Indeed, Horace Walker, Jakob, and I, animated by the uninterrupted series of successes by which our efforts during the previous month had been rewarded, considered the thing as good as done, and rejoiced accordingly. Mr. Walker was also fairly sanguine, and Mathews was willing enough to concur in the roseate view we took of things. Melchior alone declined to share our confidence. The fact is, he had not in the least changed the opinion which he had formed in 1863, but, seeing that upon this occasion he would stand alone, and that no remonstrance would make us abandon our purpose, he confined himself to indulging in observations of a Cassandra-like character, such as he thought calculated to check our premature exultation. His gloomy vaticinations had little effect upon us, and still less upon Jakob, who, notwithstanding his almost idolatrous respect and admiration for his cousin, ventured to deride his fears, and to chaff him generally in a free, not to say irreverent, manner.

At 10.10, on the morning of July 14th, we quitted the hospitable portals of Bertolini's Hotel, a rather imposing party of eight,—our four selves, Melchior, Jakob, and two porters, named respectively Jean Michel Lagnay and Julien Grange. Of both of these men, especially of the latter, we can speak in terms of unqualified commendation. Although compelled to carry loads of much above the average weight over very rough ground, their cheerfulness and good humour never varied, while they lost no opportunity of making themselves useful. Both, too, seemed to us to be very fair mountaineers. Following first the path to the Col de la Seigne, and then a track over the collection of débris and old moraine, overgrown with brushwood, below the end of the Brenva Glacier, we passed the châlets of La Brenva at 11.30, and, striking into the scanty forest immediately behind them, wound round the hillside above the glacier, pausing, as we went, to collect wood for our night's bivouac. Two or three awkward corners· were turned by steps regularly cut in the rock, and there was always some sort of track, until after a slight descent, which was necessary to cross a swollen torrent, when it finally disappeared. On the rocks beyond this torrent we halted for half-an-hour, and then, fairly turning our backs upon the valley, commenced the ascent of a series of stony slopes, occupying a sort of neutral ground between the ice and the base of the bounding ridge to the east. Nothing could be pleasanter than this part of our way, the ascent, though steady, being easy, and the surrounding scenery very fine. The rugged range on the other side of the glacier, comprising the Mont Peteret, and other points scarcely less striking, assumed grander proportions at every upward step we took, while the great lower ice-fall of the glacier, which was immediately on our left, was a constant source of enjoyment, the avalanches tumbling over the Heisse Platte, or patch of rocks in the middle of the fall, with a regularity which at last became almost monotonous. The stone slopes after a time gave place to a mixture of snow, moraine, and, at last, ice, where a few steps had now and then to be cut, and care generally taken to avoid stones sent down by the moraine higher up, which was in rather an excited state. But there was no difficulty of any sort, and at 3.20, or in about four hours' actual walking from Courmayeur, we came upon a little grassy plain, lying at the base of the ridge we had been skirting, and on the south side of a sort of bay which the glacier here forms. The appearance of the place was so irresistibly tempting, that, by tacit consent, we took off our respective loads, and were soon stretched at our ease on the soft grass. So far we had been on ground familiar to our two porters, who had more than once penetrated to this spot. The excursion may be recommended to all fairly active walkers, and the return to Courmayeur may be varied by climbing over the ridge behind, and descending by the slopes on its further side.

As we lay basking in the sun, the question was discussed whether we should take up our quarters for the night where we were, or seek a resting-place further on. Our next forward movement must evidently be across the bay just mentioned, to the base of a wall of rocks, which supports the upper glacier, and divides it into two branches, the western one being very much the most extensive. If these rocks were likely to afford a fairly eligible site for a gîte, it would clearly be advantageous to go on at once, in order to save time in the morning, but their appearance was not very promising, so, while we luxuriated, Melchior started off alone to examine their capabilities. At 4.10 a shout was heard, which was interpreted as a signal to advance, so the traps were gathered up, we crossed a perfectly level bit of glacier to the foot of the rocks, and, having with some difficulty effected a lodgment on them, had a severe scramble to their summit, which was gained at 5.15. Here we found a small platform, with a huge boulder perched in the middle of it, under the lee of which were divers articles belonging to Melchior, indicating that we were to pitch our camp. As the night promised to be fine, a more eligible spot could scarcely have been desired; for, although the big boulder afforded no shelter overhead, it completely protected us from the rather keen north wind which was blowing. But even had its intrinsic merits been less considerable, the view which our position commanded would have reconciled us to it. As we sat, looking south, the great upper ice-fall of the main branch of the glacier was on our right, at a depth of about a thousand feet below, backed by the cliffs and buttresses of Mont Blanc itself, the Mont Blanc de Courmayeur, and the Mont Peteret, not to mention other pinnacles of even more fantastic form. The ridge shutting in the glacier basin on the left is scarcely less imposing, but the grand view was in front, where, beyond the Val d' Aosta and over the top of the Cramont, was seen the entire range of the Graian Alps, from the Grivola and Grand Paradis to and beyond the Aiguille de la Sassiere, the great snow field of the Ruitor being specially conspicuous. In point of elevation, we seemed to be rather higher than the Cramont, or about 9400 feet. Melchior, after summoning us from our first halting-place, had gone off on a " reconnaissance," and did not make his appearance until some time after our arrival, but was at last seen bounding down the snow slope above us in a state of unusual animation. Our eager inquiries as to the result of his expedition were met by a series of sentences, which he was far too excited to make coherent, whose burden was " Ein schöner eisfall ! " "Einen solchen eisfall, habe ich niemals gesehen !! " When he had a little calmed down, we elicited that the ice-fall, which lay between us and the base of the buttress by which we hoped to climb to the upper regions, was of unusual magnificence and extent, and that he very much doubted whether we should be able to cross it. He even suggested that, instead of trying to do so, it might be better, in the morning, to descend the rocks again, and endeavour to find a passage below instead of above them. But this proposition did not meet with much favour, as, not to mention that the appearance of the ice-fall lower down was not by any means such as to encourage the belief that its passage there would be found at all easy, its adoption would involve a descent, one way and another, of more than a thousand feet, and a long and difficult scramble under the cliffs on the other side of the fall, exposed to a raking fire of avalanches from the hanging glaciers above. Nothing definite was settled on the subject, but it was understood that an attempt, at least, should be made to cross up above. Meanwhile, our efforts were directed to the improvement of our night-quarters. A level floor was constructed with very little trouble, and a wall was, with more labour, built along one side of the platform, where the wind was rather inclined to make itself felt. When we took up the positions we intended severally

A A

to occupy, the general result of our labours was unanimously
agreed to be a decided success, and we supped and contemplated
the sunset, in our respective berths, with serene satisfaction. To
an Alpine audience there is no need to rehearse the glories of an
Alpine sunset, and I shall say but little of the night which followed.
With such an arrangement as the Hesse Platte below, of course
"the solemn silence" was broken by avalanches innumerable, and,
equally, of course we heard the inevitable dog barking down in the
valley. Otherwise the night passed without incident. We were by
no means cold, and altogether fairly comfortable, until the moon
got round into our faces and murdered sleep most effectually.

At 1.15 the guides began to move, and at 2.45, after swallow-
ing some hot wine and coffee mixed (to me a nauseous mixture,
but approved of by the majority of the party), we started. Julien
Grange volunteered to go with us to learn the way, but his
companion, not seeming to see how, unaided, he was to carry all
the "impedimenta" down to the valley, our friend had to curb
his desire, which Melchior afterwards cruelly suggested, would
not have been so ardently expressed, had he not foreseen the
obstacle which would arise to its gratification. The rocks on
which we had slept are connected with others higher up by a
series of snow slopes, up which we went in Melchior's steps of
the previous day, keeping rather to the left. At 3.15 the rope
was put on, and then, bearing still more to the left, we made our
way, by 3.35, to the edge of the ice-fall, which had so much
excited Melchior. Had our purpose been different, we might,
by keeping a more straightforward course, have gained the
upper névé of the glacier above the fall without any difficulty at
all, but, when there, we should have been above the buttress we
had to steer for, and quite out of our proper direction. From the
head of the glacier, a pass, worth attention, might be easily made
over the low ridge west of La Tour Ronde to the Glacier du Géant.
It was still dark when we started, but now, as our difficulties
were commencing, there were signs of dawn. Gorgeous as
had been the sunset, the sunrise was more gorgeous still, the
gradations of colour over the eastern horizon before the appearance of the luminary being indescribably beautiful, while, as
the sun rose, the great wall of precipices before us glowed again
as its beams crept down them. The ice-fall certainly was worthy
of Melchior's respect and admiration, for a grander and more
broken one I have rarely seen, but, when we fairly attacked it,

we got on with less difficulty than had been feared. Of course, there was the usual up and down sort of work, but, in spite of one or two checks, we progressed steadily, and, finding ourselves more than half-way across, were about to indulge in a crow of exultation, when we came to what looked like a full stop. We had worked ourselves into a position from which there appeared, after several trials, to be no way of extrication except by returning in our footsteps, always a disheartening proceeding. We pottered about for some time without result, and then Melchior cast off the rope, and went alone to seek out a way, leaving us in rather a blank state of mind. We shivered miserably, but were finally rejoiced by a distant cry, which evidently meant " come on." The ground in front did not look promising, but, following in Melchior's steps, we gradually left the worst bit behind, and struck a broad causeway between two huge chasms which led us out of the labyrinth to where he was waiting for us.

One of the doubtful points in connection with our expedition was thus happily solved. The glacier was crossed, and all was plain sailing in front as far as the base of our buttress, which was not far above us. A smooth slope of snow between the foot of the cliffs on our left and the ice-fall offered an easy line of march, but, as we went, we had ocular evidence of the propriety of keeping out of the way of the hanging glaciers already spoken of, as a large mass of ice from one in front fell before our eyes, its débris rolling right across our path. At 5.30 we were at the base of the buttress. The rocks were approached by a steep slope of hard snow, intersected by the usual bergschrund. The latter gave us little trouble, and we were soon hard at work with the rocks. For nearly two hours we were engaged in a scramble, which, though not difficult, was sufficiently severe to be interesting, some care being required in places where snow was lying. At first we kept straight up, but later bore away to the left, ascending diagonally, until, at 7.20, when not far from the crest of the buttress, we halted for breakfast. We had risen very rapidly, and must have been at an elevation of more than 12,000 feet. Our position, therefore, commanded an extensive view in all directions—but details would be uninteresting.

The guides were in a hurry, so, cutting our halt shorter than would have been agreeable, we resumed our way at 7.55, and, after a few steps up a slope at an angle of 50°, found ourselves on the crest of the buttress, and looking down upon and across the lower part of a glacier tributary to the Brenva, beyond which towered the grand wall of Mont Maudit. We turned sharp to the left along the ridge, Jakob leading, followed by Mr. Walker, Horace Walker, Matthews, Melchior, and myself last. We had anticipated that, assuming the possibility of gaining the ridge on which we were, there would be no serious difficulty in traversing it, and so much as we could see a-head led us to hope that our anticipations would turn out correct. Before us lay a narrow, but not steep, arête of rock and snow combined, which appeared to terminate some distance in front in a sharp peak. We advanced cautiously, keeping rather below the top of the ridge, speculating with some curiosity on what lay beyond this peak. On reaching it, the apparent peak proved not to be a peak at all, but the extremity of the narrowest and most formidable ice arête I ever saw, which extended almost on a level for an uncomfortably long distance. Looking back by the light of our subsequent success, I have always considered it a providential circumstance that, at this moment, Jakob, and not Melchior, was leading the party. In saying this, I shall not for an instant be suspected of any imputation upon Melchior's courage. But in him that virtue is combined to perfection with the equally necessary one of prudence, while he shares the objection which nearly all guides have to taking upon themselves, without discussion, responsibility in positions of doubt. Had he been in front, I believe, that, on seeing the nature of the work before us, we should have halted and discussed the propriety of proceeding, and, I believe further, that, as the result of that discussion, our expedition would have then and there come to an end. Now in Jakob, with courage as faultless as Melchior's and physical powers even superior, the virtue of prudence is conspicuous chiefly from its absence, and, on coming to this ugly place, it never for an instant occurred to him that we might object to go on, or consider the object in view not worth the risk which must be inevitably run. He, therefore, went calmly on without so much as turning to see what we thought of it, while I do not suppose that it entered into the head of any one of us to spontaneously suggest a retreat. On most arêtes, however narrow the actual crest may be, it is generally possible to get a certain amount of support by driving the pole into the slope below on either side. But this was not the case here. We were on the top of a wall, the ice on the right falling vertically (I use the word advisedly), and on the left nearly so. On neither side was it possible to obtain the slightest hold with the alpenstock. I believe, also, that an arête of pure ice is more often encountered in description than in reality, that term being generally applied to hard snow. But here, for once, we had the genuine article—blue ice, without a speck of snow on it. The space for walking was, at first, about the breadth of the top of an ordinary wall, in which Jakob cut holes for the feet. Being last in the line, I could see little of what was coming until I was close upon it, and was, therefore, considerably startled on seeing the men in front suddenly abandon the upright position, which, in spite of the insecurity of the steps, and difficulty of preserving the balance, had been hitherto maintained, and sit down " à cheval." The ridge had narrowed to a knife edge, and for a few yards it was utterly impossible to advance in any other way. The foremost men soon stood up again, but, when I was about to follow their example, Melchior insisted emphatically on my not doing so, but remaining seated. Regular steps could no longer be cut, but Jakob, as he went along, simply sliced off the top of the ridge, making thus a slippery pathway, along which those behind crept, moving one foot carefully after the other. As for me, I worked myself along with my hands, in an attitude safer, perhaps, but considerably more uncomfortable, and, as I went, could not help occasionally speculating, with an odd feeling of amusement, as to what would be the result if any of the party should chance to slip over on either side—what the rest would do—whether throw themselves over on the other or not—and if so, what would happen then. Fortunately the occasion for the solution of this curious problem did not arise, and at 9.30 we reached the end of the arête, where it merged in the long slopes of broken névé, over which our way was next to lie. As we looked back along our perilous path, it was hard to repress a shudder, and, I think, the dominant feeling of every man was one of wonder, how the passage had been effected without accident. One good result, however, was to banish from Melchior's mind the last traces of doubt as to our ultimate success, his reply to our anxious inquiry whether he thought we should get up, being, "We must, for we cannot go back." In thus speaking, he, probably, said rather more than he meant, but this fact will serve to show that I have not exaggerated the difficulty we had overcome.

At 9.40 we started up the slopes of névé which rose with ominous steepness in front of us, and for the next two hours and a half the work was rather monotonous. There was no particular difficulty beyond what arose from the extreme steepness of the slope, necessitating almost continuous step-cutting, the labour of which fell upon the two guides, who, naturally enough, did not consider the way easy. Sometimes there was snow enough to help us, but as often as not it was too thin and powdery to give secure footing, and I suppose that altogether about every other step had to be cut in ice. The Corridor all the time was hidden, but we knew it to lie far away to our right, and, therefore, worked generally in that direction. Two ridges of rock, running parallel to each other, but separated by a broad expanse of ice, crop out from the face of the slope. We passed underneath the first, and cut our way across to the second, and, on reaching it, ascertained our exact position. On our right below was the upper part of the lateral glacier so often mentioned, beyond which was the wall of the Mont Maudit, the depression marking the head of the Corridor being apparently at about the same level as we were. There was our goal in full view, but between us and it was a great gulf, which there was no obvious way of crossing. Beneath the Corridor the glacier falls away very rapidly. At the foot of the Mur de la Côte the difference of level is but a few feet, but, under the Mont Maudit, a precipice of some two thousand feet intervenes. It is, therefore, only practicable to pass from one to the other at the former point. Unfortunately *we* were nearly opposite the Mont Maudit, and the glacier lay at a corresponding depth below us. From where we were standing it was not possible to descend on to it, nor, if it had been possible, would it have been profitable, as, just above the point we must have struck, was a great wall of ice running right across, and completely barring the way upwards. Our position was, in fact, rather critical. Immediately over our heads the slope on which we were terminated in a great mass of broken séracs, which might come down with a run at any moment. It seemed improbable that any way out of our difficulties would be found in that quarter. But where else to look? There was no use in going to the left—to the right we *could* not go—and back we *would* not go. After careful scrutiny, Melchior thought it just possible that we might find a passage through these séracs on to the higher and more level portion of the glacier to the right of them, and, there being obviously no chance of success in any other direction, we turned towards them. The ice here was steeper and harder than it had yet been. In spite of all Melchior's care the steps were painfully insecure, and we were glad to get a grip with one hand of the rocks alongside which we passed. The risk, too, of an avalanche was considerable, and it was a relief when we were so close under the séracs that a fall from above could not well hurt us. We passed close to a curious formation—a pinnacle of ice, in shape exactly like a man's head and neck. The neck in length and thinness was sadly out of proportion to the head, and was momentarily growing thinner, so that it was a question of time how soon the two would part company. Melchior had steered with his usual discrimination, and was now attacking the séracs at the only point where they appeared at all practicable. Standing over the mouth of a crevasse, choked with débris, he endeavoured to lift himself on to its upper edge, which was about fifteen feet above. But to accomplish this seemed at first a task too great even for his agility, aided, as it was, by vigorous pushes "a tergo." At last, by a marvellous exercise of skill and activity, he succeeded, pulled up Mr. Walker and Horace Walker, and then cast off the rope to reconnoitre, leaving them to assist Mathews, Jakob, and myself in the performance of a similar manœuvre. We were all three still below, when a yell from Melchior sent a thrill through my veins. "What is it?" said we to Mr. Walker. A shouting communication took place between him and Melchior, and then came the answer, "He says it is all right." That moment was worth living for. But every man here can realise without anything further from me what were our feelings after so many hours of alternate hopes and fears. Our difficulties were indeed over. Before us was a narrow shelf of névé, stretching from the base of a perpendicular wall of ice, fifty feet high or more, to the edge of a huge crevasse, or rather dislocation, in the glacier. Over our heads was an immense projecting fringe of icicles, but we paid no head to them, and, hurrying along as fast as was consistent with not slipping into the gulf below, emerged in a few minutes upon gently sloping snow fields,—the same upon which, in 1864, I had looked so longingly from the Mur de la Côte. From here we might have struck the top of the Mur, or, as I believe, the actual summit of Mont Blanc. But the adoption of either course would have involved an amount of step-cutting to which, after their already arduous labours, we should have been scarcely justified in exposing our two men. Besides which, we were all heavily laden, and the idea of depositing our burdens at the foot of the Mur was too alluring to be resisted. The intervening distance was traversed at a trot, and at 1.20 we stepped on to the head of the Corridor. The height of the Corridor, according to the French Survey, is 4301 mètres, or 14,112 feet. We had, therefore, made the highest, as it is certainly the grandest, pass across the chain of Mont Blanc. No one's satisfaction at our success was more profound than that of dear old Melchior, notwithstanding that his predictions had been falsified, and the expedition shown *not* to be "Eine miserable Dummheit" after all. Of the behaviour of both him and Jakob it is impossible to speak too highly. But to sing Melchior's praises is needless, while of Jakob it is enough to say that, upon this as upon many previous occasions, he had proved himself worthy of his name.

I have not much to add. We reached the summit at 3.10, and found ourselves safe at Chamouni at 10.30, after encountering the usual troubles in the dark in the forest below the Pierre Pointue. Our day's work had thus extended to nearly 20 hours, of which 17½ hours were actual walking. As regards practical utility, I fear that the Brenva route up Mont Blanc possesses few advantages over that by the Mont Blanc du Tacul. But it has one merit, which the latter lacks,—that of directness. It is also incomparably more interesting and exciting. I trust, therefore, that some one will be found sufficiently enterprising to give it another trial. The ice arête is the only *very* serious difficulty on the route, but that might very easily be found insuperable, in a high wind for instance, or after fresh snow. For this reason, he will be a rash man who attempts to descend to Courmayeur by this way, as the position of a party having got down so far, and then finding it impossible to get any further, would be, to say the least, unpleasant.

LONDON: VICKERS & HARRINGTON, 7, MARK LANE, E.C.